INSIGHT GUIDES

THE FRENCH
RIVIERA

Discovery
CHANNEL

APA PUBLICATIONS   L
Part of the Langenscheidt Publishing Group

M000248209

INSIGHT GUIDE
FRENCH RIVIERA

Editorial
Project Editor
Freddy Hamilton
Editorial Director
Brian Bell

Distribution

UK & Ireland
GeoCenter International Ltd
The Viables Centre, Harrow Way
Basingstoke, Hants RG22 4BJ
Fax: (44) 1256 817988

United States
Langenscheidt Publishers, Inc.
46–35 54th Road, Maspeth, NY 11378
Fax: 1 (718) 784 0640

Canada
Thomas Allen & Son Ltd
390 Steelcase Road East
Markham, Ontario L3R 1G2
Fax: (1) 905 475 6747

Australia
Universal Press
1 Waterloo Road
Macquarie Park, NSW 2113
Fax: (61) 2 9888 9074

New Zealand
Hema Maps New Zealand Ltd (HNZ)
Unit D, 24 Ra ORA Drive
East Tamaki, Auckland
Fax: (64) 9 273 6479

Worldwide
**Apa Publications GmbH & Co.
Verlag KG (Singapore branch)**
38 Joo Koon Road, Singapore 628990
Tel: (65) 6865 1600. Fax: (65) 6861 6438

Printing

Insight Print Services (Pte) Ltd
38 Joo Koon Road, Singapore 628990
Tel: (65) 6865 1600. Fax: (65) 6861 6438

©2003 Apa Publications GmbH & Co.
Verlag KG (Singapore branch)
All Rights Reserved
First Edition 1992
Third Edition 2001
Reprinted 2003

CONTACTING THE EDITORS
We would appreciate it if readers
would alert us to errors or out-
dated information by writing to:
**Insight Guides, P.O. Box 7910,
London SE1 1WE, England.
Fax: (44) 20 7403 0290.**
insight@apaguide.demon.co.uk
NO part of this book may be reproduced,
stored in a retrieval system or transmitted
in any form or means electronic, mechanical, photocopying, recording or otherwise, without prior written permission of
Apa Publications. Brief text quotations
with use of photographs are exempted
for book review purposes only. Information has been obtained from sources
believed to be reliable, but its accuracy
and completeness, and the opinions
based thereon, are not guaranteed.

www.insightguides.com

ABOUT THIS BOOK

This guidebook combines the interests and enthusiasms of two of the world's best-known information providers: Insight Guides, whose titles have set the standard for visual travel guides since 1970, and Discovery Channel, the world's premier source of nonfiction television programming.

The editors of Insight Guides provide both practical advice and a general understanding about a particular destination's history, culture, institutions and people. Discovery Channel and its popular website, www.discovery.com, help millions of viewers explore their world from the comfort of their own home and, by doing so, encourage them to experience it first hand.

How to use this book

This updated edition of *Insight Guide: French Riviera* is structured to convey a rich understanding of the region as well as to guide readers through its best sights and activities:

◆ The first two sections, **History** and **Features**, cover the culture of the Riviera in a series of lively, informative essays.

◆ The main **Places** section is a complete guide to all the sights and areas worth visiting. All places of special interest are coordinated by number with the maps.

◆ The **Travel Tips** section provides a handy point of reference for information on travel, hotels, shops, restaurants and more, throughout the region.

The contributors

This fully revised edition of *Insight Guide: French Riviera* was masterminded in the series' editorial headquarters in London by **Freddy Hamilton**. He also updated the chapters on the Western Riviera.

The original edition of the book was edited by **Rosemary Bailey**, who lives in the South of France and has edited and contributed to a number of Insight Guides. Bailey also wrote some of this book's original pieces, covering Riviera history and the areas she knows best along the coast: Antibes, Grasse, Cagnes, Vence, Cap Ferrat and the *villages perchés*. For this edition, she updated most of the History and Features sections as well as the Travel Tips.

Two other writers contributed to this edition. **Deirdre Mooney** lives in Cannes and has written for newspapers such as the London *Evening Standard* for many years. She updated the chapters on the Cannes Film Festival and Wheeling and Dealing. **Lanie Goodman** lives in Villefranche-sur-Mer and writes regularly on all aspects of the Côte d'Azur. She contributed research for the update of the Eastern Riviera chapters and wrote features on the Nice Jazz Festival and Matisse.

Many photographers provided images for this book, but **Douglas Corrance**, **Catherine Karnow** and **Bill Wassman** deserve special mention.

Contributors to the earlier versions of *Insight Guide: French Riviera* – and a substantial part of their work still appears in this edition – included **Lisa Gerard-Sharp** (The British Invasion; Lost Caviare Days; Monaco; Menton; Border Country), **Rowlinson Carter** (The Riviera at War), **Barry Miles** (Brigitte Bardot; Literary Visitors; The Riviera on Canvas; Picasso Country; Cagnes, Vence and the Var Valley), **Joel Stratte-McClure** (Wheeling and Dealing), **Peter Graham** (Graham Greene's War; Taste of the Coast), **Chris Peachment** (The Cannes Film Festival), **Sophie Radice** (Hyères and the Massif des Maures), **Philip Sweeney** (St-Tropez and its Peninsula; St-Raphaël, Fréjus and the Argens Valley), **Tony Rocca** (Cannes, Nice) and **Mike Meade** (Riviera Yacht-Watching).

For this edition, editorial assistance was provided in London by **Graham Meikleham**. The proofs were read by **Anne Esden** and the index compiled by **Isobel McLean**.

Thanks go also to the following, who provided assistance along the way: **David Singleton** (in St-Tropez), **Sophie Brugerolles** (in Cannes), **Sandrine Legendre** (in St-Raphaël).

Map Legend

– ·· –	International Boundary
– – – –	Département Boundary
⊖	Border Crossing
– • –	National Park/Reserve
– – – –	Ferry Route
✈ ✈	Airport: International/Regional
🚌	Bus Station
❶	Tourist Information
✉	Post Office
† ✝	Church/Ruins
†	Monastery
☾	Mosque
✡	Synagogue
▲	Castle/Ruins
⌂	Mansion/Stately home
∴	Archaeological Site
∩	Cave
🛉	Statue/Monument
★	Place of Interest

The main places of interest in the Places section are coordinated by number with a full-colour map (e.g. ❶), and a symbol at the top of every right-hand page tells you where to find the map.

INSIGHT GUIDE
French Riviera

Maps

CONTENTS

Fishing boats docked
in Cannes' old port

Travel Tips

Information panels

Places

THE BUSINESS OF GAIETY

For years, people have flocked to the Riviera for the cobalt seas, golden sands, soft light and glitzy reputation

The Côte d'Azur, the French Riviera: the names alone retain an enduring allure. Strung along the Mediterranean coast of France is a glittering necklace of exotic towns redolent of glamour and luxury: Cannes, Nice, Monte-Carlo, Antibes, St-Tropez.

The coast's plentiful pleasures include not only sun and sea, but magnificent art and architecture, glorious perfumes and flowers, world-class yachts, casinos, film and jazz festivals, food, wine and spectacular scenery. As one of the world's most glamorous holiday destinations, the French Riviera has attracted visitors for over two centuries, from Queen Victoria to Madonna, Picasso to Brigitte Bardot.

The actual geographical limits of the region are a matter of debate. Traditionally, the Côte extends from Menton to Cannes. The French Riviera usually designates the coast, despite its infinite variety, all the way to Marseille. Certainly property developers like to think so.

This guidebook takes a middle path, starting from Hyères and its islands in the west, one of the destinations first favoured by early visitors such as Queen Victoria. It extends as far as Menton and also includes the Haut-Pays in the east, where the villages close to the border are more Italian than French – appropriate, since the Italian influence is a significant aspect of the region.

The Côte d'Azur for most people is the classic image of a summer holiday. Its clichés persist: glorious blue sea, virtually guaranteed sunshine, waving palm trees and serious suntans. For most of its visitors, the Côte d'Azur continues to supply all in liberal quantity – satisfaction guaranteed. Today, however, tourism is no longer the region's sole *raison d'être*. It has also become a hub for high-tech industry and a year-round venue for business conferences.

We have tried in this guidebook to present an accurate picture of the contemporary Côte d'Azur, from its yacht culture to Grimaldi gossip; from the best restaurants to the crime figures; from where the financial investment is coming from to the best museums and the most perfect gardens, views and beaches. We have also delved into its history to put it all in context: its early beginnings; the influence of the British; the hedonistic jazz age of the Americans; the sun cult of Bardot and St-Tropez. We describe the many writers and artists who have been inspired by the region, and those, like Graham Greene, who have sometimes been enraged by it.

We have tried to be honest, to acknowledge the problems as well as exploring the pleasures, because it is these issues, as much as its traditional diversions, that make the Côte d'Azur today such a fascinating place to explore. ❏

PRECEDING PAGES: the private jetty of the Carlton Hotel in Cannes; St-Tropez artist; bikers on the St-Tropez quayside; bodies on the beach in Nice.
LEFT: a summer fête in the village of Biot.

Decisive Dates

circa **400,000 BC** Human settlement on the Riviera, as confirmed by bones and tools found in a cave complex near the harbour in Nice (on display in Nice's Musée de Terra Amata).

1800–600 BC Ligurians and, later, Celts occupy the region.

circa **600 BC** Greek Phocaeans from Asia Minor found Massalia (Marseille).

6th–4th century BC The Greeks set up a trading centre at Nikaia (Nice) and build settlements at Hyères, St-Tropez, Antibes and Monaco.

ROMAN TIMES

118 BC Provincia (Provence), the first Gallo-Roman province, is founded.

1st century BC The Via Aurelia from Rome to Genoa is extended as far as Cimiez, Antibes, Fréjus and Arles.

49 BC After a victorious campaign against the Gauls, Julius Caesar conquers Massalia and founds Forum Julii (present-day Fréjus).

14 BC Ligurians and other tribes are defeated by Emperor Augustus.

68 AD A Roman centurion named Torpes is beheaded by Emperor Nero for converting to Christianity. Legend has it that his body, cast to sea, comes ashore at the port now known as St-Tropez.

3rd century Christianity gains in importance.

410 The Lérins Monastery on the Île St Honorat, near Cannes, is founded.

5th century Collapse of the Roman Empire. Vandals, Visigoths, Burgundians, Ostrogoths and Franks invade the coastal zones.

536 Franks take over the region.

8th century Saracens attack the coast; the first *villages perchés* are built on inaccessible inland sites in the hinterland by coastal inhabitants fleeing the pirates.

THE MIDDLE AGES AND RENAISSANCE

End of 10th century The Saracens are expelled from the area by Guillaume le Libérateur.

1032 The region becomes part of the Holy Roman Empire.

12th century Troubadour poetry reaches its heyday.

1246 Charles d'Anjou becomes Count of Provence, beginning the 235-year Angevin dynasty.

1308 A member of the Genoese Grimaldi family acquires Monaco from Genoa.

1348 The Black Death devastates the region.

1388 Nice is ceded to the dukes of Savoy, to be ruled from Italy, on and off, until 1860.

1434–80 Reign of Good King René.

Late 15th century Artists of the Nice School, especially Louis Bréa, gain prominence.

1481 Charles du Maine hands over Provence to King Louis XI of France.

1539 French becomes the region's official language.

1543 An unsuccessful siege of Nice by joint French and Turkish forces is led by François I.

1545–98 The Wars of Religion ravage France. Protestants are massacred in Provence.

1691 The French conquer Nice, but the town is handed back to Savoy in 1715 after the Spanish War of Succession.

THE REVOLUTION

1789 The French Revolution. The South joins in with enthusiasm.

1793 Nice is occupied by French government troops. A young Napoléon Bonaparte defeats troops loyal to the king at Toulon and is promoted to general.

1814 The Congress of Vienna returns Nice to Savoy.

1815 Napoleon arrives back in France after exile on Elba. Landing in Golfe-Juan near Cannes, he marches northwards to Paris through the mountains via Grasse. The present Route Napoléon (N85) follows more or less the Emperor's itinerary.

1820 The Promenade des Anglais is built in Nice.

EARLY VISITORS

1834 Lord Brougham settles in Cannes and the French Riviera becomes the preferred winter residence of the English nobility.

1850 Arrival of the railway reduces the hardship of travel through France to the Riviera.

1860 Piedmont-Sardinia (formerly Savoy) cedes Nice (now Alpes-Maritimes) to France. Monaco sells Menton and Roquebrune to France.

1863 Monte-Carlo Casino opens its doors.

1864 The Paris-Lyon-Mediterranean railway line is extended to Nice.

1879 The Monte-Carlo opera is opened.

1892 Artist Paul Signac discovers St-Tropez.

1895 Queen Victoria has the Hotel Regina built in the Cimiez district of Nice and winters there from this year onwards.

1906 Renoir arrives to live in Cagnes.

1912 The Carlton Hotel is built in Cannes.

1913 The Romanian Henri Negresco builds the Negresco Hotel in Nice with a vast dome designed by Gustave Eiffel. Albert Camus, Françoise Sagan, Jean Cocteau and Ernest Hemingway are among the many luminaries who stay on its famous third floor.

1924 Scott and Zelda Fitzgerald visit the Riviera.

1925 Coco Chanel arrives and introduces the fashion for sunbathing. Colette moves to St-Tropez.

1928 Jean Médécin becomes mayor of Nice. The Médécin dynasty will rule Nice for 62 years.

1929 Monaco holds its first Grand Prix.

1934 The Prince of Wales entertains Wallis Simpson in Cannes.

1940 Italians occupy Alpes-Maritimes.

1942 German troops advance into the Riviera.

1944 The Allies land between Toulon and Esterel on 15 August. Toulon and Nice are recaptured.

POST-WAR RIVIERA

From 1945 The coast ceases to be a playground for just the rich and famous – mass tourism arrives.

1946 The first Cannes Film Festival is held. Picasso sets up a studio in Antibes.

1947 The French-speaking upper Roya Valley, which remained part of Italy in 1860, is handed over to France.

1956 Brigitte Bardot stars in *And God Created Woman*, filmed in St-Tropez. Prince Rainier III of Monaco marries Hollywood actress Grace Kelly.

PRECEDING PAGES: tuna-fishing has a long history in the Mediterranean. **LEFT:** temple columns bear witness to the Roman occupation. **RIGHT:** Prince Rainier and Princess Grace pose for the press.

1959 The Malpasset dam near Fréjus bursts, claiming 400 lives.

1966 Jacques Médécin becomes mayor of Nice.

1969 Sophia-Antipolis science park is founded.

1973 Picasso dies in Mougins.

1980 The A8 (La Provençale) is opened, joining the region to the French motorway system.

1982 Princess Grace dies in a car accident.

1986 The National Front wins more than 20 percent of the Côte d'Azur's vote in national elections.

1990 The Musée d'Art Moderne et d'Art Contemporain is opened in Nice. The controversial mayor of Nice, Jacques Médécin, flees to Uruguay after charges of tax evasion and corruption.

1994 Jacques Médécin is extradited to France. Anti-corruption campaigner Yann Piat is gunned down in Hyères, "the Chicago of the Côte".

1995 After serving a brief sentence, Médécin backs the successful candidate for Nice's municipal elections, Jacques Peyrat, a close friend of the National Front leader, Jean-Marie Le Pen.

1998 The National Front is split by internal feuding and an extreme-right breakaway party is formed. Nice mourns death of disgraced former mayor Jacques Médécin.

2001 The high-speed TGV rail network reaches Marseilles, cutting journey times to the Riviera.

2002 The euro replaces the franc as France's national currency. ❏

FROM BRONZE AGE TO BIKINIS

Ligurians, Greeks, Romans, Saracens and Genoese all occupied the coast in succession, and Nice itself wasn't strictly French until 1860

"It is to be tranquilly overwhelmed to see the Mediterranean just before dawn, stretching out beneath your windows. There will be the grey satin of the sea, the mountains behind, the absolutely convincing outline of Reinach's Greek villa at the end of Beaulieu Point. And the memory of Greek gods…

"It is one of the greatest pleasures of my life that a legend avers that Ulysses once sheltered in the sea cave below my garden. If I close my eyes I can see Pallas Athene with shield and spear stand in the sky and brood above her sea. Or if you quote to me, *Saepe te in somnis vidi…* or merely mention to me the name of Catullus you will have me in such a state that I must leave my writing and walk from end to end of the terrace for some minutes."
– Ford Madox Ford, *It Was The Nightingale* (1933)

At first glance at the stretch of Mediterranean coast which we now call the Côte d'Azur suggests that little evidence of the past can remain amongst the super-highways and shopping centres. While it is true that this region of France is not as rich in antiquity as some, it does have a past and the clues are there for those who wish to imagine the lives of earlier inhabitants.

Early gazetteers

The history of travel to the region is a story in itself; antiquarian travel books abound from the days when 18th-century visitors like Tobias Smollett were more concerned with discovering antiquities or restoring their health than with suntans and casinos.

The writers of these books, rattling about in their horse-drawn carriages along dusty roads lit only by fireflies or moonlight, or clambering over headlands still rich with fragrant *maquis* in search of Roman inscriptions and rare butterflies and plants, supply us with a wealth of classical learning and acute observation about the

region, both as it used to be in ancient times and as it appeared to them in their own time.

Some of the most fascinating include the Rev. Hugh Macmillan's scriptural reflections in his 1885 *The Riviera*; Edward Strasburger's *Rambles on the Riviera*, with its loving detail of the long-lost flora of the region; Sir Frederick

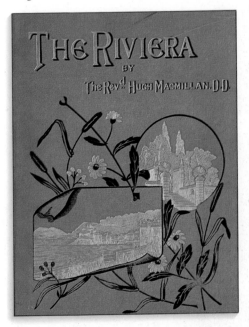

Treves's highly coloured historical anecdotes in *The Riviera of the Corniche Roads* (1923); or the altogether racier picture painted by Charles Graves in *The Riviera Revisited*, written just after World War II, and rather more concerned with the price of a good *coq-au-vin* than with anything else. Their tales of hoary peasants, newly discovered ruins or 1946 menus provide us with an excellent reference point for linking the rich history of the region with its all too present reality.

The first settlers

Some of the very first signs of human habitation have been discovered here. In the Vallée des Merveilles are Bronze Age rock carvings,

LEFT: stone bas-relief showing Roman legionnaires.
RIGHT: 19th-century guide to the Riviera.

evidence of Cro-Magnon man has been found in caves around Grasse and even earlier remains can be seen in the Musée de Terra Amata in Nice.

Some of the earliest known settlers along the coast were the Bronze Age Ligurians but little survives of their passing except the faint remains of their forts, built of unworked stone, and some fragments of pottery and beads. Anyway, according to Norman Douglas: "Their reputation was none of the best; they were more prompt, says Crinagoras, in devising evil than good."

It is not until the time of the Greeks that we have much knowledge of everyday life. They

traded throughout the Mediterranean and founded both the city of Nice, which they called Nikaia after Nike, the goddess of victory, and subsequently, Antibes, called Antipolis, meaning "the city opposite" (to Nice). Traditionally, all trading was done outside the city walls and today the Antibes covered market is still located in almost the same place on the Cours Masséna.

Roman years

The Roman occupation began in 125 BC and there is considerable evidence to be seen today. Although their primary intentions were military, the Romans can in a sense be regarded as the first visitors to appreciate the pleasures of

the coast, building themselves luxurious villas on the shore of St-Raphaël, near to their headquarters at Fréjus.

One of the most magnificent sights in the entire region is the Trophée des Alpes at La Turbie, which still towers over the landscape today, dwarfing the little village of the same name, and providing an enduring emblem of the power and self-confidence of the Romans. On the base of the monument, a long inscription lists all the subjugated tribes of the region.

The Via Aurelia, the main Roman road from Rome to Arles, passed through Menton, La Turbie and Cimiez, part of the route following what is now the Grande Corniche. La Turbie was the highest point of the road and a landmark that was visible for miles. What is today a charming backwater of a village was then an important staging-post, bustling with merchants, centurions, slaves and gossip from Rome.

The Romans set up their capital in Narbonne and founded substantial towns throughout Provence including Arles, Nîmes and Fréjus. Everywhere they built arenas, baths and temples of which substantial ruins still remain today. In some cases entire towns like Cimiez have been excavated, and everywhere there are stones with Latin inscriptions which have been re-used in later buildings.

In Fréjus, the amphitheatre and arena is one of the largest built in Gaul by the Romans. The cathedral in Vence was built on the site of a Roman temple and throughout the town are scattered fragments of blocks with Roman inscriptions. Vallauris was founded by the Romans and was famous for its pottery even then, thanks to the quality of the red clay of the surrounding mountains.

Saracen invaders

Roman rule brought peace to the region for a time and the hill tribesmen ventured down from their fortified hill settlements to establish themselves in towns along the coast. However, with the fall of the Roman Empire chaos reigned once again, and Goths, Vandals and Lombards ravaged the area, leaving little in their savage wake.

Marauders also came from the sea. The Saracens were to devastate great swathes of the Mediterranean coastline from Rhodes to Spain, and foray inland as far as the Loire river. They were Arabs originating from North Africa and the Eastern Mediterranean coast, and appear to have been exceptionally violent and terrifying. By about the year 800 they had taken power in Èze, La Turbie and Ste-Agnès, and by the 10th century occupied nearly all the coast.

Finally in 980, a concerted effort was made to drive them out by the Count of Provence, Guillaume le Liberateur, who numbered among his soldiers a Genoese named Gibellino Grimaldi, the first mention in the region of a Grimaldi, the name of Monaco's ruling house today.

It was a period of internal strife in which everybody fought with everybody else for dominance. The history of Èze in particular is an astonishing summary of violent attack and subjugation, with

Siege of Nice

The famous long-running conflict between the Guelphs and Ghibellines, defenders and enemies of the Pope, also engulfed the towns and villages of the region. Nice itself has been a constantly shifting pawn on the Mediterranean chessboard, and was frequently besieged, often by the French. On one memorable occasion, usually referred to as *the* siege of Nice in 1543, the town was saved by the heroic action of a stout laundrywoman, who beat back the Turkish invaders scaling the walls, with her washing stick. From the 14th century, Nice and the surrounding region was under the protection of

generations of inhabitants being murdered and pillaged, the village itself continually burnt and razed to the ground. What is remarkable is the tenacity with which the village has always risen from its ashes – and today continues to flourish on the lucrative proceeds of tourism.

Neither France nor Italy was united in the way we know them today. Instead, both were divided into warring fiefdoms, with towns constantly at war with each other, Pisa at war with Genoa, and Genoa at war with Nice, even tiny Gorbio, north of Monaco, at war with nearby Roquebrune.

LEFT: 19th-century Cagnes. **ABOVE:** Nice in its nautical heyday, as seen in the city's Musée Naval.

Savoy and did not elect to become part of France until 1860. The Italian influence is apparent everywhere, in architecture, place names and the Niçois dialect.

Penitents, saints and monks

Religion, of course, played a great part in the area's early history, and a wealth of religious art survives. It sometimes seems as if almost every village has a religious festival or procession to celebrate, often revived for the benefit of tourists, but authentic nonetheless. One curious example is "*La procession aux escargots*", which takes place in Gorbio. It is not in fact a promenade of snails, but a festival celebrated by the White Penitents when all the streets and houses are illuminated by oil flames lit in a multitude of snail shells.

There are Penitents' chapels in Nice, Cannes and Sospel near the Italian border. These were lay brotherhoods that appeared in the 14th century and proliferated throughout the Midi. They were denoted by the colours of their hoods, the most important being Penitents Gris, Blancs and Noirs, and were devoted to charitable and sacred duties.

All over the Côte d'Azur are sanctuaries and pilgrimage centres, often in high mountain reaches, and heavily festooned with votive

offerings. The Knights Templar also had a presence here and there are vestiges of their castles near Vence and La Gaude.

One of the most interesting ecclesiastical locations is the Île St-Honorat, near Cannes. The island's monastery was for hundreds of years after it was founded in the 5th century the centre of Christianity in Southern Europe, described by the Rev. Hugh Macmillan as "the Iona of the South".

St Honorat was, like St Columba, a man of noble birth, born in Belgic Gaul in the 4th century. He renounced his worldly life and went off on a pilgrimage to the East with his brother. Here, he was inspired to return to the Îles de Lérins to found a monastery. The island he chose was swarming with snakes, crawling in and out of the Roman ruins that remained. Undeterred, Honorat established himself, and his holy life attracted many followers. A well was rediscovered, a church built and a garden planted. Honorat's sister, Marguerite, also started a convent on the next island, now named after her.

St-Honorat rapidly became a centre of learning and was in the thick of the great religious controversies of the Middle Ages. It was a centre for missionaries and supplied bishops to Arles, Avignon, Lyon, Fréjus and Nice. Many ecclesiastical names are associated with St-Honorat, including that of St Patrick, who, according to tradition, was educated at the monastery.

The institution became very wealthy, and owned land right along the coast from Grasse as far as Barcelona, including the village of Cannes itself. At one time, nearly 4,000 monks lived on the island. But such riches were a great temptation and attacks by pirates and quarrels between the monks and Pope-appointed abbots undermined the monastery. By the 17th century it had finally collapsed, and eventually the island was bought by the Cistercians, who built a new monastery.

Damsels and pirates

Romantic stories also abound. The history of the region is awash with pirates, troubadours, distressed damsels, grand feats of bravery, dramatic betrayals, and princesses both pure and poisonous. Even today, among the high-rises and pink villas, the remains of a staircase, a curiously carved door lintel or a Renaissance window can evoke a past both humble and heroic.

As Sir Frederick Treves observed in 1923, it was a time of "general and brilliant disorder... a time to read about rather than to live in; a period that owes its chief charm to a safe distance and to the distortion of an artificial mirage. In any case, one cannot fail to realise that these scenes took place in spots where tramcars are now running, where the *char-à-banc* rumbles along, and where the anaemic youth and the brazen damosel dance to the jazz music of an American band". And little did he know what was yet to come. ❏

LEFT: *La Brigue*, by Louis Bréa (c.1450–1523), a reminder of the region's religious traditions.
RIGHT: a fountain in Mougins.

SERPOLLET

THE BRITISH INVASION

The Riviera is in large part a British creation. Here, the Brits recreated decorous anglophile enclaves in balmy, lemon-scented surroundings

"Cannes is for living, Monte-Carlo for gambling and Menton for dying." Such was the Victorian popular wisdom on the Riviera. During the days of the Grand Tour, France was considered a mere antechamber to classical Rome. But in the 1850s, the South of France replaced Italy as the British home from home.

The peaceful colonisation was led by Tobias Smollett, the Scots doctor and writer who pioneered sea-bathing as a cure for consumption. During his stay in Nice from 1763 to 1765, Smollett enjoyed the climate but deplored the uncultured locals, especially the "pot-bellied" women. He also found fault with the garlicky Niçoise cuisine, but his ill-humour melted on contact with fruit sorbets. These "sorbettes, which are sold in coffee houses and places of public resort… are very agreeable to the palate".

Escaping the northern winter

In Smollett's day, medical fashion favoured spas such as Bath and Cheltenham, but the prescription in the following century was for Riviera resorts. The avowed travel motive was health but, as William Chambers noted in 1870, "Fashion, *ennui* and love of gaiety seem to send quite as many abroad as absolutely bad health." At any rate, visitors in search of health were followed by social-climbers and pleasure-seekers. According to David Cecil, the British merely wanted to escape from "the chatter and clatter and hustle and guzzle of literary and fashionable London". One hidden impulse was the Victorian restlessness Alfred de Musset called "*la maladie du siècle*", the desire to flee.

The British migrated south in autumn and north in spring. As the American novelist W. D. Howells commented: "October was the month of the sunsets and the English." From May to September the Riviera villas were shuttered and the resorts deserted by all but unfashionable merchants, gamblers, prostitutes and, horror of horrors, the locals. But the British stranded on the Riviera out of season were vocal. Christopher Home Douglas, in Nice in May, was distressed by "a toilet table festooned with spiders' webs; decayed boots and chicken bones are also objectionable in a bedroom, even though under the bed and supposed to be out of sight".

The journey south

By the 1830s, the days of corsairs and Barbary pirates were over and the civilised world could travel freely once more. For the British upper classes this meant travelling by private carriage to the Riviera, stopping at inns along the way. In 1832, the wealthy Boyle family travelled south in a drawing-room on wheels and, at a maximum speed of 55 km (34 miles) a day, there was time to admire the view. Money bought only comfort and convenience, not speed. The journey to the Riviera took up to three weeks, as long as in the time of the Roman Empire.

Alternatively, visitors could hire a *voiturin*, a French contractor, who provided coaches and

PRECEDING PAGES: steam-powered car, Nice, 1903. **LEFT:** Lord Brougham, who "discovered" Cannes for the British in 1834. **RIGHT:** a 19th-century stroll in Nice.

horses all the way to the Côte. As late as 1875, Dr James Bennet described this option as "the most comfortable, pleasant and hygienic of any for tourists not much pressed for time or very particular about expense".

From the 1830s, steamships linked the Riviera ports, and the British often opted for the sea voyage. Despite the *fin-de-siècle* opulence of the later steamers, there were justified complaints about vibration and noise. In calm conditions the French steamers were fine, but in light seas the ships swayed dangerously. British voyagers cried discrimination at every turn. In the 1880s the Rev. John Aiton complained that "the passengers are actually starved; English passengers are insulted by Frenchmen… and as to a Frenchman lending an English voyager a spyglass or telling him the name of an island, he would rather spit in his face".

Taking the train

The arrival of the railway in the 1850s dramatically reduced the hardships of travel to the Riviera. Yet horse-power was not rendered obsolete overnight since key stretches of railway were not complete before 1870. Until then, carriages bridged the gaps. Diligences would be placed on a rolling platform and hitched to a train: a

A NECESSARY DILIGENCE

Passengers who could not afford private transport to the Riviera were forced to use the diligence, a contraption built like an overgrown haywagon. Weighing up to five tons, the diligence carried 15 to 30 passengers and travelled at little more than walking pace. In 1829, one disgruntled passenger, Dr James Johnson, likened French diligences to "locomotive prisons… in which one is pressed, pounded, and, what is worse than all, poisoned with mephitic gasses and noxious exhalations from above, below and around". Passengers faced a choice between the outside *banquette*, the cold, hard seat beside the driver, or the cowshed odours of the seats in the *intérieur* and the *coupé*.

forerunner of the modern Motorail service. Dr Bennet enthused about the new service: "Railways have all but annihilated space… A traveller may leave the London Bridge station at 7.40 on a Monday morning, by mail train for Paris, and be at Nice or Menton for supper the following day." The most luxurious trains included private saloon carriages, each containing a bedroom, sitting-room, smoking-room and study.

Royal patronage

Queen Victoria, travelling incognito as the Comtesse de Balmoral, arrived in such style that her identity was no secret. The royal train was hung with silk and was partly decorated with Louis XVI furnishings. Naturally, the Queen travelled with supplies of familiar foods, including Irish stew, kept lukewarm in red flannel cushions. In the mornings, the train was halted to allow the Queen an hour to dress and her male staff to shave. From 1882 onwards she was a regular winter visitor.

Health was the Queen's motive for visiting the Riviera since her son, Prince Leopold, suffered from consumption. Until the 1870s, consumption was the killer disease in Victorian Britain. The only remedy was believed to be a warm climate. Climates were labelled as "tonic and exciting" or "sedative and relaxing". As tonic

Louis Stevenson came in search of a southern cure and settled in the romantic retreat of La Solitude. Luxuries were cheap but essentials were dear. By this token, the British freely purchased carriages, villas, wine and entertainment but stinted on fuel, food, servants and travel. By the 1890s, Hyères' date palms incongruously sheltered an Anglican church, English estate agencies and public tennis courts.

The Brits in Nice

Compared with the privacy of Hyères, Nice was a more ostentatious resort, with British residents living in grand hotels in the public eye. By the

climates, Hyères, Menton and Cannes were considered ideal for invalids suffering from such esoteric illnesses as consumption, delicacy, gout and clergyman's sore throat. In no time, the Paris-Riviera Express became known as an ambulance train to death's waiting-room.

Queen Victoria wintered in Hyères before finding a more desirable address in Nice. Hyères was the first Riviera resort to be patronised by the British. Although later upstaged by Nice and Cannes, Hyères had a solid British clientèle from the 18th century onwards. Robert

1820s, Nice had a flourishing British community who sketched and botanised their way through the mild Mediterranean winters. Visitors indulged in literary readings, *soirées musicales*, "quantities of gossip and a great deal of dressiness".

The Victorian obsession with standards and public works soon had an impact on Nice. Winter residents insisted on better roads, English plumbing, new bandstands and public parks. The British imported nurses and ladies' maids, gardeners and grocers, lawyers and estate agents, but the local labour force had to conform to quirky British requirements. Hotels advertised "drainage executed by English engineers". French hoteliers grumbled about the demands

LEFT: the Nice shoreline in the 19th century.
ABOVE: verandah view of Monte-Carlo.

of English hygiene, the frostiness of English manners and the sibilance of English speech.

Yet British philanthropy was also grudgingly acknowledged. After the failure of the olive and citrus crops in 1821, the impoverished locals were offered employment by the Rev. Lewis Way and Charles Whitby. Funded by British families, the scheme subsidised the building of Camin des Anges, the coastal road now known as the Promenade des Anglais. Only the uncharitable questioned British motives: the Promenade provided better access to the shore and effectively shielded Victorian strollers from the hordes of beggars.

The development of a British quarter known

Cordiale as his mother. The Prince of Wales and his yacht *Britannia* were regular fixtures from 1878. "I go to the Riviera as I would a club," he'd say. "It's a place with good company where everyone mingles, just like a garden party."

However, it was an earlier and more endearing Englishman who put Cannes on the map. In 1834, Lord Brougham "discovered" this charming fishing village while looking for a suitable home for his invalid daughter. Brougham built several villas in Cannes and wintered there for almost 35 years. Under his patronage, the village became one of the Riviera's most British resorts and was home to over 1,000 English

as Newborough attracted a new wave of Victorian visitors, as did the arrival of the railway link in 1864. Queen Victoria set the tone, wintering in the palatial Hotel Regina in the Cimiez district of Nice from 1895 onwards. There she entertained the Emperor Franz Josef, other European royals and heads of state.

Dens of iniquity

Regal Nice was eventually eclipsed by stylish Cannes – in British eyes, at least. Queen Victoria's son, the future Edward VII, was not alone in thinking Cannes' Cercle Nautique the most exciting club on the Côte. Still, in his inimitable way, Edward did as much to keep the *Entente*

residents shortly after the arrival of the railway in 1862. The atmosphere, heavy with Victorian divinity and charitable works, changed with the Prince of Wales. By the Naughty Nineties, Cannes was a cosmopolitan resort with a reputation for vice second only to Monaco's.

Baptist ministers, such as Charles Spurgeon, condemned Monaco as "the serpent in paradise". Queen Victoria was not alone in refusing to stay in this "moral cesspool". Dr Bennet also feared "the proximity of a gaming table" in this warm and wicked resort. Before the end of the century, Monaco was labelled "a sunny place for shady people", the haunt of arms dealers, courtesans and gold-diggers. But the glamour drew British gamblers such as Charles Wells, the fortune-hunter who became famous as "The Man Who Broke the Bank at Monte-Carlo". Cora Pearl, the Duke of Hamilton's extravagant mistress, was an *habituée* at the casino in the 1860s.

The Riviera's sanatorium

The archetypal British resort was Menton. In its heyday, in the 1890s, it boasted the largest British colony on the Continent. As the main Riviera sanatorium, the resort had at least 50 British doctors and several rest homes. It was quieter and cheaper than Cannes and combined a dowager-like atmosphere with a seductive setting. Yet the heady, Italianate exoticism could not be openly acknowledged in a resort favoured by Anglican clergymen and consumptive ladies. Instead, "Everyone indulged in *à la mode* church-going excess, with all its formality and display."

Menton's dullness could be attributed to Dr James Henry Bennet, an eminent Victorian doctor who came "to die in a quiet corner". Instead, his consumption was cured by "the bracing, stimulating climate". From 1859 to 1891, he promoted Menton as the ideal health resort and his book, *Winter and Spring on the Shores of the Mediterranean*, became a European bestseller.

Consumptives were told to wrap up warmly but to have as much fresh air and exercise as possible. Invalids followed the strict regime prescribed by local British doctors. Flannel underwear and woollen clothes were obligatory, as were shoes with india-rubber soles, designed to insulate one against cold stone floors. For the invalids, there was little light relief: "Bath chairs monopolised the Promenade du Midi by day, and by night their premature retirement imparted a hospital hush to the atmosphere." Despite John Pemble's sombre comments, Menton, like Brighton, had British appeal.

British habits

Anglo-Saxon names flattered the insular vanity of the British, and stores stocked British delicacies such as Guinness and port, York ham and smoked goose breast, as well as "strange red, green or blue sauces in boxes marked 'by royal appointment'".

In between shopping and prayer-meetings, there were sketching trips and rides in donkey-drawn buggies. The British introduced donkey rides to Menton. Even in cold weather, the "*Miss Anglaises*" took part in donkey races on the beach or went on picnic trips to perched villages. Much to the astonishment of the locals, the young ladies still had enough energy to ride

LEFT: Queen Victoria on one of her many visits.
ABOVE: high society in a Monte-Carlo restaurant.

all the way down to the Italian frontier before returning to Menton. From her Chalet des Rosiers overlooking the Bay of Menton, Queen Victoria also found time for donkey rides. In the event of a chill in the *Entente Cordiale*, the Queen had a carriage ready to whisk her to safety in Bordighera, just over the Italian border.

In Victorian times, Britannia literally ruled the waves. Such was British chauvinism that the Franco-German War of 1870 was interpreted in Britain as a capitulation of the south to the north. On the Riviera, belief in British supremacy was widespread, and British values reigned: deference was expected and granted. In 1879 Dr

FOOD FIT FOR A QUEEN

The British rarely ventured into "foreign" shops and subsisted on safe English staples. Their eating habits and appetites were notorious. Queen Victoria's typical Riviera lunch included risotto and mutton chops, chicken with noodles, followed by tapioca, meringue and strawberries. Dr James Bennet wrote that "the dinners we positively require every day" were considered "festive dinners" by the natives. To supply the daily British intake "the country had to be ransacked for a hundred and fifty miles around". The Prince of Wales also had an enormous appetite and, as the unwitting inventor of *crêpes suzettes*, probably lost no time in polishing off both the *crêpes* and Suzette herself.

Edward Sparkes wrote: "English tastes are well understood and carefully consulted in all the hotels." English was often used as a generic term for all foreigners. As such, the "*Miss Anglaises*" were sometimes Russian or German.

Victorian life on the Riviera was deeply institutionalised. The British day followed a pattern: breakfast, early stroll, correspondence in the hotel, lunch, afternoon stroll and 5 o'clock tea. In Nice, there were English signs for "5 o'clock tea – any time". Afternoon variants included gentle shopping or a concert at the bandstand. The British community organised regattas and whist drives, while the big hotels held weekly tea dances and balls.

Depending on taste and morals, residents spent their evenings in the casino, cabaret or at home, reading. Victorian music hall was popular as were theatrical performances by Sarah Bernhardt. By Edwardian times, Folies Bergères and Moulin Rouge troupes were often in residence in casinos along the Côte. Yet after Menton opened a casino, it incurred the wrath of the moral minority. The Rev. Eustace Reynolds Ball found Menton guilty of *fin-de-siècle* decadence, "infected by the Monte-Carlo contingent".

Sporting expats

But Victorian puritanism was often outdone by patriotism. Well before the end of the century, British competitive sports played a major role in life on the Riviera. The British upper classes were serious about sport but defensive about games in a sunny climate. Author Charles Kingsley scorned "the English hedge-gnats who only take their sport when the sun shines". Still, there were enough hedge-gnats to indulge in horse-racing at Cannes, skating in Menton and Nice, as well as golf in Monte-Carlo and Sospel.

Sea-bathing was not in vogue on the Riviera until the 1930s. Although the Italians had been swimming just down the coast in San Remo since the 1850s, the British regarded this as an Italian perversity. The British swam at home, of course, but believed that the Riviera's hot climate was suitable only for seaweed and anemone hunting.

The Menton Lawn Tennis and Croquet Club was founded in 1901 and held international tournaments. The dominance of British cultural values ensured a copycat reaction: King Gustav V of Sweden and the Queen of Siam were dedicated yet hopeless players.

Politicos and oddballs

The British drawn to the Riviera included sportsmen and statesmen, royals and writers, artists and intellectuals: in short, the missing apex of the British social pyramid. British politicians were part of Riviera life from Victorian times onwards. When Lord Salisbury was in his villa at Beaulieu and Victoria in residence at Cimiez, state business moved from London to Nice. The Queen bombarded the Prime Minister with her views on heads of state, foreign affairs, church and army appointments. A monument on Avenue George V in Nice pays tribute to the warmth of royal Franco-British relations

War II. Nora, Lady Docker, flew in the face of post-war austerity by flaunting zebra-skin upholstery in her Daimler (she found mink was just too hot to sit on).

However, if one had to select the quintessential Briton abroad, it would be Dr Bennet. As well as pioneering the Riviera as a sanatorium, James Bennet was a linguist, writer, botanist, environmentalist and man of action. He represented the best face of the eminent Victorian abroad: duty led him to set up a medical association which monitored public health and instigated street-cleaning services, sewers and abattoirs. It was largely thanks to his efforts

on the Riviera: "*À la mémoire des membres augustes de la maison royale de Windsor qui depuis deux siècles furent nos hôtes.*"

British eccentrics were not thin on the ground either. Trahorne Moggridge, the Victorian entomologist, published a book on indigenous spiders. James Bruyn Andrews translated local legends and wrote works on the Mentonnais language. Edward VII's presence assured the Riviera of style. In more recent times, Amy Paget, an elderly Riviera resident, flew the Union Jack from her villa throughout World

that in 1892 the Association for the Advancement of Science declared Menton to be the cleanest, most efficient town in France.

Botanical pursuits

Bennet also personified the British love of gardens. He pressured Menton council into creating public parks and funding nature campaigns to protect plants and wildlife. Queen Victoria and Princess Beatrice often sketched and strolled in Bennet's exotic garden, created with the help of "an intelligent peasant... raised to the dignity of head-gardener".

In Menton's Jardin Botanique, Lord Radcliffe, the Governor of Malta, favoured a didactic

LEFT: relatively revealing beach fashion.
ABOVE: a more cautious approach.

approach, with thematic gardens illustrating the range of Mediterranean flora. Miss Campbell, a later owner, introduced exotic plants from Asia and Central America. Just around the corner, Major Lawrence Johnston changed the Riviera landscape by introducing rare trees from China, Japan, Asia and Africa. Sir Thomas Hanbury, a Victorian spice trader, made his fortune in China and retired to the hills on the French-Italian border. There, he introduced Norfolk pines and exotic plants from all corners of the British Empire. In Cannes, an early Victorian, Thomas Woolfield, introduced the gooseberry and the sweet potato, eucalyptus and acacia.

transplanted, they remained rooted to a British social code. Even for D. H. Lawrence and Somerset Maugham, the lotus-eating south was a miasma. Outsiders viewed the British on the Riviera more critically. Locals on the Côte d'Azur disliked patronising references to "our Gallic friends". Berlioz rued the day he married an Englishwoman on the Riviera. Stendhal saw the men as morose killjoys and the women as philistines or prudes. Henry James commented on the British "insular faculty to gush".

Katherine Mansfield confined herself to mocking English insularity, with a liking for Dundee cake and familiar nursery foods.

The British landscaped large sections of Nice, Cannes, Menton and Cap Ferrat. To some locals, Somerset Maugham is merely the person who introduced the avocado to the Riviera. When it comes to garden snobbery on the Riviera, it is hard to know whether it is a British import or a French anomaly.

The literati

But the British visitors offered more than blue blood and green fingers. For British writers and artists, the Riviera became a place to express smothered sensibilities. Enchanted by the soft light and dramatic scenery, these hot-house plants hoped to stretch out in the sun. Yet, once

Mansfield, living in Menton in the 1920s, avoided the most anglicised spots, such as Monaco. Even so, she couldn't fail to notice the pervasive British influence. The Riviera was home to British charities, lending libraries, boarding schools and Scottish tea houses. Local British animal protection societies made sure bull-fighting did not spread to the Riviera. By 1928, Menton competed with Monaco in welcoming Girl Guides and Brownies.

Glitz and glamour

Despite the virtuous Girl Guides, pleasure not duty was the keynote of the 1920s. A poster in Menton contrasts an ailing Victorian gentleman with an elegant 1920s flapper: "In the old days visitors apparently came here for their health. Today, it is a town of luxury and gaiety." If the Edwardian visitors were dutiful, the Americans embodied the pleasure principle. Residents were now judged on the size of their pools and yachts, not their consciences. The British played only supporting roles in a glittering American show.

Although the Americans wrote the script, the British occasionally upstaged them. Glamorous stars such as the Duke of Westminster regularly sailed the Côte d'Azur. "Whose yacht is that?" Amanda asks in *Private Lives*. Elyot replies: "The Duke of Westminster's, I expect. It always

discreet ceremony, far from the ... ground. The couple later spent thei... exile in a luxurious villa on the C...

In 1945, the Windsors' villa proved a major embarrassment to Winston Churchill. After her fraternisation with German officers, Coco Chanel was arrested as a collaborator but was quickly released after threatening to expose Churchill. He had made secret payments to the Germans to secure the protection of the Duke of Windsor's villa during the war.

Even so, Churchill was the best-loved British star of the period. Towards the end of his life he was an honoured guest on the Onassis yacht.

is." Noël Coward and Gertrude Lawrence rehearsed the play in Edward Molyneux's villa on Cap d'Ail in 1930.

In 1934, the Prince of Wales stayed in Cannes with Wallis Simpson's party and presented her with a diamond charm as a sign of his infatuation. It was to Cannes that Mrs Simpson retreated when it became clear that the King would abdicate rather than give her up. The couple even contemplated marriage on the Riviera but bowed to George VI's wishes for a more

LEFT: Aristotle Onassis (left) and Winston Churchill boarding the millionaire's yacht in 1959.
ABOVE: the Duke and Duchess of Windsor.

Patrick Howarth in *When the Riviera was Ours* describes how Aristotle Onassis could be seen feeding the enfeebled Churchill caviare, a symbolic tribute from "the new power on the Riviera to the most famous representative of the grandeurs of the past".

Social changes

From the 1950s, a new wave of expatriates settled in Haut-de-Cagnes, Vence and Grasse, attracted to the arts and crafts traditions in the foothills. In the 1970s, the British built Isola 2000, the skiing resort, and invested heavily in Cannes and St-Tropez. A more recent boom town is Sophia-Antipolis, the Riviera's Silicon Valley. Here, there is little sign of the tweed-suited matron, the elderly naval captain, the Anglican clergyman or other British Riviera stereotypes. Mike Meade, editor of *Riviera Reporter*, claims never to have met "the retired colonel who doesn't speak a word of French, scowls continually at the natives, and thinks that the Queen's Birthday should be a national holiday here."

If this Riviera stereotype is extinct, *tant mieux*. In today's Riviera, the emphasis is on integration, aided by bilingual psychiatrists and dual-language colleges. There are Anglo-American schools in Mougins, Nice and Sophia-Antipolis. Monte-Carlo's Riviera Radio can be heard from

St-Tropez to the Italian border and the station claims that four out of five English speakers regularly tune in.

Socially, expatriates can choose from the Riviera Singles Group, the Conservatives Abroad, the Oxbridge Set or the Dog Exchange Club. The Anglo-American Group of Provence indulges in Scottish dancing and Marseille cuisine. The Franco-Irish Friendship Group competes fiercely with the Association Franco-Irlande. The British Association has branches in Cannes, Nice, Menton and Monaco.

The Riviera Establishment survives, nonetheless. One English agency supplies British nannies, housekeepers and butlers. British antique

dealers regularly advertise for "1920s cocktail watches, Fabergé enamels and Edwardian gem set jewellery".

English lending libraries exist in Menton and Vence, as do English bookshops in Cannes, Antibes, Monaco and Sophia-Antipolis. Anglican churches are active in most large resorts, including Nice, Menton and Monaco. Elsewhere, there are British banks, pubs and the long-established John Taylor & Son estate agency. The British distrust of French plumbing remains as a relic of a bygone age. Still, one sign of the times is the existence of an Anglo-American hospital for alcoholism and drug dependency.

For some Britons, the Côte d'Azur was the place to die – D. H. Lawrence in Vence, Aubrey Beardsley in Menton. But today it is a place for the living, a second home to countless British celebrities, though Joan Collins, Ringo Starr, Michael Caine, George Michael and Elton John are hardly a typical cross-section of ·British expatriates. Nor is the image of the retired English colonel, playing golf and downing snifters at sundown, very accurate either.

Tea, lawn tennis and churches

The British simplified the south yet were deeply affected by it. The aesthetic sensibilty was not the fey whim of the consumptive artist or the cultural élite. It was a creative urge to leave a lasting mark, whether a gallery or garden, a civic statue or a treatise on spiders. Even retired Empire-builders, spice traders and clergymen succumbed, becoming art collectors, landscape gardeners or benefactors.

The Noël Coward song *I Went to a Marvellous Party* was inspired by his visit to a high society gathering on the Riviera. Yet the British legacy encompasses more than glamour. Frederic Harrison, a Victorian visitor, defined the British contribution more prosaically: "tea, tubs, sanitary appliances, lawn tennis and churches". Rather like a grand jumble sale, the British gift was a magnificent white elephant. Glorious gardens vied with eccentric institutions, alien churches and curious new games. British names and niceties, philanthropy and prejudice are part of the job lot. In the words of Edward VII, that notorious Riviera adventurer, *"Vive l'Entente Cordiale."* ❏

LEFT: a languid moment under the pines at Juan-les-Pins. **RIGHT:** the winter season in Nice.

NICE

HÔTEL N

SITUATION SPLEN
RESTAURANT D

ANTIBES
SA PLAGE DE JUAN-LES-PINS
SON CAP.
STATION D'ÉTÉ ET D'HIVER

ROGER
BRODERS

LOST CAVIARE DAYS

In the 1800s, the crowned heads of Europe flocked to the Riviera for gaiety, glamour and gambling. By the 1920s, the stars of the American Jazz Age had taken over

"The resplendent names – Cannes, Nice, Monte-Carlo – began to glow through their torpid camouflage, whispering of old Kings come here to dine or die, of rajahs tossing Buddha's eyes to English ballerinas, of Russian princes turning the weeks into Baltic twilights in the lost Caviare days."

Tender is the Night is a champagne toast to the end of an era. Published in 1934, F. Scott Fitzgerald's novel is infused with the American glamour that flooded the Riviera from the 1920s. This seductive vision of the "hot sweet south" is not a true mirror but a montage of magical moments. Strictly speaking, the kings, princes and rajahs ruled an earlier age and a moral climate conditioned by Victorian values. Even then, the balmy Mediterranean climate wrought its own magic: these were Victorian values on vacation.

The post-war Americans may have invented the summer season, but the Victorians and Edwardians were pale winter migrants. Renoir called this winter sanatorium "a hothouse into which fragile people take refuge". During the *belle époque*, from 1862 until World War I, the Riviera became the royals' winter retreat. The arrival of the railway link to Cannes in 1863 stamped the Riviera with the public's seal of approval. Invalids were the pioneers of the Côte d'Azur, a trend started by the British in the 1850s. Within 10 years, Hyères, Cannes and Nice had large foreign colonies in the winter. A few years later, Beaulieu, Menton and San Remo competed for the aristocratic clientèle while Monte-Carlo catered exclusively to the rich and pleasure-loving.

Royals aplenty

"Princes, princes, nothing but princes. If you like them, you're in the right place," complained Guy de Maupassant of Cannes in 1884. The royals were headed by Queen Victoria, the

Empress of Russia and Emperor Frederick of Germany. At the turn of the 20th century, Menton alone received the Kings of Italy, Sweden, Saxe, Belgium and Bulgaria, as well as visits by Count Pushkin and Russian Grand Dukes. The Shah of Persia and President Kruger of South Africa stayed in Menton at the same time. They

narrowly missed Emperor Franz Josef of Austria and his wife. Sometimes the royals literally crossed paths: while on a carriage drive near Villefranche, Queen Victoria passed King Leopold, out on his regular daily stroll.

In the same year, the young Aga Khan III arrived on a steamer from India and found Queen Victoria in Nice and the Emperor Franz Josef at Cap Martin. In addition, there were "a score or so Russian Grand Dukes and Austrian Archdukes in their villas and palaces, half the English peerage with a generous sprinkling of millionaires from industry and finance; and most of the Almanac de Gotha from Germany, the Austro-Hungarian Empire, the Balkan

PRECEDING PAGES: poster for the grand Hôtel Negresco in Nice. **LEFT:** 1920s advertising for Antibes and Juan-les-Pins. **RIGHT:** a fashionable cocktail, depicted by Edmond Lahaye.

countries lately emancipated from Ottoman rule, and Tsarist Russia". As the Aga Khan modestly put it: "The young man from Bombay was dazzled and awed."

Homes and hotels

The royals visited not as Grand Tourists of the 18th century, explorers on a unique adventure, but as *habitués*, comfortable in their second homes. Second palaces would be a more accurate description. Queen Victoria had a huge residence in the Cimiez quarter of Nice. Menton's magnificent 18th-century Palais de Carnolès was owned by the Queen of Prussia in the 1860s

a Parisian orchestra played Gregorian chants or gypsy music before Anastasia's afternoon nap.

The regal lifestyle

When the Riviera was Ours, Patrick Howarth's wonderful but unashamedly chauvinistic account, argues that even foreign royals followed an English lifestyle on the Riviera. Prince Albert of Prussia regularly attended Anglican services at Christ Church in Cannes, where he made it known that he hoped the hymns would include *The Son of God goes forth to war*. Tea and tennis were immovable fixtures; Russian Grand Dukes wore starched

and by Prince Metternich shortly afterwards. But given the difficulties of finding suitable French servants, royal visitors often preferred to spend the whole winter season in hotels.

Unsurprisingly, such hotels were known as *les palaces de la Côte d'Azur*. Amongst the grandest were L'Hermitage in Monte-Carlo and the Victoria Hotel on the Promenade des Anglais in Nice. Charles of Prussia stayed in the Victoria in the 1860s while Tsarevitch Alexander made it his home until his accession to the Russian throne in 1881. In Menton, the Winter Palace was favoured by Oriental royals, while Grand Duchess Anastasia occupied the Riviera Palace. In the lovely *salon de musique*,

white linen; Belgian and Swedish aristocrats challenged one another to jolly polo matches.

Chauvinism aside, the royal way of life on the Riviera was not so much English as regal. Crested dice were thrown in the Monte-Carlo Casino; coroneted carriages paraded the Promenade des Anglais in Nice; the *jeunesse dorée* dined on caviare, blinis and pink champagne in the Hôtel de l'Hermitage. Leopold I of Belgium was Queen Victoria's domineering uncle but it was his son who made an indelible mark on the Riviera. As an ageing playboy, Leopold II wintered on the Riviera from the 1890s to his death in 1909. He resided at a villa on Cap Martin and filled the grounds with lush vegetation he had transplanted from the Belgian Congo.

Princess Daisy of Pless described Leopold peeling grapes with "a look of cruelty on his face as if he were skinning alive all the members of the Aborigines Protection Society". Apart from orchids and palms, Leopold's main hobby was young girls. Princess Daisy describes how his lecherous pursuits were hampered by a dangling white beard and grotesquely long fingernails.

Eugénie and Sissi

Empress Eugénie of France, often described as the *doyenne* of the Riviera royalty, also held court on Cap Martin in the 1890s. Although

Eugénie quietly advised a variety of foreign sovereigns and ministers on world politics.

Eugénie's neighbour and contemporary was Elizabeth, Empress of Austria, married to Franz Josef I. Known as Sissi, Elizabeth was a daughter of a Bavarian duke and married her cousin at the age of 15. Sissi led a troubled life and, as Queen of Hungary, had a high political profile that was her downfall: she was assassinated by an Italian anarchist in Geneva. Sissi's restlessness and spontaneity offended Viennese society so she was delighted to find that the Riviera was not etiquette-bound. Considered the most beautiful Princess in Europe, she nonetheless

Spanish-born and married to a French Emperor, Eugénie was an anglophile who had been educated in England. After the Empire collapsed in 1870, she left Deauville for Kent. By the 1890s, her husband and son had died and Eugénie relished her role of *grande dame* in exile, even managing to charm Queen Victoria. Eugénie had long been a diplomat behind the scenes and, after a dull period of suburban exile in Chislehurst in England, found the Riviera a more satisfying stage. From her rococo-style Villa Cyrnos,

---

LEFT: gamblers at the Juan-les-Pins casino, captured by Edmond Lahaye. **ABOVE:** the Grand Hotel, facing the beach at Juan-les-Pins.

had an unhappy marriage and was labelled neurotic. Her secluded villa, the Grand Hôtel du Cap Martin, represented comfort and privacy, and she found solace walking the long coastal path around the Cape. Having no wish to meet her husband in Monaco, she usually walked the other way, towards Menton.

German visitors

Teutonic aristocrats regularly wintered on the Riviera, particularly after a German edition of Dr Bennet's *Winter and Spring on the Shores of the Mediterranean* appeared in 1863. In the same year, Maximilian II of Bavaria bought a huge Niçois villa that had previously belonged to the Russian Empress Alexandra Feodorovna.

Cap Martin became a Germanic haunt by the end of the century. The Grand Duke of Saxe-Weimar bought a villa there in 1894 and was soon joined by an exceedingly minor royal, Jean II, Prince of Lichtenstein. Frederick William, the last Crown Prince of Germany, wintered on the Cap and was known as "Little Willie" long before he retired to England in 1918. However, the German aristocrats were generally more discreet than their British and Russian counterparts. When a German claimed to be on the Riviera for health, not high jinks, he was generally believed.

RUSSIAN ROULETTE

The Russians were enthusiastic gamblers. Princess Souvorov arrived in Monaco in 1869 with an "infallible" method. At casinos across Europe she had made notes of every winning number in all the games she had seen. But despite thousands of files, she lost 300,000 francs in a couple of hours. Suddenly, her luck changed and she won for eight nights in succession, breaking the bank twice.

To celebrate, she scandalised high society by holding a party for complete strangers. The only entry requirement was that guests should be amusing. The locals refused to let her rent a room for the party so she bought a villa instead and simply gave it away the next day.

From Russia with money

The same could not be said for the Russians. Before World War I, the Russian community was second only to the British in size and influence. In 1856, Alexandra Feodorovna, the widow of Tsar Nicholas I, bought Villa Acquaviva on the Promenade des Anglais and forged the early Russian links with Nice.

Not that the Russians needed much encouragement. French was the language of the Russian court and the Riviera made a restful second home, a welcome change from Russian winters and rebellious serfs. Alexandra's son, the Grand Duke Constantine, followed in his mother's footsteps and bought Villa Lavit, also on the Promenade des Anglais. The seafront and the Boulevard Tzarewitch soon became distinct Russian colonies, set at a safe distance from the English camp at Cimiez. The Russians congregated in the Ferme Russe, Russian tea rooms run by the formidable Madame Chirikov.

The pastries provided stiff competition to the cream cakes in Perrimond-Rumpelmayer, the favourite German haunt. Below the domed winter garden of La Ferme Russe, imported Russian servants worked the samovars while their mistresses discussed upcoming charity balls or the dangers of rheumatic gout.

The opening of the railway to Nice in 1864 had an immediate impact: Tsar Alexander II arrived a week later and was soon enthralled enough to consider building a Russian Orthodox church in Nice. The flamboyant green-and-gold domes remain a testament to the importance of the Russian community in the 19th century. In 1880, Grand Duchess Anastasia, Tsar Nicholas II's aunt, founded the Association Orthodoxe Russe which looked after consumptive soldiers and students. After the Revolution, the home became known as the Maison Russe and, linked to the Russian Red Cross, still welcomes Russian émigrés.

The Russian women had a particularly high social profile on the Riviera. One *grande dame* was the Princess Kotschouby whose ochre *belle-époque* villa is now the Chéret Museum in Nice. The Princess Caramachimay abandoned her troublesome Russian estates and emigrated to Cap Martin at the turn of the 20th century. Princess Anna Chervachidzé settled on a grand estate nearby; it later sheltered a skulking Greta Garbo and is now owned by a Lebanese millionaire.

Agas and maharajahs

Non-European royals were also drawn to the Riviera, including the Princess of Siam and the Bey of Algeria. One of the most eccentric visitors was the Maharajah of Kaputhala. In 1897, he arrived at Monte-Carlo's Hôtel de Paris with a vast retinue. One servant, dressed in national costume and bedecked with gold and jewels, would stand behind the Maharajah's chair at dinner. When signalled, he sprinkled flakes of real silver on the royal curries. A later maharajah was instrumental in opening the Martinez Hotel in Cannes in 1926: he insisted on Louis XVI bedrooms for all the guests.

where "the only unguarded exit is the chute from the swimming pool to the sea".

Us and them

Foreigners maintained a frontier mentality. The only local people they met were shopkeepers and servants; even this problem could be circumvented by importing staff or living in hotels. Expatriates further down the social scale often ignored all other foreign residents. "You may see English, German and French families pass many weeks together in the same house, eat twice a day at the same table, and sit for hours in the same salon without even exchanging

Sir Mohammed Shah, the Aga Khan III, was one of the few hereditary rulers whose affection for the Riviera has been echoed by his descendants. In 1908, the Aga Khan married an Italian dancer and installed her in a Middle Eastern-style villa above Monaco. Their son, Major Aly Khan, was a member of the Free French forces that helped liberate the Riviera. Aly then went on to marry Rita Hayworth, while his father competed by marrying Yvette, a "Miss France" bathing belle. The current Aga Khan lives in an art deco mansion in Antibes

a word." Such was Frederic Harrison's view of sour-faced Victorian visitors in 1887.

The Riviera was only relatively free from social restraints; in Menton cemetery, each nationality and religion was given a separate burial tier. Nor were the pleasures of the South egalitarian; the Riviera was the preserve of the rich until the Edwardian era. In the 1840s, a house in Nice could be rented for £300 a year, while in the 1880s it cost £1,200 for the winter season. In 1896, the writer Augustus Hare commented approvingly: "Nice is a home for the millionaire and the working man. The intermediate class is not wanted. Visitors are expected to have money, and if they have to look at pounds, shillings

LEFT: Tsarina Maria Alexandrovna, a frequent visitor, in 1865. **ABOVE:** the casino on the pier in Nice.

The Blue Train

A long with the Santa Fe Superchief, the Orient Express and the Trans-Siberian Express, the Blue Train was never just a train; to travel on it from London to the Côte d'Azur in the 1920s and '30s represented the epitome of style and fashion. It was said that, for a woman to have made it in the world, she should have dined at the Ritz and Colony restaurants in New York, the Everglades Club in Palm Beach, the Ritz in Paris, Claridge's in London and the Hôtel du Cap in Antibes, sailed on the *Berengaria* and the *Aquitania*, and, of

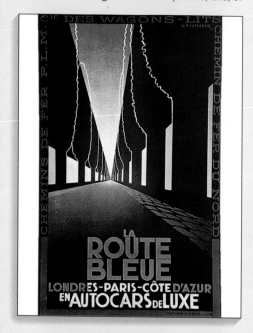

course, travelled on the Blue Train. It was the *only* way to travel to the Côte d'Azur.

From the 1850s onwards, the South of France was opened up to foreign visitors as trains reduced travelling times from about three weeks by carriage to just a couple of days by train. All that was then needed was sleeping accommodation, of the type pioneered by Pullman in the United States.

The first manufacturer of sleeping cars in Europe was the Compagnie Internationale des Wagons-Lits, founded by an enterprising Belgian, Georges Nagelmackers, in 1872. Its sleeping cars became famous, and the Calais-Nice-Rome Express, the first train to the south to be equipped with sleeping accommodation, began operating in 1883, about

six months after the Orient Express. The Italian section was little used and the train eventually became known as the Calais-Mediterranean Express. It was popularly known as the Blue Train after 1922 when blue and gold painted sleeping cars first appeared. The words "*Train bleu*" were painted on the carriages only after 1949.

This luxurious palace on wheels, whose carriages catered to only 10 passengers, would leave Calais at 1pm, arriving in Monte-Carlo at 9.30 the following morning. For early British visitors travelling south for the winter, nothing could beat the pleasurable contrast of boarding under the grey skies and smog of London and waking the next morning to the blue skies, terracotta roofs and orange trees of the Mediterranean.

It became known as the "millionaires' train" with some justification. The American James Gordon Bennett, owner of the *New York Herald* and famous for his profligacy, once, to the horror of his valet, tipped the conductor 20,000 francs. The conductor used the money to open a restaurant in Boulogne. When Charlie Chaplin came to stay with Frank Jay Gould, he arrived on the Blue Train. The Duke of Windsor had a carriage with a specially designed bathroom. When the casinos brought girls down from Maxim's in Paris they were guaranteed return tickets on the Blue Train (to be used if they failed to snare a rich husband). The fame of the Blue Train has been enshrined by the arts; Agatha Christie set a Hercule Poirot story on it, *The Mystery of the Blue Train*. Diaghilev directed a musical called *Le Train Bleu*, which was written by Jean Cocteau, with bathing costumes by Chanel and curtain by Picasso.

For Charles Graves in *The Riviera Revisited*, his account of the Côte d'Azur after World War II, being able to board the Blue Train again meant the war was truly over. He even records the menu: "Off to the Gare de Lyons, where the Blue Train itself is waiting with a six-course dinner of clear soup, red mullet, pâté with truffles, chouxfleur au gratin, cheese, fruit and coffee. Then bed in a speckless sleeping compartment which has miraculously survived all bombing by the British and American aircraft."

Today the Blue Train is no more, though its name endures. Monte-Carlo Casino has a restaurant called Le Train Bleu, using its traditional decor. However, it is still possible to travel in considerable comfort overnight through France, half-waking at dim-lit stations in the dead of night and rising to the golden sunlight glinting off the Mediterranean. ❏

LEFT: advertising poster for the Blue Train.

and pence, had much better remain at home."

Victorian and Edwardian visitors were not exclusively aristocratic. "Money increases quickly," wrote Trollope in 1866, "and distances decrease." Bourgeois visitors were, however, in the minority until the 1920s.

American takeover

While the flow of royal visitors continued during the inter-war years, a new élite emerged: the American dollar kings. Dr Bennet's *Winter and Spring on the Shores of the Mediterranean* was published in New York in 1870 and provoked a new wave of wealthy visitors. The simple yet sophisticated pleasures of the Mediterranean appealed to jaded American tycoons. In 1898, Dr Allis, the art collector, was attracted to the unspoilt site of the Palais de Carnolès in Menton. After adding two new wings and replanting the gardens, Allis installed his priceless paintings.

James Gordon Bennett, the proprietor of the *New York Herald*, started a European edition of the paper as a pretext for living on the Riviera. As well as running the *International Herald Tribune*, Bennett found time to indulge fellow-Americans at his Beaulieu villa. As for his yacht, *Lysistrata*, even Vanderbilt was impressed. Manned by a 100-strong crew, the yacht had three decks, Turkish baths and a resident Alderney cow. The millionaire once invited Drexel, Biddle and Vanderbilt to dine at the Café Riche, his favourite restaurant in Monte-Carlo. The Americans were turned away from the restaurant terrace when the management decided that only cocktails should be served there. An outraged Bennett immediately bought the restaurant for $40,000 and sacked the manager. In appreciation for well-cooked lamb chops, Bennett promptly handed over the restaurant to Ciro, his favourite waiter, by way of a tip. The fortunate Ciro then went on to open successful restaurants all over Europe.

Easy dames

Colourful courtesans such as Mata Hari and "La Belle Otéro" worked their way through the foreign ranks. Although Mata Hari's spying was beyond the pale, until 1914 courtesans had an accepted status in Riviera society. As Mata Hari, the Dutch show-girl Gertrud Zelle came to Monte-Carlo to perform "exotic dances".

Her stage name, meaning "sunrise" in Malay, was matched by exotic looks that captivated the French and German Ministers of Information. One night in the Casino, an agent accused her of secreting stolen documents in her bodice. Mata Hari promptly shot him and was excused on the grounds of self-defence.

By contrast, La Belle Otéro was apolitical. At the age of 14, Caroline Otéro, a Spanish gypsy, married an Italian baron and spent her honeymoon in Monaco. After her husband had lost in the Casino, she removed all the gold buttons from her dress and, as well as causing a stir, amassed a fortune on the tables. Caroline quickly abandoned

GAMBLERS ANONYMOUS

J. P. Morgan, the American steel magnate, was a notorious gambler at the Monte-Carlo Casino. On one occasion he asked if the individual limit for bets could be doubled to 20,000 francs. When the director refused, Morgan left on the spot, complaining that he wouldn't waste his time with such paltry amounts. Morgan went on to form the US Steel Corporation. Charles Schwab, the Corporation's President, was also an inveterate gambler. After tales of Schwab's profligacy reached the American press, Morgan hypocritically took him to task. Schwab's defence – "But I sin openly, not behind closed doors" – was countered with, "But that's exactly what doors are for."

RIGHT: poster for the Riviera Express, which ran between Berlin and Monte-Carlo.

her husband and began a new career as a *grande horizontale*. Her voluptuous figure was appreciated by Edward VII and Kaiser Wilhelm II. One of her lovers was a hideous German millionaire but, as La Belle Otéro pointed out, "Such a rich man can never be ugly." Caroline retired to Monaco in 1922 but her legendary figure lives on in Cannes' Carlton Hotel: the twin domes are said to have been inspired by La Belle Otéro's perfect breasts.

American eccentrics

There was a distinct change of climate after World War I. The courtesans were no more; the Russians were dead or in exile; the Kings of Italy,

Spain, Albania and Yugoslavia clung to their thrones; most royals were in financial straits. Only the Americans had the means to live out their fantasies. With the glamorous new arrivals, winter was banished and the summer season launched. Writer E. Phillips Oppenheim slept aboard a yacht, which was known as the floating double bed; the women were expected to stay awake at night to deal with the mosquitoes.

There was no shortage of eccentrics on the new summer stage. Mr Neal, an American millionaire guest at the Hôtel de l'Hermitage, installed an artificial moon in his window to remind him that it was night and therefore time to go to the Casino. One of his milder whims

was to invite 80 guests to a free dinner, provided that they laughed at his jokes. His peremptory method of summoning staff consisted of firing one pistol shot for room service and two shots if he required a chambermaid for personal services.

Henry Clews, the wealthy American sculptor, was also a noted eccentric. In La Napoule, his Saracen castle, Clews recreated a medieval setting, complete with minstrel gallery and staff dressed in Provençal costume. His wife's pet peacocks were notorious, frequently straying onto the railway line where they often brought the Blue Train to a halt. As Patrick Howarth remarks, "It happened so frequently that the SNCF felt obliged to make a formal demand that the peacocks shouldn't be allowed on the line."

Writers, dancers and artists

Not for nothing were the 1920s known as *les années folles*. Even if the bodies of bankrupt gamblers were no longer immured in the Casino walls, fortunes could still be won or lost on a dropped gold button. But, amidst the wanton partying, creativity seemed to flourish. Colette, Scott Fitzgerald, Somerset Maugham, Katherine Mansfield and Blasco Ibañez were writing themselves into different patches of the Riviera.

In Monte-Carlo, the impresario Raoul Gunsbourg was the first to stage Wagner outside Bayreuth and, as Director of the Monte Carlo Opera, also introduced the public to works by Berlioz, Massenet and Tchaikovsky. Ravel was invited to compose for the orchestra and created the *Ballet Pour Ma Fille*, based on Colette's work. But Gunsbourg's greatest coup was to convince Sergei Diaghilev and his Ballets Russes to settle in Monaco. In turn, Diaghilev persuaded the greatest composers of the age, including Debussy and Stravinsky, to write for the Ballets Russes. The company, starring Pavlova and Nijinsky, danced to such modern classics as *L'Après-midi d'un Faune* and *The Firebird*.

As if this were not enough, the costumes and sets were designed by Picasso and Matisse, Utrillo and De Chirico, Georges Braque and André Derain. Unsurprisingly, the ballets ran at a financial loss but Diaghilev was not deterred: "I don't spend a sou on myself. I have very simple tastes: only the best is good enough." Diaghilev praised Isadora Duncan for breaking with classical tradition but she spurned an invitation to see the Ballets Russes: "I don't care much for acrobats." Instead, she ran up huge hotel bills at the Negresco in Nice and, before her tragic entanglement with a silk scarf, indulged her penchant for chasing young men.

The beautiful people

In the 1920s and '30s, the Riviera was in glamorous American hands. Scott Fitzgerald enthused about "the soft-pawed night and the ghostly wash of the Mediterranean far below." Gerald and Sara Murphy, the originals for Dick and Nicole Diver in *Tender is the Night*, had discovered it some years before. After being introduced to the Riviera by Cole Porter, the couple bought Villa America on the Cap d'Antibes and there

herself. Although long treated as *arrivistes*, the couple exerted great influence over the Riviera for 50 years. The tasteless splendour of Juan-les-Pins is their lasting imprint.

World War II drew the curtains on old American glamour but the Riviera has proved irresistible to Hollywood stars. The Hôtel du Cap-Eden Roc provides the sumptuous link. Situated on the tip of the Cap d'Antibes, this gilded white palace has long been the mecca for the American set, from the Murphys onwards.

A new wave brought such stars as Clark Gable, Humphrey Bogart and Rita Hayworth. At different times, John Wayne and Charlie

entertained the Lost Generation. Dorothy Parker, Hemingway and the Fitzgeralds needed little encouragement to sample the sea and sun.

The Goulds, along with the Murphys, entertained *le beau monde*, welcoming André Gide and Giraudoux as well as American high society. Frank Jay Gould, heir to a railway empire, virtually created Juan-les-Pins. For Florence, his Californian wife, the Riviera was also a *coup de foudre*: she quickly opened a casino and hotel and created a neo-Gothic villa for

LEFT: Frank Jay Gould and his wife, Florence.
ABOVE: guests at the Grand Hôtel du Cap-Eden Roc, photographed in 1929.

Chaplin were entertained by the hotel's private funicular to the beach. While indulging in cocktails and caviare, John F. Kennedy admired the exotic gardens from the gigantic stone terrace.

The star-spangled tradition continues. The Cote d'Azur has not lost its glamour, and continues to attract the rich and famous who rent or own villas on Cap Ferrat or Cap d'Antibes. Rock stars and supermodels still flock to St-Tropez, to dine at the beach clubs or sip cocktails on quayside yachts. The grand hotels retain their legendary status and helicopters, private planes and limousines still provide luxury transport for the privileged percentage to keep the dream of caviare days alive for everyone else. ❏

THE RIVIERA AT WAR

In 1940, the Riviera spirit was severely dampened when Hitler marched into France, but the coast bounced back to become a hotbed of Resistance activity

The 1939 summer season on the Riviera attracted the customary cosmopolitan crowd and, enlivened by the novelties of water-skiing and skin-diving, was said to have been the best yet. Colonel Josef Beck, the Polish Foreign Minister, rubbed shoulders with Sir Robert Vansittart of the British Foreign Office and Crown Prince Umberto of Italy. The Duke of Windsor, licking the wounds of the abdication which had ended his brief reign as Edward VIII of England, took a 10-year lease on a villa near Cannes.

There were, however, intimations of the sinister clouds gathering over Europe. The shadowy face within a large car which cruised around San Remo – and was once seen parked advantageously above the annual military parade in Nice – belonged to Hermann Goering. In the Hôtel Beaulieu in Cannes, Dr E. Wightman Ginner gave a series of lectures on what to do in an air raid. Rumour spoke of secret landings at Cap Ferrat and Cap Martin – spies! Hitler occupied Austria, the Czech Sudeten, and then invaded Poland. World War II was on.

The Phoney War

While Hitler gathered strength for his attack on Western Europe, the Riviera prepared for the inevitable. Two British colliers arrived in Cannes to evacuate British subjects but some, such as the septuagenarian Miss Amy Paget, chose to stay put and ran up the British flag over her Cannes villa.

The Windsors, who also remained, invited Maurice Chevalier to their villa "in the perhaps forlorn hope," the controversial duchess wrote later, "that he might be inspired to supply a last flash of lightheartedness in that dismal atmosphere". The local labour force, on which the expatriate colony depended, was swallowed up by France's mobilisation. Waiters and tradesmen were transplanted to the concrete bunkers of the Maginot Line. Yet still no shots were fired.

LEFT: Resistance fighters in Hyères.
RIGHT: American troops rounding up Germans.

On 10 May 1940, Hitler's army simply side-stepped the Maginot Line by marching through the Low Countries and attacking France from the north. The Nazis marched into Paris on 14 June. From there, they pushed south to Nantes, Vichy, Dijon and Lyon and west to Bordeaux and the Spanish frontier.

Something Vichy

The Axis advance was suspended when the French government resigned and Marshal Pétain asked for, and was granted, an armistice. France was divided into two zones. Germany occupied the Atlantic coastline from Spain to the Low Countries and the industrial north above a line drawn roughly between Tours and Dijon. The unoccupied zone consisted of the relatively barren mountain areas, the Rhône valley, the Mediterranean coast and a puppet government named after its "capital", Vichy.

There was, of course, no certainty that Germany would not renege on the armistice and take over "Free France" as well, but in the

circumstances it was very much more conge-
nial than the north for stranded soldiers,
downed Allied air crews and persecuted minori-
ties like Jews, gypsies and Communists. For
the following four years, the war in the South of
France was mostly about providing a safe passage for these fugitives. Many of the civilians
were helped across the Mediterranean to French
North Africa. The escape route for Allied military personnel, including those arriving from
Central Europe via Switzerland, was along the
Riviera to neutral Spain.

Once the evaders had crossed the demarca-
tion line into Vichy France, they were still liable

Covert operations

With a long history of underhand survival, the
Marseille Mafia was fitter than most. To make
contact with these dubious characters, British
Intelligence turned to Nubar Gulbenkian, the
son of the legendary Iranian oil dealer. Young
Gulbenkian tackled the undertaking with the
help of Bailey, his English valet, and it nearly
came to grief at the outset in the Hôtel des
Ambassadeurs in Vichy. Bailey, having bor-
rowed an iron to press his employer's clothes,
bumped into a delegation of German officers
and dropped the iron on the foot of Field Marshal von Brauchitsch, Commander-in-Chief of

to arrest by the police but were not normally in
danger of being handed back to the Germans.
There were plenty of Vichy officials ready to
give them a nod and a wink, but if caught they
were assembled in Fort St-Jean in Marseille or,
later on, at St-Hippolyte du Fort at Nîmes or La
Turbie, outside Monte-Carlo. They were then
neither quite prisoners nor free. In Marseille,
for example, Allied officers reported on Monday
mornings for a roll call, collected their rations,
sold them on the black market, and applied the
proceeds to renting lodgings in the city. Their
ambition was somehow to slip away to Spain,
and British Intelligence created a branch known
as MI9 to help them realise that objective.

the German Army. Brauchitsch stared at Bailey, assumed he must be American, and chose
not to pursue the matter.

The pair were instructed by London to go to
Perpignan and look out for a garage proprietor
named "Parker". In time-honoured fashion, he
would be reading the newspaper *L'Indépendant*
upside-down. In case he was not alone in this
curious habit, a test question was provided:
"Have you got a Parker pen? A Parker Duo-
fold?" The reader in question passed with flying colours. Within 20 minutes Gulbenkian had
negotiated a price for guides to smuggle men
across the frontier: £40 for an officer, £20 for
other ranks. Payment was by results and the

money would be deposited in England for collection after the war. "Parker" was clearly willing to bank on the ultimate outcome.

Several British officers who had recently escaped from France were sent back under the auspices of the Special Operations Executive (SOE), a unit established by Churchill to keep the enemy on its toes by organising and supplying national resistance movements. They arrived by parachute, by submarine and from Gibraltar either in an armed British trawler flying false colours or in feluccas manned by Polish crews so exuberant that even the Polish Navy preferred to manage without them.

When not pretending to be Damon Runyon, Churchill was "Pierre Chauvet", estate agent. Flush with British War Office money, he moved into a comfortable flat in Cannes and had a regular table at Chez Robert. Churchill's memoirs are a litany of *pièces de résistance* and the search for a complementary wine. A bottle of 1911 Château Chambord was just the ticket to wash down a herb omelette and M. Robert's miraculous chicken on the occasion of Churchill's lunch with a charming "Madame Rondet". At their next meeting – at Chez Robert again, of course – they are joined by "an aristocratic Frenchman with a monocle". Churchill

A local Churchill

The Poles did not deign to conceal their activities. "The reception mob is there every night and… carry on like a Bank Holiday crowd on Derby Day," reported Peter Churchill, one of the British agents. Like many of the SOE operatives, he was in his early 20s and the whole affair was treated like a game. Churchill (no relation to Sir Winston) affected Damon Runyon prose in his official reports, the dubious theory being that any Germans intercepting his messages would be completely baffled.

LEFT: the American landings. **ABOVE:** the beach at Juan-les-Pins, a minefield in 1944.

divides his attention between "an excellent *loup de mer*… with a dry white wine", Madame Rondet's beautiful face, and "the vast expanse of the blue Mediterranean, calm and untroubled below a cloudless sky". He has to tear himself away from the cheese, coffee and brandy – "all as delicious as the rest of the meal" – to mount his bicycle and race off to the station to attend to some urgent undercover business.

Churchill soon made the acquaintance of Lise, an agent who arrived by felucca and was, if possible, even lovelier than Madame Rondet. "This girl's dynamite," he noted in his journal and, as things turned out, he later married her. But it was about then, November 1942, that the

Allies invaded North Africa. Hitler immediately terminated the French "free" zone, the occupation of which was entrusted to the Italians.

SOE had worked out plans to blow up roads, tunnels and bridges in such an eventuality, but these were countermanded by superiors in London who were pleased at the prospect of troops being absorbed by garrison duties away from the active battleground. The disappointed saboteurs took up positions on the Rue du Canada to witness the arrival of the Italians. "Below the feathers of the Bersaglieri hats," Churchill observed, "their faces seemed ready enough to break into an answering smile." He

subsequently conceded that under the Italian occupation forces, "if anything, a greater atmosphere of peace prevailed in the district and all persecution of the Jews came to an end".

The resistance continues

When Italy surrendered in September 1943, the Germans themselves took over the occupation. By then the combined efforts of SOE and the French Resistance were devoted to the repatriation of downed air crews and escaped prisoners-of-war and to longer-term planning of an uprising in support of an Allied invasion, whenever that happened. The most famous of the escape routes was the so-called "Pat Line" run

by a "Lieutenant-Commander Patrick O'Leary" who was in reality the Belgian Count Albert-Marie Guerisse. Hacksaws and other useful implements were smuggled to interned air crews at La Turbie to facilitate, in one instance, a mass escape down a coal-chute and through the sewers. About 90 percent of the 3,000 Allied airmen shot down in northwest Europe before the Normandy landings (the majority Americans) managed to avoid capture and were smuggled back to base via the Riviera.

Joint operations with the Resistance were complicated by the exiled General de Gaulle's notorious prickliness about foreigners, even friendly ones, giving orders to Frenchmen on French soil. The artist André Girard, who as "Carte" ran a section of the Riviera Resistance, shared these feelings and claimed to have no fewer than 300,000 Frenchmen under his independent command and ready to take up arms when the word was given. In the event, the word was cloaked in confusion as it rested on the misconception, which in the end may have been deliberately left uncorrected, that the Allies would crush the German forces in France between simultaneous and equal operations from north and south, "Hammer" against "Anvil".

The change in plans, Winston Churchill declared later, was "the first important divergence on high strategy between ourselves and our American friends". A simultaneous invasion of the Côte d'Azur would have drawn Allied troops from Italy, and he was keen to push through Italy and into the Balkans before the Russians got there. Nor were there sufficient invasion craft to mount two assaults.

Invasion plans

The Normandy operation was renamed "Overlord". "Anvil" was put back a few months and became "Dragoon". Even so, says Patrick Howarth in *When The Riviera was Ours*, the plans for the invasion of the south "were among the less well kept secrets of the Second World War, not least because of the frequency with which officers who were to take part in the operations themselves, or in their planning, asked for guidebooks to southern France in the bookshops of Rome".

The German defence strategy in the south was to concentrate forces around Marseille and Toulon while at the same time making an Allied landing anywhere along the coast as difficult as possible. Villas, hotels and restaurants overlooking the shore were bricked up and turned into strong-points.

Any spot that looked suitable for a landing was sown with "Rommel's asparagus", underwater posts tipped with explosive charges set to detonate on contact. The beaches were lined with trenches, tank traps and emplacements for flame-throwers; secondary defences ran 30 km (19 miles) inland and included sharp stakes to impale paratroopers and wires to impede glider landings.

Of the German 19th Army in the south, three divisions were withdrawn to fight in Normandy, leaving about 250,000 men made up largely of

yards and the St-Roch freight depot in Nice in a raid which killed 283 civilians and destroyed 500 houses. St-Tropez suffered too, and the Carlton Hotel in Cannes was only spared, so the story goes, by Herbert Matthews of the *New York Times* telling American naval gunners that in his opinion it was the best hotel in the world and they ought to take special care not to hit it.

German commanders were inclined to think that one of the most likely places for the seaborne invasion which had to follow was below La Croisette in Cannes, and they accordingly reinforced their positions with heavy gun emplacements disguised as bathing huts and beach cafés.

battle-weary veterans of the eastern front and non-Germans pressed into Hitler's service. German Intelligence estimates put the number of Allied troops available for Operation Dragoon at 500,000. The Allies enjoyed enormous superiority in aircraft: 5,000 based in Corsica and Italy against 186 German aircraft.

Aerial bombardment

Dragoon was preceded by naval and air bombardment which began towards the end of May 1944. On the 26th, bombers hit marshalling

---

LEFT: liberation in 1944. **ABOVE:** Churchill watches the St-Tropez landings from the destroyer *Kimberley*.

A TRAGIC MISTAKE

Taking the Allied bombardment from the skies as a signal for insurrection, the Resistance swung into action by blowing up bridges, which isolated St-Laurent, Cagnes-sur-Mer, Antibes and Cannes. They cut power lines and attacked factories and German installations. When no invasion materialised, the reprisals were swift and unselective: 99 hostages were hanged at Tulle after the shooting of an SS officer; even schoolboys were rounded up in Vence and deported to concentration camps, many of them never to return. For their part, the Resistance fighters, who were soon uncomfortably aware that they had jumped the gun, were not slow to execute suspected collaborators.

Some officers were convinced they were facing a double-pronged assault on Marseille and Genoa, a deception encouraged by the pattern of pre-invasion bombing and, as time went by, the thousands of rubber mannequins dropped by parachute over the mouth of the Rhône.

For weeks on end, however, the action remained stubbornly in the air, although the targets changed. "In the blue August sky," wrote an eye-witness subsequently, "formation after formation of silver planes no longer contented themselves flying overhead with that majestic indifference which until now had only drawn the glances of the curious: now the whole coast

was itself attacked, point by point." Between 28 April and 10 August, the Allies flew more than 10,000 sorties over the Côte d'Azur and dropped 12,500 tons of bombs on it.

The landings at last

On 14 August the cryptic "personal messages" which followed the BBC news bulletin provided what the Resistance had been waiting for. "Gaby is sleeping on the grass" and "Nancy has a stiff neck" signalled an Allied invasion the next day. The American 7th Army under General Patch and the French 1st Army led by General de Lattre de Tassigny landed along a 55-km (34-mile) stretch of coast east of Toulon

while an airborne division dropped inland near Le Muy. The invasion force was carried in 500 troop transport ships and 1,200 smaller craft backed up by six battleships, four carriers, 21 cruisers and more than 100 destroyers.

Sir Winston Churchill, a regular pre-war visitor to the Riviera, watched the landings on Pampelonne Beach near St-Tropez from the destroyer *Kimberley*. He was frustrated to learn that his ship would remain 9 km (6 miles) off St-Tropez for fear of mines. Had he been told in time, he said, he would have arranged a launch to take him ashore. "As far as I could see or hear," he wrote, "not a shot was fired either at the approaching flotillas or on the beaches."

It was not so quiet nearer Cannes, where Germans and Americans fought for possession of the beaches at Agay and Dramont. The unluckiest unit in the invasion force were French commandos who landed on the Pointe d'Esquillon. Their mission was to climb the rocky Estérel and blow up roads to prevent German reinforcements from moving west. They had been led to believe that the area was free of mines, but hours before their arrival German sappers had laid a new field. Eleven out of a unit of 67 were killed, 17 badly wounded and the rest captured. Ten were rescued by the daring intervention of the Resistance.

German sappers had actually wired up charges to blow up every hotel, public building and monument in Cannes in the event of their withdrawal. The Carlton Hotel alone was sitting on 50 canisters of explosive, but it seems that a senior German officer relented at the last moment and revealed the whereabouts of the central detonator to the Resistance. It was in the wine cellar of the Hôtel Splendide.

Grenoble was retaken by elements of the US 6th Corps on 23 August, while the Germans put up a fight along the coast. Marseille and Toulon were liberated after two weeks' fighting, and on 1 September Nice, to which many of the German forces had withdrawn, was regained after stiff street fighting between the Germans and the Resistance. On 12 September a Free French patrol near Châtillon-sur-Seine ran into scouts from General Leclerc's French 2nd Armoured Division coming south. That emotional encounter meant the invasions of Normandy and Provence had finally met in the middle. ❑

LEFT: a US soldier lends a helping hand.
RIGHT: local children greet their liberators.

THE SUN CULT

The 1950s paradise is now an over-developed but still popular holiday spot

For over a century British, American and European visitors flocked to the Côte d'Azur in search of status, health and pleasure, not to mention rare spiders and Roman antiquities. But after World War II the spotlight shifted to the French. Picasso moved to Antibes in 1946 and spent the rest of his life on the Côte d'Azur. The artists Arman, Klein and Raysse, all born in Nice, created the School of Nice, diametrically opposed to what was happening in the Paris galleries. Parisian bohemian stars like Juliette Greco began to visit St-Tropez in the footsteps of Colette, Poiret and Anaïs Nin.

The first Cannes Film Festival in 1946 attracted world-wide attention, publicising the Riviera as the land of the bikini. This was reinforced by Brigitte Bardot's 1956 film *And God Created Woman*, in which her unabashed sensuality and penchant for nude sunbathing scandalised the world. It popularised the sun worship which had started in the 1920s, as people began to associate health with a golden tan.

Even these days the dangers attributed to sunbathing appear to have made little impact and sun-worshippers continue to baste themselves slowly on the sand, as if, in Françoise Sagan's words, they are "nailed to the beach by the forces of summer".

Sagan's highly successful novel *Bonjour Tristesse* also helped to popularise the region. With the advent of the post-war youth culture, and paid vacations for French workers, the Côte d'Azur entered the late-20th century. It was opened up to everyone, beyond the wealthy aristocracy who had frequented its glamorous hot spots for more than 100 years, and the show business people and shipping tycoons who dominated the scene immediately after World War II.

The Côte d'Azur was the quintessence of glamour: sun, sea, sand and sex, with the added frisson of famous film stars who just might be

PRECEDING PAGES: 1953 Cannes Film Festival – Dany Robin, Kirk Douglas, Olivia de Havilland, Edward G. Robinson and members of the festival jury.
LEFT: Brigitte Bardot at Nice's Victorine Studios in 1959.

sunbathing on the next *matelas*. But with a sun-tan, a bikini and a pair of sunglasses, who was to know the difference anyway. Here was a whole new swinging lifestyle that was emulated by millions, all hoping that two weeks on the French Riviera would somehow rub off, making them richer, more beautiful or at least more suntanned.

Fun in St-Tropez

As Roger Vadim described St-Tropez: "It was the happy mixture of old and young, wealth and class. A person with no money could live like a millionaire and a millionaire could have fun living like a bohemian."

In her autobiography, *With Fondest Regards*, Françoise Sagan captures the rapid change that took place in the formerly quiet fishing port in the late '50s, "a village that triggers off a day-dream". When she arrived in 1954 with a crowd of young, wild Parisians, they were the only young, wild people there; they found a scene of timeless calm with village women knitting and fishermen bringing home their catch.

But the very next year she describes "wild and disorderly groups of urban bathing beauties as they rush from street stall to street stall in search of a swimsuit, speed-boats and the rowdy screaming and shouting of young people

PLAYING CHICKEN

An incident in Roger Vadim's autobiography typifies the period. "It was 1958. Tahiti beach in St-Tropez. One evening the sound of a Ferrari drowned out the crickets. The roar of a Mercedes 300 SL replied to the Ferrari. It was a duel." Roger Vadim and Gunther Sachs started up their cars positioned either side of a bend in the road with a huge parasol pine in the middle. Neither driver could see the other car and had to guess which way the other would turn at the tree. If they both found themselves on the same side of the tree there would be a head-on collision unless one of the drivers yielded. "It was a sort of Russian roulette with wheels," writes Vadim. He was driving the Ferrari, and the

judges included Françoise Sagan, Christian and Serge Marquand and Marlon Brando.

In the second round, the two cars came face to face and a split second before they crashed Sachs lost his nerve, jerked the wheel and plunged his Mercedes into the ditch. He wasn't hurt and the next day a crane hauled the car out. Sachs, who later became Brigitte Bardot's third husband, was very wealthy and could easily afford to cover the damage. That evening he gave a celebration dinner at the Restaurant Tahiti; an enormous dish was served which turned out to be Serge Marquand decorated with mayonnaise and gherkins.

who roar off in unruly disarray – all for the feeble purpose of lying on the sand five hundred metres farther down the beach." Suddenly St-Tropez was the "metropolis of illicit pleasures". She concludes, nonetheless, that St-Tropez has an indestructible beauty with its tonic winds, its peaceful yellow sun, and "the red-hued coastline with its intricate inlets".

It was in St-Tropez that Roger Vadim and Brigitte Bardot shot *And God Created Woman*, the film that made her a star and created a look copied by young girls everywhere. Bardot is still held largely responsible for starting the sun cult on the Côte d'Azur.

from Arab oil sheiks and wealthy Europeans.

What the French termed "caviarisation" began, as every rich globule on the coast began to connect up. Soon there was barely an inch of coastline left that was not built on. Vast marinas were constructed, and the coast became a mecca for boat owners everywhere. Every fat cat from Aristotle Onassis to Donald Trump had to have a yacht as big as a ferry moored in Antibes or Monte-Carlo.

Instead of mere luxury villas, huge apartment blocks rose everywhere. For a while it was a free-for-all, with ugly results. By 1980, the development had reached its zenith and the

Rampant development

Being the world's favourite holiday destination naturally took its toll. Millions flocked every summer, renting anything from exclusive *pied dans l'eau* villas to caravans, from sailing yachts to surfboards, and from motocyclettes to Mercedes. The property market boomed. What began as merely good investment was rapidly exploited by developers, and by the 1970s property prices were sky-rocketing, with luxury villas in areas like La Californie and Super-Cannes commanding record prices

government began to crack down. Bardot also put her foot down, threatening to leave St-Tropez if the mayor went ahead with a new development scheme. She insisted that the town must decide who was the greater tourist attraction. The mayor backed down.

From 1980 new building was forbidden within 100 metres of the sea; high-rise apartment buildings were banned, and new ones limited to seven floors; nothing was to be built in designated "natural zones" of virgin woods and fields. In many areas now, new houses can only be built using traditional materials and methods.

The permanent exception to this rule is Monaco, where skyscrapers cram the tiny prin-

LEFT: aspiring starlet in Cannes. **ABOVE:** Robert Mitchum playing for the paparazzi in 1954.

Brigitte Bardot

W hen the film *And God Created Woman* appeared in 1956, it made the young Brigitte Bardot a world-famous star and a sexual icon. "You are going to be the respectable married man's unattainable dream," her director-husband Roger Vadim told her.

It also put St-Tropez on the map and sun worship on every budding starlet's agenda. Today the film seems tame, but in 1956, when sexual union was represented by fireworks or waves crashing on to rocks, its nudity and love scenes caused a furore,

particularly in the US. In 1957, it earned over $8 million, more than France's biggest export, the Renault Dauphine. It was Bardot's 17th film, and hers was by no means a rags-to-riches story. Her parents were well-to-do: her father was an industrialist and her mother ran a clothes boutique in Paris. At 14, Brigitte, having done some modelling, was recruited as a cover girl for *Elle*. Her parents insisted she could only be identified by her initials, "B.B."

Film-director Marc Allegret was developing a film-script written by a 19-year-old White Russian, Roger Vladimir Plemiannikov (known as Vadim). He asked Vadim to investigate the new *Elle* cover girl. While they made a formal visit to Brigitte's parents, the 15-year-old Brigitte and Vadim sneaked out onto the balcony together. Although the resulting screen test was a flop, Vadim and Brigitte soon became lovers, though Vadim had to change his religion and wait until Brigitte was 18 before they could marry.

Enthusiastically promoted by Vadim, Brigitte was given a number of small parts in a series of mediocre films. Her fifth film, Anatole Litvak's *Act of Love*, starring Kirk Douglas, was promoted at the 1953 Cannes Film Festival. It was the opportunity Vadim had been waiting for. The United States aircraft carrier *Midway* was in Cannes to show the flag, entertaining the best known film stars on deck: Edward G. Robinson, Gary Cooper, Lana Turner, Olivia de Havilland and Leslie Caron all paraded for the cameras, smiling and waving in time-honoured tradition. But the cameramen began to slip away, turning their backs on the stars and focusing instead on a slender girl in a raincoat who had not been invited on board. Brigitte let slip her coat to reveal a tiny little-girl outfit, tossed her pony-tail and smiled. The next day her face and figure were on the front pages of newspapers around the world.

She became an international star with a British film, *Doctor At Sea*, starring Dirk Bogarde, and caused a sensation with the press. When they asked her what wardrobe she had brought with her she replied, "Several nightdresses because I hope someone will take me out." Her role received rave notices, and young girls everywhere copied her pony-tail and affected her famous pout.

Her movies became more and more daring, until *And God Created Woman*, which was such a *succès de scandale*. It was after this that Brigitte bought La Madrague, a large villa near St-Tropez, where she still spends part of the year.

The presence of the most famous woman in France drew the tourists, and an enterprising American tourist agency offered Riviera tours with the "possibility" of seeing B.B. bathing in the nude. Her fame attracted other celebrities and jet-setters, whose presence transformed the tiny fishing port.

After three marriages and numerous love affairs, Bardot declared that she preferred animals to men. She began to devote her life to various animal causes, from saving the whales to rescuing her neighbour's donkey. Since then, however, she has shocked the world again, first by marrying Bernard d'Ormale, a leading member of the National Front. Then she published an autobiography that caused so much furore her ex-husband and son tried to have it suppressed. ❑

LEFT: the young Bardot.

cipality like Hong Kong or Manhattan, the most recent of them built on landfill, often blocking light and views from older properties. Since many of Monaco's residents are domiciled there for tax purposes, nobody seems to complain.

Enduring charm

Today, within the Alpes-Maritimes *département*, 94 percent of the housing stock is located along the coast, although villages further and further inland are being enthusiastically restored. But, despite such unbridled development and the inevitable problems generated, in many essential respects this charmed coastline offers to the visitor the same interest and pleasures as ever. It has a near-perfect climate resulting from its blessed geographical position nestling between snow-crowned mountains and palm-fringed sea. The scenery remains sensational, eclipsing even the most grotesque architectural mistakes. The same bare red porphyry rocks and glittering turquoise sea, silvery olive trees and fragrant broom greet new arrivals as they have always done. Matisse's "glaring festive light" still bathes everything in a luminescent glow that he felt was so strong that no one would believe such intense colours were possible.

Inland, the mountains are covered in lavender and broom, high mountain plateaus remain silent and windswept, and if the medieval villages are less desolate than they were, so much the better. The current wave of restoration has preserved many buildings which would otherwise be reduced to rubble. The more hedonistic latterday attractions still hold good; Scott Fitzgerald's "lost caviare days" endure for some. In Monte-Carlo the casinos still draw the gullible rich; the nightclubs of Juan-les-Pins continue to attract swarms of young people for whom a day on the beach, a good suntan, the latest fashion in beachwear (or even no beachwear at all), followed by a night of dancing, constitutes a perfect holiday. For the gourmet francophile, the area abounds in fine restaurants and top-flight chefs, and those with cultural aspirations cannot fail to be stimulated by a huge number of museums and art galleries. Even at the height of the summer season, it is perfectly possible to enjoy the Côte d'Azur, though you may need to be a little offbeat if you want to be alone.

RIGHT: Monaco's high-rise real estate.

A mecca for business

The glamorous image of the Côte d'Azur undoubtedly remains. Perhaps what is most remarkable about the region is that it has, somehow, tenaciously hung on to its image and not gone slithering downmarket, the almost invariable fate of other popular holiday destinations.

Image, after all, is what it is all about, and it is the image of the Côte d'Azur that attracts not only 9 million tourists a year but swarms of business visitors, and entices companies to relocate here. Increasingly, the Côte d'Azur has become the centre of the European sun-belt and a high-tech paradise along the lines of Califor-

nia's Silicon Valley. (The Provence-Alpes-Côte d'Azur region is formally twinned with California and the Var aims to become, somewhat dubiously, the "Florida of Europe".)

In fact, business receipts now actually outweigh revenue from tourism. Traditional tourist attractions have been repackaged. Business tourism is very successful and there is a huge year-round conference trade. The region is second only to Paris in the number of new companies created. They relocate here, attracted by the climate, lifestyle and image of the Riviera, and take advantage of improved transport and communications systems – the second largest airport after Paris, and the densest telephone system in regional France.

The high-tech sector, in particular, has boomed. The attractions are not hard to understand; the so-called "beach boffins" enjoy all the advantages of a high-tech working environment with in-house swimming-pools, good weather, palm-fronded villas and frequent trips to the sea, not to mention reflective jogs round the Provençal countryside, landscaped for their convenience.

Overcrowding and corruption

But a "technological Eden" it is not. Despite such visionary developments, the Côte d'Azur can often look as if it is approaching its zenith.

beaches and empty restaurants. In 1992 major floods throughout the region caused severe devastation, washing away bridges, roads, houses and several miles of railway track.

The political scandals that beset the region in the last decade of the 20th century have not done much for its image either. Most infamous was Jacques Médecin, mayor of Nice from 1965 until 1990. He was indicted for financial corruption in 1990 and fled to Uruguay, but was finally extradited in 1994 and sent to prison. On his release, he fled again, and died in November 1998.

He was not alone; throughout the region, mayors and public officials have been indicted,

Although the tourist authorities continue to talk in traditional terms about increasing the number of visitors, anticipating an increase from 9 million to 10 million a year, they do concede that it is important now to focus on "quality rather than quantity" and stimulate interest in art and culture as well as sun and sea.

There is now some recognition that to carry on regardless would be to risk killing the golden goose. The besetting problems of overcrowding and increasing pollution will eventually put off even the most weathered sun-worshipper. The 1990s saw several disastrous seasons, with the Gulf War, fear of recession and a particularly ill-timed oil slick resulting in deserted

and even imprisoned for corruption and underworld dealings. Hyères became known as the "Chicago of the Côte" after a series of bomb attacks and the mysterious assassination of a local official campaigning against corruption. The mayor of Cannes was brought to trial over a casino scandal and the mayor of Frèjus was investigated for financial irregularities. Maurice Arreckx, mayor of Toulon from 1959 to 1985 was also sent to prison for misusing public funds in 2000. Politically the region is leaning further to the right, and now has the highest number of National Front voters in France. In the 1998 regional elections they accounted for 27 percent of the votes.

Environmental concerns

Pollution continues to be a volatile issue, and beaches now have flags to warn bathers of excess contamination. Even so, there is a general tendency to try to minimise the problem rather than tackle it fundamentally. Toxic algae in the sea has become an increasing problem, due in part to yacht anchors damaging the sea bed, and new jetties and marinas affecting currents. The algae, first detected in 1984 has multiplied at an astonishing rate, now affecting over 4,000 hectares (10,000 acres) between Toulon and Genoa, posing a grave threat to marine fauna.

Forest fires are another growing problem, with and fire-fighting technology has become increasingly sophisticated, with water-filled planes and motorbikes equipped with hydraulic pumps.

Appalling traffic means the coast roads are frequently choked, and parking is a nightmare. Transport remains the key to the development of the region. A new airport is planned, as is a tramway system for Nice, due to be in service in 2005. An extension of the TGV as far as Nice has long been on the cards, though there has been controversy over the environmental effects of its routing, and the development has been stalled. A relief autoroute further inland from the A8 is also planned, to improve communications along the

more financial resources being required every year to combat them; they destroy up to 50,000 hectares (125,000 acres) of land in the French Mediterranean every year. While fire has always been a threat, the scale of disasters has grown because incendiary material in the forests is no longer cleared by local inhabitants. Owners of forest land are now required to clear their own grounds and from 1 July to 15 October, the *période rouge*, no fire kindling is permitted in high-risk zones. Air surveillance is used to spot fires

crucial Barcelona–Genoa Mediterranean axis. But this, too, has run into political difficulties.

It remains to be seen whether the Côte d'Azur can retain its allure while exploiting it enough to survive. There are many contradictions in this richly endowed and over-exploited region of France. When a proud new villa-owner happily pays 1,000 euros for an ancient olive tree to be planted in his designer-landscaped garden, while centuries-old olive groves are ripped up to make way for new building, it is time to invoke the spirit of Renoir, who bought his land at Les Collettes with the express intention of preserving the grove of olive trees that had been growing there for centuries. ❏

LEFT: welcome heat on the Plage de Pampelonne in St-Tropez. **ABOVE:** unwelcome heat: forest fires are a constant threat.

WHEELING AND DEALING

Thanks to various scandals in the 1990s, the Riviera has a reputation for corruption,

but with all the money floating around even legitimate businesses can clean up

Wheeling and Dealing on the French Riviera doesn't just mean bicycle riding and blackjack. It is also the euphemism for a Mediterranean style of life that prompted Somerset Maugham to call Monaco "a sunny place for shady people".

It is endemic in both legitmate and illegitimate business sectors and evident in everything from cocktail party bravado and taxi-driver stings to corrupt commercial practices and crude political machinations.

If Maugham considered Monaco shady he must have thought Nice and Marseille were pitch black. The fact is, everyone on the Côte d'Azur, from much-maligned Marseille to spick-and-span Monaco, wheels and deals to some extent.

Some people even get caught. Jacques Médecin, former mayor of Nice, ran the city known as the Riviera's Big Olive like a personal fiefdom. Then he was fingered for financial shenanigans and had to flee to Uruguay and sell T-shirts on the beach. Extradited eventually, he served a short prison sentence. Despite the fact that he had pocketed millions of francs of the city's money, when Médecin died in 1998, Niçoise society forgave him and turned up in their thousands for his funeral.

Also in Nice, customs agents at the airport, who regularly pilfered from passengers' baggage, were themselves searched, confiscated and sent from the Big Olive to the Big Prison. Elsewhere, a crop of croupiers at the Cannes casinos were nailed red-handed for helping selected "customers" to cheat. In fact, hardly a day goes by without a story in *Nice-Matin*, the Riviera's monopolistic daily paper, about drug-smuggling, prostitution or other shady enterprises.

Drugs, fraud and bribery

A number of villas near Mougins lack patriarchs because they are serving time for running dope. Drug busts are so common that a haul of

120 illegal immigrants pushing heroin barely merited a line on the front page of *Nice-Matin*. Even a Monaco bank was shut down, with its bosses earning interest in the slammer, when it was discovered laundering drug money. Creating fraudulent bills, which has landed other members of the Nice political and business

community in jail, and accepting bribes, are all part of doing business in many Riviera communities. Try to work a deal with some local municipalities and you may find yourself allocating a part of your budget to a local youth project, or some equally undefined cultural scheme, in order to get the contract. Try to pay your plumber with a cheque and you get a look that would block any respectable drain.

Mouillot's story

To the shock of all, the once-clean town of Cannes must now join the the list of corrupt municipalities after the fall from grace of the mayor Michel Mouillot.

PRECEDING PAGES: conspicuous wealth along the quay in St-Tropez. **LEFT:** high-rollers stay at the Carlton in Cannes. **RIGHT:** a hard day's work.

The charismatic Mouillot was arrested at his home in the Var on 17 July 1996 for corruption involving the Carlton Casino and a number of planning permission projects. In the case of the casino, it was alleged that he had demanded a bribe before granting permission for the installation of one-armed bandits.

The planning-permission story was more complicated. Back in 1992, Mouillot had ordered a police inquiry into corruption in the town's planning department and stopped all work on the latest palace being built for a nephew of Saudi tycoon Adnan Khashoggi. Planning officers had discovered that the

marble colossus was twice the size it should have been. Another luxury villa for a leading member of the Qatar Government was also found to be illegal. The estate agent who carried out the negotiations was charged with fraud.

Mouillot feared that many of the sprawling buildings littering the hills had been built without proper permission or had exceeded their permitted size. Little did he know that he would end up taking most of the rap.

At the time, Yves Paoli, chairman of the Cannes Planning Committee, who was arrested at the same time as Mouillot, said, "It is a very sensitive matter. The police were called in after it was found that the planning permission for the

Khashoggi palace was false. We also discovered there were three or four more important dossiers affecting other buildings which were not correct."

After years of court hearings the Khashoggi palace is finally going ahead, with the town owing a considerable amount of money in damages to the owner. As for Mouillot, he spent 18 months as a guest of Grasse Prison and was finally released after going on a hunger strike. His case has still not been heard.

Getting away with it

This type of activity occurs throughout the world, of course. But like many other endeavours, it is much more prevalent on the French Riviera. The good climate, the glare from the morning sun or perhaps a plethora of *pastis* at sundown makes everyone feel they can get away with absolutely anything. Something on the Riviera seems to encourage an abundance of excess. A plumber in Valbonne, for example, was imprisoned because he tried to collect his bill in sexual favours rather than French francs.

Not everyone gets nailed, of course. A number of restaurants in St Laurent-du-Var were burned down mysteriously and no one claimed responsibility or even explained why. The apprehension of a bag snatcher would merit a front-page story because it happens so infrequently.

Typically, the wheelers and dealers will swear they don't cheat any more or less than the local priest, and most are pretty straight (except when it comes to taxes, where the people on the Riviera play a little more with their returns than their northern brethren). But legitimate businesses complain on a regular basis that they pay hefty taxes to support the Riviera's unceasing growth.

Naturally, not all business is illicit. The Cannes Film Festival is just a good-natured "stick a cigar in your mouth and sit on the Carlton Terrace" business. Not all the yachts sold in Antibes go to drug-runners, and some agents selling those 40-million-euro homes on Cap Ferrat are making an honest buck. The paparazzi in Monaco waiting to get a compromising photograph of the royal family are just doing a hard day's work. And people operating in the seasonal business *need* that seasonal profit.

Fleecing the tourists

There is also legitimate big business on the Riviera, generating huge amounts of economic activity. Tourism and high technology are two highly visible money spinners, but other traditional areas, from public works to perfume, remain important. Tourism brings about 9 million visitors to the region each year and provides plenty of seasonal employment. But the down side has always been the string of shoddy buildings and unattractive developments that line the coast.

The problem with tourism is that it remains concentrated between May and October, when events like the Cannes Film Festival and the Monaco Grand Prix set the pace. During the summer season it is rare to find a hotel, restaurant or service business that does not jack up

plus Arabs who take up quarters in Cannes in August. Riviera drivers, who tailgate throughout the year and take it very personally when a light turns red, get remarkably aggressive in the summers with visitors who do not know the right of way.

Foreigners on vacation are, by nature, dumber than locals. They are prime targets for stings – usually unsophisticated bag snatchings but also elaborate burglaries that bring back the delightful era of Cary Grant and Grace Kelly in *To Catch a Thief*. Thievery (check your bag – *now*!) is very much alive and well.

Yet nothing is more nonchalant than a local

the price a bit. This is the period when people like Ivana Trump will happily pay 70,000 euros a month to rent on Cap Ferrat.

But there is a transformation in more than just prices. The normally sensible people on the coast go crazy with the summer influx of Americans (who talk too loud), Brits (who are too polite), Italians (who wear their furs in July) and Scandinavians (who crowd like lemmings on the beaches). And in the past ten years there has also been a huge influx of rich and poor holidaymakers from Eastern Europe,

policeman's shrug when a foreigner comes in to report a crime. There is some improvement in the crime area though – the forestry department have begun cleaning up the carcasses of stolen cars out of the Esterel valleys, the traditional graveyard of many heisted vehicles.

Summertime blues

What's worse is that so much of the infrastructure, especially the road and sanitation systems, simply cannot cope with the surge of visitors during the summer. By September the Riviera can, and often does, look like a garbage dump.

The authorities are trying to spread some of the tourism to the hills and are planning events

LEFT: apartments for sale in Cannes.
ABOVE: Jacques Médecin and friends.

throughout the year, but they face a summer seaside tradition that has been alive and well since the 1920s. And most locals manage to tolerate three months of heated hell and the invasion of the body-watchers because it has led to a proliferation of services and income they can enjoy all year round.

Indeed, about the only good tradition that has withstood the test of money and tourism is that most shops still close between noon and 2 or 3pm for lunch. And restaurants like Barale or La Mérenda in Nice still coolly close their doors during the high-flyer month of August, when they might actually get the most custom.

Conventions and conferences

Business tourism continues to boom: the Acropolis in Nice and the Palais des Festivals in Cannes both attract a huge variety of conventions and congresses. The Palais has been extended to almost twice its original size and has some sort of convention taking place every month, plus, of course, the famous Film Festival. Monaco has carved out a niche as the venue for insurance conferences.

There is growth everywhere. The Nice-Côte d'Azur International Airport has been completely renovated and now sees almost 12 million passengers a year. The Arénas business complex ("Off the plane and into the office" was the pro-

motional slogan) was created across from the airport almost overnight and is now one of the leading business sites in the South of France.

Property, of course, is one area that remains ripe for exploitation. A foreign stooge will get taken not only by the estate agent (there are more pages of estate agents than restaurants in the telephone book) but also by everyone down the line – plumber, gardener, maid and electrician. They will pay exorbitant prices, which will wreck the prices for locals – who must then, of course, wheel and deal with even greater dexterity.

"The demands from the clients are the same as always – an address with cachet, like Cannes or Cap d'Antibes, a sea view, isolation from neighbours and enough rooms and salons to invite guests during the season without anyone getting in the way of each other," explained José Tauzia, an architect based in Cannes.

Foreign business

Foreigners still like the place because of the sun. Japanese investors bought the golf course in Valbonne and instantly made the green fees the coast's most expensive. Setting up business here is an attractive proposition. For one thing there is an eager and wealthy local market that has not only attracted more financial services than elsewhere in France – the Côte d'Azur now has the greatest concentration of French and foreign banks after Paris – but also many entrepreneurs.

For example, Lebanese businessman Nabil Boustany spent $300 million completely rebuilding the Metropole Palace Hotel in Monte-Carlo. "Every whim – from chocolates to diamonds, from a brasserie to royal cuisine, from a junior suite to your own apartment – can be satisfied under one roof," he boasted, claiming that despite the price the development is still considered a great investment.

And in the land that helped form Picasso, Chagall, Matisse and Renoir, art continues to be a lucrative commodity, with a proliferation of art galleries, many of them foreign, often situated in the smallest villages.

In one of these villages, away from the coastal frenzy, a poster went up reading "The back country must not be a victim of the coast's frenetic development." The big question remains: how long can the Riviera keep its goose alive and the golden eggs forthcoming? ❏

LEFT: playing to win.

Beach Boffins

There has been nothing more prominently touted in the evolution of the French Riviera over the past 30 years than Sophia-Antipolis. The high-technology park built just off the autoroute between Nice and Cannes derives its name from the Greek words for wisdom and Antibes. "Sun, silicon and software" and "Silicon Valley South" are typical descriptions of the 2,300-hectare (5,700-acre) park with its constantly expanding mix of buildings – from high-tech pyramids to banal low-tech monstrosities – natural forests and brand new road networks.

Brainpower, the argument goes, works better in a good climate and since Sophia was founded by Pierre Laffitte (now a senator) in the early 1970s, there has been a flood of companies from Allergan to Zamboni, and self-employed individuals, from architects to zoologists, proving the premise that only fools or Eskimos prefer London or Stockholm.

Laffitte was inspired to build Sophia after a visit to Stanford University in California in the late 1960s. He wanted to duplicate the ingredients of Silicon Valley and create a technopole with a university, a strong infrastructure, good communications, established companies and high-tech start-ups in a pleasant environment.

Sophia grew quickly, not least because it became the focal point of the local government's efforts to diversify away from tourism and attract educational institutions, scientific ventures and high-tech industry. Aided by the national and regional governments (almost every politician has since claimed to be behind the impetus of Sophia-Antipolis), Laffitte's vision became a combination of dream-come-true and nightmare.

To start with, there were teething problems. In 1975, Sophia Antipolis contained only five companies in an area spanning the communes of Antibes, Biot, Mougins, Vallauris and Valbonne. Rolling hills and greenery were more prominent than concrete.

Sophia recovered, though, and today it is described as Europe's leading science park, two-thirds of which is landscaped open space, and it is soon to expand northwards. There are currently 1,200 companies on site – including 110 foreign-owned – providing 25,500 jobs to 63 different nationalities. Forty percent of the businesses work in research and development in information technology, life sciences and environmental sciences.

These companies employ 14,000 engineers and technicians. Information technology acounts for over 25 percent of the companies and close to 50 percent of all jobs. There are also 10 higher education establishments on site, headed by UNSA, the University of Nice Sophia-Antipolis, with students specialising in industrial economy, pharmacology, immunology and a variety of other disciplines.

"Sophia Antipolis is a magic site with an ambience that makes it a great place to build a solid team. The pleasant environment results, I think, in a higher quality of work and improved level of productivity," says Pascal Ozanne, e-marketing director at Marconi Communications.

But not everyone agrees. The infrastructure has not kept up with the advertisements and many locals feel the park is a development nightmare. The authorities, for example, did not always respect the edict to maintain a certain percentage of natural greenery and forests, and Sophia has stretched many local resources to the limit. Despite advances (such as the computerised touch-screen directional finders at the entrances), there are still numerous complaints about parking, roads, housing costs and schools. Recently, though, companies such as Wellcome, Dow France, Allergan and France Telecom banded together to form a "Club des Dirigeants" to resolve many of the problems. The results of their work have yet to be seen. ❑

RIGHT: the Sophia-Antipolis technology park.

LITERARY VISITORS

Writers such as Hemingway, Huxley and Somerset Maugham came here for the easy life. The beauty of the Riviera inspired them to new literary heights

Our vision of the Riviera was first shaped by a handful of writers, most of all by F. Scott Fitzgerald and his portrait of life on Cap d'Antibes in the glittering 1920s. The French themselves have a different vision; the Riviera for them is not glamorised and mythologised as it is for the British or Americans. In 1927, the writer Colette moved into a villa in St-Tropez where she wrote *La Naissance du Tour*, set in the then unspoiled fishing village.

It wasn't until the 1950s, however, that a double impact did wonders for local tourism. In 1955 the 18-year-old Françoise Sagan had huge success with *Bonjour Tristesse*, in which Cécile, the spoiled teenage narrator, manipulates her father's love-triangle in a villa somewhere between Fréjus and Cannes. A year later, Brigitte Bardot's film *And God Created Woman* did the rest.

But British and American artists have long made the Côte d'Azur a port of call. The Americans arrived in France in the 1920s, in the aftermath of the Great War. A combination of reasons prompted their arrival: Prohibition, puritanism and the cultural wasteland that was then America. This, combined with the buying power of a strong dollar against a weak franc, meant that a poverty-stricken young writer could live very well on very few dollars and in luxury on a moderate income.

Scott and Zelda

Scott Fitzgerald and Zelda first arrived in France in 1924, on the *Aquitania*, docking at St-Raphaël where they stayed at the Villa Marie in Valescure, the wealthy annex where villas and hotels are scattered over wooded hillsides overlooking the sea. They had found themselves with $7,000 in the bank and realised that, given their expensive lifestyle, it would not go far in Great Neck, Long Island, but they could live very reasonably in Europe for some time. "We were going to the Old World to find a new rhythm for our lives," Fitzgerald wrote, "with a true conviction that we

had left our old selves behind forever." Initially, all went well and that June Fitzgerald wrote: "We are living here in a sort of idyllic state among everything lovely imaginable in the way of Mediterranean delights... I am content to work and become excruciatingly healthy under Byron's and Shelley's and Dickens's sky."

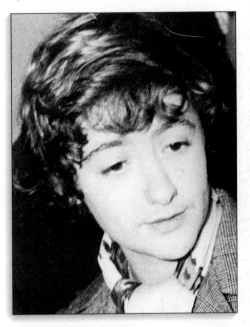

They saw their wealthy American friends Gerald and Sara Murphy, who were in the process of having their Villa America built. They had invited Gilbert Seldes and his new bride to spend a few days at the Villa Marie. Seldes recorded the experience: "The road from their villa had been built for carriage traffic and there was one point at which it dangerously narrowed and curved. Every time, just at this point, Zelda would turn to Scott, who was driving, and say, 'Give me a cigarette, Goofo'." In the terrified silence that followed, Fitzgerald was always able to give Zelda her cigarette, and manoeuvre the Renault around the turn to safety. Clearly, not all of their old selves had been left behind forever.

LEFT: Colette, who lived in St-Tropez.
RIGHT: Françoise Sagan, the teenage prodigy.

Boredom and adultery

The climate and relaxed lifestyle proved beneficial to Fitzgerald, who was able to unwind and concentrate on getting some work done on *The Great Gatsby*. Zelda, however, was not so happy. With Fitzgerald writing every day, she became bored and began a casual affair with a handsome young French aviator named Edouard Josanne. Everyone could see what was happening, it seemed, except Fitzgerald, and it was only when the Frenchman proposed marriage and Zelda asked Fitzgerald for a divorce that something was done. Fitzgerald asserted himself. Zelda acquiesced and Josanne

DRASTIC MEASURES

On their first sojourn on the Riviera Fitzgerald and Zelda dined with Sara and Gerald Murphy at La Colombe d'Or in St-Paul-de-Vence. There is a sheer drop away from the walls of the restaurant terrace and Murphy sat with his back to the parapet from which 10 stone steps led to a path. Isadora Duncan sat at another table and Fitzgerald went over to introduce himself. Seeing him kneel at the dancer's feet, and knowing by the way that Duncan ran her fingers through his hair that she had selected him as her partner for the night, Zelda, without warning, stood on her chair and threw herself into the darkness of the stairwell. She reappeared, with blood all over her dress.

departed, but the affair soured their marriage. Long after the event, Fitzgerald wrote in his notebook, "That September 1924, I knew something had happened that could never be repaired." The Fitzgeralds spent the winter in Italy and in April went to Paris.

In August 1925, they returned to the Riviera, staying with the Murphys at the now completed Villa America just below the lighthouse on Cap d'Antibes. The terrace of the villa was the model for the Divers' in *Tender is the Night*. Gerald Murphy himself became the unwitting model for Dick Diver, the book's hero.

Fitzgerald brought the Jazz Age to the Riviera and gave a name to the frivolity, hedonism and arrogance of the rich young people who arrived daily on the Blue Train – people like Dick Diver in *Tender is the Night*: "I want to give a really bad party. I mean it. I want to give a party where there's a brawl and seductions and people going home with their feelings hurt and women passed out in the *cabinet de toilette*. You wait and see."

In 1926, they settled into the Villa Paquita in Juan-les-Pins, but it was not large or comfortable enough for the Fitzgeralds so they moved to the Villa St-Louis, which was nearer to the casino and had a private beach.

Three's a crowd

They passed the Villa Paquita on to Ernest Hemingway and his wife, Hadley, who had to leave the Villa America because their son, Bumby, had contracted whooping cough and had to be quarantined. Everything was going well for Fitzgerald, but Hemingway and Hadley were less tranquil. They had been living in a *ménage à trois* with the American heiress Pauline Pfeiffer in Austria. With Bumby in quarantine, the Hemingways were stuck in the Villa Paquita, but Pauline Pfeiffer suggested that, having had whooping cough as a child, she was not afraid of catching it again and proposed that she join them. Hemingway was enthusiastic and Hadley soon found herself living in a threesome again.

When the lease ran out, they all moved to the nearby Hôtel de Pinède. Hadley wrote: "Here it was that the three breakfast trays, three wet bathing suits on the line, three bicycles were to be found. Pauline tried to teach me to dive, but I was not a success. Ernest wanted us to play bridge but I found it hard to concentrate. We spent all morning on the beach sunning or swimming, lunched in our little garden. After siesta time there were long bicycle rides along the Golfe de Juan." Hemingway set much of *The Garden of Eden* at La Napoule, which they visited on an automobile drive with the Murphys.

By June, the Hemingways and Murphys had moved on to Pamplona and the Fitzgeralds were back in Paris. In August, the Hemingways returned to the Villa America, all pretence of being happily married gone. Their return trip to Paris was their last together, divorce from Hadley followed and Pauline Pfeiffer soon became the second Mrs Hemingway. The Fitzgeralds returned to the States, lured by Hollywood.

by Katherine's plight, and hoping to convert her to Roman Catholicism, Connie Beauchamp invited her to move to Menton, where the weather was warmer, and installed her in a nursing home. The home was noisy and far too expensive and it was not long before she and Ida were being fussed over in Connie and Jinnie's Villa Flora on the outskirts of Menton.

Mansfield spent the four summer months in England with Murry, then in September 1920, she and Ida returned to Menton where they had arranged to rent the Villa Isola Bella, another of Connie and Jinnie's places, which was built at the other end of their garden. Here, Katherine

Convalescing on the Côte

The New Zealand writer Katherine Mansfield moved to the Riviera to find relief from the tuberculosis that eventually killed her. She went first to San Remo, on the Italian Riviera, in September 1919 with her husband John Middleton Murry and her close friend Ida Baker. Murry returned to London where he edited the *Athenaeum*, leaving the two women to spend the winter alone. Katherine Mansfield's father had a cousin, Connie Beauchamp, who spent her winters in Menton with an elderly friend, Jinnie Fullerton. Touched

relaxed and wrote many of her best short stories: *The Young Girl*, *The Stranger*, *Miss Bull*, *Passion* and *The Lady's Maid*.

Two days after Christmas 1920, she wrote in her journal: "I went out into the garden just now. It is starry and mild. The leaves of the palm are like down-drooping feathers; the grass looks soft, unreal like moss. The sea sounded, and a little bell was ringing, and one fancied – was it real, was it imaginary? – one heard a body of sound, one heard all the preparations for night within the houses. Someone brings in food from the dark, lamp-stained yard. The evening meal is prepared. The charcoal is broken, the dishes are clattered; there is a soft

LEFT: Ernest Hemingway.
ABOVE: Scott and Zelda Fitzgerald in 1932.

movement on the stairs and in the passages and doorways. In dusky rooms, where the shutters are closed, the women, grave and quiet, turn down the beds and see that there is water in the water jugs. Little children are sleeping."

Having failed to convert her to Catholicism, Connie Beauchamp was rather hoping to have the villa for someone else, and since Katherine had grown dissatisfied with Menton, it was mutually convenient when, on 4 May 1921, Katherine and Ida departed for a Swiss chalet, high in the mountains. Katherine Mansfield never again saw the Mediterranean. She died in January 1923.

Memories of war

One of the most prominent English writers to settle in the South of France after the Great War was Ford Madox Ford, who arrived with his partner, Stella Bowen, at St-Jean-Cap-Ferrat in the winter of 1922. After three days of freezing rain in Paris and sitting up all night in a second-class railway carriage they were astonished by the light and warmth of the south. Their villa had been lent to them by Harold Munro, the owner of the Poetry Bookshop in London, and they delighted in its simplicity and charm. Stella described it in her autobiography *Drawn From Life*: "You climbed to it by a rough mule track, or alternatively by long flights of stone steps of a giddy and exhausting steepness… The garden terraces which overhung Villefranche harbour appeared to have been levelled and stoned up since the dawn of history. The front windows opened wide on to a great luminous sky with a Saracen fortress on the skyline opposite… Behind the villa you looked over Beaulieu towards Monte-Carlo and Italy."

It was on a still night while walking among the ancient olive trees in Munro's garden that Ford conceived and began work on his masterpiece, the war tetralogy *Parade's End*. Ford was afraid that his memory of the war and his creative powers "might have deteriorated" and wrote, "There remained then for me, under Munro's olive-trees, a final struggle with my courage… one day I sat down at Munro's grandfather's campaign-secrétaire – it had been on the field at Waterloo – I took up my pen: saluted St Anthony who looked down on me, in sheer gratitude for his letting me find my pen at all, and I wrote my first sentence." *Parade's End* is both Ford's most highly acclaimed work and – at four volumes – his largest. It is the basis for his reputation as one of the greatest novelists of World War I.

Huxley, Mann and Connolly

Aldous Huxley lived in the South of France from 1930 until 1937, when he moved to California believing that the climate would help his eyesight – his near-blindness had been a constant burden. Though he lived in the writers' colony of Sanary, near Bandol, he often visited friends in the Riviera or accompanied his wife Maria to Nice to get her red Bugatti fixed. It was in Sanary that he wrote *Brave New World*, and *Eyeless in Gaza* is set there: "The eye was drawn first towards the west, where the pines slanted down to the sea – a blue Mediterranean bay fringed with pale bone-like rocks and cupped between high hills, green on their lower slopes with vines, grey with olive trees, then pine-dark, earth red, rock-white or rosy-brown with parched heath…"

Huxley's neighbours included Thomas Mann who, together with other German intellectuals and writers, moved here in 1933 to escape the Nazis, and also Cyril Connolly who was writing his first and only novel, *The Rock Pool*, set further along the coast in Cagnes-sur-Mer and Juan-les-Pins. Connolly and his American wife Jean adored the South of France and spent the years before the war living an idyllic bohemian life, supported by Jean's small income and whatever

Cyril made as a book reviewer for the *New Statesman*. They lived simply, surrounded by their ferrets and lemurs, drinking brandy before lunch (to Huxley's horror) and eating dinner with their fingers while reading beside the fire.

Idyllic days

Connolly had lived in Cagnes in the 1920s after coming down from Balliol College, Oxford and *The Rock Pool* is in many ways a *roman-à-clef* about his experiences among the English and American community there. In the book, Cagnes becomes Trou-sur-Mer, but Juan-les-Pins, Antibes and the other settings all retain

concerned with futility, when heroes were called Denis and Nigel and Stephen and had a tortured look… I think I may claim to have created a young man as futile as any."

Connolly's love of the Riviera is nowhere more evident than in his wistful memories in *The Unquiet Grave*: "Early morning on the Mediterranean: bright air resinous with Aleppo pine, water spraying over the gleaming tarmac of the Route Nationale and darkly reflecting the spring-summer green of the planes; swifts wheeling round the oleander… armfuls of carnations on the flower-stall… Now cooks from many yachts step ashore with their market-

their proper names including the beach at La Garoupe: "This time he bathed at La Garoupe, floating on the waters of the wooded cove and looking across at the remote and snowy Alps beyond. It was his favourite beach: for him the white sand, the pale translucent water, the cicadas' jigging away at their perpetual rumba, the smell of rosemary and cistus, the corrugations of sunshine on the bright Aleppo pines, held the whole classic essence of the Mediterranean." It is very much a 1920s book, as Connolly says: "It was a period when art was

baskets, one-eyed cats scrounge among the fish-heads, while the hot sun refracts the dancing sea-glitter on the café awning, until the sea becomes a green gin-fizz of stillness in whose depths a quiver of sprats charges and counter-charges in the pleasures of fishes."

Living large

Somerset Maugham bought a house on Cap Ferrat from King Leopold II of Belgium for $48,500 in 1926. He called it the Villa Mauresque, after its Moorish architecture and lived there for at least six months each year until his death in 1965. Here, served by a cook, a butler, a footman, a chauffeur, two maids and

LEFT: Katherine Mansfield. **ABOVE:** Thomas Mann and his wife, who moved here to escape the Nazis.

seven gardeners, he created the Maugham legend. His hand of Fatima trademark was painted on the gatepost and above the door through which passed many of the most famous people in the arts, letters and society of the time: his neighbour and friend Winston Churchill, Jean Cocteau, Noël Coward, Harold Nicolson, Ian Fleming, the Aga Khan and even a few famous women. Edna St Vincent Millay looked out over the Bay of Villefranche from the terrace and exclaimed, "Oh, Mr Maugham, but this is fairyland!" She was not intending to pun, but the fact was, Maugham was able to live with his lover on Cap Ferrat without the

scandal this would have attracted in England.

However, political events were transforming Europe, and by 1939 there was an anti-aircraft battery on Cap Ferrat and Nice golf course was covered with soldiers' tents. By the time the war ended, the Villa Mauresque had been badly damaged by a combination of German and Italian occupation, shelling by the British fleet and looting by the French. The Germans had drunk the contents of the wine cellar, stolen Maugham's cars and mined the garden, part of which had been destroyed by an incendiary bomb. After the American Seventh Army landing of 15 August 1944, the villa was used as a rest house for officers on leave. Undaunted,

Maugham started again from scratch, restoring the villa to its former glory so that the gardens were once again filled with the chatter of rent boys, reprobates and royalty.

Short stories on the side

Among the most celebrated expatriate writers was Graham Greene, who moved to France to "escape the braying voices of the English middle-class." Greene lived quietly in Antibes, where it was his habit each day to leave his modest flat at the Résidence des Fleurs and walk to the gates of the Old Town. There, at Bernard Patriarch's café, he would buy *Nice-Matin* and a copy of *The Times* and then make his way to Chez Félix for lunch. He once wrote: "Since 1959, Chez Félix was my home-from-home. I found short stories served to me with my meal."

One of these he titled *Chagrin in Three Parts*: "It was February in Antibes. Gusts of rain blew along the ramparts, and the emaciated statues on the terrace of the Château Grimaldi dripped with wet, and there was a sound absent during the flat blue days of summer, the continual rustle below the ramparts of the small surf. All along the Côte the summer restaurants were closed, but lights shone in Félix au Port and one Peugeot of the latest model stood in the parking-rank. The bare masts of the abandoned yachts stuck up like tooth-picks and the last plane in the winter-service dropped, in a flicker of green, red and yellow lights, like Christmas-tree baubles, towards the airport of Nice. This was the Antibes I always enjoyed; and I was disappointed to find I was not alone in the restaurant as I was most nights of the week."

The short story which follows reads as if he simply transcribed the conversation of the two women in the restaurant. In the dialogue, he found a way to introduce the proprietor: "But before Madame Dejoie could reply, Monsieur Félix had arrived to perform his neat surgical operation upon the fish for the bouillabaisse…" Shortly before his death in April 1991 at the age of 86, Greene travelled to Switzerland for his health. In a letter to the Mayor of Antibes, Pierre Merli, he said: "I have always been very happy in Antibes. It is the only town on the Côte d'Azur where it was possible for me to live… I am going to keep on my apartment there in the vain hope of returning to it one day." ❏

LEFT: Somerset Maugham at his Cap Ferrat home.

Graham Greene's War

The novelist Graham Greene caused a minor sensation in 1982 when he took up the cudgels for Martine Guy, a friend's daughter who was living in Nice. In a booklet entitled *J'Accuse – The Dark Side of Nice*, he bitterly attacked Martine's husband, Daniel, for his behaviour in a dispute over the custody of their children; he threw doubt on the way Daniel had got rich quick; and he accused local police and magistrates of corruption.

Nice, he said, was "the preserve of some of the most criminal organisations in the south of France". He concluded, sarcastically: "Of course Nice has its sunny side also, but I can leave it to the Mayor of Nice, Monsieur Jacques Médecin, to talk about that side of the city."

At the time Médecin dismissed Greene's booklet as an "extraordinary hotch-potch of fiction and rumour" and made the absurd claim that the illustrious 77-year-old author was trying to "get some free publicity for himself". He called a meeting of Nice city council to decide whether to sue Greene. But in the end it was Daniel Guy who took Greene to court – and won damages from him and his publishers. Subsequent events showed that Greene's half-voiced suspicions about the mayor of Nice were well-founded: in September 1990, he was indicted for financial corruption and fled to Uruguay.

The story of the rise and fall of Jacques Médecin is the stuff that novels are made of. His father, Jean, became mayor of Nice in 1928, the year Jacques was born; and he held the post until he died in 1966, when his son took over. The citizens had loved "*le Roi Jean*", and did their best to regard Jacques with equal fondness.

Like his father, he ran the city as though it were his own preserve and built up a large network of faithful, and often grateful, supporters. Questions began to be asked about his use of public money. Between 1983 and 1989, seven paramunicipal associations, headed by Médecin himself, together received some £100 million from the city of Nice, which they spent more or less as they wished. Médecin, nicknamed "Monsieur 10 Percent", set up a nexus of letter-box companies both in France and in the United States, where he passed himself off as "le Comte de Médicis" *(sic)*. He even succeeded in spending up to six months a year away from Nice without the Niçois noticing or caring.

RIGHT: Graham Greene – crusader against corruption.

By the mid-1980s, the storm clouds were gathering. Claudette Berke, who had fallen out with Médecin after representing his interests in the US, denounced Médecin's business practices. Médecin began lengthy libel proceedings. Berke told friends she was determined to reveal all. Early in 1989, just before the case was due to be heard, Médecin withdrew his suit. A few months later, Berke was found dead in her California jacuzzi. Cause of death: unknown.

After finally being forced to flee in 1990, Médecin wrote, in a letter which was read out before the city council: "I am now in a position which few people, I suppose, have experienced before me. I am a dead man, yet I have the enormous privilege of being

present at the kill and of observing from a distant planet what men and women who owe me everything are doing with my effects and my legacy." If by that time Graham Greene's animosity had turned to *Schadenfreude*, he could surely be forgiven.

Greene's campaign was finally vindicated when Médecin was extradited in 1994 and brought to trial in France, where he served a short prison sentence. He disappeared again, fleeing further corruption charges and finally died in 1998. There was a lot of political fall-out after his downfall, as Nice began to discover the extent of the corruption. Indeed, several more of the region's mayors have since been exposed for corruption and financial irregularities, further vindicating Greene's brave battle. ❑

THE RIVIERA ON CANVAS

From Monet to Matisse, some of the world's most famous artists have tried to capture the intense light and vivid tones of the Côte d'Azur

Picasso's nymphs and sea urchins; the Promenade des Anglais seen from Matisse's balcony; Dufy's triangles of white sails on a blue sea; golden light through the olive trees of a Renoir landscape; Bonnard's red-tiled roofs and palm trees from an open window; Léger's doves – the visual image of the Côte d'Azur has undoubtedly been created by the many painters who have been inspired by the light and colour of the region.

It is the Impressionists who first come to mind, because it was their business to paint light itself. Although best known for his waterlilies and studies of Rouen cathedral, Claude Monet also painted in the South of France, which he visited for the first time with Renoir in 1883.

Mediterranean light

The "glaring festive light" was so strong that Monet feared the critics, who had not seen it for themselves, would be angered by his bright palette, even though he pitched his tones somewhat below the intensity of the real thing. He compared the light to the colours on a pigeon's throat or that of a flaming bowl of punch – shimmering, evanescent films of coloured light.

In 1888 he returned, staying in Antibes and Juan-les-Pins, where he relied upon tourist guides to show him picturesque spots as he did not know the region. By painting local beauty spots, he also made his work more saleable as collectors liked to buy paintings of familiar places, rather like buying up-market postcards. He spent the winter and early spring in the south, as was the custom in those days. He only worked when the weather was good, believing that this was a landscape which demanded the sun. He exhibited his Antibes paintings at Theo van Gogh's gallery in the early summer of 1888, causing his friend, the poet Stéphane Mallarmé, to write to him in admiration, saying: "This is your finest hour."

It was not until old age that Auguste Renoir moved to Cagnes-sur-Mer. He was born in 1841 in Limoges and moved to Paris four years later. Claude Monet, Alfred Sisley and Renoir were all students together at the École des Beaux-Arts. Under Courbet's influence, they tried to paint what could be seen with the eyes as accurately as

possible. They painted outdoors, and soon realised that the colour of objects changed with the lighting conditions. It was their attempt to capture this light that gave rise to Impressionism.

Renoir heads south

In 1889, Renoir suffered an attack of rheumatoid arthritis which forced him to spend the winter months in the south. He first settled in Magagnosc, near Grasse, in 1899, then moved to Le Cannet in 1902. Hearing that a venerable old olive grove overlooking Cagnes was to be pulled up and built over, Renoir saved it from the developers to use as an outdoor studio. Finally in 1905, he decided to live there and had a modern house built for himself and his large family. He lived here for the rest of his life but not without some disturbance – hotel porters suggested his house as one of the sights to tourists and he was often disturbed by businessmen wanting him to paint their wives and children. Sometimes he did.

Illness and old age took their toll. By 1904 he weighed only 48 kg (106 lb) and found it difficult to sit. He used crutches to get about but by 1910 onwards even this was too painful and he became a prisoner of his wheelchair, his hands deformed and bandaged. His paintbrush had to be wedged in between rigid fingers and yet, day after day, he continued to paint. In his lifetime,

on painting, working in the Post-Impressionist manner which he quickly made his own. He studied at the Paris École des Beaux-Arts and came under the influence of Gauguin and Monet. But it was from Degas and his paintings of women at their toilet that Bonnard created his own "intimist" style of interiors.

Bonnard first discovered the Midi in June 1909 when he took a villa in St-Tropez. From then on, he returned practically every year, staying in St-Tropez, Grasse, Antibes, Cannes or Le Cannet, where he rented the Villa Le Rêve. In 1925, shortly after marrying his model, Maria Boursin, with whom he had lived for the previous

he painted more than 6,000 pictures, making him almost as prolific as Picasso. Even in the last two painful decades he still painted an Arcadian wonderland of light and colour, naked girls bathing in shallow ponds, washed by the Mediterranean light. "I'm still making progress," he said a few days before his death. On 3 December 1919 as an assistant arranged a still life for him, he uttered his last word: "Flowers."

Post-Impressionist influx

Born in 1867 in Fontenay-aux-Roses, Pierre Bonnard's early career included furniture design, theatre posters and book illustration but from 1905 onwards he concentrated principally

30 years, he moved to Le Cannet permanently.

Le Cannet is a small village on a hill, which has now been engulfed by Cannes. There, Bonnard bought a small pink house called Le Bosquet, nestling high among the trees on the Avenue Victoria. The mountainside climbed above it, covered with olive trees where herdsmen tended their flocks of goats. He delighted in his garden which was filled with birds and plants – mimosa in January, the flowering almond tree in spring and the fig tree in October. He made more than 200 paintings, his subjects including every inch of the interior of the house and the views from its window out across the red-tiled roofs and palm trees of Le

Cannet to the bay and surrounding mountains.

Other Post-Impressionists to arrive in the south included Paul Signac, who painted a number of important works on the Riviera using the divisionist colour theory, or Pointillism, in which the picture is literally made up of coloured dots using the rainbow palette - colours that are found only in nature.

Then came the Fauves ("Wild Beasts"), known for their unnaturally bright and wild colours and deliberately unrefined painting technique: Henri Matisse, André Derain, Georges Braque and Raoul Dufy.

In 1908, Raoul Dufy spent the summer in close collaboration with Braque at L'Estaque (near Marseille), which caused him to abandon Fauvism for the Cézannesque palette from which he developed his mature style – his *Bâteaux à L'Estaque* can be seen in the Musée des Beaux-Arts in Nice. It is the work produced between 1926 and 1929 that makes us associate him with the Riviera. During this time he worked first in Nice and Golf-Juan, painting panoramic beach scenes and his characteristic views through windows. In 1927, he also made ceramics in the pottery town of Vallauris.

Between 1928 and 1929, he executed mural decorations for a semi-circular room in Arthur Weisweiller's Villa L'Altana at Antibes and did a number of paintings of Nice and Cannes. At the same time, he continued to design fabrics and make lithographs. The archtypical Dufy view remains a patch of pure blue sea, dotted with triangular white sails, as seen from a hotel window with a few palms neatly framing the picture. A deceptively simple and attractive picture, perhaps, but as Gertrude Stein said in 1946: "One must meditate about pleasure. Raoul Dufy is pleasure."

Greatest painters

Two giants of 20th-century painting were Picasso and Matisse, both of whom settled on the Riviera. *(For details of Picasso's work, see pages 192–3.)* Henri Matisse was born in 1869 and studied law in Paris. Strangely, he showed no interest in art and during his two years of law studies did not visit a single gallery. He took a job as a clerk in a law office in St-Quentin where his family lived. It was not until

he was 20 years old, and convalescing from an appendix operation, that he started to paint. The man in the bed next to him spent his time copying popular colour prints and Matisse asked his mother to buy him a paintbox. He began by copying prints and on leaving the hospital began taking lessons. Even after such a late start, Matisse clearly felt that painting was his vocation. Against his father's wishes he gave up his secure job and moved to Paris where he enrolled in the Académie Julian. He failed the entrance examination for the École des Beaux-Arts and went to study with Gustave Moreau.

At the end of 1898, he and his new wife,

Amélie, visited Corsica. He marvelled at the light and the climate of the Mediterranean. He wrote: "It was in Ajaccio that I became enchanted with the south." The paintings made in Corsica were his first attempts to escape the realist tradition; his colours and shapes are simplified and more evenly distributed. His compositions became bolder and, most important, his range of colours was widened. Matisse, the great colourist, was beginning to emerge.

For Matisse, 1904 was a key year. He spent the summer in St-Tropez, where he was again exposed to the Mediterreanan light, and there he met Paul Signac and Henri-Edmond Gross, both strict practitioners of Georges Seurat's

LEFT: *Antibes* (1888), by Claude Monet. **RIGHT:** *La Baie de Nice*, painted in 1918 by Henri Matisse.

Pointillist technique. Matisse tried it, and though he did not respond well to such a systematic approach to painting, he produced some important work, particularly *Luxe, Calme, et Volupté*.

The use of the rainbow palette finally set him free from the formal constraints of outline and into a realm of pure colour. Matisse could not abide the use of small, even brush-strokes and soon gave up Pointillism. His paintings were now filled with luminous colours, often clashing. His *Portrait of a Woman*, done in 1905, was subtitled *The Green Line* because an olive-coloured line ran from the top of her forehead to the tip of her nose.

Colourful wild animals

Matisse and his friends Derain, Vlaminck, Manguin and Louis Valtat all exhibited together in Room VII of the Salon d'Automne in 1905. The critics were aghast and dubbed them "Fauves", wild animals, and proclaimed Matisse their leader. Fauvism lasted only three years in France, after which the artists went their own ways, but traces of Fauvism always remained in Matisse's work even at its most decorative.

By now Matisse was well known, and collectors such as Sergei Shchukin and Leo and Gertrude Stein were buying his work. It was shown in London, Stockholm, Moscow and at Stieglitz's famous 291 gallery in New York.

Matisse was well off and able to concentrate entirely on painting. His work consisted of colourful portraits, often of his daughter or wife, nudes, bathers and groups of nudes. The human figure was always an essential starting-point for him, though he did sometimes paint a few landscapes. Cubism also made its impact on his work, and many of his figures have the "African mask" face of pre-Cubist Picassos.

Matisse's move to Nice at the age of 48 was to precipitate a change in his work because at no previous time in his career did his physical environment play so powerful a role in his art, or contribute so much to the appearance of the resulting paintings. The proximity of North Africa enhanced his interest in the exotic and resulted in the wonderful odalisque series.

But most of all it was the light. He had experienced the Mediterranean light many times before, most notably in L'Estaque where he and his old friend, Albert Marquet, spent December 1915 sketching and painting. He returned again in December 1917 and later wrote: "I left L'Estaque because of the wind, and I had caught bronchitis there. I came to Nice to cure it, and it rained for a month. Finally I decided to leave. The next day the *mistral* chased the clouds away and it was beautiful. I decided not to leave Nice, and have stayed there practically the rest of my life."

He first stayed at the Hôtel Beau-Rivage, 107 Quai des États-Unis, an extension of the Promenade des Anglais past the market and the old town. Here, he had an uninterrupted view of the sea, the beach and the full trajectory of the sun. At least nine paintings made in this hotel room survive. "Most people came here for the light and the picturesque quality. As for me, I come from the north. What made me stay are the great coloured reflections of January, the luminosity of daylight." He rented a studio in the building next door and began painting.

When his hotel was requisitioned for soldiers, he moved his family to the Villa des Alliés in the hills which rise steeply above the old port of Nice, on the pass over to Villefranche. Here he took to painting landscapes and watching the dawn arrive. He wrote, "Ah! Nice is a beautiful place! What a gentle and soft light in spite of its brightness!" For the next three years he spent the summer travelling, then returned to Nice where he always stayed at the Hôtel Méditerranée at 25 Promenade des Anglais – now demolished. During the winter of 1918–19 he employed the 18-year-old model Antoinette Arnoux, who was to figure in many nude and costume paintings made at the hotel, often posing in front of the huge windows with their decorative iron grilles, a palm tree silhouetted against the blue sea. A model, posed against a room interior, became one of his favourite themes and there are literally dozens from this period

The odalisques appear

The year 1920 saw the arrival of Henriette Darricarrère, who became Matisse's primary model for the next seven years. It was Henriette who

He remained in this building until 1938, posing his models against the window or using the spacious interiors. He loved the densely patterned wallpaper and introduced it into many of his paintings. To it, he added his own collection of masks, fabric hangings and mirrors, so the studio had the lush atmosphere of an oriental bazaar. The period 1927–1931 was characterised by decorative odalisques in highly stylised settings

After a year-long visit to the United States in 1930, his style changed and he used more and more areas of flat tone. After a variety of models, in 1935 he settled upon Lydia Delectorskaya who remained his model and assistant for the

entered most fully into Matisse's exotic odalisque fantasy and he painted her dozens of times in this role. Having painted and repainted his Niçoise model, and explored the limits of hotel interiors, Matisse now felt ready to become a resident, and took a large flat on Place Charles-Félix, in the old town. It overlooked the old market and had an uninterrupted view of the sea, the Promenade des Anglais curving round to the west with its elegant rows of palms and the rooftops of old Nice.

LEFT: Henri Matisse's *The Green Line* (1905), a portrait of his wife.
ABOVE: *Femme au Divan* (1920), also by Matisse.

rest of his life. In 1938, he moved to the Hôtel Regina in Cimiez, and it was here, being too disabled by arthritis to paint, that he began to work seriously at the paper cut-outs. "Cutting straight into colour reminds me of the direct carving of the sculptor," he wrote. He began his cut-outs at the age of 70 and was 84 when he did the last one. He made the medium his own, creating several important works: the famous "Jazz" series, which he executed betwen 1943 and 1944 at the Villa Le Rêve in Vence and his wonderful monochrome *Blue Nude* of 1952, which showed that all the subtlety of painting could be brought to this simple medium. Matisse died on 3 November 1954 at Cimiez.

Léger's legacy

Though the work of Fernand Léger appears throughout the region, particularly in the impressive museum devoted to him in Biot, Léger always worked from the studio on Rue Notre-Dame-des-Champs in Paris that he first took in 1913 and retained until his death. He first visited Biot in 1949 with his former pupil Roland Brice to design their first ceramics together and the next year set up a small factory-workshop there, which he visited until the end of his life on 7 August 1955. His intention was to find a way of using ceramics for monuments. Together with Brice, he found a method since, as he observed in 1942: "My work continues to develop and is in no way dependent on where I am situated geographically."

Inhumane solitude

On the corner of Rue de Revély in Antibes, close to the city wall and the Château Grimaldi, is a small 19th-century house that the road encircles. It is the only flat-roofed house on this part of the wall and in the 1930s a loggia was built on the roof with a terrace, to make an artist's studio. It was here that artist Nicolas de Staël spent the last six months of his life.

He arrived in September 1954 and began

of accentuating the figures or abstract forms he was using by underlining them with black rings, a technique which enabled him "to house sun in my ceramic works and simultaneously to give a light, airy quality to the relief".

The large ceramic panel set in the terrace wall at La Colombe d'Or restaurant in St-Paul-de-Vence is a very good example of his success. The museum in Biot exhibits his monumental work to good effect, beginning with the 45-metre (150-ft) long ceramic originally designed for the Olympic Stadium in Hanover. But, in his case, there is no reason to believe that living in the South of France would have appreciably altered his work

getting to know the town, making sketches and painting small-scale landscapes. He felt lonely, an "inhumane solitude"; he was 40 years old, cut off from his family and devoted every hour of the day to working on his outdoor terrace, from sunrise – which is the only time of day that Corsica is just visible, shimmering on the horizon, to sunset – when the Garoupe lighthouse on Cap d'Antibes begins its regular sweep across the seascape. With de Staël's work less is more: "I paint as I can and each time I try to add something by removing what encumbers me." He made 354 paintings in six months: "One has to get used to finishing more, without finishing," he wrote.

On 5 March 1955, he made a short trip to Paris where he saw a Webern concert. In the programme from the Théâtre Marigny he noted, "red, red/ochre violins". Upon his return to Antibes, he began work on a huge canvas, 6 by 3 metres (20 by 10 ft), designed to fit a wall in the Musée Picasso next door, in the room which nine years before had been Picasso's studio.

After preparing the canvas, and making preparatory sketches, de Staël worked feverishly for three days on *The Grand Concert*, which was to be his *chef-d'oeuvre*. It is composed of two elements: a horizontal black piano to the left and a vertical cello to the right

been his studio for the past six months. *The Grand Concert* now hangs on the wall he intended it for, among a collection of his other works from the same period.

Chagall's return

After escaping to the United States for the duration of the war, Marc Chagall returned to France in 1948 with his companion, Virginia Haggard, and their son David. They lived in Orgeval, near Paris, then in the early spring of 1949 settled in a *pension en famille* in St-Jean-Cap-Ferrat where the light and the sight of the Mediterranean released an explosion of new ideas in Chagall.

painted in ochre, but it is the background that causes astonishment. Behind the stage is a backdrop composed of 12 sq. metres (130 sq. ft) of bright transparent red paint, spread across the canvas in one bold gesture.

The day after completion, de Staël wrote three letters, including one to his daughter, then, on 16 March 1955, "as a spiritual act, inoffensive, as it were, and undertaken in a spirit of total goodness towards humanity", he threw himself to his death from the terrace which had

LEFT: *Intérieuré à la fenêtre ouverte* (1928), by Raoul Dufy. **ABOVE:** *Women Running on the Beach* (1922), by Pablo Picasso.

ALWAYS THE BRIDESMAID

Marc Chagall was always deeply jealous of Picasso and Matisse. So when he moved to the Riviera, their territory, he wanted to show the world he was their equal. In order to compete, he decided he needed somewhere grand to live. As he put it, "Chagall can't live in a house that has cow dung on the driveway," although, even then, there was very little cow dung to be found on the Côte d'Azur.

In 1950, he eventually chose a house called Les Collins in Vence, a fine property with a long driveway lined with cypresses and wonderful views of the sea. Unfortunately, Matisse lived on the same road and not long after Chagall moved in the road was renamed Avenue Henri Matisse.

The influence of the Riviera is less obvious in Chagall's work than in that of other artists. He continued to paint fish climbing ladders and upside-down trees, and his greatest inspiration remained the Old Testament. After seeing Matisse's chapel in Vence, however, he went to some lengths to find and decorate one of his own, but it was not until 1973, when he completed his Musée Message Biblique in Nice, that he achieved this aim, though many churches in the region contain examples of his mosaics.

Aimé Maeght, the art dealer, and his wife, Marguerite, lived near Chagall, though they had not yet opened their foundation, and it was not

long before Maeght was Chagall's sole dealer. Chagall married Vava Brodsky and moved to St-Paul which remained his home until 28 March 1985, when he died at the great age of 97.

New style

In the 1950s, Nice produced its own school of artists, the Nouveaux Réalistes: Yves Klein, Arman, Martial Raysse (all from Nice) and César (born in Marseille but settled in Nice), plus Ben Vautier from Naples and a group of associated artists, Tinguely, Niki de St-Phalle, Daniel Spoerri, Chubac, Rotella, Sosno and others. The Nouveaux Réalistes came as a reaction to American Abstract Expressionism and the more refined Parisian Lyrical Abstraction.

Born of Neo-Dadaism and experiments with Minimalism, the Nouveaux Réalistes were united by a common appropriation of the material surfaces of contemporary life: paint tubes, trash, packaging, the contents of the industrial junk heap. Arman packed trash into transparent containers, freezing them in acrylic so they seemed set in aspic. He created a flock of birds, made from identical heavy-duty pliers, and exploded and deconstructed violins in every possible way, including a violin and its case, neatly sliced like an onion and set in concrete.

César presented automobiles, compacted into neat cubes by a scrapyard. What the Nouveaux Réalistes also had in common was a light-hearted, easy-going approach to art: "Although we of the school of Nice are always on vacation, we are not tourists. That's the essential point. Tourists come here for vacations; we live in a land of vacations, which gives us the spirit of nonsense. We amuse ourselves without thinking of religon, art or science," wrote Yves Klein.

Klein was the acknowledged leader of the movement. In 1955, when abstract painting ruled the world, Klein set up an easel on the Promenade des Anglais. Gazing out to sea, he covered the canvas with blue pigment – one of his famous monochrome paintings. It was not abstract, it was real, literally just a canvas covered in blue paint. His *International Klein Blue*, or IKB as it is known, became his symbol, used over and over in different contexts. During his brief life, from 1928 to 1962, Klein astonished and irritated critics and the public with his radical inventiveness, particularly with his *Anthropometries*, in which he coated the bodies of nude models with paint, usually IKB, and either pressed them against the canvas or gave them directions to move their limbs or crawl. Some paintings were made before a live audience, with a 20-piece orchestra.

He worked on *Cosmogonies* in which the painting was shaped by the wind, rain and other natural phenomena, and made portraits by casting his subject in plaster. He worked with fire, sometimes combining the effect of fire with his *Anthropometries*. His stated aim was to sensitise the whole planet, to return to the state of nature in a technological Eden – as good an aim as any in an artist's paradise. ❏

LEFT: the Musée Picasso in Antibes. **RIGHT:** Picasso and Françoise Gilot at Golfe-Juan in 1948.

THE CANNES FILM FESTIVAL

Every year, Cannes is transformed into Hollywood-sur-Mer as the movie industry takes over for 12 frenetic days of screenings, parties, deals and prizes

There still persists in the public's mind a notion that the Cannes Film Festival is a sedate affair, where the very best of world cinema is screened to film critics so they may report back on the state of the art, where prizes are awarded by a jury composed of international alumni of the film world, where judgements are made, followed perhaps by a little lunch on the beach.

Nothing could be further from the truth. Of the 70,000 foreigners who descend on this small seaside resort every May, only 5,000 are journalists and photographers. Another proportion are budding or fading starlets, chancers and liggers, while the great majority are businessmen. What they all have in common is that they are all here to make a deal.

For 12 days, Cannes becomes a mini-Hollywood with the big American studios occupying whole floors in the four palace hotels, the Majestic, the Noga Hilton, the Carlton and the Martinez. These movie moguls don't look like the businessmen you might expect to see in the City of London or Wall Street. Everywhere there are men in sharkskin suits, crocodile shoes, pony tails, and Hawaiian shirts that look like a nosebleed on a road map. They lie around the hotel pools, puffing huge cigars, sipping from Perrier bottles and murmuring to each other, hoping their shades will mask the fact that they are watching the topless sunbathers.

Evey so often one of them will break off to do a quick calculation on a hand-held PC. He will then say something like, "But I get the satellite rights on this one", or something to do with a "four walls deal". They then shake hands on the movie deal and say, "I'm sure we can get into bed on this one." But each party knows that the handshake will not be binding once they return to the real world and that the balance sheets look a bit different away from the glare of the noonday sun.

PRECEDING PAGES: the lights of Cannes. **LEFT:** French actress Catherine Deneuve poses for the press. **RIGHT:** guests arriving for a festival party.

The early days

The origins of the festival lie in the French distrust of the Venice Film Festival. Mussolini had launched the Venice festival in the 1930s, and it soon became clear that it was just an exercise in propaganda, with all the prizes going to the Fascist films. France proposed retaliation, with

an international festival at Cannes set to begin in September 1939. However, the timing was not right. Mae West and Norma Shearer arrived on the steamship *Normandie* to be greeted with the outbreak of War. They re-embarked almost immediately and sailed home again.

After this false start, the festival had its première in September 1946 and was France's first important cultural event after the war. To start with, it was more a film forum than a competition as almost all the films presented received a prize. Apart from 1948, 1951 and 1968 (when it was stopped by protests on the first day), the festival has been held every year since 1946. In 1951, it was decided to change the timing to May.

The 1950s

With its post-war première, the festival was consciously designed to be part of the general optimism in a new Europe. In those days Cannes was still part of the playground favoured by the Riviera set. It was common to see the Aga Khan strolling in to screenings. One British critic records that, as late as 1955, he was invited to a small screening of *The Cranes are Flying*, only to discover that he shared the auditorium with just two other men, Pablo Picasso and Jean Cocteau.

Throughout the 1950s, it was possible to fit everyone involved in the festival into a small boat and head off for an island lunch. It was also

interest in the festival. And Brigitte Bardot made such an impact on the festivals of 1955 and 1956 that there were complaints about her hogging the limelight, much as there were in 1991 over the appearance of Madonna. How female stars dress or undress is now a permanent feature of the festival photographers' lenses.

A growing festival

In the early years the festival was mainly a tourist and social event for the few hundred participants attending the parties organised in the palace hotels of La Croisette and the various villas of Cannes. But owing to the great

common for the jury to include illustrious members of the Académie Française – one particular member gave an opening speech in which he said he was delighted to return to watching cinema since the last film he had seen had been in 1913.

The festival may have been small in those days, but it still attracted its share of publicity. An English starlet, Simone Silva, made history by ripping off the top of her bikini and thrusting her talents into the surprised arms of Robert Mitchum, who just happened to be strolling by. There also happened to be a corps of press photographers present, and the pictures were duly printed worldwide, leading to the horror of the American leagues of decency and to general

increase in participants and the new economic stakes involved, the festival soon became an annual gathering of the entire cinema industry. In Cannes, the professionals found the resort a unique opportunity to meet colleagues, build up future projects and do business with partners from an increasing number of countries.

It was in 1959 that the festival began to take on its modern crowded aspect. There was a large American presence for the first time. They had realised that Cannes was a perfect opportunity to set up a European shop window for American products, and very soon the *marché* was established, showing films to the world's distributors and journalists outside the official festival.

The art of film

The films were originally chosen for the festival by their countries of production, but in 1972 the festival began to select the films itself from the recent productions in each country, a decision that marked a turning point and has since been taken up by many other festivals.

Thanks to a balance between the artistic quality of the films and their commercial impact, the festival gained its fame and became the meeting place for the international film scene. Not only does the presentation of a film in Cannes guarantee international publicity, but the festival also reflects the evolution of

for their star-studded blockbusters and the excuse has always been that they wouldn't be ready in time for Cannes.

The prizes

An international jury, composed of a president and nine artists, is appointed by the board of directors. The jury members draw up a prize list from the feature films in competition and in the official selection. The jury is required to award the Palme d'Or, the Grand Prix and prizes for best actress, best actor, best director and best screenplay. The jury is also empowered to confer one more award called the Jury Prize.

cinematic trends. Many film schools and new developments in world cinema owe their reputations to Cannes, and the festival has discovered, established and honoured directors, who by their presence in Cannes also contribute immensely to the prestige of the event.

Although nobody will admit it now, there has been a kind of 'cold war' between the big American studios interested only in the bottom line and the more arthouse-oriented festival committee. The movie tycoons often prefer to use the Deauville and Venice festivals as showcases

The best film in competition each year is awarded the Palme d'Or. Outside Hollywood, it is the highest award a film can receive. It confers upon the film considerable prestige but this is usually the limit of its effect. Only an Oscar can have a noticeable effect on the box-office take.

In 1993, for the first time in the festival's history, two Golden Palm awards were handed out. They went to *The Piano*, directed by Jane Campion, and to the Chinese film *Farewell my Concubine*, directed by Chen Kaige. Other recent Palme d'Or winners include *Pulp Fiction* by Quentin Tarantino (1994), *Secrets and Lies* by Mike Leigh (1996) and *The Pianist* by Roman Polanski (2002).

LEFT: photo call for the stars. **ABOVE:** Celebrity handprints in the pavement outside the Palais des Festivals.

Fighting the crowds

The main films in competition used to be screened at the Grand Palais, a magnificent old cinema with a marble foyer and one of the best projection systems in the world. Since each film was usually a brand-new print, and the projection was pin sharp, the viewing often took on an almost hallucinatory quality. It was like watching a moving, three-dimensional piece of sculpture.

Alas, the numbers of people clamouring to get into the relatively small cinema meant that a larger venue had to be built. In 1982, a new Palais des Festivals emerged, a hideous piece of neo-brutal architecture designed by a British

For the novice hack with a lesser entrance card, life can be especially tiresome. A stout 'Non' from a doorman barring your way is often the opening round to a vicious battle. Protestations that you do indeed have the right card and that the auditorium is half empty usually produce nothing more than a shrug. A little barging often produces the desired result, although this has to be done carefully. The doormen at Cannes seem to be recruited from the lower ranks of the French riot police. A frustrated critic was once spotted trying to take a flying leap over the phalanx at the door. He failed and was led away in disgrace.

architect whose name is now mercifully lost to history. It was immediatedly nicknamed "Le Bunker". And while it contained many screening rooms of various sizes, nothing quite matched the quality of the old Palais. Finding one's way around inside the maze-like space takes either years of practice or a good guide map.

Getting into the screenings themselves is even more difficult. It takes many years of assiduous reporting for quality newspapers before the lucky journalist is allotted the coveted *pastille d'or* (gold spot) on his or her press card. This, when waved at the doormen, will allow entry into most, if not quite all, the screenings, many of which are at 8.30 in the morning.

Alternative venues

The debarred critic can always take refuge on Rue d'Antibes. Here there are three multi-screen cinemas, and film companies hire them to show their films around the clock in the hope of attracting distributors and exhibitors. Hopping from screen to screen without checking what is on, can often yield surprise catches.

There also used to be unlimited screenings of hard-core pornography, although these are now banned. After their banishment the hard-porn brigade mounted their own award ceremony in a hotel outside Cannes, but in the past few years the event, called the Hot d'Or, has been held on a huge yacht anchored in the bay.

Nothing in moderation

Cannes today is all about excess – excessive posing, excessive indulgence and excessive spending. Cannes had never been a real town at all. La Croisette, the main promenade along the shore, with its rows of *grande luxe* hotels, was created largely to please the English taste for the Riviera in a more gracious age. Even the beaches are false: sand is imported to cover the pebbles and is raked each morning by a hotel *plagist*. Each section of the beach is privately owned and visitors will pay heavily for lunch in the restaurant at the back of the beach, or for the mattresses and parasols invitingly laid out near the water.

this do, while the rest of the hacks are caged in "American style" and almost kill each other trying to get a picture or a few words from the stars sipping champagne and nibbling canapés nearby.

It is possible for journalists to survive the two weeks simply by party-hopping, if they don't mind existing on a diet of vol-au-vents. The parties are thrown by distributors, exhibitors, PR companies, producers – anyone who wants to show everyone else they can afford it. By the end of the festival, though, you realise that the parties are all the same, that the same faces turn up at each one, no one enjoys them, and that it's definitely time to go home. ❏

Few complain since everyone is on expenses.

Then there are the parties. One particular star-studded affair that has now become a regular feature of the festival is the huge fund-raising party organised by AMFAR, the American Foundation for Aids Research, of which Elizabeth Taylor is chairman. Tickets for the event cost around £1,600 (US$2,250). The A to Z of Cannes stars turn up, and the event is usually held at the world famous Moulin de Mougins restaurant.

Only the top film journalists get invitations to

LEFT: the red carpet is rolled out at the Palais des Festivals. **ABOVE:** Roman Polanski brought a pirate ship to Cannes to publicise his 1986 film *Pirates*.

PUNCTURED EGO

In 1994, film star Bruce Willis got a sobering reception at a Cannes press conference to promote the eminently forgettable psychological thriller *Color of Night.* The press were locked into the ballroom of the Martinez Hotel and plied with food and drink. When Willis and his co-star, Jane March, renowned mostly for taking her clothes off on screen, finally showed up, two hours late, the journalists were treated to a ten-minute preview of the film. Afterwards, a young journalist from Philadelphia asked Mr Willis, "Aren't you ashamed of yourself for getting so much money for such crap...?" Aghast, Mr Willis muttered, "f...f....," and headed straight for the exit.

TASTE OF THE COAST

Combining readily available seafood and the flavourful produce of the Provençal hinterland, the Riviera produces a cuisine that is as good as any in France

"**M**y accent has a touch of garlic," says the film actor Charles Blavette in his book of memoirs, *Ma Provence en Cuisine*. The remark is not surprising coming from a native of the Midi. In no other part of France are the characteristics of a regional culture so closely bound up with food.

Characters in the films of Marcel Pagnol, for example, not only put down their cultural markers by using quaint Provençal expressions and speaking with thick southern accents, but often refer to local dishes and the ritual of making them. Indeed, the lilting words for many such specialities – *bourride, bouillabaisse, ratatouille, rouille* and *ailloli*, for example – might almost have been designed so that Pagnol's favourite actors could wrap their tongues around them.

The legendary bouillabaisse

The cuisine of the Côte d'Azur does not differ much from that of Provence, except that it is a little more fish-orientated and has the added attraction of Nice's idiosyncratic specialities. It was forged long before the Côte became a string of seaside resorts, at a time when transport was difficult and people relied on local ingredients. Its most famous – and most often traduced – dish, the fish stew *bouillabaisse*, often used to be cooked on the boat after the catch. Many kinds of Mediterranean fish both great and small – whose kaleidoscopic hues before cooking have inspired more than one painter – should go into *bouillabaisse*, each providing its own special flavour.

Fish soup, which when properly prepared consists of more or less the same ingredients as *bouillabaisse*, but sieved to remove the bones, is equally filling. Once again, the grated cheese can be dispensed with. In *bourride*, another delicious fish stew, *ailloli* is used to thicken the cooking liquid at the last moment, producing a creamy and perfumed sauce to go with the fish (which is sometimes filleted). A

ubiquitous dish on Côte d'Azur menus is fennel-flavoured grilled *loup* (sea bass), which is often overcooked and dry. Grilled fresh sardines with a squeeze of lemon are a better bet. On no account miss sampling that most delicately flavoured of Mediterranean fish, red mullet *(rouget)*, best cooked very simply.

BOUILLABAISSE LORE

There are no strict rules about which fish are mandatory, but there seems to be a consensus that no *bouillabaisse* worthy of the name can do without *rascasse* or conger eel, while spiny lobster is regarded as historically unsound. Other ingredients include olive oil, onions, garlic, tomatoes, fennel and saffron. *Bouillabaisse* usually comes in two courses (first the broth, poured over croûtons, then the fish) and is served with *rouille*, a fiery, chilli-laced version of the garlic mayonnaise *ailloli*. The grated cheese often served with the dish is a naff, recent innovation. Be warned: a good *bouillabaisse* makes an ample meal on its own (and so it should, given the price it commands).

PRECEDING PAGES: olives by the bucket load.
LEFT: Le Café, a traditional bistro in St-Tropez.
RIGHT: a café on Cours Saleya in Nice.

In the old days, it was difficult for people living in the hinterland to get hold of fresh fish, so on Fridays they tended to make dishes using salt cod *(morue)*. If salt cod sounds dreary, you will change your mind after tasting *brandade*, a rich blend of cod, olive oil, garlic and potato. Poached salt cod is often the centrepiece of a *grand ailloli* or *ailloli garni* (sometimes just called *ailloli*), a cold dish that's great on a hot summer's day.

Ailloli and garlic

Ailloli (or *aioli*) is just a sauce, of course, but like *pistou* (of which more in a moment) it has also come to denote a whole dish. In addition to

tomates provençales – indeed, in restaurants all over the world the term "*à la provençale*" or "*provençale*" tells customers to expect lashings of garlic. Garlic also goes into *ratatouille*, that resonant mixture of tomatoes, onions, courgettes, peppers and aubergines which can range in quality from the practically inedible to the sublime.

Local produce

A dish that combines so many vegetables is symptomatic of the way the cuisine of the Côte d'Azur revels in the ingredients which the region produces best, whether they be vegetables, fruit or herbs. Local sun-gorged tomatoes taste of the

the salt cod and garlic mayonnaise, it consists of cooked vegetables (potatoes, French beans, carrots, small local artichokes), hard-boiled eggs and, sometimes, cold poached snails.

A word here about garlic. Gone, fortunately, are the days when most British people regarded garlic with distaste and a Pelican book on herbs written in 1949 could write: "Anyone who travels in Italian buses might be forgiven for deciding never to grow this evil-smelling plant." The classier restaurants on the Côte d'Azur are careful in their use of garlic, but that is not the way it is eaten by the locals: they rub it enthusiastically into croûtons, pound it into *ailloli*, pile it into meat stews, strew it chopped on baked

sweet fruit they really are. (Surprisingly, in view of the important role they now play in the cuisine of the Côte d'Azur, tomatoes were initially viewed with suspicion and became widely used there only from the 19th century on.)

Baby courgettes, with their orange-yellow flowers still attached to one end, form the basis of a subtle gratin called *tian*. The flowers alone are also sometimes stuffed with a rice-based, Parmesan-flavoured mixture. Also on sale in markets and at greengrocers all along the Côte d'Azur is *mesclun* (or *mesclum*), a mixture of baby salad plants which includes all or some of the following: rocket, dandelion, lettuce (Cos, oak-leaf), watercress, chicory, radicchio and chervil. *Mesclun* has been something of a success story: it is now common, if not *de rigueur*, on the menus of restaurants all over France.

The luscious, almost caramelly flavour of melons from Cavaillon is unrivalled. The taste of fresh figs belies their dull appearance; startlingly complex and not too sweet, the fig is sometimes exploited in meat dishes. Most households boast several pots of lovingly watered basil. Aromatic rosemary, savory, fennel and thyme grow wild on the parched hillsides. The herbs and other vegetation of the *maquis* are ideal food for the sheep that graze there: the lamb of the Côte d'Azur is justly celebrated.

even a very good burgundy like a Pommard in the dish, remarking that "what you put into the casserole you'll find in your plate."

In the Niçois version of *daube*, dried *cèpes* (mushrooms) add a further distinctive flavour. All wild mushrooms, and especially *cèpes* and *sanguins* (the aptly named *Lactarius deliciosus*, or saffron milk cap), are highly prized on the Côte d'Azur.

Thrushes and blackbirds and other small birds are regarded as very tasty by locals, who still hunt them. But under French law they can no longer be served in restaurants. Tinier birds that Blavette recalls eating with relish, such as

A hearty stew

Generally, though, meat does not feature prominently in local cuisine – until recent times there was little available – though *daube*, a wonderfully rich-flavoured beef stew, is a great favourite. In his book, Blavette gives a recipe for it: a large quantity of shin is put for 24 hours in a marinade of red wine, bay leaf, thyme, pepper, zest of an orange, cloves and grated nutmeg, then cooked gently for five or six hours with salt pork, a calf's foot, garlic, onions, tomatoes and pork rind. He recommends using

the robin and the cirl bunting, are now, fortunately, protected even from hunters.

This taste for our smaller feathered friends is an Italian trait. Italian culinary influences are strong on the Côte d'Azur, partly as a result of considerable immigration from Italy in the early part of the 20th century. They are particularly noticeable in Nice – though the proudly individualistic Niçois would deny it. The Comté de Nice (Nice and its surrounding area) has been French only since 1860. Before that it was part of the Kingdom of Sardinia, which also included Savoy, Sardinia and Piedmont. From a culinary point of view, Nice straddles several cultures but has retained its own special character.

FAR LEFT: Nice market trader. **LEFT:** the makings of *bouillabaisse*. **ABOVE:** a Côtes-de-Provence vineyard.

Delicacies of Nice

The best way to get an idea of what Niçois food is all about is to stroll through the old quarter of the city, which is packed with small food stores. Cheese shops are stacked high with Parmesan and mature Gouda, as well as local cheeses like fresh *brousse* (often made from ewe's milk) and the rare *tome de Rouré*. Tubs of capers and salted anchovies serve as a reminder that it is in Nice that the finest version of *anchoïade*, a sauce served with vegetables in the same way as *ailloli*, can be sampled (it contains not only anchovies, olive oil and garlic but capers, unlike its cousin found along the Côte to the west).

pissaladière (a cousin of pizza consisting of black olives, cooked onions and anchovy spread on a bread dough base) and *pan bagnat* (a small round loaf cut in half and stuffed with the ingredients of *salade niçoise* – tomato, hard-boiled egg, anchovy, tuna, spring onion, cucumber and green peppers).

There is a wide range of Niçoise *charcuterie* that can only excite admiration – your gaze may even be returned by the spectacular *porchetta*, a boned, stuffed and reconstituted roast piglet, which is cut into huge slices from the back end. Greengrocers always have a good stock of fresh basil, handfuls of which go into

Alongside slabs of salt cod, you may see large, curiously emaciated fish that seem to be screaming (their open "jaws" are in fact the gill-bones of the beheaded fish): this is stockfish, the wind-dried cod that goes into *estocaficada*, a pungent fish stew that is Nice's proudest speciality. Shops displaying fresh pasta and gnocchi often also sell the strange cuttlebone-shaped *panisses*, made from chickpea flour, deep-fried and served with salt and pepper. Chickpea flour, a peculiarity of Niçois cooking, also goes into *socca*, a very thick, tasty pancake sold in chunks by street vendors.

Other snacks that can be eaten on the move in Nice and in many resorts along the coast are

that truly wonderful Niçois soup, *pistou* (though *pistou* strictly refers to the paste of pounded basil, garlic and Parmesan that is usually added to the minestrone-like soup at the last moment).

Fine dining

With its wealth of top-quality ingredients the Côte d'Azur is also renowned for its restaurants. If you want to splurge, you cannot go wrong. The Louis XV, in the Hotel de Paris in Monte-Carlo, combines the peak of luxury with sublime food and towering prices. Roger Vergé's Moulin de Mougins and Jacques Maximin's eponymous restaurant in Vence offer similar fare in more relaxed surroundings. Le Chantecler in the Negresco Hotel in Nice stars Alain Lorca, typical of a new generation of Provençal chefs, who bring an original light twist to the region's delicacies. Another is Bruno Oger, of the Villa de Lys in the Majestic Hotel in Cannes.

All these establishments offer dishes that reflect or reinterpret local culinary traditions, as is the fashion nowadays. Problems begin to arise when it is a question of choosing restaurants in the middle or lower price ranges. Chancing one's arm with a village bistro or tiny restaurant tucked away in some Cannes or Nice backstreet may not be too hazardous. But as soon as you decide to eat on or near the beach, or in some otherwise

Taking the flavours home

To ensure that your stay leaves a pleasant taste in your mouth, it is a good idea before leaving to browse round a street market or food store and stock up with the kind of preserved or dried staples which any good kitchen requires and which are more expensive and/or of inferior quality at home. There is a wide range of olives available, the best being the tiny black Niçois olives marinated for six months in thyme and bay. These are available in jars from Alziari in Nice, a company celebrated for its smooth and subtly flavoured olive oil, unquestionably the best on the Côte d'Azur.

fashionable location, an apparently honest establishment can turn out to be a tourist trap. Our advice is to consult one of the specialised food guides like the Michelin or the Gault-Millau (many hotels have them at reception). Otherwise, you may find yourself paying through the nose for watery, overcooked *ratatouille*, thin tasteless fish soup, *bouillabaisse* that is little more than a fish soup – at five or six times the price – with a few flakes of fish and a couple of fish bones in it, and a bottle of Côtes-de-Provence rosé that produces instant heartburn.

Other possibilities include fragrant local honey, crystallised flowers from Grasse, dried *cèpes*, Parmesan cheese, anchovies in jars and maybe a bottle or two of good Côtes-de-Provence (Jas-d'Esclans and Château Minuty are reliable growers) or that rare and surprisingly strong port-like Niçois wine, Bellet.

But there is one widely available product which, once you are back home, can conjure up memories of those lazy holiday meals more powerfully than any other, when for example spread on warm toast or used as a stuffing for hard-boiled eggs: *tapenade*, a smooth purée of capers, black olives and anchovies with olive oil, plenty of pepper and a little thyme. ❑

LEFT: tempting Provençal produce. **ABOVE:** dining *al fresco* at the Plage de Pampelonne near St-Tropez.

PLACES

A detailed guide to the entire region, with principal sites
clearly cross-referenced by number to the maps

From the world-famous beaches of the French Riviera to the lavender fields of its Provençal hinterland, here we explore the region in depth. From the ancient stones of Roman ruins to the villas of present-day inhabitants fully equipped with swimming pools and satellite dishes, we look at every aspect of this rich and complex area – its past, present and future.

The contrasts are legion: the cool, clear waters of the Golfe de Giens, the ultra-chic beach clubs of St-Tropez, the glitzy heights of Cannes and the medieval charms of its old town, Le Suquet, the millionaire's yachts of Antibes' Port Vauban and the fabulous Château Grimaldi Picasso collection. Other facets include the perfumes of Grasse, the high-tech industry of Sophia-Antipolis, the pulsating beaches of Juan-les-Pins, the exclusive luxury of Cap d'Antibes, the art galleries of St-Paul-de-Vence, the street markets of Nice and its stunning modern architecture. Here, too, are the exotic gardens of Cap Ferrat, the fishermen of Menton, the sophisticated hotels of Beaulieu, the winding streets of ancient fortified towns, the rococo facades of Monaco, the celebrated perched villages of Èze and Roquebrune and the remote secret places in the mountains.

Play *boules* in the village square or roulette in the casino; eat three-star *haute cuisine* or a *pan bagnat* on the beach; windsurf for recumbent admirers or wander a lonely hillside; investigate medieval villages or watch dolphins at play; sunbathe by the pool in isolated splendour or head for the shore.

Whatever your inclination, the Côte d'Azur encompasses such a variety of landscapes, culture and facilities that every whim can be satisfied. And if all you want to do is spend your entire time sea-gazing, no beaches are better designed for the purpose. You can rent a parasol-shaded *matelas* for the day and only rise for an ice bucket of Provençal rosé and *moules marinière* in the beach restaurant. Should your activities stretch to some light exploration, this Insight Guide will give you all the ideas you need.   ❑

PRECEDING PAGES: exotic flora in the village of Èze; the rooftops of Nice, the Riviera's largest city; dinghies waiting for sailors beneath the towers of Antibes. **LEFT:** the beach and old town of Menton.

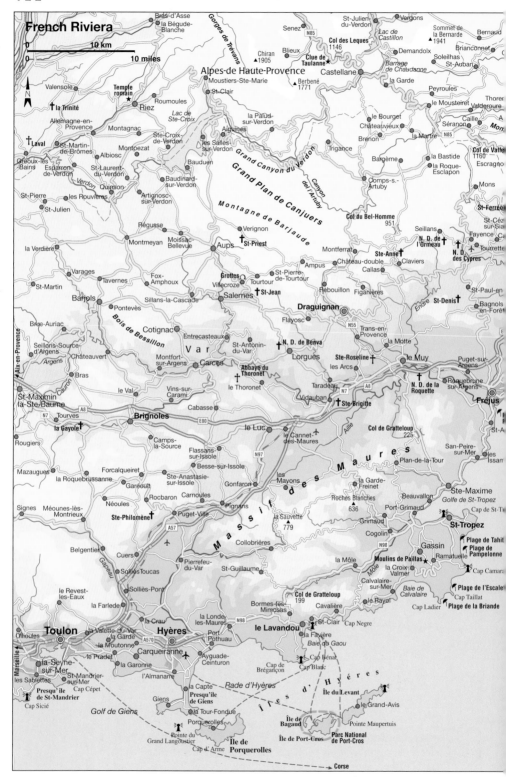

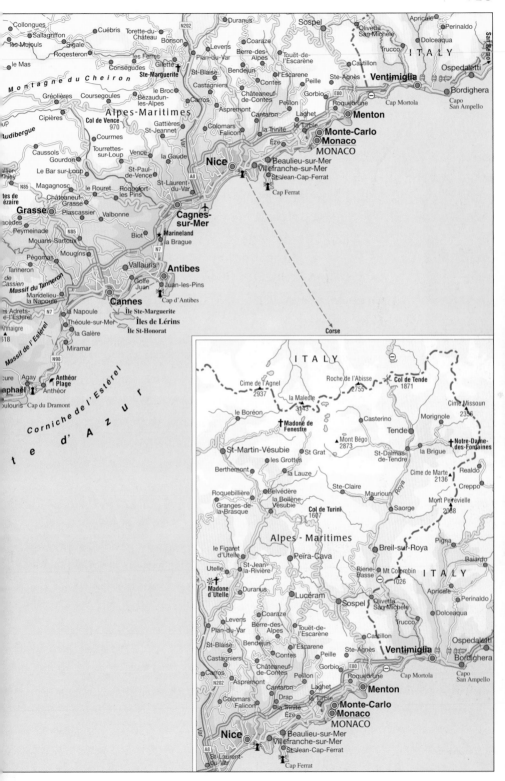

Collongues · Cuébris · Torette-du-Château · Bonson · Duranus · Sospel · Olivetta San Michele · Trucco · Apricale · Perinaldo

Sallagriffon · Sigale · les Ferres · Levens · Coaraze · Berre-des-Alpes · Touët-de-l'Escarène · Castillon · Dolceaqua

les Mujouls · Roqesteron · Gilette · Plan-du-Var · Ste-Marguerite · St-Blaise · Bendejun · Escarène · Peille · Ste-Agnès · **Ventimiglia** · Ospedaletti · **ITALY**

le Mas · Consègudes · Castagniers · Contes · Gorbio · E80 · Roquebrune · Cap Mortola · Bordighera

Gréolières · Coursegoules · Bézaudun-les-Alpes · le Broc · Châteauneuf-de-Contes · Pellon · Capo San Ampello

Cipières · **Alpes-Maritimes** · Carros · Aspremont · Cantaron · Laghet · **Menton**

Audibergue · **Col de Vence** 970 · Gattières · St-Jeannet · Colomars · Falicon · la Trinité · la Turbie · **Monte-Carlo**

Caussols · Courmes · Tourrettes-sur-Loup · Vence · la Gaude · Èze · **Monaco**

Gourdon · Le Bar sur-Loup · St-Paul-de-Vence · **Nice** · Beaulieu-sur-Mer · **MONACO**

Magagnosc · le Rouret · Roquefort-les-Pins · St-Laurent-du-Var · A8 · Villefranche-sur-Mer · St-Jean-Cap-Ferrat

Châteauneuf-Grasse · **Grasse** · Piascassier · Valbonne · Cap Ferrat

Peymeinade · N85 · Biot · **Cagnes-sur-Mer** · Marineland · la Brague

Mouans-Sartoux · N7

Pégomas · Mougins · **Vallauris** · **Antibes**

Tanneron · Golfe Juan · Juan-les-Pins

Massif du Tanneron · Mandelieu-la Napoule · **Cannes** · Cap d'Antibes

les Adrets-de-l'Esterel · la Napoule · Île Ste-Marguerite

Théoule-sur-Mer · **Îles de Lérins**

Vinaigre · la Galère · Île St-Honorat

Miramar

N98

Corniche de l'Estérel · Agay · **Anthéor Plage** · Anthéor

aphaël · Anthéor

oulouris · Cap du Dramont

Côte d'Azur

Corse

ITALY · Cime de l'Agnel 2937 · Roche de l'Abisse 2755 · **Col de Tende** 1871 · Cime Missoun 2356

la Malédie 3143 · le Boréon · Casterino · Morignole · Tende

Madone de Fenestre · Mont Bégo 2873 · **Notre-Dame-des-Fontaines**

St-Martin-Vésubie · St Grat · St-Dalmas-de-Tendre · la Brigue

les Grottes · Cime de Marte 2136 · Realdo

Berthemont · la Lauze · Ste-Claire · Creppo

Roquebillière · Belvédère · la Bollène-Vésubie · Maurioun · Mont Perrevielle 2068

Granges-de-la-Brasque · **Col de Turini** 1607 · Saorge · Roya

Alpes - Maritimes · Pigna

le Figaret d'Utelle · Peïra-Cava · Breil-sur-Roya · Baiardo

Utelle · St-Jean-la-Rivière · Riene-Basse · Mt Colombin 1026 · **ITALY**

Madone d'Utelle · Duranus · Lucéram · Sospel · Olivetta San Michele · Apricale · Perinaldo

Levens · Coaraze · Touët-de-l'Escarène · Trucco · Dolceaqua

Plan-du-Var · Berre-des-Alpes · Castillon

St-Blaise · Bendejun · l'Escarène · Peille · Ste-Agnès · **Ventimiglia** · Ospedaletti

Castagniers · Contes · Gorbio · E80 · Bordighera

Carros · Châteauneuf-de-Contes · Pellon · Roquebrune · Cap Mortola · Capo San Ampello

N202 · Aspremont · Cantaron · Laghet · **Menton**

Colomars · Falicon · Drap · la Trinité · la Turbie · **Monte-Carlo**

Èze · **Monaco**

Nice · Beaulieu-sur-Mer · **MONACO**

A8 · Villefranche-sur-Mer · St-Jean-Cap-Ferrat

St-Laurent-du-Var · Cap Ferrat

HYÈRES AND THE MASSIF DES MAURES

The western end of the Riviera is still relatively unspoilt, especially if you stay off the beaten track and head for the pristine Îles d'Hyères, the wild hills of the inland massif or the hidden beaches near Cap Bénat

Map on page 128

One of the longest established of the Côte d'Azur resorts is **Hyères ❶**, although it is often viewed as an unfashionable and slightly shabby cousin of the "real" Riviera towns of Cannes or Nice. This unfair reputation has its seeds in Queen Victoria's flippant patronage of Hyères in 1892, for no sooner had hotels and palm-lined avenues been built in honour of Her Majesty and her entourage than she decided to move on to Cimiez, near Nice, rendering the town *passé* almost overnight.

However, the French never ceased visiting Hyères-les-Palmiers, and it has long been a centre for the seriously *sportif*, who take advantage of the sub-tropical climate to sail, scuba-dive, windsurf and water-ski. There are now three vast leisure ports and 35 km (22 miles) of beaches to be sampled. The town is not wholly reliant on tourism and is surrounded by vast greenhouses cultivating early fruits such as strawberries, peaches and kiwis, as well as ornamental plants, rare flowers (orchids in particular) and potted palms. Close by are many good vineyards which thrive in excellent growing conditions. The busy atmosphere of the modern town combines charmingly with its backdrop of faded *belle-époque* grandeur.

The medieval town centre

Before setting off on a steep climb through the medieval streets of the old town, built on the slopes of the Castéou hill, pause for a coffee under the plane trees of the Place de la République. Facing the Place is the 13th-century **Eglise St-Louis**, named for Louis IX, who recuperated here in 1254 when the now disused port of L'Syguade was a base for returning crusaders. The calm, elegant church is an example of a successful marriage between Italian Romanesque and Provençal Gothic.

Not far from the southern end of Place de la République is a 13th-century gate, **Porte Massillon**, which gives access to Rue Massillon and the Vieille Ville. Gate and street are named after the great preacher of the court of Louis XIV who was born in nearby Rue Rabaton. On Rue Massillon produce merchants use street-side tables to tempt passers-by with North African and Provençal delicacies.

Further on is Place Massillon, a café-filled square overlooked by the 12th-century **Tour St-Blaise** (open Wed–Mon; free). The tower is the last remnant of a Knights Templar command post, set up in Hyères with the blessing of Charles I of

Anjou after the town gained royal status. The rooftop terrace gives a good overview of the medieval streets below.

Towards the château

Continuing up the hill, you come to Place St-Paul, where more expansive views open up across the rooftops. Steps lead up to the **Collégiale St-Paul** (open Wed–Sat) which has an Gothic nave and Romanesque bell-tower. Beside the church is a Renaissance house and turret built over a gateway.

From the church take Rue Paradis and continue up a calf-achingly steep track which snakes past the **Parc St-Bernard**

(open daily), an attractive garden containing hundreds of varieties of Mediterranean flowers and plants. Above the park is the **Villa Noailles**, a Cubist house designed by Robert Mallet-Stevens. In the 1920s, the villa was visited regularly by members of the Dada and Surrealist movements – Man Ray's bizarre film *The Mysteries of the Château de Dé* was filmed here in 1929. The villa is undergoing restoration but still manages to put on regular art shows (open during exhibitions only, Wed–Sun; free; tel: (04) 94 65 22 72).

The track continues uphill to the ruins of the 13th-century **château**. The castle's

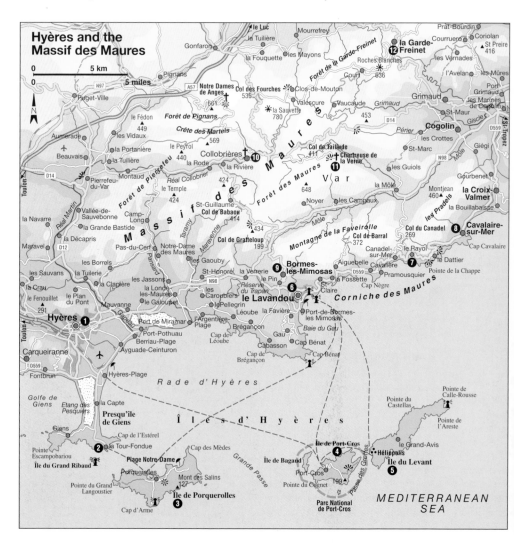

Map on page 128

foundations sit on a Greek defence wall dating from the 4th century BC; at the time a Greek trading-post called Olbia existed on the coast at Almanarre (just south of Hyères). The castle was established by the Lords of Fos and passed to Charles I in 1257. In 1662, the castle was pulled down during the Wars of Religion. Without its stronghold the importance of the town was drastically reduced in favour of Toulon.

The view from the turrets provides a strong sense of the local geography. To the east are the dark curves of the Massif des Maures, to the south the Giens peninsula and the Îles d'Hyères. The American novelist Edith Wharton fell in love with the view when she first visited Hyères in 1915. She returned after World War I and wrote that she was ravished by "views of land and sea such as were never seen before".

A newer castle

Edith Wharton is also associated with the **Castel Ste-Clair**, a 19th-century castle surrounded by exotic gardens, on the southern slopes of the same hill (gardens open daily; free). She lived here for 10 years, devoting much of her time to restoring what was once a Clarisses convent. Her friend Bernard Berenson pronounced the castle and its views to be "sheer paradise… with the incense-like fragrance of the pines and cypresses and the artistic beauty of the rocks." Other literary figures to visit Ste-Clair were Henry James, H. G. Wells, Aldous Huxley and Kenneth Clark.

Another famous inhabitant of old Hyères, with a tomb in the grounds of Ste-Clair, is Olivier Voitier, the 19th-century naval officer who discovered the statue of the *Venus de Milo*, now in the Louvre, when on a maritime campaign in Greece.

The modern town

The modern town has its own attractions, including many Moorish-style buildings, such as Villa Tunisienne (1 Avenue de Beauregard) and La Mauresque (2 Avenue Jean Natte). On Avenue Jean Jaurés is the shiny **Casino des Palmiers**, restored to its

former grandeur and filled with the usual gaming tables and one-armed bandits.

South of the town centre you can see just-married couples posing for photographs against the tropical plants, flowers, peacocks and ornamental lakes of the **Jardin Olbius Riquier** (open daily).

Heading for the islands

For the town's beaches, head further south, beyond the airport, to Hyères-Plage or the long sandy expanse of **La Capte**, on the isthmus of the Giens Peninsula. The safe, shallow waters here make it very popular in summer. Behind La Capte is the Salins des Pesquiers, the coast's only working salt marsh. In Roman times this strange narrow strip was probably underwater, and it was flooded again in the great storms of 1811.

On the end of the peninsula is **La Tour-Fondue ❷**, where ferries leave regularly for the Hyères islands. At the foot of the tower, which the young Napoleon reestablished as a stronghold when he was an artillery officer at Toulon, day-trippers and divers congregate for the crossing.

It is a half-hour trip to the beautiful and densely vegetated **Îles d'Hyères**, also called the Îles d'Or, because of the mica or "fool's gold" which sparkles in the sand and rocks of the islands.

In the 16th century, François I granted the right of asylum to convicts provided they would live on the islands and protect them against corsairs and pirates. However, the criminal underclass flooded the islands and turned to piracy themselves, rewarding the king's generosity by trying to capture one of his ships.

Troubles on the mainland have also been felt on the islands. In 1793, the British landed on Porquerolles and blew up the fort, and in August 1944 American troops landed on the islands of Port-Cros and Le Levant to fight off German batteries.

Unspoilt havens

Île de Porquerolles ❸, named after the wild boar that once roamed here, is the largest and most popular of the islands. It

BELOW: Moorish-style architecture in Hyères.

Map on page 128

offers the most amenities for families, pleasure-craft owners and the less intrepid, while its white sandy beaches and woods of pine, eucalyptus and myrtle remain remarkably unspoilt. Porquerolles has been protected from developers by State ownership, with a large conservation area established in 1972.

The island's village, also called Porquerolles, has a strong colonial flavour in the simple style of its houses, built by the military in the mid-19th century. The small village church has a wooden Stations of the Cross carved by a soldier with his penknife. Inexpensive lunches can be enjoyed at the many restaurants around the main square.

Alternatively, hire mountain bikes (beware of uncompromising seats) or the gearless *classique* and set off with a picnic to the fine beaches on the north coast or the lighthouse on the south. Climb the lighthouse to enjoy dramatic views of the hills of Le Grand Langoustier to the west, Fort Ste-Agathe to the north and, beyond it, Hyères and the Maures massif.

Île de Port-Cros ❹ is quieter and more rugged and is worth a whole day's visit. The island is named after the hollowed-out (*creux*) shape of its harbour. Explore the island by walking through the Vallon de la Solitude to the best hotel on the island. Le Manoir d'Hélène is named after the heroine in Melchoir de Vogue's novel *Jean d'A-grève*, which is set on the island. It was here that D. H. Lawrence is supposed to have met the Englishwoman whose confessional post-coital conversation inspired *Lady Chatterley's Lover*. Continue to **Fort de l'Estissac**; the botanical path is overgrown with wild flowers whose scent accompanies you down to the sheltered beach and turquoise waters of La Palud.

Île du Levant ❺ is a strip of barren rock only 8 km (5 miles) long and less than 1.5 km (1 mile) wide. Here you can bare all at the nudist village and beach of Héliopolis, which used to be the "Mecca of Naturism". The nudist colony was founded on the island (once inhabited by Lérins monks) in 1931 by the doctors

BELOW: the crossing to Porquerolles.

Gaston and André Durville who urged their patients to enjoy the physical and psychological benefits of "the childlike liberation of nakedness". Since it has become acceptable to take off your swimsuit on many beaches around the Mediterranean, the island has lost some of its *risqué* reputation, but is still popular with dedicated nudists. There is not much of the island to explore as most of Levant is owned by the navy, but there is the strange sight of shopkeepers, estate agents and waiters going about their daily routine in a G-string or less.

The Corniche des Maures

Back on the mainland, the coast east of Hyères, from La Londe to Cap Bénat, hides a number of relatively uncrowded beaches. Some cannot be reached by road, but exploration on foot will be rewarded by unspoilt stretches of sand. **Cap Bénat** itself is France's equivalent of Camp David. The rocky promontory, with its two ruined castles, is a military training

ground and includes the official summer residence of the President.

The main resort of the corniche is **Le Lavandou ❻**, further east, whose name refers to the lavender fields on the banks of the River Batailler. It is now a resort catering mainly for the teenage holiday market and the owners of pleasure-craft, although it does still function as a fishing port. It is a mixture of nightclubs, bars, cheap hotels and leather-jacketed *mecs* on motorbikes. The town's best point is its sandy beach and long, tree-lined promenade. Ferries leave regularly from here for the Hyères islands.

Quieter beaches can be found, east of Le Lavandou, at the less built-up resorts of **St-Clair**, **Aiguebelle**, **Cavalière** and **Pramousquier**. In particular, look out for the Plage du Layet, hidden in the trees west of Cavalière.

Further east, in **Canadel-sur-Mer**, a narrow road, the D27, turns away from the coast and twists steeply up into the Pradels range (follow signs to La Môle). Just when

BELOW: beach on the Golfe de Giens.

Map on page 128

you've had enough of the stomach-churning hairpins, the road reaches the top of the ridge, where it crosses the GR 51 hiking route. Here the views are stupendous – from the St-Tropez peninsula in the east to the Île de Porquerolles in the west.

In **Le Rayol** ❼, the next village along the coast, is one of the area's highlights, the 20-hectare (50-acre) gardens of the **Domaine du Rayol** (open Jan–Nov: daily; entrance fee; tel: (04) 98 04 44 00). Created in 1910, the Domaine is now a showcase for plants from exotic places that share the Mediterranean climate, including China, Australia, South Africa and California. The unspoilt setting, the exquisite landscaping and the bewildering array of shapes and colours will tempt you to linger.

Beyond Le Rayol, a rare stretch of undeveloped road will bring you to **Cavalaire-sur-Mer** ❽, a town built for the convenience of boat-owners. It has mooring for 1,200 yachts, good shops and a long sandy beach. In the summer, you can catch a ferry from here to the Hyères islands or St-Tropez. The Wednesday market on Place Jean Moulin offers an abundance of regional produce: honey from the forest, olives, olive oil, *saucisson* and the essential local rosé.

Away from the coast

Just inland from Le Lavandou, via an avenue of mimosa and eucalyptus, is the village of **Bormes-les-Mimosas** ❾, whose coral-coloured houses and steeply sloping streets give a delightful flavour of Provence. In Place St-François is a statue of Francesco di Paola whose visit to the town was said to have miraculously ended an outbreak of plague. In the chapel of St-François there is a monument to the landscape painter Jean-Charles Cazin whose works are on display both in the town hall and in the small Musée d'Art et d'Histoire (open Wed–Mon; Sun am only; free). At the top of the town there are excellent cafés and magnificent views of the coast and, to the north, the forest of Dom.

BELOW: street in Collobrières.

Exploring the Massif

North of Bormes is the oldest range of mountains in Provence, the **Massif des Maures**. The mainly schist rock was originally part of the huge Tyrrhenian massif, which once included Corsica and Sardinia. The name *Maures* is not an allusion to the Moors (Saracens), who occupied the area for more than a century and who were finally driven out in AD 973, but to the Provençal word *Maouro* which describes the dark density of the cork oak, chestnut and pine forest.

The glorious views and abundance of flowers and plants such as yellow gorse, lavender and wild roses are enjoyed by drivers, walkers and cyclists who use the Massif's villages to shape their route through the mountainous forest.

One such village is **Collobrières** ⑩, reached from Bormes by a tortuous road over the thickly wooded Col de Babaou. The village center is not the attractive main square with its Spanish feel, or the main boulevard with its grand mercantile

houses, but the extensive bouledrome by the Collobrier River. A 12th-century bridge crosses the river nearby, and beside it is the **Confiserie Azuréenne**, a delicious-smelling shop famous for its chestnut sweets and purées. At the east end of the village is the romantic-looking ruin of the 12th-century Eglise St-Pons.

North of the village one can take an 11-km (7-mile) detour to the eccentric Merovingian priory of **Notre-Dame-des-Anges**, which shares its high point with a large communications tower and transmitter mast. The 19th-century chapel is filled with offerings made by pilgrims who have climbed to the spot where a statue of the Virgin Mary was found by a shepherd in the 11th century. Babies' bonnets and pictures of the sick being cured cram the dark chapel and, more mysteriously, two stuffed alligators hang from the ceiling.

Deeper into the woods

The road east of Collobrières (the D14 towards Grimaud) is spectacular. Winding through forests of oak and chestnut, it climbs high into the heart of the Massif. Along the route there are points for cars to stop and admire the breathtaking views or simply to let an impatient hill-farmer overtake in his van. Tracks and paths are clearly marked for walkers.

These forests are particularly prone to devastating fires, sparked spontaneously by thoughtless visitors, or, as some locals think, by arsonists. From the road you may see blackened and twisted trees, and fire-fighters carrying out their daily duties of strimming down the undergrowth and creating fire-breaks.

About 6 km (4 miles) from Collobrières, an even narrower and more tortuous road turns off to the south and climbs to a desolate and brooding Carthusian monastery, the **Chartreuse de la Verne** ⑪ (open Feb–Dec: Wed–Mon; entrance fee; tel: (04) 94 43 48 28). This forbidding-looking structure, standing on a plateau overlooking the forest, dates mostly from the 17th and 18th centuries, but some vestiges remain from its 12th-century beginnings. During the Revolution, the monks fled and the monastery remained unoccupied until

LEFT: traditional café in La Garde-Freinet.

Map
on page
128

1983, when nuns from the order of Bethlehem took up residence. Restoration work is still in progress but visitors can wander through the beautiful semi-ruin and see the blue-green serpentine cloisters, empty monks' cells and 17th-century church.

Capital of the Maures

The D14 continues to Grimaud *(see page 148)*. From here, a more substantial road leads north to **La Garde-Freinet** 12, the main village of the Massif and fashionable among second-home owners and expats escaping the crush on the coast.

In the 19th century, the village produced more than three-quarters of France's bottle corks. The industry has declined dramatically since then, but the cork-oaks in these hills are still harvested, and you will often see them stripped of their bark on the side of the road. The light, impermeable and elastic outer bark is cut off and sent to factories in Fréjus and further afield.

You can pick up ornaments crafted from cork on Rue St-Jacques, which also tempts visitors from the coast with local antiques, pottery and flower shops. Look out for the exquisite but expensive jewellery made from the local serpentine stone.

The Saracens were at one time credited with building the **fortress** on a high point to the northwest of the village, but it is now thought to be of a later period (12th–16th century). A small museum above the tourist office on Place Neuve (open Tue–Sat; entrance fee; tel: (04) 94 43 08 57) contains a model of the fort as well as archaeological finds from the area. The tourist office also provides information on the many superb hiking routes in the surrounding hills.

If you're visiting in early June, try to be here on the day of the *transhumance* festival, when the village celebrates the departure of the local sheep for higher summer pastures. In many places, this is now carried out in vehicles, but in this area the shepherds still walk all the way with the sheep, often spending several days on the march. ❑

BELOW: the rooftops of Bormes-les-Mimosas.

Maps:
Area 145
Town 140

ST-TROPEZ AND ITS PENINSULA

*The quayside and beaches of legendary St-Tropez attract thousands
in the summer, but the rest of the peninsula offers more peaceful
pursuits among the vineyards and traditional hilltop villages*

Like Hollywood, **St-Tropez** ❶ ranks among an élite handful of place-names to have achieved practically mythical status. To large numbers of French, the myth is still one of the *ne plus ultra* of summer chic. To others, St-Tropez typifies over-commercialism and vulgarity. Needless to say, the reality is somewhere between the two, and varies in any case according to the season.

Crammed with between 45,000 and 60,000 daily visitors in July and August, in winter St-Tropez's population returns to a placid and neighbourly 5,400. Though obviously not for those in search of rustic serenity, at least in summer, a visit to St-Tropez can be considerable fun, if taken in the right spirit, and preferably equipped with a generous budget. Perhaps the best approach is to think of the town as a sort of Mediterranean extension of the Left Bank of Paris, with all that this implies in terms of parking problems and expense.

St-Tropez's original attraction was based on the beauty of the dusky pink and ochre houses of the old town, its position on the southern curve of its large, sheltered gulf, and the climatic conditions which contribute to its beautiful, clear light. Uniquely on the French Riviera, St-Tropez faces north, so that the quayside cafés receive the famous golden evening light, as well as the bay's stunning sunsets.

As neither railway nor major trunk roads passed through the town due to its peninsular position, it escaped the late 19th-century development of earlier resorts such as Juan-les-Pins and Cannes. Its restricted road access is now a mixed blessing – in summer traffic jams run the length of the N98 to the huge roundabout at La Foux, and, sometimes, the whole way round the bay to Ste-Maxime. (The times absolutely to be avoided on this road are late morning until early afternoon, and between 6 o'clock and 10 o'clock in the evening.)

PRECEDING PAGES: Le Café, St-Tropez.
LEFT: first encounters.
RIGHT: rooftops of the old town.

Early history

St-Tropez is named after Torpes, a Christian Roman centurion, steward of the Emperor Nero's palace at Pisa who, according to legend, was beheaded for his faith and cast adrift with a dog and a rooster in a boat which eventually drifted to the site of the present port. The early town was sacked and its population killed or dispersed by Saracen raiders who occupied the region in the 7th and 9th centuries. In the 15th, St-Tropez was ceded to a Genoese nobleman, Raphaël de Garezzio, with rights tantamount to those of a republic, and was populated by a number of Genoese families, some of whose descendants remain today.

The citadel overlooking the town dates from the ensuing period of well-organised

security, provided by an elected "town captain" and militia. In 1637, this militia successfully defended the town against a raiding force of 22 Spanish galleys.

By the late-19th century, St-Tropez was primarily involved in tuna fishing, shipping wines from the region to Marseille and Toulon, and making corks from the bark of the local oaks. A handful of large houses outside the town had been restored or constructed by prominent individuals such as Napoleon III's minister Émile Ollivier, who retired to the Château de la Moutte, in whose grounds his tomb stands, "seeking only peace, but finding delight".

The artists arrive

In 1887, the writer Guy de Maupassant arrived in St-Tropez aboard his boat *Bel Ami* and found it "a charming, simple daughter of the sea" with "sardine scales glistening like pearls on the cobblestones." It was the painter Paul Signac, however, who, sailing into the port on his yacht in 1892 and falling in love with the

light, acquired a small house overlooking the beach of Les Graniers and began to attract friends and painter acquaintances: Matisse, Bonnard, Camoin, Dunoyer de Segonzac. In 1927, the novelist Colette moved to her villa La Treille Muscate. She was followed by 1930s *beau monde*, such as the couturier Paul Poiret, the writer Anaïs Nin, and after the interruption of World War II, when the long Pampelonne beach was used for the Allied liberation landings, by the first of the St-Germain bohemian stars, Juliette Greco.

In 1955 Roger Vadim shot *And God Created Woman* in St-Tropez, with the sex-kitten Brigitte Bardot wreaking havoc around the old port, and the floodgates of the town's modern showbusiness invasion were opened. The *yé yé* industry – pop stars led by Johnny Hallyday and record magnate Eddie Barclay – followed the film world, and in 1969 the opening of the luxurious Hôtel Byblos marked a turning point in the transformation of the hitherto simple fishing village into a fully paid-up

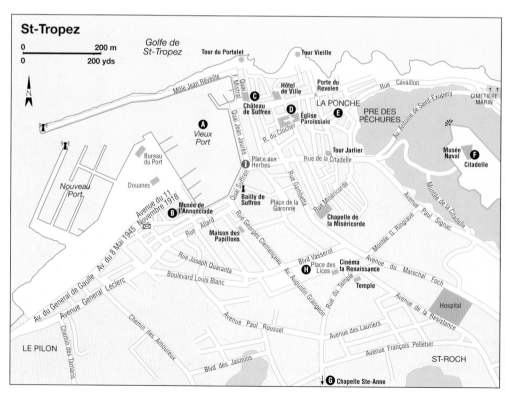

Map
on page
140

jet-set destination. It only remained for the masses to follow, and the seriously rich to move out of town to luxurious and secluded villas, or the staterooms of their substantial yachts.

The St-Tropez season traditionally starts at Easter, peaks in the frenzy of the national holiday month of August and continues until the end of Les Voiles de Saint-Tropez, a fashionable yacht-racing week at the end of September. The quiet winter months are interrupted by a substantial mini-season around Christmas; many shops, restaurants and hotels close during the off-peak period.

Sights of the old town

The centre of St-Tropez is the renovated **Vieux Port Ⓐ** (Old Port), enclosed by the long stone jetty, the Môle Jean Réveille, extending outwards from the squat, round 15th-century **Tour du Portalet**. The quays (Suffren, Jean Jaurès and Frédéric Mistral) are lined with restaurants and fashionable cafés, notably the all-red

BELOW: view of St-Tropez and the gulf beyond.

Sénéquier, formerly a pâtisserie and still famed for its nougat. Beside it is the more youthful **Le Gorille**, open 24 hours a day in the summer, making it *the* place to go for post-clubbing hunger pangs. Both are ideal venues for people-watching.

Behind Sénéquier is the small **Place aux Herbes**, reached through an archway beside the tourist office. Every morning a flower, vegetable and fish market is held here.

Stern to the quay are the great yachts – futuristic white plastic gin palaces or gleaming teak classics – with uniformed crews and, increasingly, non-sailing corporate charterers. Throughout the old, and adjacent new, ports is a wide range of craft, from vintage sailing yachts to the long, spearhead-shaped, V8-engined, offshore "cigarettes" that drone across the bay at 100 kph (60 mph).

On the west side of the old port is the **Musée de l'Annonciade Ⓑ** (open Dec–Oct: Wed–Mon; entrance fee; tel: (04) 94 97 04 01), a 16th-century chapel attractively converted to house a large and excel-

lent collection of paintings and sculptures by artists who lived or worked in the town. Partly donated by the Tropezien philanthropist Georges Grammont, the museum's collection constitutes one of the most important assemblages of neo-Impressionist and Fauvist art outside Paris. Signac is represented by a rotating collection of 10 watercolours and five oils, and other high points include works by Van Dongen, Matisse, Seurat, Bonnard, Dufy, Vuillard and Braque. Many of the paintings depict scenes of St-Tropez itself.

A little way beyond the Annonciade is the **Quai Suffren**, with its bronze statue of one of St-Tropez's most illustrious adopted citizens, the Bailly de Suffren. De Suffren's late-flourishing nautical career ended with a famously successful Indian campaign in the 1780s and the command of the French navy. His name was retrospectively applied to the 10th-century square tower, the **Château de Suffren ❻**, just behind the Quai Mistral. The tower was used along with a similar building in Ste-Maxime by the Knights Templar to protect the gulf's settlements from the North African Barbary pirates whose raids plagued the region until the 15th century. It is sometimes used for art exhibitions.

Away from the quayside

Behind the tower is the attractive ochre-coloured **Hôtel de Ville** (Town Hall). From here you can explore the lovely narrow stone streets of the old town, those nearer the port lined with shops and restaurants, those further back residential and surprisingly quiet and unspoilt even in August.

In the centre of the old town is St-Tropez's 18th-century neo-Baroque **Église Paroissiale ❼** (Parish Church; open daily; am only), whose distinctive pink and yellow bell tower and typically Provençal wrought-iron belfry have become a symbol of the town. The church contains statues of Torpes, the town's patron saint, both headless and recumbent, plus menagerie, in his boat, invariably festooned with votive offerings of flowers and hearts.

BELOW: repairing a fishing boat on the Quai Mistral.

Map on page 140

The quiet, old *quartier* of **La Ponche** **Ⓔ**, reached through the 15th-century stone gate, the Porte du Revelen, was once the haunt of Tropezien fishermen. In years gone by they would beach at the Port des Pêcheurs and sell their catch from nearby stalls. The tiny corps of remaining fishermen now use the Quai Mistral and trade at the covered market on Place aux Herbes.

The narrow streets of La Ponche are home to a couple of fine hotels frequented by the Sagans and Vadims in the pre-Byblos 1950s and '60s. Hôtel La Ponche, with its terrace restaurant, and the similarly elegant Yaca Hotel have both managed to update their facilities and decor with great taste, retaining the charm of the lovely old buildings.

Other points of interest in the centre of St-Tropez include the 16th-century semi-ruined **Tour Jarlier** and the 17th-century **Chapelle de la Miséricorde** with its blue, green and gold tiled belfry. Best of all, though, is the general effect of the little streets, warm pastel walls enlivened by pots of geraniums (once put on the window ledge to keep out mosquitoes) and glimpses of oleander peeking from walled gardens.

The outskirts

Ten minutes' walk from the centre, overlooking the bay from its grassy, pine-dotted hillock, is the triangular, 16th-century **Citadelle Ⓕ** (open Dec–Oct: Wed–Mon; entrance fee; tel: (04) 94 97 59 43), surrounded by an extensive wall and dry moat, and patrolled by peacocks. Apart from the superb view from the ramparts, the maritime museum within the citadel has displays of torpedoes (the weapons are still made at a factory just outside St-Tropez) and of maps, uniforms and guns relating to the 1943–45 Resistance and Liberation. Below the citadel, on the opposite slope of the hill from the town centre, is the **cemetery**, its rows of white headstones outlined strikingly against the blue of the sea it overlooks.

Excellent views of the town (and, in the other direction, of Cap Camarat) can be

BELOW: hanging out at the Sénéquier café.

had from the 17th-century **Chapelle Ste-Anne** 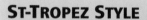 (closed to public), 20 minutes' walk uphill south of the town centre.

The fabled nightlife

Facing the floating palaces of the Old Port, the famous café duo of Sénéquier and Le Gorille, plus the newer, trendier establishments such as Café de Paris (redesigned by Phillipe Starck with red velvet, bare metal and chandeliers) and the retro-chic Bar du Port, are St-Tropez's supreme breakfast and all-day people-watching haunts. For the evening buzz, they are often rivalled by the cafés on the **Place des Lices** 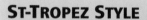, five minutes' walk away. Under the five rows of big plane trees (many of which are on their last legs, supported by metal props), hundreds of people play *boules*, stroll, sit on benches, or in the case of younger holidaymakers, pose on Harley-Davidsons and scooters.

One of the favourites is Le Café, on the site of the legendary *boules*-players' hang-out, the Café des Arts. Its busy bistro-like interior is a good place to dine well at a medium price with a view of the fascinating bustle in the square.

Around midnight, queues start to form outside St-Tropez's nightclubs, which range from the exclusive and glamorous Caves du Roy at the Hôtel Byblos and the classic 1960s favourite, Papagayo, to the newer, hipper VIP Room. All can be difficult to get into; dressing up will help.

The beaches

St-Tropez itself has very limited beach areas, being centred around the port. The famous golden beaches are on either side of the town, and, in the case of the biggest, Plage de Pampelonne, 5 km (3 miles) to the southeast, in the commune of Ramatuelle. Most of them are occupied by a series of beach "clubs" which are usually not clubs at all, but concessions rented by their proprietors from the local council and offering their bars, restaurants, parasols, loungers, and some cases shops, hairdressers, and tenders to pick up customers

LEFT: panamas for sale on the Place des Lices.

ST-TROPEZ STYLE

St-Tropez is a barometer of style for the well-heeled, a summer alternative to the catwalks of Paris or the ski slopes of Mégève. Getting the measure of the St-Tropez look is deceptively complex. Informality has always been the keyword, but *studied* informality – this is not a place to go if you don't want to bother about what you look like. Everyone stares at everyone else all the time, and it's not always clear whether it's out of contempt or admiration.

Once chic, the shops on the quayside now cater to the tour groups. Set back from the port, however, in little shopping streets, the cream of European *prêt-à-porter* is available to those who can afford it. Hermès has a shop here, as does Louis Vuitton; Joanna sells Alexander McQueen, Dolce & Gabbano and Dries van Noten; elsewhere boutiques offer Tommy Hilfiger, Versace, Anna Sui, Emilio Pucci, Prada, and much more.

The surprising thing is how popular St-Tropez remains with the super-rich. Like much of the Côte d'Azur, it is often seen as overcrowded and over-rated, but for many people (usually the ones with the yachts and private villas) it has remained as desirable as ever. Star-spotters will not be disappointed – the likes of Robbie Williams, Naomi Campbell and Jack Nicholson still wander the streets.

Maps:
Area 145
Town 140

from their offshore yachts, to anyone who is willing to pay for these services.

This is not to deny they can seem as cliquey and exclusive as clubs, with different social sets patronising different establishments. Beach life tends to begin late morning, proceed to a leisurely lunch at the restaurant and peak during the post-prandial mid- to late-afternoon lazing time.

The beaches actually forming part of St-Tropez are: to the west of town the **Bouillabaisse**, where the action centres on two concessions, upmarket La Bouillabaise, one of the town's best restaurants, and Les Catamarans, frequented by a younger crowd; **Les Graniers**, a simple local beach just below the Citadel favoured by native Tropeziens; further east the slightly larger **Plage des Canebiers**, overlooked by Bardot's villa, La Madrague; and on the eastern edge of the peninsula, the rather crowded **Plage des Salins**. For less populated sands, head for the **Plage de la Moutte**, reached by a separate road just north of Salins.

RIGHT: ochre
facades at
Ramatuelle.

Legendary Pampelonne

Along the 5-km (3-mile) golden sands of the **Plage de Pampelonne ❷** the popularity of the beach restaurants/concessions is subject to the flighty whims of fashion. Current favourites, from north to south, are: Tropezina; Tabou-Plage; Tahiti, a big, long-established showbiz favourite including a hotel and shops; Bora Bora and the very chic Moorea; Liberty and Neptune, both naturist; Club 55, the oldest (founded in 1955 by the de Colmont family) and classiest; Key West Beach; Nioulargo-Kaï Largo, with its traditional and Asian restaurants; La Plage des Jumeaux, noted for its Provençal food; Cachalot, also offering good local cuisine; La Cabane Bambou; funky and laid-back l'Esquinade; and Tropicana, another showbiz favourite with excellent local cooking. Although much of Pampelonne is taken up by these establishments, there are also small stretches of public beach where you can enjoy the sands without shelling out for lounger, parasol and cocktails.

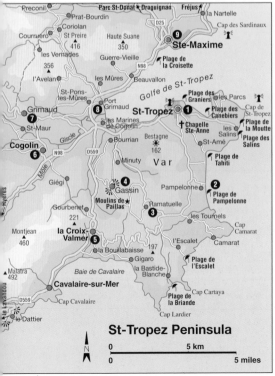

St-Tropez Peninsula

Further round the peninsula, there is a small, attractive beach at **L'Escalet**. If you walk south from here to the next bay, the **Baie de Briande**, you'll find a beach that not many others have discovered.

Peninsular hill villages

If you tire of the beaches, head for the interior of the peninsula. Here you'll find the beautiful hilltop villages of **Ramatuelle** and **Gassin**, their old stone centres rising above the surrounding oak and beech woods to command superb views of the sea, and on a good day, far back to the north, glimpses of snow on the peaks of the lower Alps. In and around them are opulent holiday homes and, in their centres, pretty, chic, tree-shaded restaurants offering a slightly more secluded alternative to those of St-Tropez.

The Saracens are said to be responsible for the name of **Ramatuelle ❸** (from *Rahmatu 'llah*, Arabic for "God's Gift"), which retains two 10th-century doors in the remains of its fortifications from the Saracen occupation. Other significant episodes in the village's martial history include the unusual use of hives of bees hurled from the ramparts to repel a Royalist siege in 1592, and during World War II, its role as a point of contact for the Resistance with Allied submarines, attested to by a monument near the cemetery.

A pretty, tile-roofed, flower-bedecked village of narrow, winding streets, Ramatuelle is also noted for its summer festivals of jazz, classical music and, especially, theatre, all held in an open-air auditorium on the southern slope of Ramatuelle's hill. On Place de l'Ormeau, the Romanesque village church contains furnishings taken from the Chartreuse de la Verne *(see page 134)*, including a 17th-century doorway carved from serpentine. Just outside the village, a magnificent view is available from the road running past three ruined windmills known as the **Moulins de Paillas**.

Ramatuelle's neighbour, about 4 km (2.5 miles) to the northwest, **Gassin ❹** is the

BELOW: Tabou-Plage, at the north end of Pampelonne.

Map on page 145

more elevated of the two. It is an exquisite little town with a 16th-century church and town hall, a pretty central square planted with African lotus trees and surrounded by a warren of tiny roads and alleys, and a circular boulevard with great views over the entire gulf. Gassin's position was its early *raison d'être* – as a look-out post, it was manned from the 10th century by the Knights Templar, who did not, however, prevent a Saracen raiding party carrying off 33 of the village's inhabitants in 1394.

Fruit of the vine

The lower slopes of the peninsula are dominated by vineyards. Viticulture accounts for 40 percent of the agriculture of the region, and the peninsula is an important part of the Côtes-de-Provence *appellation contrôlée* area. Running through this region is the "Route des Côtes-de-Provence", a signposted itinerary passing by some of the most important individual *domaines*, all of them open for visits and sales. Favourites just north of Gassin include the elegant Napoleon III **Château de Minuty** (open Easter–Oct: daily, Nov–Easter: Mon–Fri; free; tel: (04) 94 56 12 09) off Route D61, and the nearby **Château de Barbeyrolles** (open Easter–Oct: daily, Nov–Easter: Mon–Sat; free; tel: (04) 94 56 33 58). The wine co-operative **Les Maîtres Vignerons de Saint-Tropez** (open Mon–Sat) at the La Foux junction near Port Grimaud is the best place to taste a range of local wines, and to pick up other regional products.

On the southern slope of the peninsula, looking down across vineyards, reed-beds and pine groves towards the Baie de Cavalaire, the village of **La Croix-Valmer** ⑤ contains few vestiges of its Roman past. Its name, however, is believed to derive from the legend that Emperor Constantine, while passing en route to Italy, was persuaded by the vision of a cross in the sky to convert to Christianity. For the most part dating from the early 20th century, La Croix-Valmer contains some striking modern buildings, including the parish church. In addition to its role as a centre for vacation homes, it is an important wine-producing centre.

West of St-Tropez, just before the coastal plain begins its long mutation into the hills of the Massif des Maures, sits the town of **Cogolin** ⑥, General de Lattre de Tassigny's headquarters during the 1944 battle to liberate Provence. Although possessed of a pretty old centre with a 16th-century church, numerous serpentine doorways and vaulted passageways, Cogolin is also a working town. In addition to wine, it produces furniture, hand-woven carpets, clarinet mouthpieces from the surrounding reed beds and pipes carved from the roots of local mountain heather.

Foothills of the Maures

Just as the Massif de l'Estérel, to the north, acts as a buffer against the urbanisation of the coast between Cannes and St-Raphaël, so the great wild bulk of the **Massif des Maures** counterbalances the St-Tropez build-up. Indeed, until the seaside boom in the early 1900s, the presence of the Maures kept the coastline isolated and undeveloped for centuries.

RIGHT: red wine on tap at a cellar in Cogolin.

The Maures are among the areas of the Riviera worst afflicted by brush fires, however, and long stretches of the roads which wind north through the low hills pass acres of fire-blackened, dead trunks, protruding from the thistle, thyme and broom scrub. Patrolling fire engines and look-out points are a common sight in summer.

Just where the massif begins to rise northwest of Cogolin is the typical fortified village of **Grimaud** ❼, flower-decorated and immaculately maintained by a population that seems to consist largely of four-wheel-drive-owning architects. The name of the village derives from that of Gibelin de Grimaldi, a knight who was given lordship of the area in the 10th century as a reward for his part in the expulsion of the Saracen occupiers; the name is also that of the Monaco royal family.

Modern-day Grimaud, clustering around the ruins of its medieval castle, has a simple but impressive Romanesque church, St-Michel, once used by the Templars, after whom the lovely arcaded street

nearby is named. There is no shortage of chic and pretty hotels, one of the prettiest being the small, traditional Coteau Fleuri, with its flower-packed garden and wonderful views. The hike up to the castle is worth braving for even better views in all directions. The romantic ruins themselves are notable for their sharp-edged serpentine window-frames, which seem to hold their own while the rest of the edifice crumbles around them.

Grimaud's scene-stealing seaside extension, **Port Grimaud** ❽, is 5 km (3 miles) to the east, at the head of the Gulf of St-Tropez *(see opposite)*.

Ste-Maxime

Further around the gulf, opposite St-Tropez, is **Ste-Maxime** ❾, a prosperous and pleasant resort of over 12,000 inhabitants with a marina and pretty seafront marred only by the traffic passing along its main coast road. The centre is occupied by the massed striped parasols of the main beach, the pastel bulk of the casino, with an art deco bas-relief of swimming girls, and well-kept gardens of palm trees, mimosa and oleander.

Just behind the centre, the old town is pedestrianised, if busy in the summer; on its edge is the cool, immaculately kept 19th-century parish church and a square 16th-century tower, the Tour Carrée, now a local history museum (open Wed–Mon; tel: (04) 94 96 70 30). For sun-worshippers, Cherry Beach, 3 km (2 miles) east of the marina, is the chic choice, and further on, Plage des Eléphants is more affordable.

On route D25, about 10 km (6 miles) northwest of Ste-Maxime, in the foothills of the Massif des Maures, look for a sign on the right indicating the privately-run **Musée du Phonographe et de la Musique Mécanique** (open Easter–Oct: Wed–Sun; entrance fee; tel: (04) 94 96 50 52). In a shed behind a lovingly crafted folk-kitsch facade, one woman has collected around 400 assorted antique record players, barrel organs, and other mechanical music-makers, including an 1860s clockwork songbird, all displayed in an amiable jumble. If you're lucky, Madame will demonstrate some of the still-working pieces. ❑

LEFT: the game of *boules* is as popular as ever.

Port Grimaud

Port Grimaud inhabitants like to ask visitors jokingly if they have ever visited St-Tropez –"you know, that little village across the bay". The implication of the newer resort's fame is by no means all hyperbole: it now rates as one of the most popular tourist attractions in France, averaging over a million visitors a year – not bad going for a town that did not exist before 1966.

Port Grimaud, furthermore, is the creation essentially of one man, architect François Spoerry, whose reputation was made by this little Provençal Venice, and who went on to consult on similar schemes in New York, Mexico and Japan. Spoerry's idea for Port Grimaud was nurtured in the 1950s at his parents' holiday home along the coast in Cavalaire. "I found it dreary to have to get up in the middle of the night, if there was a storm, and go to the port to secure our boat's mooring." He determined to design a leisure port, with yacht-owners primarily in mind, on the model of Venice, where the "ground floor" of the buildings serves as a reception area and mooring for the owners' boats and those of delivery men.

In 1962, Spoerry obtained a stretch of marshy land by the mouth of the little river Giscle at the end of the Gulf of St-Tropez in the commune of Grimaud. The area was a mosquito-infested sand-pit, and it took Spoerry four years to obtain building permission for a project widely regarded as crazy. The earliest houses went for as little as 150,000 francs. These days you would be lucky to get a studio apartment for four times that value, and the houses sell for over a million euros.

Spoerry's guiding principles were those of what he describes as *architecture douce* (soft architecture). Buildings, he believed, should be unassuming, human in scale, and functional, and should avail themselves of local traditional materials and techniques. He therefore designed Port Grimaud in the traditional local style, with terracotta tiled roofs, and facades painted in the wonderful shades of ochre and cream that characterise so many Provençal villages.

Every house has a waterfront and boat mooring – later "streets" have small front gardens with lawns and trees – and access roads at the rear permit vehicle access for deliveries, but not in theory for parking. Movement between the 2,500 houses, two squares, 30-odd bars and restaurants and several dozen shops is on foot, via the little wood or stone-clad bridges connecting the little islands, or by the small electric-powered boats used as runabouts.

Port Grimaud is an impressive achievement and in many places extremely pretty, but ultimately it is a stage-set. The French, German, Italian and British owners of the huge yachts moored outside the houses are absent for a large part of the year, consigning their properties to resident caretakers.

If the development lacks the soul of a true Provençal village, however, its convenience attracts numerous buyers. The buildings are acquiring a patina of age, and cicadas now chirrup in the main square, adding the quintessential Midi soundtrack to the pastiche.

Spoerry himself died in 1999, and is buried in Port Grimaud's striking church. The house he built for himself in the "floating" village sold for 35 million francs. ❑

RIGHT: a 20th-century Venice.

ST-RAPHAËL, FRÉJUS AND THE ARGENS VALLEY

Away from the glitzy resorts of St-Tropez and Cannes, this region offers Roman ruins in Fréjus, unspoilt highlands in the Massif de l'Estérel and superb Côtes de Provence wines around Les Arcs

Map on page 154

If the region around Fréjus and St-Raphaël is rather overshadowed by world-famous neighbours such as St-Tropez and Cannes, it is by no means totally eclipsed. Economically and demographically, the area is booming – the local population, rate of employment and small business sector all grew substantially in the 1990s.

In Fréjus, it possesses a visible Roman heritage of national importance as well as a medieval centre the equal of any on the Riviera. And the wild, forested hills of the Massif de l'Estérel have helped the Var retain its reputation as the green *département*. Even the coast here, while built up and crowded in summer, is relatively lightly so.

Hugging the coast

The Fréjus-St-Raphaël conurbation can be reached inland from Cannes via a sprint down the A8 autoroute *(La Provençale)*, a slightly longer but still brisk drive along the pretty, winding N7 just south, or via the Corniche de l'Esterel road (N98) which twists along a narrow strip between the sea and the steep red rock edges of the massif. The corniche road, and the railway line it approximately accompanies, pass beside a succession of coves, small beaches and villages surrounded by a scarcely interrupted fringe of villas, hotels, restaurants and campsites: in July and August the traffic is heavy. To one side rear the red porphyry peaks of the **Pic de l'Ours** and the **Pic du Cap Roux**. To the other, the sea is dotted with little islets, forming part of the same ancient rock mass.

At the eastern edge of the Massif de l'Estérel, just west of Cannes, is **La Napoule ❶**, in effect just a seafront extension of the Cannes satellite, Mandelieu. La Napoule possesses three sandy beaches, a leisure port and the **Château de la Napoule** (open Mar–Oct: Wed– Mon; pm only; entrance fee; tel: (04) 93 49 95 05), an arts foundation set in a converted medieval castle filled with the idiosyncratic sculptures of American artist Henry Clews.

The series of increases of building density which follow along the coast – for this is what the formerly separate villages have become – are distinguishable from each other by features such as a 19th-century soap factory turned château at **Théoule**, attractive beaches at **Le Trayas** and **Anthéor**, and the deeper than average natural harbour at **Agay ❷**. This former Roman port, with its lovely bay shaded by pines and red cliffs, is one

of the region's most laid-back resorts.

Just west of Agay, covering the long slope of the hillside above the wide beach of **Le Dramont** (a key landing point of the American 7th Army in August 1944), is a development which symbolises the nadir of the rampant over-building of the 1970s and '80s, but also represents its belated check. **Cap Estérel**, a huge concrete complex of holiday apartments, centred around a pair of stadium-sized swimming-pools, was obliged to limit itself to just half its planned size after a regional tribunal revoked building permission, a landmark decision in an area long milked with impunity by French property companies.

In even the most densely touristed places, however, oases of calm subsist, surprisingly near to the beaten track. At **Boulouris** ❸, a resort of pine-shaded villas just outside St-Raphaël, the **Plage d'Arène Grosse** is a pleasant spot to sip an evening apéritif and watch the pin-prick shimmer of lights on the far-off St-Tropez peninsula. A seafront walk here is pretty and quiet. Gardens of umbrella pine and yucca stretch down to the path. The occasional dog races in and out of the gentle waves.

St-Raphaël

The earliest citizens of **St-Raphaël** ❹ came looking for sea air and relaxation. They were wealthy Romans from the important naval and military settlement of Fréjus, and they built terraced villas decorated with mosaics close enough to enjoy the restorative properties of the sea.

In the Middle Ages, the settlement was sacked by the Saracens; it was re-inhabited by monks from Marseille, placed under the protection of the Knights Templar and subsequently attracted a small fishing and agricultural community. In 1799, Napoleon entitled St-Raphaël to one of its rare entries in the history books by disembarking here on his return from Egypt.

In the 1860s, the celebrated Parisian journalist, Alphonse Karr, moved along the coast from already-crowded Nice and began to invite down the advance guard

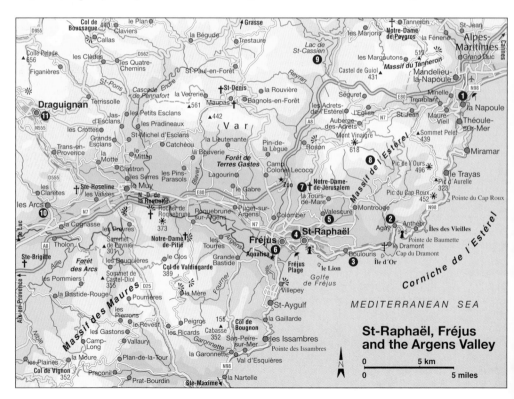

St-Raphaël, Fréjus and the Argens Valley

MEDITERRANEAN SEA

0   5 km

0   5 miles

Map on page 154

of metropolitan intellectual trendsetters (including writers Dumas and Maupassant, and composers Berlioz and Gounod) who, rapidly augmented by rich English, made St-Raphaël a fashionable resort.

Along the seafront

As you approach from the east, you pass St-Raphaël's purpose-built yacht harbour, **Port Santa Lucia**, with its 1,600 berths and modern Palais de Congrès (conference centre). A little further along, on the **Boulevard de Gaulle** and the **Promenade René Coty**, are the few early 20th-century hotels and slightly shabbier apartment blocks that lend the town its air of a little Cannes. Here and there, curlicued art nouveau balconies look out over the tall palms that line the raised promenade.

At the end of this sweep stands the **Casino**, in front of the dome of the late 19th-century church of **Notre-Dame-de-la-Victoire-de-Lépante**, the two main features (with a large block of flats characteristically obscuring both) that mark out the town if approached from the sea. The casino represents St-Raphaël's most recent mass-tourism phase, as well as the town's heyday of bourgeois gentility, and its earliest origins, too, as the site was occupied by the first Roman settlement.

The **"Vieux Port"** in front of the casino is actually late-19th century. It is home to a small fishing fleet, a number of pleasure-craft, the occasional visiting naval vessel and regular ferry services to Port Grimaud, Ile de Port-Cros, Ile Ste-Marguerite and St-Tropez. (The 50-minute journey to the latter is the nicest, and in August the fastest, way of getting there.)

The fishing boats' daily catch is on sale every morning from a line of market stalls set up alongside the quay on **Cours Jean Bart**. This broad boulevard, with its stone benches and double row of big plane trees is the night-time centre for strolling and café life. Entertainment is provided in the high season by the usual panoply of itinerant pavement artists, street performers, Senegalese fake Louis Vuitton pedlars,

BELOW: Notre-Dame church, behind the St-Raphaël Casino.

and, in some of the cafés, resident entertainers on Yamaha keyboards. At its western end, marked in summer by a plastic reproduction 18th-century Venetian fairground carousel, the bustle of activity merges with that of Fréjus-Plage.

The old town

Heading away from the port, you come to the wood-beamed market on **Place Victor Hugo**. Here, fruit and vegetable traders rub shoulders with traditional *charcuteries* and fishmongers. Nearby, the simple La Bouillabaisse restaurant, with its check tablecloths and ivy-covered terrace, is an excellent place to consume good value bouillabaisse and langoustes.

Continuing northeast you reach the pretty, but minuscule and unkempt, old town. Here, the 12th-century **Église St-Raphaël**, from which the town took its name, provides a link with the period of the Knights Templar. The small, plain, single-nave church was used as a fortified refuge in case of attack by pirates, as its

military-looking watchtower suggests.

Traces of the town's Roman past are restricted to a collection of amphoras in the **Musée Archéologique** (open Tues–Sat; entrance fee; tel: (04) 94 19 25 75), beside the church. Most have been lifted from the sea bed by local diving teams. The museum also contains prehistoric material as well as documents and photos from the town's 19th-century heyday.

In the leafy hillside suburbs to the north and east of the town centre are the Edwardian-Provençal villas surrounded by gardens built for the early moneyed English visitors. These are concentrated particularly around the suburb of **Valescure ❺**, with its famous golf course – the fifth oldest in France – whose perimeters feature a now common Riviera phenomenon – holiday apartments for visiting golfers.

Roman metropolis

If present-day signs of St-Raphaël's medieval past are limited, and of its Roman past virtually non-existent, the

BELOW:
windsurfers in
the waters off
St-Raphaël.

Map on page 154

reverse is true of **Fréjus 6**. The larger town (48,000 inhabitants as opposed to St-Raphaël's 30,000) retains extensive remains from the period during which it was second only to Marseille in size and importance as a Roman military port. Fréjus was founded by Julius Caesar as a stopping place on the main route to Spain, but was rapidly expanded by Augustus Octavius, and at its Roman zenith had almost as large a population as it has today. The town's medieval centre bears even more visible and impressive testimony to its status in the early Christian world: Fréjus was a bishopric as early as AD 374 and remained one until 1957.

Seaside extensions

Though Fréjus lost its maritime functions in the 10th century as the sea receded, it has responded to the demands of modern tourism by acquiring two offshoots radically different in style from the old town, and both closer to St-Raphaël.

Fréjus-Plage is a 1960s and '70s devel-opment of apartment blocks and hotels running the length of a fine, flat sandy beach bordered to the east by St-Raphaël and to the west by the new yacht basin of Port de Fréjus. Its attractions are by day quite simply the beach, and by night the numerous cafés, shops and stalls, which stay open, and thronged, until 1 or 2am, along with various nightclubs.

Port de Fréjus was built in 1989 to provide accommodation for 10,000 peo-ple, mooring for 700 yachts and various restaurants and shops. Port de Fréjus is at the mouth of the original Roman port, which was connected to a second basin inland, beside Fréjus proper, by a broad channel. Demand for more space in Port de Fréjus has prompted developers to expand away from the sea, re-excavating this same channel. Unfortunately, the waterway will not be extended to the site of the original inland port.

Just west of Port de Fréjus are two attractions popular with kids: **Base Nature** (open daily; free) is a former

BELOW: the land of the disposable bikini.

military base converted into a 120-hectare (300-acre) open-air sports centre, offering everything from mountain-bike trails to basketball courts; **Aquatica** (open daily, entrance fee; tel (04) 94 51 82 51), on the main road to Ste-Maxime, is a water amusement park.

The medieval centre

The old central area of Fréjus has considerable charm, particularly by contrast with the brashness and the crowds of summertime St-Raphaël and Fréjus-Plage. At the centre of the old town, beside the 14th-century **Hôtel de Ville** (formerly the Bishop's Palace) on Place Formigé, is the **Cité Episcopale**. This medieval complex includes a 12th-century, double-naved **cathedral** (open daily), a small stone **baptistry** – one of the oldest in France, dating from the 5th century – and a lovely two-storey **cloister** with its ceiling composed of hundreds of painted wooden tiles.

Visits to the baptistry and cloister (open Tues–Sun; entrance fee) are fascinating,

particularly the tall, sombre octagonal baptistry with its separate entry and exit doors, octagonal baptismal pool and dolium for liturgical oil. The cloister, by contrast, with its white marble columns, central tile-roofed well and laurel bushes, is serene and sunny. If you take the guided tour you will be shown a pair of 17th-century wooden doors (normally covered up), which are beautifully carved with scenes of a Saracen massacre.

Beside the cloister is the **Musée Archéologique** (open Mon, Wed–Sat; free; tel: (04) 94 52 15 78), which displays a fine collection of Roman and early Ligurian tiles, mosaics and sculptures. Highlights include a complete mosaic floor with a leopard as its centrepiece and a fine double-faced head of Hermès, discovered in 1970, which Fréjus has made its symbol.

Just to the west is the triangular **Place Paul Albert Février**, which contains the prettiest open-air restaurants, though not necessarily those with the best cuisine; nonetheless, tables can be hard to obtain by 9pm in summer. The Saturday market (local peaches and roses a Fréjus speciality) takes place on the square. Further west is the other main centre of café life, the **Place de la Liberté**, with its fountain and two big plane trees. This is the best place for coffees, mid-afternoon beers, apéritifs and midnight café-cognacs. Much later Fréjus closes down, and you have to head down to the seafront.

The streets and alleys surrounding the pedestrianised medieval centre and the Rue Jean Jaurès, which circles downhill through town bearing a constant stream of traffic, are extremely pretty, with numerous ornate doorways, cats peering through lace curtains and windowsills spilling over with geraniums.

Roman remains

Fréjus's major Roman remains are no less interesting for being dispersed around the edges of the town. To the south, beside Boulevard Decuers, is the base of the western citadel, known as the **Butte St-Antoine**, which once overlooked the inland port and is now overgrown with vegetation. A partly-ruined wall leads east

LEFT: fountain in Fréjus.

Map on page 154

from the Butte to the stump of a tower, the **Lanterne d'Auguste**. This structure once held a flame marking the entrance to the port, and at night was the anchor point for an iron chain across the canal which denied access from the sea. North towards the town centre is the **Porte d'Orée**, a decorative arch, probably once the entrance to the baths.

North of the centre, on Avenue du Théâtre Romain, are the enclosed remains of the 2,500-capacity Roman **theatre** (open Wed–Mon; free). It is largely destroyed, but the low remaining section has been renovated and is used, with scaffolding benches, for concerts and theatrical productions. Northeast of the theatre are the remains of the **aqueduct**, which once supplied the whole city with water. Large, impressive sections can be seen on either side of Avenue du XV Corps d'Armée.

The 2nd-century AD **amphitheatre** (open Wed–Mon; free), half resting against a grass knoll beside Rue Henri Vadon, has suffered from centuries of looting, and is neither as large nor as sumptuous as those at Nîmes or Arles. The arena is in regular use for concerts and, several times a year, bullfights. Fréjus is the eastern outpost of the sport in France, and the highlight of the year is the *féria*, a bullfighting festival that takes place in July and August and includes music and other entertainment.

On the outskirts

North of the aqueduct is the Palladian-style **Villa Aurélienne**, set in a fine small park. The villa hosts temporary art exhibitions in the summer.

Nearby are two architectural curiosities connected with the town's military past. Both buildings acknowledge the role of troops from France's former colonies. The **Mosquée Missiri de Djenné** (closed to public), on Rue des Combattants d'Afrique du Nord, is a replica of a West African mosque, while the Buddhist **Pagode Hong Hien** (open daily; entrance fee) on Rue Henri Giraud commemorates France's Vietnamese operations.

BELOW: medieval cloister in Fréjus's Cité Episcopale.

Ten minutes' drive outside town on the N7 is the small circular chapel of **Notre-Dame-de-Jerusalem** (open Mon, Wed–Fri: pm only, Sat all day; free; tel: (04) 94 53 27 06), designed by Jean Cocteau in 1961. The beautiful cool, blue and pastel murals inside are among the poet's last work.

The wild massif

The interior of the **Massif de l'Estérel** ❽ is easily explored by car, with walks of between half an hour and an hour and a half on scrub-surrounded paths to reach the panoramas available from the tops of the main peaks: the Pic de l'Ours, Pic d'Aurelle and Pic du Cap Roux. Further inland, **Mont Vinaigre**, the highest point at 618 metres (2,027 ft), can be approached via the N7. The roads in the massif wind prettily through a landscape of low but massive hills, with open stretches of scented thyme, thistle broom and eucalyptus interrupting the wooded expanses of cork oak and chestnut.

Leaving your car behind, the hills are best encountered on foot, horseback or mountain bike. Excursions can be arranged at the St-Raphaël and Fréjus tourist offices.

Further inland, the D837 road passes through Les Adrets-de-l'Estérel, crosses the autoroute and shortly afterwards arrives at the **Lac de St-Cassien** ❾, an extensive stretch of water, still relatively wild in aspect but heavily patronised by fishermen, picnickers and dinghy sailors in summer.

Up the Argens Valley

Northwest of Fréjus, the N7 follows the valley of the River Argens through fields of flowers and vegetables, gradually climbing through vineyards and rockier olive, pine and oak groves.

About 10 km (6 miles) from Fréjus a smaller road leads to the pretty village of **Roquebrune-sur-Argens**. In the village centre, almost every house is over 400 years old and many are joined by covered passageways and arcades. Vestiges of the 16th-century ramparts also remain.

BELOW: Roman arch, Fréjus.

Map on page 154

West of Roquebrune, in the heart of the Côtes-de-Provence wine region, is the small town of **Les Arcs** ❿. Here, the **Maison des Vins** (open Apr–Sep: daily, Oct–Mar: Mon–Sat), beside the N7, provides copious information and free tastings of the many *crus* of the region.

Les Arcs' medieval village, known as the **Parage**, is as lovely as any in the region. The former château complex is now occupied partly by exquisitely pretty little houses and tiny olive-shaded squares, and partly by a beautiful hotel and superb restaurant, the Logis du Guetteur. The hotel's vine-draped terrace and shuttered bedroom windows offer stunning views over the red roofs of the town to the vineyards beyond.

Among the vineyards northeast of Les Arcs is the **Chapelle de Ste-Roseline** (open Tues–Sun; pm only; free), a former abbey of which the chapel and cloisters remain. The Baroque chapel was beautifully restored by art patron Marguerite Maeght, who commissioned pieces from Marc Chagall, Diego Giacometti (brother of Alberto) and other artists to decorate the space. The Baroque altarpieces, Renaissance rood screen, huge Chagall mosaic, Giacometti sculptures and modern stained-glass together create an astonishingly harmonious synthesis. For fans of the macabre, however, the highlight is the preserved body of St Roseline, on display in a glass coffin. The 13th-century nun, whose body miraculously refused to decompose, still attracts pilgrims, over 600 years later.

To the north is **Trans**, with its little 18th-century town hall, perched on the edge of the boulder-strewn River Nartuby. Beyond is **Draguignan** ⓫, the former departmental capital and one of the biggest army bases in France. It is a solid, pleasant country town with an old centre and two worthwhile museums: the **Musée des Arts et Traditions Populaires** (open Tues–Sun; entrance fee; tel: (04) 94 47 05 72) covers traditional local industries and the **Musée Municipale** (open Mon–Sat; free; tel: (04) 94 47 28 80) houses paintings, furniture and archaeological finds. ❏

BELOW: the pristine hills of the interior.

Maps:
Area 176
City 166

CANNES

Every May, Cannes pulsates with action as the stars and paparazzi hit town for the Film Festival. At quieter times, you'll find Provençal tradition, Edwardian elegance and, offshore, a pair of unspoilt islands

"In his 1921 book *The Twenties: From Notebooks and Diaries of the Period,* the American literary critic Edmund Wilson wrote: "Cannes: Côte d'Azur. Some gleaming town of rose and white, there where the Alps like elephants come down to kneel beside the calm and azure sea. On the sky and the water lies a hard glaring glaze of gold. The Mediterranean, level and smooth, lips the shore with a slow rise and fall of sound like the breath of a sleeper – a gentle insistent rhythm – brushing the beach with sound. The cactus clumps (aloes) like spiky octopi. The palms that stud the Croisette at Cannes with tignasse tufts and thick pineapple stems. At night the pale dark peppered with stars like the finest of silver tinsel. The last soft red streamers of the sunset faded behind the gray silhouette of the Estérel, and from the jetty I saw the green trees and the red roofs of the houses that mount the little hill to the square Saracen tower grown somber and black above the silver blue-gray water of the harbor, where the little boats were neatly moored in a fringe about the shore: above the boats was the low avenue of lindens and along between their trunks were the lights of the shops."

Cannes ❶ has undoubtedly developed since Edmund Wilson recorded its charms. The surprising news is that in a changing world where the character and soul of lesser oases have been swept away in a tide of mass tourism, Cannes sparkles miraculously as a jewelled survivor of a bygone age.

Early visitors

Earlier, though, the place wasn't even on the map. Three roads with fishermen's houses, a tower on the hill and an inn serving bouillabaisse were all there was to Cannes before a chance incident altered its destiny late in 1834. Fatigued after six years as Lord Chancellor of Great Britain (where among other achievements he championed the abolition of slavery), Henry, Lord Brougham, resigned and set off from London with his sickly daughter Eleonore in search of a mild climate on the Riviera, where the British were already making their presence felt in increasing numbers.

He intended to go to Nice, travelling in a six-horse berlin as far as the River Var, which then formed a formidable frontier between Provence (France) and the Kingdom of Sardinia (Italy). However, he found more than a raging torrent barring his way. Soldiers refused to let him through as cholera had broken out in Provence. They forced him to turn back, first to Antibes which displeased him, then to Cannes where an

inn which had previously accommodated Victor Hugo and Pope Pius VII proved more to his liking. Brougham was so captivated by the countryside that he bought a plot of land within a week and soon built the Villa Eleonore. It still stands, tastefully converted into flats, on Avenue du Docteur Picaud.

Escaping the riff-raff

So began the Anglicization of Cannes. Other rich and influential British visitors soon followed, encouraged to find an alternative winter retreat to Nice where an "inferior class" was establishing itself, and a highly cultivated society took root. Quite literally, it seems: they even had their new villas' lawns relaid annually with turf brought from England by boat. Brougham extracted one million francs out of King Louis-Philippe – 33 times the town's municipal budget – to fund a new harbour so the boat could dock.

Royalty was not far behind. Though Queen Victoria did not disdain Nice, it was here that her sons Leopold, Duke of Albany, and Edward, Prince of Wales, discovered the more entertaining aspects of Riviera life. Poor Leopold, who was a haemophiliac, vaguely remembered for having introduced croquet to the coast, died after falling down stairs at Cannes' Cercle Nautique. Edward (later King Edward VII) on the other hand is hugely famed for having indulged his appetite for gambling, tobacco, food and sex.

Brougham died in 1868, two years before the railway came to town and spelled the end of an idyll. A statue of him stands in the Allées de la Liberté, not far from another, of Edward VII, as if emphasising the diverse roles which the British have played in the city's history.

The city today

But what of Cannes today: its conventions and congresses, its beaches, its shopping, its "Season"? Everyone knows "the Festival": two weeks in May when the movie world turns this dowager resort into a

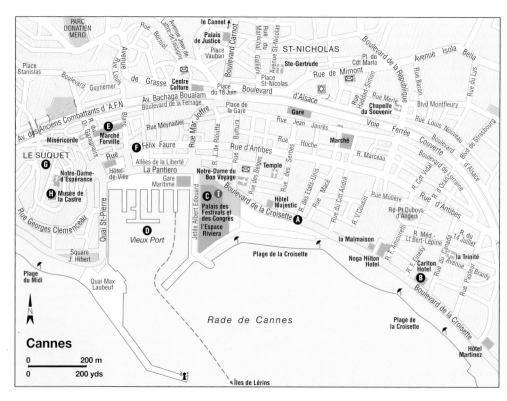

Map on page 166

painted lady, starlets cavort topless on the sands and big deals are clinched by moguls clenching big cigars in their even bigger teeth. The images are the same every year and the ritual would be dismissed as quaintly amusing but for the revenue – upwards of £60 million – that the event generates for the area.

Casual it may seem, but behind the scenes a huge effort goes into ensuring that those 70,000 people visiting this affair, with all its hype and hoopla, are not disappointed. The golden sands, for instance, are raked and disinfected fastidiously every day, and on the private beaches are groomed to perfection before the *beau monde* gathers for cocktails beneath pastel-coloured parasols.

Likewise the floral arrangements. The municipality grows 400,000 bedding-out plants a year and out on the Croisette they are replanted four times a year. Notice, too, how the streets are mercifully free of parking meters – scrapped years ago in favour of "pay and display".

Nature also plays a part. In February and early March mimosa spreads yellow fire across its hills. Boughs of mauve wisteria snake around its old ochre facades in April. Gardens burst with oleander pinks in summer and for much of the year splashes of purple and red bougainvillaea everywhere are taken almost for granted.

Heat and light

The Season, of course, puts a great strain on the city from mid-July until the end of August, and many find the crush intolerable, though thousands of masochists love it here then. The sand disappears under the press of near-naked bodies. "Full" signs go up in restaurants and hotels. The thermometer soars and hot winds often blow, sometimes to disastrous incendiary effect.

Yet, there are six evenings in July and August which provide moments of light relief. Three of them celebrate important dates: Bastille Day (14 July), Assumption (15 August) and Cannes Liberation Day (24 August). On all six evenings, crescen-

BELOW:
cocktails at the
Carlton Hotel.

does of fireworks and classical music burst around the Croisette in a spectacular celebration lasting half an hour, provided free by the city council. Each show is different, involving tons of explosives launched from barges, and if you don't have your own personal yacht as a vantage point (some coming into the bay are the size of cross-Channel ferries) there are alternatives. Exceptionally, the beach restaurants, which normally close at night, offer superb dinners and a front-row seat under a sky that suddenly erupts in a storm of light. Or for a dress-circle view, you could retreat inland to a hill and watch the pyrotechnics while listening to the music on local radio.

A tour of the sights

Your first port of call to soak up the sophisticated atmosphere should be **La Croisette** Ⓐ, the broad boulevard that runs alongside the manicured beach. It is lined with haughty palms and pristine flower-beds tended 12 months of the year by over 100 full-time gardeners. Despite being one of the most internationally-recognised of all beachfront promenades, its Edwardian elegance has remained remarkably unsullied by adverts for fast food or tanning cream.

La Croisette is home to Cannes' four so-called palace-hotels, the *grandes dames* of the seafront, frequented by the rich and famous, particularly during the Film Festival. The oldest and most glamorous is the 1912 **Carlton Hotel** Ⓑ, whose wedding-cake facade has barely changed since it was built. The pepper-pot cupolas at each end are said to be modelled on the breasts of La Belle Otero, a famous dancer and courtesan of the period. The edifice symbolises Cannes as much as Big Ben does London, its name a synonym for comfort and grace.

Further down the drag, at No. 73, is the **Hôtel Martinez**, built in 1929. Many of its original Art Deco details, both inside and out, have been lovingly restored. Heading in the other direction, you come

BELOW: the blue Med from a balcony at the Carlton.

Map
on page
166

to the least attractive of the four, the **Noga Hilton Hotel**, at No. 50. The concrete eyesore was built in 1992 on the site of the old Palais des Festivals, where Vadim launched Brigitte Bardot.

Beside, and virtually swamped by, the Hilton, is **La Malmaison**, the only surviving part of the original Grand Hotel, a 19th-century forerunner of today's seafront giants. The elegant building now houses temporary art exhibitions (open Wed–Mon; entrance fee; tel: (04) 93 99 04 04). Further west, at No. 14, is the 1926 **Hôtel Majestic**, which is famous for its bar. During the Festival, movie deals are struck here under the gaze of huge, faux sarcophagi, which evoke the kitsch, but grand ambitions of Hollywood heroes like Cecil B. DeMille.

Festivals and fish

Virtually opposite the Majestic is the vast concrete bunker of the current **Palais des Festivals D**, home to the Film Festival since 1983 (tours by arrangement: Wed pm; tel: (04) 93 39 24 53). In recent years, Cannes has used its film-circuit fame to sell itself as a top venue for business conferences and other media gatherings, and the Palais is in almost constant use, hosting over 100 events per year.

Beyond the Palais is the **Vieux Port D**, where you'll see Cannes' fishing fleet tied up to a jetty parallel to Quai St-Pierre, their nets piled high on deck. The fishermen are an endangered species. Dwarfing their boats are the dazzling white hulls, shining brass and polished teak of the bigger vessels sharing the little basin. Further threat to the fishing industry comes from a new 150-metre (490-ft) cruise ship quay, built here by the city to capture some of the lucrative cruise market.

For the moment, the *manja pei* (literally, "fish-eaters") still chug past the huge status symbols to bring in their catch in the early dawn, every day of the year. Strange Mediterranean fish with names like *rascasse, rouquier* or *blavier*, some of which have poisonous, spiny fins and are

best enjoyed in a bouillabaisse on the quay, flip and flop as they always have done.

To see the catch being sold by the fishermen's wives, head away from the port to the **Marché Forville** **Ⓔ** (open Tue–Sun; am only), where *coquillages* spill from the open-air displays. Elsewhere in the market, smallholders from the back country proudly mark their produce with the name of the village of origin instead of bothering with a sell-by date. Nobody cares; it is always dew-fresh. The traders' clamorous cries and good-natured banter fill a pitch the size of a football field with their twanging Provençal accents.

This festival predates the film festival by 100 years. Long before the stars lived in Beverly Hills its French twin's roots were firmly established in the dark red earth of the Midi. Here they run a continuous performance – a free spectacle for the eyes, ears and nose.

Just to the east of the market is **Rue Meynadier**, a boisterous pedestrian thoroughfare where local gourmands have always shopped for the best home-made pasta, the freshest cheese, and the most mouth-watering delicacies its master *traiteurs* can produce. The street is now also home to a growing number of inexpensive clothing outlets and tourist emporia, but the likes of La Ferme Savoyarde at No. 20 still hold their own and tempt the taste buds of passers-by.

Prince of Cannes

They say the Duke of Windsor, when he was Prince of Wales, deliberately gave his bodyguards the slip on one of his many visits to Cannes in the 1930s. There was panic, of course, and for hours his friends and courtiers scoured his favourite haunts. The places they looked have not changed much over the years.

They tried the restaurants of **Rue Félix Faure** **Ⓕ** and the flower stalls facing them, both of which still attract locals and visitors today. They scanned the *boules* pitch on the nearby **Allées de la Liberté** (still frequented today by die-hards of

BELOW: vintage yachts compete in the bay off Cannes.

Map
on page
166

the quintessentially Provençal game, except on Saturdays when an antiques market takes over). They combed the boutiques of **Rue d'Antibes** further east – still one of Cannes' most fashionable retail addresses.

Finally, someone had the wit to eschew the ritzy side of life and investigate the market and the old streets to the west. There, in the back lanes, he found the future King of England sitting in the sun outside a tiny *auberge*, eating sea urchins in garlic sauce. Pleased with himself for his few hours' freedom as a commoner, the Prince looked up and said (according to local history, which must have had a reporter present): "Cannes is like a beautiful woman. Charming, but full of secrets." How much *aïoli* he had consumed by that stage is certainly not recorded.

The old town

The Prince had discovered the oldest part of town, **Le Suquet ⑥**, which still has secret alleys, passages and half-hidden

auberges and bistros, especially on Rue St Antoine. Le Suquet's hill and moorings were used in Roman times (they named the site Canoïs Castrum because of the reeds and canes growing there). At the top of the hill is the **Place de la Castre** where you can appreciate commanding views along the shore in both directions and inland to the hill of La Californie. However, to get this far is an achievement – the cobbled lanes are steep and narrow, and the temptation to emulate the Prince has spelled the ruin of many a latter-day photo expedition.

Facing the Place de la Castre is a 19th-century church, **Notre-Dame d'Espérance**. Behind the church are a castle and square tower dating from the 11th century and built by the monks of Lérins to guard against Saracen attack. Also here is the 12th-century Romanesque Chapelle Ste-Anne. Castle and chapel house the **Musée de la Castre ⑪** (open Wed–Mon; entrance fee; tel: (04) 93 38 55 26), which contains varied displays covering ethnology,

Mediterranean archaeology, art of the region and a fine collection of musical instruments from around the world.

Villas in the hills

Another secret Edward must have remarked upon lies in the city's residential streets away from the seafront. Mrs Simpson took sanctuary in a villa here when the King was preparing to abdicate, and they planned to move into one of their own which they rented on a 10-year lease but never took up because of the outbreak of war.

Now, these same bourgeois houses, hiding their charms behind sentinel palms and wisteria-entwined pergolas, are a dying species. They are the last bastions of the *belle époque*, under siege in a less-mannered age when site values are appreciating faster than the properties standing upon them. No matter how sweetly they evoke a lost chapter of history, it counts for little with unsentimental property developers who are changing the face of Cannes remorselessly.

Another area which has succumbed to development is the old village of **Le Cannet ❷**, now effectively engulfed by the city. However, wander around and you will still find intriguing little lanes and pretty squares with 18th-century houses. Place Bellevue is worth a visit for its great view of the bay and good-value restaurants. Originally, Cannes formed part of the commune of Le Cannet, and the little village still insists on the definite article prefixed to its name. The village's musical evenings are a big draw in summer.

Havens of the super-rich

Skirting the skies above Cannes, sumptuous summer palaces glitter like golden eggs. Here, in the wealthy enclave of **Super-Cannes ❸** there is a hidden lane, the **Corniche du Paradis Terrestre**, the road to Heaven on Earth, which hardly figures on some maps. The bumpy corniche has one of the best views of the city of stars. And it is precisely to deter hoi polloi that the road has been left unpaved.

Much of the wealth up here is Arabian and royal. If you can afford to live here or in next-door **La Californie ❹** you have to think big. Twin marble palaces built here in the early 1980s for two brother princelings were not occupied for a single night before they were demolished and resurrected as apartments in classic Palladian style for sale at over £3 million each, including individual swimming-pools. Disgracefully, there was but one, shared, helipad.

The islands

Every day, boats leave the Gare Maritime beside the Palais des Festivals for the pretty **Îles de Lérins**, which make a peaceful contrast to the buzz of the city. **Ste-Marguerite ❺**, the larger of the two islands, is the more touristy, but if you head away from the crowded port you will find quiet paths through the woods and rocky inlets for bathing. Near the port is the 17th-century **Fort-Royal** (open Wed–Mon; entrance fee; tel: (04) 93 43 18 17), identified as the prison of the mythical Man in the Iron Mask, made famous by Alexandre Dumas. The fort

LEFT: al fresco dining in Le Suquet, the old part of town.

Maps:
Area 176
City 166

displays artefacts salvaged from nearby wrecks, including a 1st-century Roman ship and a 10th-century Arab vessel.

Monastic seclusion

St-Honorat ❻, just 400 metres (1,300 ft) wide and mainly covered by parasol pines, eucalyptus trees and cypresses, is much more secluded. The island has an impressive ecclesiastical history commencing with the monastery originally founded by St Honorat in the 5th century.

For hundreds of years, St-Honorat was a centre of religious life for the whole of Southern Europe, and was so powerful that it owned much of the land along the Mediterranean coast, including Cannes itself. At one time 3,700 monks lived on the island, and the monastery was responsible for the training of many important bishops, including Ireland's St Patrick. But its wealth meant it was subject to constant raids from pirates, as well as papal corruption, and its decline was inevitable. In 1869, it was bought by the Cistercians, who built a

new monastery on the site of the old one.

The **monastery** and **church** can be visited (open daily; closed for Sunday services; entrance fee Jun–Sep only), but the island is the private domain of the monks, who grow lavender, grapes and oranges and are pleased to sell you their own honey and Lérina liqueur. The 11th-century tower of the earlier fortified monastery can be seen behind the complex, and of the seven chapels originally scattered across the island, the **Chapelle de la Trinité** at the eastern end still celebrates mass. Only one ferry company serves the island, and as there are no restaurants here you are advised to bring a picnic.

St-Honorat is the last secret. Out here on a summer's day only the distant jet-wash of planes approaching Nice airport reminds you that the centuries have marched on. It is a negligible price to pay, because a sound as old as time, that of the cicadas, quickly reasserts itself to convince you that here you have indeed found that elusive prize: a true little corner of Heaven on Earth.   ❑

BELOW:
remains of the
11th-century
monastery on
St-Honorat.

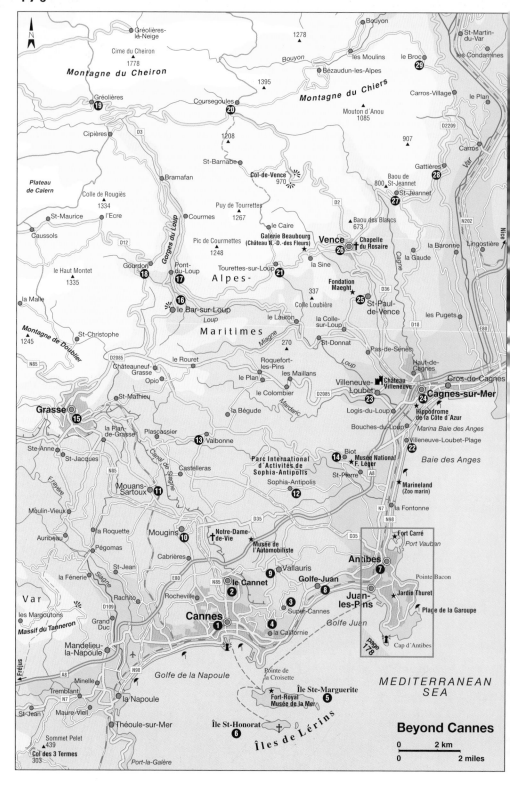

Beyond Cannes

0 — 2 km

0 — 2 miles

Maps on pages 176 & 178

ANTIBES AND THE PLATEAU DE VALBONNE

With its sprawling villas, gleaming yachts and celebrity-filled Hôtel du Cap, the Antibes peninsula is one of the most exclusive addresses on the coast. Inland are the picturesque villages once frequented by Picasso

Cap d'Antibes has secured its legendary status through the work of Scott Fitzgerald and its popularity with American expatriates in the 1920s and '30s. Although it is sometimes hard to imagine the original attraction of the quiet beaches and clear sea as one sits in a traffic jam in the middle of Juan-les-Pins with music blaring and beach shanty towns rising on all sides, it is still possible to discover and understand its special charms and sample its undoubted luxuries.

It must be said, however, that its real pleasures remain reserved for the rich, with their *pied dans l'eau* villas, hotels and private beaches, from which they can contemplate the sea, forgetting the milling crowds outside. The coast itself is nearly always crowded, and venturing on to a public beach should be done with people-watching firmly a priority. Inland, the popular towns of Vallauris and Biot also draw crowds of visitors to their craft workshops and glass factories. But even here, within just a few miles of the coast, the roads are quieter and one can seek respite in charming towns such as Valbonne, Mougins and Mouans-Sartoux. The region is famous for its flower production, in particular roses, carnations and anemones.

Year-round yachting

Antibes ❼ itself is surprisingly untouristy; its venerable history gives it a gravitas that is undeterred by waves of tourism, and the old town offers many instructive sights. Ultimately, Antibes is a yachting town, with the massive **Port Vauban** Ⓐ the true centre of Mediterranean yachting. Its inner harbour is home to several hundred vessels and the outer port shelters some of the world's most prestigious yachts on a wide *quai* known as "millionaires' row". The presence of these yachts, and the consid-

erable crew and services required to support them, means that Antibes functions all year round, and is not as limited to seasonal visitors as are other parts of the coast. Graham Greene, who was a longtime resident, always preferred the winter. In *May We Borrow Your Husband?* he wrote: "Then Antibes comes into its own as a small country town with the Auberge de Provence full of local people and old men sit indoors drinking beer or pastis at the *glacier* in the Place de Gaulle. The small garden, which forms a roundabout on the ramparts, looks a little sad with the short stout palms blowing their brown fronds; the sun in the morning shines without any

PRECEDING PAGES: a nautical *tricolor*. **RIGHT:** reflecting status.

glare, and the few white sails move gently on the unblinding sea."

On the north side of Port Vauban is the imposing mass of the 16th-century **Fort Carré**, where Napoleon was imprisoned for a time.

Across the bay from Nice

The main area of interest in Antibes is really quite small so you would be well advised to park in one of the multi-storey car parks as soon as you enter the town (do not forget to keep your ticket with you as you need it to pay before reclaiming the car). A good free map is available from the Maison du Tourisme on **Place Général de Gaulle**. This used to be the Place Macé, and the tourist office is in what was once the Grand Hotel and home of the Municipal Casino which opened in 1911.

Antibes, now the third largest town on the Côte d'Azur, began life as the Greek city of Antipolis, "the town opposite", facing the earlier settlement of Nice. The Greeks held only a narrow stretch between the sea and the present Cours Masséna; it was a narrow enclosure filled with warehouses and only one gate, entered opposite the present **Hôtel de Ville** on the Cours Masséna at the Rue Pardisse.

The settlement traded with the Ligurian tribes along the coast but did not allow them to enter the city so all dealing took place outside the city walls; the covered market is still located on the Cours Masséna at roughly the same spot. But nothing more, save the name and a few objects in the museum, remains of this distant period.

The Romans, in their turn, built an important city at Antibes and the ruins of the baths, the aqueduct, the circus and the theatre stood until 1691 when Vauban used the stones to construct his massive fortifications. Vauban's ramparts were demolished in 1898 except those which constituted the sea wall; today the Promenade Amiral de Grasse runs along the ramparts, beginning at the **Bastion St-André** in the south. This now houses the excellent

LEFT: Antibes' cathedral, the Eglise de l'Immaculée Conception.

Map on facing page

Musée d'Histoire et d'Archéologie ⓑ (open Dec–Oct: Tues–Sun; entrance fee; tel: (04) 92 90 54 35), two huge barrel-vaulted rooms with a well organised display of Greek, Etruscan and Roman pottery and exquisite examples of Roman glass. The remains include a large collection of amphoras, stacked as if in the hold of a Roman galley.

Picasso's studio

The original Roman camp was built on the ruins of the Greek acropolis, on a terrace overlooking the sea. In the 12th century the **Château Grimaldi** ⓒ was built on the same site (now on Place Mariejol). Many of the Romanesque features remain, including arched windows and the square tower which dominates the old town, though the building was reconstructed in the 16th century. Some of the tiny inner doorways have very attractive carving. The château is now home to the **Musée Picasso** (open Tues–Sun; entrance fee; tel: (04) 92 90 54 20) and contains a remark-able, unified collection of the more than 50 works Picasso executed here in 1946, when he was offered the keys to the château to use as a studio.

He painted solidly for five months, revitalised after spending the war years restricted to his Paris studio. The light and intense colour of the south were immediately incorporated into his work in a series of drawings and paintings of fish, sea urchins, goats, stars and the sea shore. He was captivated by the antiquity of the Mediterranean. Standing on the terrace of the ancient castle, the site of a Greek acropolis, a Roman *castrum*, the residence of the Bishops of Antiboul and the 16th-century Grimaldi, he invented a mythological cast of characters to inhabit his drawings and paintings: a faun, often playing the double flute of antiquity, a bearded centaur (undoubtedly himself) and a beautiful nymph, sometimes dancing with a tambourine (Françoise Gilot). The paintings and drawings of these figures eventually resulted in a major work,

BELOW: Port Vauban, with Fort Carré behind.

La Joie de Vivre, which symbolised his entire stay in the château.

The fishermen provided another source of inspiration, as they had done before the war in his huge painting *Night Fishing at Antibes (see pages 86–7)*. Some of these, such as *Man Gulping Sea Urchins* are on canvas, and x-rays have revealed that Picasso, holding the keys of the château, had raided the storerooms and painted over what he regarded as mediocre 19th-century paintings. It was also here that Picasso painted the *Antipolis Suite*, a series depicting highly stylised, pared-down nudes, often reclining.

In an unusual act of generosity, Picasso left virtually everything to the museum in which they were created. On display are 27 paintings, 44 drawings, two sculptures, 50 engravings (mostly from the Vollard Suite) and 75 original ceramics – a major collection and in fact the first permanent collection devoted to the work of a living artist. It is supported by works of tribute by other artists, photographs and documentation.

The museum also has one of the largest collections of the work of Nicolas de Staël, who lived in Antibes and also painted in the château. On a terrace overlooking the ramparts is a series of sculptures by Germaine Richier, César and Miró, in a fragrant Mediterranean garden with the sea providing a dramatic backdrop.

Sights of the old town

To the north of the château is the old cathedral, the **Eglise de l'Immaculée-Conception** ⓓ. The square Romanesque bell tower is a converted 12th-century watchtower but only the east end remains of the original 12th-century building, the west end being 17th-century rebuilding. The 1710 doors are worth noting.

On Cours Masséna the old town gate with its two round towers survives. In one tower is the **Musée de la Tour** (open Wed, Thurs & Sat: pm only; entrance fee; tel: (04) 93 34 50 91), a museum of popular arts and traditions, concentrating on 18th- and 19th-century costumes, furniture and *objets*.

BELOW: lunch on the ramparts in Antibes.

Map on page 178

The ramparts continue past the cathedral to the Vieux Port. Below is the small **Plage de la Gravette**, a sheltered sandy beach, separated from the Vieux Port by the Quai H. Rambaud. From the ramparts there is a gateway to the **Rue Aubernon**, where there is a regular flea market. Just around the corner, opposite the gate to the old fishing port, at 50 Boulevard d'Aguillon, is Restaurant Chez Félix, the old-fashioned bistro where Graham Greene took his lunch and often found inspiration *(see page 84)*. The restaurant remains unchanged, its decor determinedly unpretentious, with flowery tablecloths and a motorcycle parked at the bar. And there is the same proprietor, who will always show you the fish you have ordered before it is cooked.

A few streets to the south, Place Nationale is home to the **Musée Peynet** (open Tues–Sun; entrance fee; tel: (04) 92 90 54 30), dedicated to Maurice Peynet, whose delightful, somewhat coy drawings have made him a cult figure. In the same square and many of the narrow streets leading to the cathedral, there are lots of restaurants, so this is a popular place to stop for lunch after the morning market (arrive not long after midday to be sure of a table).

South again and the grid of old lanes between Rue James Close and the bus station are worth exploring; here life continues much as it has always done, with washing hanging from windows, pots full of geraniums, and children playing games between the ancient stone walls of the narrow streets.

The rest of the peninsula

Cap d'Antibes is still very much the preserve of those fortunate enough to have villas here, but as a result it has retained much of its charm, and rewards exploration. South of Antibes, there is a **public beach** with golden sand stretching from the Pointe de l'Ilet down to the Port de la Salis. Although not large, it is the only sandy beach this side of the Cap apart from the tiny Plage de la Garoupe. Most of the beach clubs here suffice with wooden decks built out over the rocks, the

BELOW: the old quarter in Antibes.

Riviera Yacht-Watching

Luxury yachting has always been part of the Riviera legend but in recent years it has become a fully fledged industry, vital to the region's economy. Nowhere else on earth is there so much extravagant floating real estate in one place. While some harbours – like Cannes or St-Tropez – see the traditional *pointu* fishing boats go happily about their business alongside sleek luxury vessels, the many new ports designed exclusively for private yachts have made the Riviera the uncontested world centre for a new type of craft, dubbed the "megayacht" – fully crewed private vessels over 36 metres (120 ft) long.

Riviera harbours are open to anyone wishing for a closer look at the lifestyles of the rich and famous. Between the Italian border at Menton and the port of Marseille 127 nautical miles (235 km) to the west there are 130 of these harbours, totalling over 52,000 moorings. Riviera ports shelter a third of the world's megayacht fleet. Yachting occupies over 1,500 local businesses and provides more than 6,000 jobs, not including crew.

Monaco was Aristotle Onassis's favourite harbour, but Antibes' Port Vauban is the true centre of Mediterranean yachting. The inner harbour is home to several hundred smallish vessels but the IYCA (International Yacht Club of Antibes) outer port, built to shelter Adnan Kashoggi's Italian-built 83-metre (270-ft) *Nabila*, is now home to some of the world's most prestigious megayachts, berthed with their sterns to the wide quay known as "millionaires' row".

Famous names still frequent Riviera ports but, except in a few cases, with cautious discretion. Some of the more flamboyant owners, however, make no secret of their possession and the name of a yacht is often a clue to who her owner might be.

The costs of running one of these boats often means that an entire offshore company is set up to own and manage the vessel, which partly explains the majority of British-flag yachts on the Côte d'Azur. Some of the owners are indeed British, but many are not and are only attracted by British tax law which, given the nation's maritime tradition, is more favourable than in other European countries.

If a taste of the seafaring life sounds tempting, a used 18-metre (60-ft) model can be had for about £1.5 million. If you want something with a bit more speed or cabin space you should be thinking in the neighbourhood of £4 million. Today, yachts worth more than £25 million are not at all uncommon and you should count on 10 percent of the boat's value as the cost of annual upkeep.

Chartering offers a cheaper solution for those on a 'budget'. For about £3,000 a day you can hire a modest 22-metre (72-ft), 4-cabin yacht, but if you plan on throwing large parties on board you'll need something bigger, with a crew included, at around £15,000 a day. Prices do not include berthing fees, fuel, food or drink. Sailing is perhaps an overstated term for the activities of many of these yachts, since they seem to spend more time quayside than they ever do at sea. Sometimes it looks as if their sole purpose is to host ostentatious cocktails on deck for the entertainment of spectators on shore.

LEFT: classy vintage yachts.

Map on page 178

lack of sand compensated somewhat by the clear waters this far out.

Beyond Pointe Bacon is the famous **Plage de la Garoupe** , more of a reference to a beach than anything else. Scott Fitzgerald's description of the "bright tan prayer rug of a beach" is most accurate in calling it a rug, and a fairly moth-eaten one at that. Had Gerald Murphy, avant-garde American painter and original model for Fitzgerald's hero in *Tender is the Night*, known the fate of his quiet little cove he may have been more inclined to cover it up with rocks than painstakingly remove all the seaweed, as he did in the 1920s. Today wooden sundecks on stilts extend the tiny beach out over the rocks with beachclubs charging for the use of a mattress.

The Murphys decided to settle here and bought a villa with a huge garden just below the lighthouse, naming it the Villa America. While the villa was being remodelled, Gerald was clearing the beach of seaweed at the rate of eight square feet a day.

One of the first visitors from the Hôtel du Cap to use it was Rudolph Valentino.

From Garoupe you can walk out to the rocks at **Cap Gros**, following the cliff path. To the southwest is the **Pointe de l'Ilette**, the southernmost point of the Cap, with spectacular rocks and a lighthouse sweeping the night sea.

Exclusive hideaway

The coast between here and the **Musée Naval et Napoléonien** (Ave Kennedy; open Nov–Sept: Mon–Fri & Sat am; entrance fee; tel: (04) 93 67 88 00), which contains model ships and Napoleon memorabilia, is the preserve of the **Hôtel du Cap-Eden Roc** , the most glamorous hotel on the Riviera, popular today with Cannes superstars. It is expensive, of course, but can be visited for drinks or a day at the pool. (Be warned, though, that credit cards are not accepted.) You can drive in, use the free parking, and stroll through the parasol pines to the restaurant and terrace bar. The most coveted part of

BELOW: entrance to a villa on Cap d'Antibes.

the hotel are its tiny wooden bungalows at the water's edge, where celebrities can relax in total privacy during the day, far from the prying paparazzi.

The hotel was originally built by the founder of *Le Figaro* newspaper, supposedly as a home for impoverished artists and musicians, but in 1863 was taken over by Russian princes who transformed it into a hotel. It was one of the first luxury hotels on the Riviera, inspiring certain scenes of Fitzgerald's *Tender is the Night*. The Murphys stayed here in 1923 and persuaded the owner to open during the summer, thus launching the Riviera summer season.

Sipping an Americano cocktail on the 1930s-style terrace with its elegant white railings and yellow cushions, watching the colour-coordinated yellow buoys bobbing about in the sea below, is the essence of luxury, as is swimming in the organic, shaped pool cut into the rocks (where mad Zelda Fitzgerald used to dive). It is as good a way as any to appreciate the enduring allure of the Côte d'Azur.

Votive offerings

Dominating the skyline of the Cap is the **Phare de la Garoupe**. The lighthouse itself is of recent date, since the retreating Germans dynamited the old one in 1944. The chapel next to it, the **Sanctuaire de la Garoupe G**, however, is old, with two naves, one 13th- and one 16th-century. Despite its setting amid luxury villas, it is still used by the local people and feels like a small village church.

For centuries, seafarers have left votive offerings in the church, which now resembles a Portobello Road junkshop of naive paintings, drawings and medals. Low on the wall to the right of the entrance is an extraordinary drawing of a wrecked car, smoking in a ditch. Its owners pray to God for their survival but unfortunately for their future prospects they are kneeling right in the middle of the road. In front of the chapel is a viewing platform; from here you can see as far as Cap St Erasmo in Italy to the east and St-Tropez to the west.

Not far from the chapel and lighthouse,

BELOW: Plage de la Garoupe: everything but sand.

Maps on pages 176 & 178

on the Boulevard du Cap, and a fairly easy walk from the public beaches of Antibes or the Casino end of the Plage de Juan-les-Pins, is the **Jardin Thuret** ⓗ (open Mon–Fri; free; tel: (04) 93 67 88 00), with its collection of exotic trees and plants, many of which have been successfully introduced to the region. Right next door is the Villa Thenard, where the Grand-Duke Nicholas of Russia died in 1929.

Back up the D2559 towards Juan-les-Pins, there is a marina at Port Gallice and the tiniest of sandy beaches reaching out to the Port du Croûton. The sheltered sandy beaches of **Juan-les-Pins** ❶ itself reach almost this far down the Cap and stretch the full length of the town, providing plenty of space for a frenetic beach life of intensive sunbathing and shoreline promenading – the palpable pleasures which for many visitors fulfil their expectations of the Côte d'Azur. This is also the place for nightlife with its casino, throbbing nightclubs and people-watching pavement cafés. In July, an annual jazz festival with a prestigious line-up of international artists is held under the shady pine trees of the seaside Pinède Gould.

Golfe-Juan

Between Juan-les-Pins and Cannes is **Golfe-Juan** ❽. The bay of the same name is famous for Napoleon's ill-fated return from exile on Elba in 1815. He apparently met the Prince of Monaco on his way to reclaim his own throne after the Revolution and said to him, "Monsieur, we are in the same business." Napoleon headed north with his troops through the rough terrain of the Alps to Paris. The path he took, via Grasse, Sisteron, Castellane and Digne is now known as the **Route Napoleon**.

On the way into Golfe-Juan there was once a strip of 1930s villas, jammed in between the railway and the coast road to Antibes, facing the beach. Now predatory tower cranes menace the buildings, and the old villas near the port are being torn down, their gardens uprooted. In their place is a row of high-rise apartment

BELOW: the essentials.

blocks which will eventually stretch all the way to Juan-les-Pins. The long beach, however, remains the same with its elegant line of palms, golden sand banned to dogs, and with a seductive Cap d'Antibes shimmering across the bay.

The part of the old fishermen's port at Golfe-Juan that faces the enclosed harbour has not changed much; the traffic on the coast road has always been busy and the fact that the old port is cut off from the main town by the railway tracks has preserved it. After the war Picasso and Françoise Gilot had an apartment overlooking the boats. It was on the beach at Golfe-Juan that Picasso met Susanne and Georges Ramié, owners of the Madoura pottery in Vallauris, an event which was to transform the fortunes of the inland town.

Heading inland

Vallauris itself is less than three built-up kilometres (2 miles) from Golfe-Juan and the coast, and resembles a seaside town with rest homes, private hospitals, and a tourist strip, except in this case, the souvenirs are pots. Vallauris has always been a potters' town, a tradition begun by the Romans and continued by Italian potters fom Grasse, but its fortunes declined drastically and did not improve until Picasso began patronising the Madoura pottery workshop. His output was prodigious, 2,000 pieces in the first year which required a whole team of people to prepare and fire. The pottery was permitted to make limited edition copies of his plates and vases, which they still do, and his presence attracted other artists, including Marc Chagall.

Today Vallauris is one of France's largest pottery centres and virtually the whole of the Rue Clemenceau from the museum to the edge of town is lined with pottery shops. Behind them are the kilns and workshops that produce the pottery, open to the public when in operation (though not at weekends).

A wide variety of pottery is for sale, some of it good value, although sadly much of it is dull and occasionally ghastly.

BELOW: potter at work in Vallauris.

Map on page 176

Basic terracotta cooking-pots are worth buying, and the Galerie Madoura on Avenue des Anciens Combattants is still the best place to shop for high-quality, though expensive pots. There are other crafts available including wickerwork, glass and woodwork, the most interesting shop specialising in perfume flasks made from rare woods.

Picasso's chapel

The **Château de Vallauris** (open Wed–Mon; entrance fee; tel: (04) 93 64 16 05), originally a 13th-century Lérins priory, houses the **town museum** and includes a chapel decorated by Picasso. It is entered through a courtyard shaded by a huge lime tree, with a 1985 Riopelle mosaic on the wall. Rebuilt in the 16th century, it has a round pepperpot tower at each end in the Renaissance style, unusual in Provence. There is also a splendid Renaissance staircase. Of the priory, only the Romanesque chapel survived intact. It has a fine barrel vaulted ceiling and round arches.

In 1952, at the request of the town, Picasso decorated it with a huge composition called *War and Peace* painted in his studio on hardboard panels which would bend to follow the curve of the roof. It is by no means Picasso's best work and is not improved by the fact that he neglected to prime his surface so the dull brown of the hardboard shows through the large fields of white paint and scrubbed brushwork. The colours seem to have sunk into the boards, sapping the painting of its vitality.

The museum also contains other work by Picasso: a collection of lithographs and a display of ceramic work, mostly glazed plates and dishes with a few larger painted jugs, produced in a limited edition by the craftsmen of the Madoura pottery to Picasso's designs. Although they carry the usual themes of the bullring, owls and faces, these, too, lack a certain vitality, the touch of the master perhaps. Also here are some very good photographs of Picasso by André Villers.

The museum also has six rooms con-

taining the work of Alberto Magnelli (1888–1971), including some of his important early abstract works from 1914.

Because Picasso saved the town's principal industry, he was made an honorary citizen. In 1950 he in turn presented Vallauris with a life-size bronze statue, *l'Homme à l'Agneau*, which stands outside the château in the Place Paul Isnard.

Around Mougins

Picasso connections abound elsewhere in the area. If you head inland from Vallauris, picking up the D35 to Mougins, you should visit the small chapel of **Notre-Dame-de-Vie** on the way. The 17th-century chapel has an outdoor porch and is on a beautiful site overlooking Mougins. The area is popular for walking, and nearby is an entrance to the Parcs de Mougins which border the Parc Départemental de la Valmasque. It is beautiful forest land and very popular for weekend picnics.

Picasso spent the last 12 years of his life in the neighbouring Villa Notre-Dame-de-Vie. It remains extremely well protected, not open to the public or visible from the road, much like most of the expensive villas in the area. The house was a former *mas*, converted before the war into a luxurious villa by Benjamin Guinness, who also paid for the restoration of the chapel.

Mougins ⑩ itself was also "discovered" by Picasso, along with Francis Picabia in 1936, and they were followed shortly after by Paul Eluard, Man Ray and Jean Cocteau. It is a pretty hill town, surprisingly small, with wonderful views of the Mediterranean, surrounded now by a rash of more recent housing, including some discreet but sumptuous villas. Today Mougins is best known for its restaurants, in particular Roger Vergé's Moulin de Mougins and his famous "*cuisine du soleil*".

Even if you forswear more serious gourmandising, Mougins is a pleasant place for a stroll and a drink. The site has been occupied since Roman times, and during the Middle Ages was owned by the monks of Île St-Honorat *(see page 173)*. All that

BELOW: the chapel of Notre-Dame-de-Vie, near Mougins.

Map
on page
176

remains of the original ramparts is a 15th-century fortified gate, the Porte Sarrasin. The church, L'Eglise St-Jacques-le-Majeur, was begun in the 11th century but has been heavily restored. The bell tower is open to the public; the key is available from the **Musée de la Photographie** (open Jul & Aug: daily; Sept, Oct, Dec–Jun: Wed–Mon; pm only; entrance fee; tel: (04) 93 75 85 67) round the corner on Rue de l'Eglise. Here there is an excellent collection of 20th-century classics, including a large number of photos of Picasso.

Southeast of the village, just off the A8 autoroute is the **Musée de l'Automobiliste** (open mid-Dec–mid-Nov: daily; entrance fee; (04) 93 69 27 80), a snazzy glass and concrete structure with everything from German military vehicles to vintage Bugattis, all on rotating display.

Two planned communities

Between Mougins and Grasse on the N85 is **Mouans-Sartoux ⓫**. The village was reconstructed in the 15th century on a grid

plan like nearby Valbonne streets in each direction and pretty square outside the church and facing the castle. The chapel has huge buttresses on its northern side facing the Château Mouans-Sartoux, which has round towers on each corner. There is also a small formal garden and an old well in the middle of a lawn.

It was from this castle that Suzanne de Villeneuve offered obstinate resistance to the Duke of Savoy in 1592 during the War of the League. He destroyed her castle and sacked the village despite the convention signed by the Duke who was in retreat. Enraged, she pursued him, overtaking him at Cagnes. Seizing the bridle of his horse, she reproached him in front of his whole army. Embarrassed, the Duke had 4000 écus counted out to her on the spot and she returned to rebuild her ruined town.

The château is now a centre for modern and contemporary art, **L'Espace de l'Art Concret** (open Wed–Mon; entrance fee; tel: (04) 93 75 71 50), with a collec-

tion of abstract and minimalist works. Next to the car park is a small chapel with a naive carved typanum over the door depicting a nativity scene with church, shepherds and dozens of sheep.

To the east, **Sophia-Antipolis ⑫** – or, to give its full name, Parc International d'Activités de Valbonne Sophia-Antipolis – covers an enormous area of the Valbonne plain – over 2,300 hectares (5,700 acres). The development, which accommodates scores of high-tech companies, is much more than just a green-site technical park. It also includes miles and miles of new roads, plus housing, shopping, schools and research institutes, many of them in futuristic buildings – horizontal cylinders, mirrored pyramids and more *(see page 77)*.

Sophia-Antipolis continues to expand, and its success reflects the region's determination to become the Silicon Valley of Southern Europe. However, the sight of eager young American executives jogging along the landscaped roads still has an inescapably bizarre quality.

Valbonne and Opio

As a result of the Sophia-Antipolis development, nearby **Valbonne ⑬** has seen its population increase dramatically. It was laid out in the 16th century by the Lérins monks, on a strict grid four blocks wide and 10 blocks long.

In the centre is a beautifully proportioned arcaded square shaded by old elm trees. The church, built on the river bank just outside the grid, began life as part of an abbey founded by the Chalais order who built it in the shape of a Latin cross. The abbey was taken over by the Lérins and the present building finally became the parish church. Sadly, the building has been very badly restored. The adjoining convent is also being restored by the commune.

The road between Valbonne and Opio, to the northwest, passes through pleasant green and shady woodland, shielding an abundance of luxury villas and hotels. **Opio** itself is a bijou village, well maintained with painstakingly restored houses and neatly trimmed hedges. Here, you can visit the Roger Michel olive oil mill, where you can see the olive-crushing in operation, and buy a variety of olive oil-based products.

Glass and Léger

On your way back to the coast, head for the ancient town of **Biot ⑭**. Although tourists are encouraged to visit its potteries and glass-making ateliers, parking provision is poor, and you would be well advised to park instead at the foot of the hill near La Verrerie de Tines, one of the glass factories for which Biot is famous, and walk up the hill to the Port des Tines.

The climb, in any case, is a more authentically medieval way to enter the town. A rather run-down cobblestone ramp takes you through the 16th-century Port des Tines and into the old walled village. Here, the narrow lanes and *ruelles* house the citizens of Biot in quiet retreat from the tourist-oriented main streets and shops.

The Rue de Mitan has a number of untouched examples of medieval shops and the entire quarter has a charm which is missing from some of the more popular hill towns. The closer you get to the church, the older the streets and houses

LEFT:
keeping cool.

Map on page 176

become. The Rue de la Vieille Boucherie still has its old butcher's shop with ceramic tiles and metal meat racks hanging in the street outside.

The village centre is the Place aux Arcades, originally the Roman forum, for this was a Roman town. It has two long 13th- and 14th-century arcades either side of an oblong plaza; one later doorway is dated 1579. The 15th-century church leads off the east end of the square and has one very unusual feature: because of the slope of the ground, the visitor is immediately faced with a flight of 20 steps, leading down into the nave. It is built upon the foundations of an earlier Romanesque church, and rebuilding continued from 1470 until 1655, when the lateral chapels were completed. The old cemetery, just a few streets to the north, is also well worth a visit.

In the Rue St-Sébastien are all the potteries and glass shops, along with cafés, tourist information and a small local history museum (open Dec–Oct: Wed–Sun; entrance fee; tel: (04) 93 65 54 54). The street is often the only part of Biot visitors ever see, which is a pity.

At the foot of the town, on a small hill, is the **Musée National Fernand Léger** (open Wed–Mon; entrance fee; tel: (04) 93 65 63 61), conceived by Madame Nadia Léger and built to hold Léger's work and archives. It contains a complete cross-section of over 300 works executed between 1905 and 1955. It suffers from the usual problems of "estate museums" in that Leger's greatest works are scattered among the major museums of the world. Though he kept examples of all periods of his work, few of them were among the very best.

It would take a retrospective exhibition to show the full range of his achievement and this museum is of most interest to those who already know his work. Still, there are enough of his early post-Cubist paintings to show his importance, and his gigantic ceramic panels and mosaics exhibited on the exterior walls of the building are a spectacularly colourful sight burnished by the strong sun of the Midi. ❑

BELOW:
a fête in the streets of Biot.

Picasso Country

Pablo Picasso was the greatest artist of the 20th century: he broke new ground in painting, sculpture, lithography, engraving, pottery and book illustration. He is an all-pervading presence, a bench-mark against which all 20th-century work is measured.

Every phase of his work has been tremendously influential; indeed it has been said that anything painted since the war can be traced back to Marcel Duchamp or Picasso. His sad Blue Period portraiture and wistful Rose Period style have both been

widely copied, ultimately by sentimental chocolate-box artists. His Cubism and collages began a line of development from Schwitters, Miró, Léger, Ernst, Dubuffet, Motherwell, Nevelson, Rauschenberg and the Pop artists to Arman and the School of Nice. De Kooning's women, early Pollock, the work of Henry Moore, Victor Pasmore, Hans Arp, Elizabeth Frink, all show the influence of Picasso.

From day one, his life attracted legends. On 25 October 1881, the midwife attending his birth gave him up for dead and turned her attentions to his mother. But his uncle, Don Salvador, blew cigar smoke in his face, thus making the baby cry and saving him from suffocation. It is a classic story of Picasso triumphing over all odds.

His first 10 years were spent in Málaga, where his painter father taught art. His father encouraged his talent until the decisive moment when, in Picasso's words, his father was so impressed with the work of his 13-year-old son that "he handed me his paint and his brush and never painted again". Picasso entered the La Longa school of art in Barcelona where he skipped the beginner's course. To take an advanced course in classical art, he had to submit a project file within a month. The other students earnestly began their month-long preparations but Picasso handed in his file of far superior work the very next day. A child prodigy, he graduated at the age of 14.

By 1896 he had his own studio and was exhibiting regularly – but the world centre of art was Paris. He took his first studio in Montmartre in 1900, painting life in Paris: old age, loneliness, poverty, and using mostly blues and greens – his "Blue Period". In 1905 he began painting circus acrobats and jugglers – the "Rose Period". By 1907 he made a major breakthrough with *Les Demoiselles d'Avignon*, which was essentially the first Cubist painting, its picture plane distorted into flat slabs and the faces simplified into African masks. He and Georges Braque took Cubism to the limit, painting the subject-matter from all angles simultaneously, then went their separate ways. Picasso developed many sides of the technique, from collage to the distortion and abstraction, which irritated so many early critics.

Picasso's love affair with the Riviera first began in 1920 when he spent the summer at Juan-les-Pins. The beach inspired him to create a series of monumental neoclassical nudes. But it was not until after the war that he moved there permanently. In the pre-war years, he often spent his summers there, returning to Paris for the winter season. In 1923 he painted harlequins in Cap d'Antibes. In the summer of 1924, he painted a series of large still-lifes at Juan-les-Pins and spent most of 1926 and 1927 at Juan-les-Pins and Cannes, working chiefly on etchings, and he continued to visit until 1939 when he made a hurried retreat to Paris as war broke out.

He had been living in Antibes working on a major painting, *Night Fishing at Antibes*, a very large work, 2 metres high and over 3 metres wide (6 by 10 ft), a format he used only for important subjects. This painting *(see pages 86–7)* summed up many of his feelings about the Riviera, a luminous nocturnal seascape with the fishermen and their boats illuminated by white acetylene lamps – a common sight in the Mediterranean. It turned out to be more of a leave-taking than a summing-up for he was not to see the Riviera again for six years.

In 1946, he left Paris to settle in the Riviera for good, going first to Antibes. Here was the same intense light and warm Mediterranean lifestyle as his native Spain, to which he could not return while Franco remained in power. He responded to the clear silhouettes of the mountains, the hard shadows and bright luminous colours. Though he rarely painted a traditional landscape – his paintings are almost always populated – he responded to the familiar. At Vallauris in 1953, for instance, he painted 13 variations of a view of the electricity transformer near his house. These post-war paintings have a freedom he could not find in his Paris studio. He felt at home and remained in the region for the rest of his life, leaving only for short visits.

Picasso country is a very small area, a few square miles between Antibes and Cannes, though he moved constantly within this area. He and Françoise Gilot, whom he met in 1943, spent the summer of 1945 at the Villa Pour Toi, facing the fishermen's harbour at Golfe-Juan, but it was not until the following year that he acquired his first property in the south.

In the early summer of 1946, Picasso and Françoise Gilot returned and Picasso was given the keys to the Château Grimaldi in Antibes to use as a studio. He and Gilot then moved to Vallauris, to La Galloise, a "small, rather ugly house", as she called it, and Picasso began his experiments with ceramics, single-handedly reviving the town's fortunes. It was here between April and June 1954 that Picasso produced his famous series of more than 30 drawings and paintings of Sylvette David, a young English girl who worked next door to his studio on the Rue de Fournas. Unusually, Sylvette posed for the paintings (his portraits were normally done from memory), and he painted her in every conceivable style from naturalistic to highly abstract Cubist variations. Her long neck, thick blonde hair held high in a pony-tail, straight nose and sloping shoulders created a fashionable, much copied style à la Picasso. The pony-tail, introduced the year before by Bardot, became all the rage.

After Picasso's relationship with Gilot broke up, he lived alone at La Galloise, painting interiors. The break-up, however, released a flood of energy, resulting in the 80-odd drawings made between 1953 and 1954 of the artist and his model, the old

artist always in the act of creation, painting the young model. It was to be a recurring theme.

Picasso then began living with Jacqueline Roque, whom he married in 1958. In 1955, he moved from Vallauris to La Californie, a large, ornate mansion overlooking Cannes. The space inspired him to invent the term *paysages d'intérieur* for the series of interiors he painted here, driven by an urge to fill the echoing empty rooms.

In 1958 he was again on the move and bought the huge Château Vauvenargues near Aix-en-Provence, but this move from the Riviera did not last long and in 1961 he returned, to Mas Notre-Dame-de-Vie, on a hill overlooking Mougins.

He remained prolific to the end. During his last five years, he created over 1,000 works of art. His Riviera period was perhaps his most obsessional; he would take a theme or a new medium and work at it until it was exhausted. The astonishing productivity continued until, on 8 April 1973, Picasso died at Mas Notre-Dame-de-Vie, at the age of 91.

Today Picasso is a constant theme on the Côte d'Azur. Antibes has a major museum in the Château Grimaldi. Mougins has an exhibition of photographs of the artist. Vallauris has his *War and Peace* in the château museum and the sculpture of *L'Homme à l'Agneau* in the centre of town. Sometimes it seems as if every town or village is anxious to claim some connection with the master. ❑

LEFT: *The Doves* (1957). **RIGHT:** *Jacqueline with Flowers* (1954).

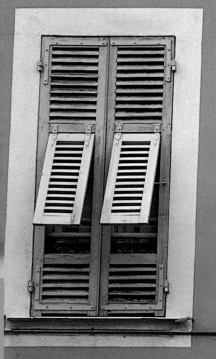
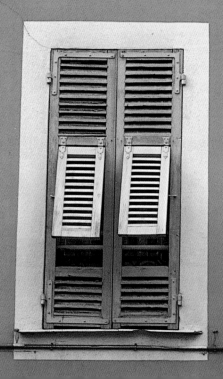

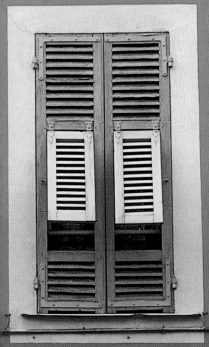
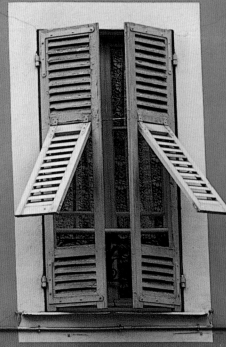

Map on page 176

GRASSE AND THE LOUP VALLEY

Famous as the centre of the Provençal perfume industry, fragrant Grasse rewards the visitor with picturesque medieval streets and museums galore. The nearby Gorges du Loup offers a more rugged, alpine experience

The ancient town of **Grasse** ⑮ is an excellent place to appreciate the acute contrast between the Côte d'Azur and its bucolic hinterland. The town is set on a fabulous site, cradled by sheltering hills and surrounded by flowers, and with splendid views all the way to the sea. Beneath its palm-fronded terraces, elegant pink villas decorate the hillside, sloping gently down to the highly populated valley below, thick with executive housing and high-technology parks. Here, the desired synthesis of modern technology with the peace and beauty of the countryside seems entirely possible.

Beyond Grasse are craggy mountains terraced with lavender, meandering river gorges, and the medieval villages of Provence. Within only a few miles, spectacular drives and walks are possible. The Gorges du Loup, in particular, makes a wonderful excursion, leading you rapidly into an altogether more elevated universe of alpine pastures and mountain mists.

It is the centre of the perfume industry, and for most of the year the air is laden with fragrance; golden mimosa flowers in March; in early summer there are acres of roses waiting to be picked and lavender to be processed; in the autumn the tiny white stars and heavy perfume of jasmine appear.

As well as being a base for the major fragrance manufacturers, Grasse is the hub of an idyllic industry of small flower farms and perfumeries. These days, Grasse concentrates more on processing raw materials from other countries, but it is still possible to see vast mountains of rose petals, vats of jonquils and spadefuls of violets and orange blossom waiting to be processed each morning.

A little history

The town has a venerable past. Between 1138 and 1227 it was a free city, allied to Pisa and Genoa, and governed by a con-

sulate, like the Italian republics. It became a bishopric in 1243 and remained so until 1791, thus becoming a focal point for local power. Its most famous cleric was the 15th-century Bishop Isnard de Grasse who was head of the monastery of the Îles de Lérins.

The town was annexed by the counts of Provence until 1481, when Provence was united with France. Grasse continued to trade with Italy, importing animal skins and selling linen and leather goods. Grasse leather was of very high quality, characterised by its greenish hue, caused by treating it with myrtle leaves. In the 16th century, the fashion for perfumed gloves (masking, along with pomanders and handkerchiefs, the undesirable smell of the populace) was introduced by Catherine de

PRECEDING PAGES: shuttered lives. **LEFT:** negotiating the narrow streets of Grasse. **RIGHT:** searching for the perfect scent.

Medici. This encouraged the perfume industry in Grasse, but it was not until the 18th century that tanning and perfumery began to develop as separate trades.

The Place du Cours

Grasse is a very satisfying town to visit. There is much of historic interest to see and perfumeries abound, but tourism has not taken over completely. Despite the usual souvenir shops selling bags of Provençal lavender, the town still has a working feel to it, and shops on the main square continue to sell everyday items to local residents.

In the architecture of Grasse the influence of the Italian Renaissance is clear. As the city guide points out, "It is to Genoa that the city is indebted for its austere medieval facades, for its Renaissance staircases, for its houses furnished with arcades…"

The town walls were not demolished until the mid-19th century, so the buildings crammed within the walls were extended vertically. The majority are six storeys high, even in the narrowest of alleys, many

of which are dark medieval tunnels reeking of garbage and poverty (a side of Riviera life rarely encountered by the tourist). The southern part of the old town houses many Algerians, bringing a lively street life and Arab music to the lanes and squares.

The **Place du Cours** is a good place to begin a tour of Grasse. Here, a bevy of museums flank a charming terraced garden full of fountains and waterfalls. The **Musée International de la Parfumerie** (open Jun–Sept: daily; Jan–May & Oct: Wed–Sun; entrance fee; tel: (04) 93 36 80 20), housed in an elegant 18th-century mansion, covers the entire history of the industry, including exquisite perfume bottles and Marie-Antoinette's travelling case. Best of all is the greenhouse garden of Mediterranean and sub-tropical perfumed plants.

Down Boulevard Fragonard is the 18th-century **Parfumerie Fragonard** (open summer: daily; winter: Mon–Sat; free; tel: (04) 93 36 44 65), a traditional perfume factory. Opposite it is the **Villa-Musée Fragonard** (open Jun–Sept: daily; Oct &

BELOW: façade of the Villa-Musée Fragonard.

Map on page 176

Dec–May: Wed–Sun; entrance fee; tel: (04) 93 40 32 64). This 17th-century villa was where artist Jean-Honoré Fragonard, who was born in Grasse, lived with his family for some years before the Revolution. The house contains drawings and etchings, and two self-portraits by Fragonard as well as copies of the famous panels made for the Comtesse du Barry which are now in the Frick Collection in New York. The building is surrounded by a charming formal garden.

More museums

Heading in the other direction from Place du Cours you quickly reach the **Musée Provençal du Costume et du Bijou** (2 Rue Jean Ossola; open daily; free; tel: (04) 93 36 91 42), the Fragonard family's personal collection of eighteenth- and nineteenth-century jewellery and traditional costume, from festive peasant dresses to frilly aristocratic frocks.

On a nearby street, Rue Mirabeau, are two townhouses that belonged to the Clapiers de Cabris family, one 17th-century and the other, now the **Musée d'Art et d'Histoire de Provence** (open Wed–Sun; tel: (04) 93 36 01 61; entrance fee), built in 1771. This museum has a good collection of regional crafts including ironwork, ceramics and furniture, and a library of Provençal documents.

North of the Place du Cours is the **Musée de la Marine** (2 Blvd du Jeu-de-Ballon; open Jun–Sept: daily; Oct & Dec–May: Mon–Sat; entrance fee; tel: (04) 93 40 11 11), the beautiful 18th-century former town house of the Pontèves family. The museum commemorates the life and career of Amiral de Grasse (1722–88) who was born locally in Le Bar and played a decisive role in the American War of Independence at the Battle of Yorktown, Virginia, the final battle of the campaign against the British. The museum contains flags and memorabilia, and has a delightful garden with neatly trimmed hedges surrounding roses and small lemon trees, and a pair of cannons captured from the British.

RIGHT: Grasse street life.

HOW PERFUME IS MADE

The flowers must be picked early, when the oil is most concentrated, and delivered immediately. It takes huge quantities of blooms to produce the tiniest amounts of perfume: about 4,000 kilos to produce 1 kilo of "essential oil."

There are a number of different methods used to extract the "absolutes" or "essential oils", which the perfumer then combines to create a fragrance. The oldest method is steam distillation, which is now used mainly for orange blossom. Water and flowers are boiled in a still, and the essential oil floats to the top. Another ancient method still used today is *enfleurage*. Here the flowers are layered with a semi-solid mixture of lard, spread over glass sheets and stacked in wooden tiers. When the fat is thoroughly impregnated with the perfume, the scent is separated out by washing the lard with alcohol. A more modern method involves immersion of the raw material in a volatile solvent. Only the perfume, colour and natural wax dissolve, and after distillation and wax-separation, you are left with a final concentrate called the "absolute."

The highly trained perfumers or "noses" of Grasse can identify and classify hundreds of fragrances. In creating a fragrance, a perfumer is rather like a musician, using different "chords" of scent to blend together in harmony.

Exploring the streets

To the north is the **Place aux Aires**, long and narrow, with shady trees and an 18th-century fountain facing the 1781 six-storey Hôtel Isnard, with its slightly incongruous portico of pillars supporting a balcony. The square dates from the 14th century but the row of arcaded buildings which are its pride and joy are wealthy family town houses from the 16th and 17th centuries, mostly six storeys with shutters and washing hanging from the windows, giving a rather Italian feel to the scene. A market is held in the square every morning.

Turning south, down the narrow steps of the Rue des Fabreries, you encounter the remains of a 14th-century mansion on the corner of the Rue de l'Oratoire. The first two floors are rusticated in the Italian Renaissance style and there is a fine two-arched window on the third floor, below which runs the line of corbels for a missing balcony. You could be in Florence.

As you continue along the Rue de l'Oratoire, you reach the **Église de l'Oratoire**,

which dates from the 14th century, although the bright yellow ochre paintwork on the walls makes the building look much more recent. Everywhere you walk, there is evidence of great age in the buildings, with blocks of stone and fragments of arches peeking through the now flaking rendering.

Now head for Place Jean Jaurès and make a right down the very narrow and rather creepy Rue Répitrel to the **Rue Mougins-Roquefort**, where a 14th-century double round-arched window survives. It has Italian Renaissance corbels and, like many of these buildings, was obviously originally arched on the ground floor. Further down, close to the cathedral, is a 13th-century house.

The cathedral

The **Place du Petit Puy** is the centre of the medieval town. Facing the square is the cathedral of **Notre-Dame-du-Puy**. It has a very high nave with a ribbed vault supported by four enormous 12th-century pillars, scarred and worn, evidence of the burning of the building in 1795 when it was transformed into a forage store. View the nave from the west door looking straight down to the altar. It was altered considerably in the 13th century and remodelled in the 17th century.

The classic Italian Romanesque facade now has a double staircase by Vauban, architect of the ramparts of Antibes; it was a failed attempt to give this crude and powerful building a touch of 17th-century elegance. The ground-floor side windows were recently restored; they had previously been cut into by insensitive "modern" windows at a higher level.

The interior features some interesting works: a rare religious painting by Fragonard, *The Washing of the Feet* (1754), in the south transept, and three works by Rubens on the south wall of the nave: *The Crown of Thorns*, *The Crucifixion* and *St Helen in Exaltation of the Holy Cross*, painted in Rome in 1601. There is also a triptych attributed to Louis Bréa, and some interesting reliquaries and church treasure.

Outside there is a good view of the south transept from the Place St-Martin. A tunnel leads through to the Place Godeau, where

LEFT: the high vaulted nave of Notre-Dame-du-Puy.

Map on page 176

the **Bishop's Palace** forms the other side of a small square. Arrow slits in the palace are aimed straight at the north doorway of the church. The Palace (now serving as the Hôtel de Ville) once had an elegant three-arched loggia in the Italian manner but this was mostly infilled in later years, leaving only the passage through from the Place Godeau. The ensemble is completed by a tall 10th-century square tower in red tufa.

To the east of the Bishop's Palace, on the Place du 24 Août, is a solitary clock tower, the remains of the 13th-century consulate (law courts).

The Gorges du Loup

The area around Grasse is traditionally dependent on the flower industry, and a good way to see a number of interesting villages is to head northeast towards the Gorges du Loup. At **Le Bar-sur-Loup ⑯**, a pair of cannons, captured by Amiral François de Grasse from the British, stand either side of the door to l'Amiral restaurant on the Place F. Pault. De Grasse was born in the 16th-century castle of Le Bar, and Rue Yorktown is named after his famous battle *(see page 199)*. Le Bar is a centre for walking, and itineraries are available from the Syndicat d'Initiatif located in the strange *donjon* in the middle of the village. The Gothic church has been extensively remodelled but has fine door panels by Jacotin Bellot. There is also an extraordinary 15th-century painting of *La Danse Macabre* (The Dance of Death) in the nave.

Pont-du-Loup ⑰, at the south end of the Gorges du Loup, is like an Alpine village with palm trees. The village is framed by mountains on either side with spectacular views, making it a good place for walking tours. It is dominated by the remains of a railway viaduct, blown up by the Germans in 1944 and never repaired; great ruined monoliths rise hundreds of feet over the houses and trees.

Gourdon ⑱, high above Pont-du-Loup and one of the most dramatic *villages perchés* of them all, is still relatively inaccessible, though the new road to it is an

BELOW: Gourdon, perched high above the River Loup.

easy ride in comparison with the steep mountain track the peasant with his mule used in centuries past. The approach gives a stunning view of the village with its sheer drop of several thousand feet below the château walls.

Today only the château's living quarters have survived, and where the tower once was, is now laid out a formal French garden, providing an almost surreal contrast between the neatly trimmed low hedges and topiary and the wild backdrop of the surrounding mountains. The castle has a museum (open June–Sept: daily; Oct–May: Wed–Mon; entrance fee; tel: (04) 93 09 68 02), which contains some very interesting (and valuable) armour: suits of plate armour, chain mail, broad swords, rifles and various types of ordnance. All the rooms have huge fireplaces, even the private chapel, certainly necessary because Gourdon is a cold and rugged place for much of the year. On the upper floor is a large and exceptionally good collection of naive paintings, includ-

ing a Henri Rousseau portrait with an excellent Proustian moustache.

The Gorges du Loup itself is glorious and terrifying by turns. The road tunnels through the rock and sweeps past magnificent waterfalls, occasionally offering views down to the rushing river far below. The footpaths along the gorge are well maintained with steps cut in the steeper parts.

Skiing near the sea

Beyond are the Clues (gorges) de Haute Provence, a barren, remote region which comes into its own in the winter skiing season. **Gréolières** ⑲ to the west is on an alpine slope, remote and quiet, the hillsides dotted with violets and spring flowers. Eighteen kilometres (11 miles) beyond is **Gréolières-le-Neige**, the nearest ski resort to the Mediterranean.

Turning east instead you will come to **Coursegoules** ⑳, a pretty town of muted terracotta stone nestling protectively against the bare rock of the mountain side, surrounded by sheep pastures and tinkling

BELOW: the village of Tourettes-sur-Loup.

Map on page 176

bells. There is a considerable amount of new building here – basic apartments, not tourist villas – and a lively school housed in a beautifully-restored old building. Remote as it may seem, Coursegoules is only 16 km (10 miles) from Vence, and the excellence of the roads means local people can commute to the coast.

A mountain village

An alternative route from Le Bar follows the D2210 to **Tourettes-sur-Loup** ㉑, clinging to the rock between two deep ravines. To the west of the village are great expanses of sheer rock, and at the cliff edge are troglodyte houses carved from the living rock. Today Tourettes is an important centre for violet production, supplying Grasse perfumeries and the factories manufacturing candied violets in Toulouse.

The village is in an ideal defensive position and began life occupied by Ligurian tribes. In 262 BC, the Romans established an observation post here: "Turres Altae", which was corrupted into "Tourettes".

The Romans left in AD 476, after which the village suffered the same series of invasions and massacres that befell its neighbours. The Saracens were responsible for fortifying the site. In 1387, Tourettes came into the hands of the Villeneuve family, where it remained until the French Revolution when the Villeneuves fled, never to return. The Black Death, the Wars of Religion and the Revolution all took their toll and by 1944 the population had shrunk to 850. Today the revitalisation of the area has resulted in a population of nearly 4,000.

The old village is quite amazingly crooked, with no two windows alike or a straight line anywhere, and the twisting streets feel completely enclosed until a cool, dim alley unexpectedly emerges on to a windblown mountain panorama. The horseshoe-shaped Grand Rue is lined with art galleries and craft shops but is not over-commercialised, and there are medieval shops, now private houses, and numerous interesting doorways still visible.

In the centre of the village a very formal Hôtel de Ville looks rather out of place. It incorporates an 11th-century watchtower, and has a pleasant courtyard with a tinkling fountain. The 11th-century church has been rebuilt on and off from the mid-16th until the 18th century and has a simple stylised *Virgin and Child* over the front door. To the north of the village is the Chapelle St-Jean, which contains recent naive wall paintings.

A little further along the D2210 towards Vence is the Château Notre-Dame-des-Fleurs, a 19th-century castle that now houses the **Galerie Beaubourg** (open Apr–Sept: Mon–Sat; Oct–Mar: Tue–Sat; entrance fee; tel: (04) 93 24 52 00). Run by Parisian art dealers Pierre and Marianne Nahon, the gallery puts on seasonal exhibitions of contemporary art. The château itself was built by a Grasse perfumer on the remains of an 11th-century Benedictine monastery, and behind the facade on the ground floor are the original monks' cells and private chapels, all beautifully restored. A vast sculpture garden features works by Niki de St-Phalle, Arman and César, but don't miss the chapel filled with sculptures by Jean Tingueley. ❑

RIGHT: the deep ravine of the Gorge du Loup.

Map
on page
176

CAGNES, VENCE AND THE VAR VALLEY

The Fondation Maeght, Matisse's Chapelle du Rosaire and the endless commercial galleries are constant reminders that some of the greatest modern artists once wandered the streets of Cagnes, St-Paul and Vence

The coastline between Antibes and Nice is perhaps the most exploited on the Riviera, even though the beaches themselves are often unappealingly pebbly. Inland, the property development from Cagnes to Vence is equally unbridled, and St-Paul-de-Vence is said to be the most visited village in France after Mont St-Michel.

Popularity should not dissuade anyone from visiting this part of the Riviera, however – its reputation is entirely justified. Both St-Paul and Vence are of great historical interest and the area has long been a thriving artistic centre; St-Paul, for example, is home to the Fondation Maeght, one of the world's great art museums (*see page 214*).

The section of the N7 highway that runs along this stretch of coast resembles a Hollywood-style strip of neon lights, hoardings, petrol stations and huge drive-in supermarkets (worth checking out by anyone with serious shopping to do). The view is dominated in all directions by the **Marina-Baie des Anges**, at **Villeneuve-Loubet-Plage ㉒**, a much reviled piece of modern architecture, built in the 1970s. Actually, it is by no means out of place, its curving terraces echoing the waves and the mountains behind.

Easiest access to the marina, crammed with hundreds of magnificent yachts, is from the N98 coast road. Next to it on one side is the Hippodrome race-track, and on the other is **Marineland**, a big marine zoo and entertainment complex with dolphins, sea-lions and whales (open daily; entrance fee; tel: (04) 93 33 49 49).

Birthplace of Escoffier

The original medieval village with the same name, **Villeneuve-Loubet ㉓**, is just off the N7, east of the river Loup.

Surprisingly, it still has an authentic feel to its steep narrow lanes and lived-in ancient buildings which have resisted renovation with layers of cement and pebbledash. They huddle at the foot of the château, restored in the 19th century and now private property. The path round the château walls offers a good view out to the Baie des Anges.

One of Villeneuve's most famous sons is remembered at the **Fondation Auguste Escoffier** (also known as the **Musée de l'Art Culinaire**), housed in the great chef's birthplace, a short way up the hill from the main square (open Dec–Oct: Tues–Sun; afternoons only; entrance fee;

PRECEDING PAGES: La Colombe d'Or, St-Paul-de-Vence.
LEFT: window-shopping in St-Paul.
RIGHT: Château Grimaldi, Haut-de-Cagnes.

tel: (04) 93 20 80 51). Exhibits include an old Provençal kitchen; gleaming copperware and kitchen utensils; some of Escoffier's own inventions, including a device for making breadcrumbs; a roomful of mouthwatering old menus; some wildly imaginative examples of sugarwork, including a haywain and a model of a Loire château; Escoffier's own hand-written recipe book and, touchingly, the master's last *toque*.

There is also a selection of old photographs, including some of Dame Nelly Melba, for whom Escoffier invented the Peach Melba while he was chef at the London Carlton Hotel. And if your visit to the culinary museum has given you an appetite, there are a couple of gratifyingly good pâtisseries in the square below.

Three towns in one

Surrounded by a tangle of highway intersections is **Cagnes-sur-Mer** ㉔, which is divided into three very distinct parts: the modern unremarkable seaside resort of Cros-de-Cagnes, a former fishing village; the modern town of Cagnes-sur-Mer (which is not in fact on the sea, as its name implies, but inland) with its shops, supermarket, public park, covered market (mornings only) and, of course, Renoir's house, Les Collettes; and the historic hill town of **Haut-de-Cagnes**, crowned by a 14th-century château.

The history of the town begins with the monks of Lérins, who founded an abbey at Saint-Véran in the 5th century, now the site of the Hippodrome. By the 14th century Cagnes became a Grimaldi possession and subject to the constant turmoil of the Middle Ages. It has always depended on agriculture for its economic survival, notably olives, vines and flowers. By the 19th century, fishermen from Menton had settled along the coast, and the town thus developed between coast and castle.

Today, as well as being a popular tourist destination, Cagnes-sur-Mer is an important artistic centre and a major flower producing centre.

BELOW: the curving terraces of Marina-Baie des Anges.

Map on page 176

A stroll in the old town

The steep, winding streets and tiny square of Haut-de-Cagnes are as carefully tended by the town's inhabitants as their own homes. Terracotta pots of flowering jasmine and geraniums glow against a backdrop of fig trees and wisteria that overhang from roof gardens, while the traditional kitchen gardens serried beneath the ramparts are still zealously cultivated.

Steps to the left of the Montée de la Bourgade, a street lined with restaurants, lead to the rue du Portis Long. This lane follows the inside of the ramparts through a long barrel vault past the ground floors and basements of the buildings. It makes for a pleasantly cool walk in the heat of summer. You can also stroll along the outside of the ramparts; just exit through one of the medieval gateways.

Cagnes has many 15th- and 16th-century houses and a number of Renaissance houses with arcades near the castle. The oldest building here is the **Chapelle Notre-Dame-de-la-Protection**, a bijou 14th-century structure on the edge of the town, erected as protection against plague and pestilence. It contains some beautiful 1530 frescoes and has a large open-sided porch offering a wide view south over Cagnes-sur-Mer to the Mediterranean and Nice airport beyond. A narrow, hidden path curves round the outside of the apse and down the hillside.

Château Grimaldi

The **Château Grimaldi**, a solid square keep built as a prison in about 1300, has been described as the finest specimen of a medieval stronghold in this part of France, but it has been badly treated and needs some sorting out architecturally. At some point, large, modern windows were cut through its great walls, destroying sections of the machicolations which are the castle's finest feature.

The castle is flanked by two squares. The Place du Château is filled with cafés and nightclubs, and to the north looks out over distant and frequently snow-covered

BELOW: the hilltop Haut-de-Cagnes.

mountains. A medieval archway takes you through to the Place Grimaldi and the entrance to the **Musée Grimaldi** (open Dec–Oct: Wed–Mon; entrance fee; tel: (04) 93 20 87 29) housed in the château.

The Musée Grimaldi is cluttered with exhibits of local history, artefacts, and paintings by local artists, admittedly mediocre but housed in wonderful rooms. One section of the museum recounts the history of the olive tree and its importance to the region, and includes a collection of old olive presses and implements. Other features to look out for include a fine fireplace, an old well, a magnificent ceiling, and the red-brick floors polished to a glassy patina by centuries of passing feet.

Portraits of a *chanteuse*

The paintings exhibited around the rest of the castle may be second-rate, but the **Donation Suzy Solidor** collection is definitely worth a look. In the 1930s, singer Suzy Solidor ran a famous nightclub in Paris known as La Vie Parisienne. A thoroughly modern woman with the signature bobbed hair, she moved in artistic circles and had the brilliant idea of having her many friends paint her. In all, she had 224 portraits painted, of which 47 are on display here. It is fascinating to see the same subject approached in so many different ways: Foujita surrounded an oriental-looking Suzy and her dog with gold-leaf panels; Van Dongen painted her in a sailor suit; Lydis treated her as a Vargas pin-up. There's an odd, rapidly executed Picabia; drawings by Raoul Dufy and Jean Cocteau; and the jewel of the collection, a Tamara de Lempicka nude of her with a Cubist cityscape background. The Lempicka alone is worth the admission charge. The **Musée d'Art Moderne Méditerranéen** on the top floor is dedicated to artists who have worked on the Côte d'Azur.

Renoir's home

In the 1920s, Cagnes became a popular bohemian haunt for artists, and was the setting for Cyril Connolly's only novel,

BELOW: Cagnes today.

Map
on page
176

The Rock Pool, in which the town becomes Trou-sur-Mer. He describes the louche doings of "the doomed tribe" of failed artists, "the mysterious jungle atmosphere… intense nocturnal life… where the hopelessness of the struggle was admitted with fatalism, yet where all fought on".

A rather more celebrated local artist is Auguste Renoir, and his house, **Les Collettes**, is a wonderful place to visit. It is surrounded by a magnificent olive grove: 2 hectares (5 acres) of 300-year-old olive trees, spread out across the hillside with superb views of the old village of Haut-de-Cagnes, the Mediterranean and Cap d'Antibes – a view which has, of course, changed dramatically since Renoir's day. The house, on Chemin des Collettes, now contains the **Musée Renoir** (open Dec–Oct: Wed–Mon; entrance fee; tel: (04) 93 20 61 07). Renoir spent the last 12 years of his life here and the building still feels like a private home. Nine of the rooms are open, including his two studios,

BELOW:
Terrasse à
Cagnes, as
Renoir saw
it in 1905.

filled with memorabilia. In the small studio is his palette, a square of white ceramic, wiped clean after use so that he could see the pure colour as it would look on a white canvas. Not for Renoir the heavily encrusted kidney-shaped wooden palette of the stereotypical artist. Even the bathroom is on view, with a wonderful tub and, low on the wall next to the bidet, a small ceramic tile of a nude, probably by his son Claude.

There are 10 original paintings by Renoir in the museum, including a large sketch for Les Grandes Baigneuses in which he roughs in the form with cross-hatch pencil work over the paint. There are also drawings, busts and other work. They are interspersed with reproductions, often quite crude ones, which give the museum a homely feel.

A walled town

On the way between Cagnes and Vence is the small but perfectly fortified town of **St-Paul-de-Vence** ㉕, now one of the

region's main tourist spots, besieged today by coach parties who invade its tiny streets and tourist shops stocked with lavender bags and T-shirts. If you drive straight to Vence in the high season you will have ample opportunity to examine St-Paul's fortifications from the traffic jam which extends all the way down the D36.

Parking is always a problem here so expect to leave your car outside the town if you drive at all; the Café de la Place just outside the main (north) gate is a good place to stop for coffee and watch a game of *boules*.

The circle of ramparts, built in 1536, remains unbroken. A walk round them gives a good view of the surrounding countryside studded with dark cypresses and azure swimming-pools, as well as a better sense of life in St-Paul than a walk down Rue Grande provides; glimpses of bougainvillaea-filled gardens and treasured terraces hint at an insider's life beyond the stout wooden doors visible from the street.

A cannon captured at the Battle of Cérisoles in 1544 defends the north gate, la Porte Royale, where a machicolated 13th-century tower houses the tourist centre. The gate opens straight on to Rue Grande, a narrow crooked street which runs the full length of the village passing Place de la Grande-Fontaine with its pretty urn-shaped fountain.

Many of the the 16th- and 17th-century houses bear coats of arms and are now "artists'" ateliers. Some of the medieval shops survive, usually as private homes; look out for a wide arch, beneath which is a doorway and an adjoining window. The window has a large marble sill which used to be the shop counter, a direct descendant of the Roman shop.

Sights in St-Paul

The building of the church (**La Collégiale de la Conversion de Saint Paul**) spanned several centuries. It was begun in the 12th century and has an 18th-century bell tower. Among its treasures is a painting

BELOW: La Colombe d'Or restaurant, St-Paul-de-Vence

Map
on page
176

attributed to Tintoretto of St Catherine of Alexandria, at the end of the north aisle. Also displayed is a 13th-century enamel virgin and child and a silver reliquary said to enclose St George's shoulder blade.

Across from the church is the donjon, a tower that completes a pleasing group of buildings. It now contains the **Musée d'Histoire de St-Paul** (open daily; entrance fee; tel: (04) 93 32 41 13), which presents local history in tableaux of wax figures – more endearing than it sounds. Much more interesting, however, is its exhibition of photographs of celebrities taken in St-Paul: Greta Garbo, Sophia Loren, Yul Brynner, Burt Lancaster, Jean-Paul Sartre and Simone de Beauvoir and many others enjoyed holidays here.

The rich and famous still come to St-Paul, most often to eat at the celebrated **La Colombe d'Or** restaurant. In the 19th century, the village of St-Paul declined and it was not until the 1920s that it was "discovered" by a group of artists which included Bonnard, Modigliani, Soutine,

Signac and others, who u café that later became L They paid for meals and i ings and sculptures and proprietors assembled an enviable, and now priceless, collection of art. The dining-room walls are adorned with works by Picasso, Braque, Miró and Matisse, the garden wall features a huge brilliantly coloured Léger mosaic, there is a Calder mobile and a Braque mosaic dove by the cypress-sheltered swimming-pool, and works by Dufy, Chagall, César and more at every turn. The hotel itself is charming, cosy even, a feast of warm terracotta, bright ceramic tiles, painted wooden ceilings and burnished wood. Dining outside on the terrace is one of the pleasures of Provence; sampling the 15 famous hors d'oeuvres and the Grand Marnier soufflé an essential – if expensive – experience.

There are further riches close by; within easy walking distance of the village is the **Fondation Maeght** (open daily; entrance fee; tel: (04) 93 32 81 63), a

BELOW:
the fortified
town of St-
Paul-de-Vence.

The Fondation Maeght

Visiting the Fondation Maeght outside St-Paul-de-Vence is a bit like finding London's Tate Gallery set in steep pine woods. It is a world-class museum of modern art, housing not only exhibition galleries but a library, workshops, and a sculpture garden. The foundation itself has an ever changing exhibition, but the permanent collection is very strong in Miró, Braque and Giacometti, and examples of their work are always on display. Giacometti's club-footed bronze figures stride across the central sculpture court and are the most photographed pieces in the collection. There is art everywhere; even the door handles were designed by Miró.

Behind the gallery is the Joan Miró labyrinth: a series of connecting spaces designed by Catalan architect Josep Luis Sert, who also built the main galleries. Each of the big humorous sculptures has its own special

setting, in water or silhouetted against the sky. Miró made the ceramics at the foundation workshop and the large concrete pieces were built *in situ*.

The tiny chapel, which contains Georges Braque's beautiful *White Bird on a Mauve Background* (1962), a delicate stained-glass panel set high above the altar, was also built by Sert. It was actually the first building on the site, erected in memory of the child of the founders of the museum, Aimé and Marguerite Maeght. Aimé came from Nîmes, where he had shown some aptitude for engraving, and he met Marguerite in Cannes. They married and set up in business together with an electrical goods shop which was very successful. Marguerite indeed had such an instinct for business that she once said of herself, "If I were cast up naked on a desert island, I'd make money."

During World War II many Jews fled to the relative safety of the South of France, bringing with them art works to sell. The Maeghts seized the opportunity and replaced the electrical appliances with paintings. The supply was increased when Pierre Bonnard, who lived in Le Cannet, noticed Aimé's engravings and asked for his assistance. Because Marguerite's father ran a grocery business, they were able to exchange scarce wartime provisions for art works. Bonnard then introduced his new friends to Henri Matisse in Vence, another artist in need of groceries.

Within 10 years the Maeghts had risen to extraordinary prominence in the art world. Their Paris gallery represented, among others, Matisse, Miró, Giacometti, Kandinsky, Braque, Chagall and Calder.

Following the tragic early death of their child, the Maeghts decided to build a chapel in his memory, which evolved into the foundation. Maeght was an art dealer who did something no art dealer had ever done before: he created a museum in his own name, paid for entirely by himself and filled with art from his own extensive stock. At the inauguration in 1964, André Malraux, the Minister of Cultural Affairs, said: "Here something has been attempted which has never been attempted before: to create, instinctively and lovingly, the universe in which modern art might find both its place and the other world once called supernatural."

LEFT: sculpture in the garden of the Fondation.

Map
on page
176

world-class museum of modern art, with works by Miró, Giacometti, Calder and many others *(see page 214)*.

Inland to Vence

A short drive up the D2 is **Vence** ㉖, a delightfully civilised town, perched high on a rock promontory, surrounded by rose farms and orange groves which are sheltered by mountains to the north. Its gentle climate has made it popular, especially with invalids – D. H. Lawrence died here in 1930 – and has resulted in property development scarring the surrounding hillsides.

Such popularity has its advantages; today Vence provides excellent food shopping for fresh fish, vegetables and pâtisserie, as well as a market twice a week, and it is always pleasant to stroll round its leafy squares and ancient streets.

Vence has a chequered history. It was occupied by the Phoenicians and the Gauls, savaged and ruined by the Saracens and the Lombards before the Romans named it Ventium and made it an important religious centre. Vence converted to Christianity early, a change usually attributed to St Trophime. The first Bishopric was founded here in AD 374 and the town quickly grew to become an important regional centre.

Much of the history of Vence has been the conflict between the power of the bishops and that of the Villeneuves, because the lords of Villeneuve-Loubet shared seignorial rights over the town with the church. Vence won a great victory in the Wars of Religion against the Huguenots, but it suffered horribly from the Black Death in 1572.

Bishops remained here until the outbreak of the French Revolution when Bishop Pisani was forced to flee the country; the see was never restored.

Vence drifted into steady decline so that by the beginning of the 20th century it was half-deserted with many houses in ruins. But tourism and sun-belt industries have transformed it into a bustling centre of more than 15,000 people.

BELOW: Place du Peyra in Vence.
RIGHT: Chagall mosaic, Vence Cathedral.

Ramparts and ancient gates

Before you reach the old town, you pass through the Place du Grand-Jardin, and Place du Frêne with its huge ash tree planted in 1538. The medieval centre of Vence is very picturesque and once you get away from the souvenir sellers, the lanes and alleyways are little changed from previous centuries – except that many of the lanes in the northeast side of the old town now have light and air where they end at the town ramparts; the walls have been cut down to waist height so that now there is a mountain view instead of a prison-like wall.

The ramparts were built in the 13th and 14th centuries and used to have a broad walk running along the top. In the northern section, this promenade still exists where it has become Boulevard Paul André. The south section of the ramparts has been repeatedly pierced to make shops along Avenue Marcellin Maurel. Vence has retained its town gates: the 13th-century Porte du Signadour incorporated into a defensive tower; the round arched Porte d'Orient pierced through in the 18th century (the date of 1592 refers to a battle during the Wars of Religion); the 14th-century Portail Levis, which once possessed a portcullis and opens on to Rue de la Coste, one of the oldest lanes in the town; Le Pontis, built in 1863; and, most impressive of all, the **Portail du Peyra** built by Good King René who died in 1480. It is much restored and in the 17th century an imposing square tower was added to its side.

The entrance through Portail du Peyra leads past a small fountain to the Place du Peyra, which has a grand and ancient chestnut tree shading the cafés. Place Godeau, named after the famous poet bishop, is outside the cathedral and was once the cemetery. Today, it is a pleasant place to stop for a drink. There is a granite Roman column in the centre of the square and some fine old houses: a 13th-century house with a two-arch Romanesque window, and another dated 1524.

LEFT: Portail du Peyra, one of Vence's ancient gateways.

IN MATISSE'S FOOTSTEPS

When Matisse wrote from these hills in 1943, "I've come on a long journey that took me from Nice to Vence," he wasn't talking in terms of geographical distance. Here in Vence, his style radically changed from reclining nudes in sumptuous flower-filled interiors to a search for purity in bold colours and decorative cut-outs.

For the first time, Matisse enthusiasts can now visit the exotic garden of the artist's Vence home, Villa Le Rêve, where the great master churned out hundreds of pen and ink drawings, plucking flowers to study the essence of their form. The guided visit is only possible as part of a tour (offered by the Atelier Soardi in Nice) that traces the artist's aesthetic evolution step by step. It begins with his arrival in Nice's Old Town in 1917, where he was so enchanted with the dazzling silver light that he ended up settling on the Côte d'Azur and spending the rest of his life here. Highlights of the tour also include a stop at the Atelier Soardi itself, where Matisse sketched the enormous mural La Danse; the Musée Matisse in Cimiez (see page 230); and the Chapelle du Rosaire in Vence, whose stark white walls are set off by the artist's sublime stained glass. For tour bookings, telephone the Atelier Soardi on (04) 93 62 33 30.

Map
on page
176

Vence's old cathedral

The 15th-century watchtower rises next to the **cathedral**, which is entered from Place Clemenceau, the old Roman forum, where a flea market is held every Wednesday. Buried in its outside walls on the Passage Cahours are reused Roman stones bearing inscriptions, one to the goddess Cybele and the ceremony of the Taurobolium, in which a bull was sacrificed to the gods, and another to Lucius Veludius Valerianus, decurian of Vence and his wife Vibia.

The cathedral was built between the 12th and 15th centuries on the site of Roman temple adapted for Christian use in the 5th century. It consists of a nave with four aisles. The roof is carried on immense square pillars, lacking in ornament. The two side aisles were roofed over in the 15th century by a wide gallery which looks down into the nave through a row of arches, built to accommodate an enlarged congregation. Either side are two more aisles where the chapels are located: one, which is said to contain the body of St Véran who died in 492, uses a carved Roman sarcophagus as both tomb and altar. Other Roman figures can be found in the walls, one in the pillar before the chapel of St Véran.

In 1499, at the same time as the roofing of the aisles, a tribune was added at the west end, housing the choir on a gallery high above the door. This contains the 51 famous wooden choir stalls imaginatively carved by Jacotin Bellot of Grasse who began work on them in 1455 and finished them 25 years later. He carved animals and plants and recorded the everyday life of the people and clergy, sometimes not at all reverently.

The cathedral also has a wonderfully carved wooden door taken from the destroyed *prévôté* or chapter house. In the baptistry there is a mosaic design by Marc Chagall of Moses in the bulrushes.

Outside the city walls, the **Château de Villeneuve** (open Tues–Sun; entrance fee; tel: (04) 93 58 15 78), has been renovated as an exhibition space for modern art.

BELOW:
Matisse's
Chapelle du
Rosaire
(1947–51).

Matisse's chapel

The other church of interest in Vence is the **Chapelle du Rosaire** (open mid-Dec–Oct: Mon–Thur & Sat; Mon, Wed & Sat: afternoons only; entrance fee; tel: (04) 93 58 03 26), designed by Henri Matisse between 1947 and 1951. The 1950s design hasn't quite stood the test of time, indicating perhaps that Matisse was more at home with the fine arts, though its most original element, the chapel's ultramarine-and-white tile roof still looks superb. The yellow-and-blue stained glass, based on a leaf motif, works very well with the simple wall decorations chosen by Matisse: instead of frescoes, he painted his designs for the walls on uniform white tiles, specially made for the building. Unfortunately, quite a few on his Stations of the Cross wall cracked when the building settled.

The drawing itself is confident and strong, remarkably so considering how old and arthritic Matisse was by the time he produced it. Of greatest interest are the details: the candlesticks on the altar and the confessional door – an assemblage of wooden shapes painted white, echoing the traditional perforated doors in medieval churches.

Up the Var valley

From Vence, the road to the northeast climbs to **St-Jeannet ㉗**, towered over by the great **Baou de St-Jeannet** (*baou* is Provençal for rock) which has inspired many painters, among them Poussin, Fragonard, Renoir and Chagall. The village nestles on a terrace at the foot of the Baou. In some lights it looks no more than a natural outcrop of the rock; at other times the rock itself looks like a craggy château.

At one time, St-Jeannet was famous for its grapes and wine but today production is concentrated on flowers. However, locally produced wines and jams are sometimes available for sale in the village; if the shop is shut you may find them left outside with a little box for payment.

St-Jeannet is a village of quiet courtyards, arched doorways and sloping lanes

BELOW: the craggy outcrop of the Baou de St-Jeannet.

Map on page 176

of stone steps. On a pleasant square with a fountain, is the Chapelle St-Bernadin, built in 1666 and lit by only three recent stained-glass windows. Behind the church is a wonderful panorama from a small platform partly covered by an old archway with thick beams. It is amazing to see how the narrow terraces below accommodate carefully tended *potagers*, parked cars and even swimming pools,

St-Jeannet has a number of fine restaurants making it a good place to stop for lunch – before or probably after, a climb. There is a path to the top of Baou St-Jeannet which starts from the Auberge St-Jeannet and takes about an hour each way. A spectacular view of the French and Italian Alps can be seen from the viewing platform at the top.

Industrial development

Gattières ㉘, further along the D2210, is a working perched village with steep streets filled with washing lines and barking dogs. The ancient buildings are there but covered in pebbledash or rendering, making it an interesting contrast to many other self-consciously picturesque villages with virtually identical housing stock.

South of St-Jeannet, on the D18, is **La Gaude**, a small, lively village built high above the River Cagne; it is the nearest village to the massive IBM Research and Study Centre on the D118 to St-Laurent. When Breuer's IBM centre was built it was highly praised for harmonising with the landscape – as well as two giant Y-shaped blocks supported by concrete pillars can. Now the area has become heavily built up and the IBM architecture no longer looks so modern or interesting.

Le Broc ㉙ is another classic perched village, this time high on a rock overlooking the River Var. The view is extraordinary because the scale of human intervention on the landscape comes as a shock; the Var has been straightened out like a canal in a gigantic feat of engineering, taming it and binding it with freeways and industrial zones on either side. ❑

BELOW: the highly developed Var valley near Le Broc.

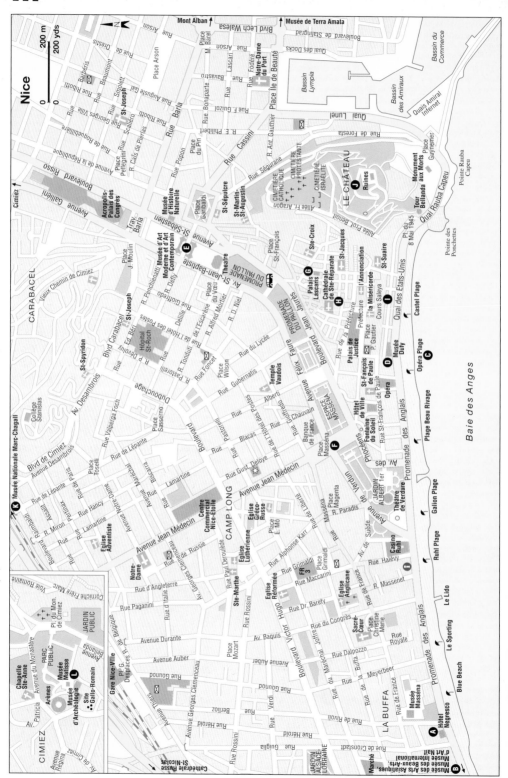

Maps:
Area 236
City 222

NICE

Facing the wide Baie des Anges, the beautiful city of Nice is the undisputed capital of the Riviera. For the art lover, there are museums aplenty, and for the wanderer, there are the markets and narrow streets of the old town

The city of **Nice** has officially been part of France only since 1860. Before that it had closer ties with Italy. Local jokers, however, like to dispute even this, saying that for 62 years up to 1990 Nice was the personal fiefdom of the Médecin men – first Jean, then his son Jacques – both of whom ruled as mayor and left indelible marks. Jacques ("Jacou") was loved by the Niçois, and when he died in 1998, they turned out in their thousands for his funeral, despite the fact that he had been indicted for tax evasion and corruption in 1990 and fled to Uruguay.

His downfall closed just another chapter in the city's see-saw history of changing management which began in 350 BC with the Greeks, who named it after the goddess, Nike ("she who brings victory"), and variously saw in power Romans, counts of Provence, dukes of Savoy and kings of Sardinia. As a tug-of-love baby, the "Maid of Provence" certainly had a turbulent upbringing, and was a ward of the Italian court for most of 500 years.

Today, Nice is essentially French but its character and temperament remain Italian, with constant reminders that the frontier is still just 32 km (20 miles) away. However, it is rightly proud of its own language, *Nissard*, its own surrounding "county" of the Alpes-Maritimes and its cuisine, which goes much further than just a famous salad.

It is now a unique city of western, medieval and oriental influences, a provincial metropolis that is the richest, most attractive tourist centre outside Paris. Nice is France's fifth-largest city and has the country's second-largest airport. It has also become a business and cultural centre to be reckoned with.

A French Bournemouth

It was the British who invented the name "Riviera". They laid the foundations for its present-day capital and were certainly in no doubt about its being the brightest jewel in the river of towns sparkling all the way from Cannes to Monte-Carlo.

A thriving English colony subsequently developed. Well-heeled British aristocrats and retired army officers zealously set about turning Nice into a kind of sanitised Bournemouth, with hotels called Westminster and West End in a sector they named Newborough.

Indeed, it is an English clergyman, the Reverend Lewis Way, whom we must thank for the Promenade des Anglais, which remains the main thoroughfare of the city. He was a skilled missionary with remarkable powers of persuasion, who talked his flock into providing construction work for men thrown out of work by a severe frost

PRECEDING PAGES:
jogging on the Promenade des Anglais.
RIGHT:
Italianate facade.

which killed the area's orange trees in 1821.

By 1887, when poet Stephen Liégeard first named the coastline the Côte d'Azur, Nice had already expanded to the size of Cannes today, and was regularly attracting over 25,000 winter visitors, mainly by train. There were shops selling trinkets made of olive wood inscribed with the words "Nice", and "*Je reviendrai*" – forerunners of today's "Nice is Nice" T-shirts and "*J'aime la Côte d'Azur*" bumper stickers.

There was an air of prosperity, electric lighting in the streets and, naturally, guidebooks. "Nice is a home for the millionaire and the working man," one proclaimed. "The intermediate class is not wanted. Visitors are expected to have money, and if they have to look at pounds, shillings and pence had much better remain at home."

A seaside promenade

The **Promenade des Anglais**, the little coastal road that was then used by about 100 English families and their carriages, has today become one of the most clogged thoroughfares in France. It is an eight-lane highway, 5 km (3 miles) long, on which only the aggressive survive, and you need to be alert. Watch your window, too, if you stop at the lights in summer: resplendent with marching palms and flowerbeds, the Prom (even the French call it that) has an automatic watering system and the sprinklers are liable to turn your car into a jacuzzi if your reflexes aren't sharp enough.

Today's scene on the Promenade des Anglais is very different from its 19th-century counterpart. When Henri Negresco's palace first opened its doors in 1913 they pointed north: 150 years after Tobias Smollett introduced sea-bathing here, it still had not dawned on anyone that the future of tourism lay in hotels with their resplendent fronts, not their backs, to the sea.

The famed **Hôtel Negresco**  remains the crown of the Promenade. It is a national monument where visiting heads of state still occupy entire floors, and the flamboyance of the exterior is only

BELOW: the elegant Hôtel Negresco.

Map on page 222

eclipsed by the jewels within. This was where F. Scott Fitzgerald stayed and although you won't find a Diamond as Big as the Ritz, there is a crystal chandelier by Baccarat with 16,309 stones and weighing more than a tonne, designed originally for the Tsar of Russia.

There are a number of fine museums stretched out along the Promenade des Anglais. Furthest west, near the airport, is the **Musée des Arts Asiatiques ❽** (open Wed–Mon; entrance fee; tel: (04) 92 29 37 00), a sleek glass-and-metal structure with a small collection of rare pieces, including 4,000-year-old Chinese jade artefacts. In the Château Ste-Hélène on Avenue Val Marie is the **Musée International d'Art Naïf** (open Wed–Mon; entrance fee; tel: (04) 93 71 78 33), with its collection of 600 works from 27 countries.

Heading back towards the city centre you'll find the **Musée des Beaux-Arts** (open Tues–Sun; entrance fee; tel: (04) 92 15 28 28), a *belle-époque* villa built for Russian royalty at 33 Avenue des Baumettes, mainly devoted to 19th-century painting. Finally, behind the Hôtel Negresco, at 65 Rue de France, is the **Musée Masséna** (open Dec–Oct: Tues–Sun; free; tel: (04) 93 88 11 34), a mixed bag including École de Nice tableaux and regional artefacts.

Also worth noting further east along the Promenade are the **Palais de la Méditerranée**, a famous 1920s casino now crumbling away, and the **Casino Ruhl**, which continues to delight gamblers every night with its gaming tables and slot machines.

On the Baie des Anges

The locals' sunny disposition derives from an ability to use the **beaches** every day in summer, in the grinding halt between noon and 3pm. The 5 km (3 miles) of curving seafront may be disappointingly pebbly, but the beaches are clean, like the sea, and run right through the heart·of town. For a quick dip, there is nothing wrong with the public beaches (with their free showers), but various private

RIGHT: the beach beneath the Prom.

NICE JAZZ FESTIVAL

The jazz tradition in Nice dates back to 1974, when American francophile, George Wein created the "Grande Parade de Jazz". Over the years, legendary artists such as Lionel Hampton, Ray Charles, Ella Fitzgerald and Miles Davis regularly appeared at the festival, making it a mecca for enthusiasts. After 1994, it saw a change of emphasis, with more world music and pop. But the festival's newest organizer, Viviane Sicnasi, has reinstated Wein's original aim, an eclectic mix of traditional and modern sounds with a prestigious international line-up.

Set in the vast Jardins de Cimiez, the event features three separate stages, where groups perform simultaneously each evening, for 12 days in July. The atmosphere is a cross between a Gallic Woodstock and a musical fair: families arrive en masse with strollers, Grandma and the dog and spread picnics under the century-old olive trees, where piping-hot *socca* (a delicious savoury pancake made from chickpea flour) and sandwiches are sold. At the other end of the park is a dramatic 4,000-seat arena – a Roman amphitheatre, built in the 3rd century BC, which once featured javelin-throwing gladiators. At the festival it sometimes gets almost as wild. For information on the festival call (04) 93 87 19 18 or contact the Nice tourist office.

establishments offer excellent facilities at half the price charged down the coast at Cannes. One favourite is **Opéra Plage** ●, which claims to be the oldest in France, run by the same family since 1906, just a towel's shake from the old Opera House.

Just east of the Opera House, at 77 Quai des États-Unis, is the small but delightful **Musée Dufy** ● (open Tues–Sun; entrance fee). The museum puts on changing displays of Raoul Dufy's paintings, a great many of which were produced in Nice.

Traffic barrelling down the seafront vanishes into a tunnel in front of the old Opera House and emerges at the **port**, a long-neglected side of Nice which, with its disciplined quays lined with terracotta and ochre buildings, bobbing yachts and excellent restaurants, is the epitome of the Mediterranean harbour.

For a city whose history depends so much on the sea, the port is disappointingly bereft of attractions, its main attribute being the bathing rocks on its eastern edge from which you can see the Corsican ferry glide by. Just beyond the port, at 25 Boulevard Carnot, is the **Musée de Terra Amata** (open Tues–Sun; entrance fee; tel: (04) 93 55 59 93), an archaeological museum built on the site where human remains from around 400,000 BC were found.

A view of the city

For the best overview of what is not really a very complicated city you should have a car and drive east, up to the ruined fort of **Mont Alban**, approached through 140 hectares (345 acres) of municipal forest on Mont Boron, a good place for picnics. It is easy to see how the city has evolved in three different parts, with the **River Paillon** in the middle.

Don't bother searching for the river on a map; it is only a trickle and the entire riverbed has been covered over with a promenade, roads, parks, and hanging gardens hiding a bus terminus and car-park. This is the site of the **Acropolis** convention centre, decorated inside and out with the work of contemporary artists. Here also is the

BELOW: a private beach with loungers for hire.

Map on page 222

Musée d'Art Moderne et d'Art Contemporain  ❸ (open Wed–Mon; entrance fee; tel: (04) 93 62 61 62), a pet project of former mayor Jacques Médecin. The museum concentrates on French and American art from the 1960s to the present and attracts topnotch temporary exhibitions. Highlights include some iconic pieces of Pop Art and a room devoted to local hero Yves Klein.

To the southwest is **Place Masséna** ❻, the modern heart of the city, with its neoclassical red colonnades. This is the new town, with shops, hotels, and a pedestrian zone housing smart boutiques with all the big designer names. **Avenue Jean Médecin**, a wide thoroughfare lined with plane trees to the north of Place Masséna, is the main business and shopping street. Beyond Place Masséna the **Jardin Albert I** is a refreshing oasis of fountains.

The old town

BELOW: well-entrenched on the seafront.

To the east of the Paillon is the old town, signposted either as **Vieille Ville** or Vieux Nice. This has to be the *pièce de résistance*:

a cracked basin of russet, yellow, pink and beige earth tones. You are now entering the Painted City, where the municipality has breathed new life into the 13th century.

There is always a busy-ness about the place. For all its medieval seductions, scaffolding is a perpetual hazard and ladders and buckets of paint are winched away with bewildering urgency in a society more at ease with the Midi spirit of *farniente* (doing nothing). Look up and admire facades adorned with *trompe l'oeils* and frescoes, especially at the so-called Adam and Eve house in Rue de la Poissonnerie; the "Pistone" building in Rue du Marché; No. 27 Rue Benoît Bunico; and in Rue Pairolière, where the Maison de la Treille (the house with a climbing vine) inspired one of Raoul Dufy's pictures. The showpiece is the **Palais Lascaris** ❼ (15 Rue Droite; open Dec–Oct: Tues–Sun; tel: (04) 93 62 05 54), a 17th-century mansion now completely restored as an elegant museum, complete with pharmacy and a splendid open staircase in the Genoese style.

The streets become darker and narrower the further in you go, with intriguing scents and smells coming from the doorways. As you advance through the labyrinth, look at the lintels, some of which are inscribed with dates and incantations; INTERNA MELIORA – "Inside it's Better" – hangs over a former brothel on Rue de la Place Vieille.

The 18th-century **Place Garibaldi**, in the northern part of Vieux Nice, echoes the style of Place Masséna; nearby is the church of St-Martin-St-Augustin, where Garibaldi was baptised and Luther celebrated mass.

Place St-François is the morning fish market. **Rue Miralheti** is the place to sample classic street food such as *socca*, a chickpea pancake not found anywhere else in France. On Place Rossetti is the painted facade (1650) of the **Cathédrale de Ste-Réparate ⑪**, dedicated to the city's patron saint. Admire the bell tower and roof of coloured tiles. The square is also the best spot in town for coffee or ice-cream – try the home-made flavours at Fennocchio.

The markets

The promenade between the old town and the sea is known as **Cours Saleya ⑪**, the site of Nice's main market. Famous residents like Matisse, who lived at the end of the Cours in a big yellow house (No. 1: it has snarling faces of plaster lions protruding from it), and Chagall loved the city and their work fills the museums.

It was from his third-floor window in the Vieille Ville that Matisse painted those cheerful little pictures of the blue sea, the palm trees and the houses with green shutters. He surely also painted the market that is still held in the Cours, 600 metres (650 yards) long, separated from sea by the Ponchettes on one side and from the older part of town by the palace of the Sardinian kings, now housing the **Préfecture**, to the north. Don't miss the famous flower market open all day, or the fruit and vegetable market which vanishes at noon. On Mondays there is a large flea market. Although bargains are unlikely there is bountiful variety of antique furniture, china and linen.

BELOW: shellfish for sale on the Place St-François.

Map
on page
222

Artistic heritage

Nice has made an impressive contribution to the history of art; it first produced a school of primitive painters in the 15th and 16th centuries; it was home to the Van Loos in the 17th; Rodin worked here in the 19th and it has given its name to the modern École de Nice centred around Yves Klein, Arman and César. This was born in the Vieille Ville and some of the best young artists of modern France now have their ateliers on **Rue Droite**, so named not because it is straight but for the fact that it directly connected the two main gates of the old city.

Don't go looking for the château, by the way; it is just a trick of the tongue. One has not existed since the illegitimate son of James II razed it in 1706 on the orders of Louis XIV, thus sealing the fate of a citadel that was more than 2,000 years old. In its place, what is now called **Le Château** ❿ is just a 90-metre (300-ft) high hill with gardens, playgrounds, an artificial waterfall and a couple of discreet snack-bars – all very welcome on a hot day; but it's the panoramic views that attract people. There is a lift from the end of Quai des États-Unis.

Cimiez, a northern suburb

On a hill north of the city, the suburb of **Cimiez** is most easily reached from the Boulevard de Cimiez. Here, the Romans built their Cemenelum to compete with rival Greek Nikaïa down the road. It is noted for its excavated Roman ruins, including baths and an amphitheatre that is a venue for Nice's famous Jazz Festival.

Before you climb the hill, don't miss the **Musée Marc-Chagall** ⓚ (Ave Dr Ménard; open Wed–Mon; entrance fee; tel: (04) 93 53 87 20), specially designed to house Chagall's masterpiece, the *Messages Bibliques*, and the biggest single collection of his work.

At the top of the hill are the **Musée d'Archéologie** (open Tues–Sun; entrance fee; tel: (04) 93 81 59 57), which displays finds from the Roman town, and the much

BELOW: ruins of the Roman baths, Cimiez.

more popular **Musée Matisse**  (open Wed–Mon; entrance fee; tel: (04) 93 81 08 08), a 17th-century villa which cunningly conceals a gallery wing beneath. The latter houses Matisse's personal collection, with works from every period, as well as the vases, shell furniture and Moroccan wall-hangings – even the giant cheese plant, which he so often included in his paintings.

Once-fashionable Cimiez still has intimations of empire. The crowned heads of Europe – Britain, Sweden, Denmark, Portugal, Belgium and the entire Russian Imperial Family – once wintered up here in nine "palais-hotels" modelled on the ghastly Regina Palace, opened by Queen Victoria in 1897.

In the western suburbs, on boulevard du Tzarewitch, you can find evidence of the once-thriving Russian colony – the **Cathédrale St-Nicolas**, the finest Russian Orthodox church outside the motherland. Its five green-and-gold onion domes pleased Tsar Nicholas II himself. Services are held here in Russian.

Nice is nice

Nice might miss its castle but not much else. Despite being top dog in the holiday league with 8 million summer visitors and a comparatively small resident population of around 450,000, it hasn't allowed its character and unique ambience to be subsumed into soul-less skyscraper blocks. The airport still has orange trees in its car-park. Coconut-icing villas hide among the olives and parasol pines on the hills overlooking the bay. Tunnels of plane trees on the main streets, Boulevard Victor Hugo and Avenue Jean Médecin, lead to shaded squares and fountained gardens. Downtown, the *fin-de-siècle* glory of the buildings, all of uniform height and rococo charm, sings to you in friezes, frescoes and domed arpeggios. The city has a human scale. Nice really is nice.

It is a real gutsy town with its own gutsy wine (Bellet, whose vines were planted by the Phoenicians who founded Marseille), a commercial life based on more than just its flower industry and a cultural richness second only to Paris. It is also surprisingly

BELOW: pebbles and bodies.

Map on page 222

efficient and clean, equipped with automatic loos with piped muzak, spotless bus shelters and public phones which actually work. There are wardens employed to prevent vandalism in its 300 hectares (740 acres) of public greenery, and hundreds of gardeners who start work at 5am daily.

A modern metropolis

And for all its Mediterranean *laissez-faire*, Nice has developed into a highly modern city with state-of-the-art facilities: the Acropolis conference centre, in the middle of town, with a 2,500-seat auditorium; the Arénas business centre opposite the airport; the expensive and carefully landscaped Haliotis sewage plant; and Nikaïa, an 8,000-seat concert hall, opened in 2001 by Elton John, who has a villa east of the city on Mont Boron.

There is plenty of action, too. The city's opera, concert orchestra and international jazz festival are famous. Carnival has become a safer event now that the confetti is made of small bits of coloured paper rather than lumps of hard plaster (confetti once meant anything from small sugar-coated sweets to rotten eggs, flour, plaster, chickpeas, to egg-shells filled with soot and sand). The practice of throwing flowers became separated from the main event, and the Battle of Flowers is now an established attraction in its own right.

The Cours Saleya market in the Vieille Ville is perhaps the best place to take the pulse of Nice, a complete antidote to the pace of life on the other side of the Paillon. The performance is never-ending, though it is transformed dramatically with the firing of a mid-day gun. To the sound of flapping pigeon wings, the scenery changes miraculously as gangs of sweepers armed with brooms and high-pressure hoses march in and the market is cleaned up. Chairs and tables come out. Hardly a piece of ground is left unoccupied as the stage is set for a bravura performance of Niçois life. The whole place is turned into a sea of happy people absorbing the scene unfolding before them. ❑

BELOW: the flea market on Cours Saleya.

Map on page 236

CAP FERRAT AND THE GOLDEN TRIANGLE

East of Nice the coast becomes steeper and rockier, and drivers are tested on the tortuous corniche roads. Along the shore are old-fashioned towns like Villefranche and Beaulieu and the exclusive enclave of Cap Ferrat

The area known as the **Corne d'Or** – Golden Horn or Golden Triangle – which includes Cap Ferrat, Beaulieu and Villefranche is very different from the Côte d'Azur to the west. The terrain changes dramatically beyond Nice, from wide bays to towering cliffs. Every view is dominated by the mountains, giving it a grandeur that would be impossible to spoil – though thankfully, apart from in Monaco, no one has really tried.

The famous corniche roads between Nice and Menton, snake one above the other round the mountain side. Along the cliff top, the spectacular **Grande Corniche** (the high road) was built by Napoleon and follows the old Roman road, the Via Aurelia, to Italy. Cut into the rocks beneath it, the **Moyenne Corniche** (the middle road) is the most recently built of the three scenic routes. The **Basse Corniche** (the lower road) was built in the 18th century. It emerges from Nice at Port Douanges, then winds its way around the Cap de Nice, offering more lovely views across Villefranche Bay to the high ridge of Cap Ferrat. This, too, is a spectacular road, but it is often jammed with nose-to-tail traffic.

A medieval town

Villefranche-sur-Mer ❷ is a surprisingly unspoiled little town, given its proximity to Nice and the fact that the American 6th fleet used it as a base until the French left NATO. Villefranche was founded in the 14th century as a customs-free port by Charles II of Anjou and British and American ships still use its wonderful harbour, which is one of the deepest in the world.

The town itself has retained a homogenous, medieval character. The old streets, citadel and port are well restored but not bijou; there is plenty of authentic laundry hanging from the balconies and inquisitive matrons leaning from their windows to gossip across the narrow streets.

The old town of Villefranche, huddled around its protective citadel, is very Italian in its architecture and atmosphere; along the front of the old Port de la Santé the houses have a cheerful, faded air, each facade a different colour ranging from terracotta and ochre to rose and magnolia with the shutters painted half a dozen different shades of green. There are lots of attractive little bars and restaurants along the quay and in the alleyways leading to it. On the Quai Courbet stands the tiny 14th-century **Chapelle St-Pierre**, with a candy-coloured facade and interior decorated by

PRECEDING PAGES: the bay of Villefranche from Cap Ferrat.
LEFT: ochre hues in Villefranche.
RIGHT: Villa Kerylos, Beaulieu.

Jean Cocteau (1889–1963), who spent his childhood in Villefranche.

The huge 16th-century stone **Citadelle de St-Elme** dominates the bay and looks impregnable enough to still fulfil its original function, though the deep dry moat is now used as a car-park. It is like an enormous quarry, with sheer walls set at an angle for greater stability and tiny watchtowers and viaducts crossing on slender pylons. Within the walls are housed the town hall, the chapel of St-Elme, and a couple of museums.

The **Musée Goetz-Boumeester** is a collection of about 100 minor works by Picasso, Hans Hartung, Picabia and Miró. The sculptor Antoniucci Volti was a resident of Villefranche and the **Musée Volti** has a good collection of his monumental smooth figurative sculptures, most of them female, some of which are displayed outside in the main courtyard of the citadel (both museums open Dec–Oct: Wed–Mon; Sun afternoon only; free; tel: (04) 93 76 33 33).

Italianate architecture

Many of the houses in the old town are built on the Italian model with large arched loggias on the ground floor, most of which have subsequently been filled in. The area around the church features the steepest, most winding streets and twisted houses. The church itself is 18th-century Italian baroque, with little evidence left of its early 14th-century origin. It features many religious statues, including one of Jesus and another of Mary, both with an electric halo.

The town seems to specialise in *trompe l'oeil* wall paintings, usually of windows, often with cats in them. There is a good window with a cat on the **Place de la République**, a charming little square with a large shady pine tree in the centre and houses dating from the 17th and 18th centuries. The chapel on rue de l'Eglise is entirely painted with a *faux* Pisan Romanesque facade, which has what appears to be a genuine Pisan-style doorway dated 1590.

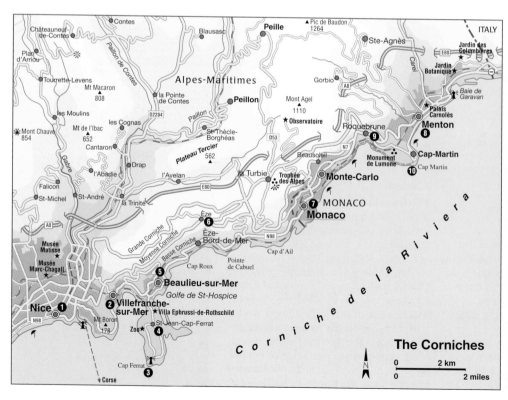

The Corniches

Map
on page
236

The main street of the old town is the **Rue du Poilu**, which leads to the tiny Place du Conseil, from which there is a good view of the harbour and Cap Ferrat. The lovely 13th-century **Rue Obscure** starts here. Steps lead down to an arched passage which has changed little since it was built; the street is almost entirely composed of covered passageways which the inhabitants could reach from back doors or intersecting streets and squares. This was the place people came for shelter whenever the town was bombarded, which, given its strategic position and excellent harbour, was often.

The point at which the Rue Obscure crosses the **Rue de l'Église** is perhaps the most picturesque spot in town. The blue waters of the harbour glint through an arch at the end of the street.

Home to a Rothschild

The turning off La Basse Corniche for **Cap Ferrat ❸** is marked, significantly, by a shop offering electronic surveillance

systems and 24-hour personal security. This is a very expensive, very private place but well worth a visit, if only to see how the other half live. The 10-km (6-mile) stretch of road that runs right round the Cap offers glimpses of luxurious villas and magnificent gardens, all hidden behind high hedges and impenetrable gates.

The narrowest part of the peninsula is dominated by the **Villa Ephrussi-de-Rothschild** (open daily; Nov–Jan: pm only Mon–Fri; entrance fee; tel: (04) 93 01 45 90), a prime example of how the other half used to live. Seven hectares (17 acres) of gardens spread right along the crest of the Cap with wonderful panoramic views on all sides. The pink-and-white *belle-époque* villa was built to house the personal art collection of the Baroness Ephrussi de Rothschild and includes a magnificent variety of mainly 18th-century furniture, porcelain, carpets and paintings. The ceilings were specifically designed around her Tiepolos.

The grand salon leads out on to a marble terrace with views to each side of the

BELOW: Villa Ephrussi-de-Rothschild on Cap Ferrat.

Cap and down to the gardens. They are perfect for gentle strolling, through the cactus grove, the Japanese garden, the Italian sunken garden with grotto, even a temple of Diana; all, it must be said, looking somewhat neglected. But sitting under the deep green shade of the umbrella pines, cooled by gentle breezes, looking out to an aquamarine sea, it is easy to understand the appeal of such a perfect place. It is an appeal felt more strongly perhaps by latter-day visitors than the Baroness herself, who didn't get around to visiting the mansion between World War I and her death in 1934.

Leopold, Somerset and Elton

Cap Ferrat has the reputation of having the most pleasant climate on the Riviera and it was for this reason that Leopold II, King of Belgium, bought it. He had a large park, Les Cèdres, laid out on the peninsula, and in its grounds built a palace for himself and three houses, one for each of his mistresses.

With so many mistresses at hand, Leopold became concerned that he might die without absolution, so in 1906, three years before his death, he built a house near his palace for his confessor Monseigneur Charmeton. In 1926, Somerset Maugham bought the house and its 3 hectares (7 acres) of terraced land. He called it the Villa Mauresque because Charmeton had had it designed in the Moorish style.

Leopold also established an exotic garden complete with a lake which has now been replaced by a small **zoo** (117 Blvd Général de Gaulle; open daily; entrance fee; tel: (04) 93 76 07 60). The animals include Himalayan bears and Siberian tigers.

In 1938, the Duke and Duchess of Windsor arrived on the Riviera, adding even more cachet to the already exclusive Cap Ferrat scene. They rented Sir Pomeroy Burton's villa where the duke dug the garden and the duchess kept house. The Duke insisted that his guests refer to the duchess as Her Royal High-

BELOW: La Radiana, a villa built for one of Leopold II's mistresses.

Map on page 236

ness, despite a strict edict from Buckingham Palace that she was not permitted to use such a title.

Soon the Cap was home to industrialists such as Singer, the sewing machine magnate, and a host of stars and celebrities like Charlie Chaplin, Edith Piaf, David Niven and Otto Preminger. More recent residents have included the Rolling Stones, who lived here as tax exiles, U2's Bono and Elton John.

Despite the predominance of private estates, a great deal of the natural beauty of the peninsula, which includes some of the oldest olive trees in France, can still be seen. There is a 10-km (6-mile) public footpath all around the headland. Most of it runs along the cliff edge, but parts of it take you down to sea level. The way is clearly marked: approaching from Villefranche, it begins at Plage de Passable and continues to St-Jean-Cap-Ferrat. Another promenade extends from the harbour at St-Jean-Cap-Ferrat around the Baie des Fourmis to Beaulieu-sur-Mer.

The village of **St-Jean-Cap-Ferrat** ❹ itself consists of little more than a beautiful yacht harbour, once home to fishing boats, lined with a few old houses and cafés, with a small residential area extending up the hillside. There is a one-way system in and out of the village and parking is often difficult. On the very tip of the Cap is the exclusive and fashionable **Grand Hôtel du Cap Ferrat**. The hotel and its gorgeous spill-over pool are set in wonderful gardens at the water's edge.

Faded grandeur

East of the Cap is **Beaulieu-sur-Mer** ❺, a town with an air of old-world refinement. Here, beach clothes anywhere other than the beach are still rather frowned upon, though all that is changing rapidly.

It always seems to be warm in Beaulieu, which claims to have the best climate on the coast, protected from the north wind by a great rock face. Hence its popularity as a retirement town, with many elegant rest homes and genteel

BELOW: old money never goes out of style.

hotels surrounded by softly waving palm trees, neatly clipped hedges and carefully weeded gardens. It is quietly stylish if a little old-fashioned, with shops offering goods of the highest quality.

It also boasts some of the best hotels on the Riviera; the Russian and British gentry spent their winters in Beaulieu, which used to be one of the most fashionable of the Riviera resorts. The elegant early 20th-century luxury hotels, known as the Riviera Palaces, in which they stayed are still there, surrounded by beautiful, well-tended gardens.

The **Promenade Maurice Rouvier** extends along the sea front and follows the coast of Cap Ferrat all the way to St-Jean-Cap-Ferrat, past villas and hotels with lush gardens. In the town the walk goes through formal flower gardens flanked by park seats looking out to Fourmis Bay.

The 11th-century Romanesque chapel near the old port is one of the few remaining indications of the town's long history. It has a fine round apse and round arches.

Also worth a visit is the **Villa Kerylos** (open mid-Dec–mid-Nov: daily; Dec–Feb pm only; entrance fee; tel: (04) 93 01 01 44), a complete reconstruction of a Greek villa with marble columns and cool courtyards open to the sky and sea, housing a large collection of mosaics, frescoes and antique furniture.

Village on a hill

Further along the Basse Corniche, the Commune of Èze has built a resort on the seafront of its land called Èze-Bord-de-Mer with its own private beach and Club Nautique. The next and last resort before Monaco is the secluded Cap d'Ail, a luxury retreat of private villas and hotels. Look out for **Plage la Mala**, a deservedly popular pebble beach.

Èze ❻ itself is accessible from the Moyenne Corniche. It is possibly the most *perché* of all the perched villages, with steep lanes, tiny twisting alleys and crooked steps. The rock upon which Èze is built is so sheer that very little fortification was ever needed and there are only two gates to the town.

The **Rue du Barri** climbs up steps, tunnels under houses and meanders over them. There are wonderful features to be seen at every turn; here a cluster of medieval chimneys, there a Romanesque window or tiny rooftop garden. Some of the houses are still dilapidated but the majority have been very well restored. With few residents remaining, Èze is more like an open-air museum, most of it given over to small shops, galleries and restaurants. From the terraces there are superb views of the surrounding cliffs and out to the Mediterranean.

A history of destruction

Èze has been on the brink of total destruction on a number of occasions, and its beleaguered past reflects the history of the region very well. For some of its history it has been nothing but a charred, empty ruin, at other times it has risen to become a great power. It began as a Ligurian settlement later fortified by the Phoenicians and developed by the Romans, who established a harbour in the bay below. After the

LEFT: the bride arrives at a wedding in Èze.

Map
on page
236

Romans came the Lombards, who in AD 578 murdered the inhabitants and burned the town to the ground. The Lombards held Èze until AD 740, when the Saracens appeared, enslaving any inhabitants they could capture and murdering the rest. It was they who built the first castle here.

Èze was one of the last strongholds of the Saracens; they were not driven from Provence until 980 and they razed the town when they left. After the Saracens, Èze was taken and retaken over and over, first by the Guelphs, then by the Ghibellines, then by the House of Anjou and the Counts of Provence. In the 14th century it was finally bought by Amadeus of Savoy, whose family retained control until the entire area was ceded to France in 1860.

During the Middle Ages, Èze became a centre of piracy, and vaulted passages and storerooms were built to hide their booty. A particularly nasty massacre took place in 1543 when the French army of Francis I aided by the Turkish fleet under the command of the corsair Barbarossa, launched an attack. Yet again, Èze was put to the sword. Street by street the inhabitants were slaughtered and the town looted then burned. The new Èze that slowly grew from the ruins, was struck again, this time by the 1887 earthquake which did more damage to the town and split what remained of the town walls. The village was abandoned and by the 1920s was almost completely depopulated.

Exploring Èze

Today there is little left of the castle, which is now surrounded by the **Jardin Exotique**, a fine collection of cacti and succulents. The village church was rebuilt in 1765, though a 16th-century font remains. The 14th-century **Chapelle des Pénitents Blancs** on the Place du Planet should not be missed. It has an unusual 1258 Catalan crucifix with Christ smiling. Other features of the village include the narrow path to the coast favoured by Frederich Nietzsche as he conceived *Thus Spake Zarathustra*. ❑

BELOW: a typically steep street in Èze.

MONACO

Ruled by the disaster-prone Grimaldi family, the principality of Monaco is a tax haven for the super-rich. Visitors can get a vicarious thrill by gazing at the huge yachts in the harbour and the big spenders in the casino

Maps on pages 236 & 246

The fiercest critic of **Monaco** ❼ was the writer Katherine Mansfield, who labelled it *"Real Hell*, the cleanest, most polished place I've ever seen." She preferred her home in sleepy Menton to this "procession of pimps, governesses in thread gloves – Jews – old, old hags, ancient men, stiff and greyish, panting on the climb, rich fat capitalists, little girls tricked out to look like babies".

Today, Mansfield might be charged with ageism, racism and snobbery. "Rich fat capitalists", for example, are now quite sleek through working out in Monte-Carlo Golf Club. And Monaco boasts an idyllic, natural setting, glamorous residents, Americanised culture and international cuisine. Yet Mansfield's repugnance does strike a chord, at least with ordinary visitors. Society runs like clockwork: toy-town guards seem to be everywhere; and multilingual signs tell visitors not to walk around "bare-chested or barefoot".

"To live in Monaco, all you need is good taste and a lot of money," proclaims the principality's *Society* magazine. Money is essential but good taste is optional, even a liability. In short, everything – except perhaps Monégasque citizenship – is available at a price. The writer Anthony Burgess, who was a long-term resident, once called Monaco "the most uncultivated community I've ever come across".

Money to burn

Mere creativity cannot compete with financial talk. Residents have the highest per capita income in the world. For its size, Monaco has arguably the greatest number of banks in the world. Its status as a tax haven has led to Monaco's claim to hold $25 billion in deposits, 60 percent belonging to non-residents. In fact, out of a population of 32,000, only 7,000 residents are Monégasques. The rest are primarily French, Italian, British and German.

This pocket handkerchief of a country could fit neatly into New York's Central Park. Monaco's critics call it a princely theme park where fairy-tale lifestyles are shrewdly sold. The principality's tourist board boasts of *"Monaco – un rêve, une réalité".* Writer Jeffrey Robinson pokes gentle fun at the nonchalant vulgarity of the Monaco jet set. "On a grand yacht, a Chinese waitress lays a buffet for 20 guests who will shortly be leaving on a two-hour cruise to nowhere, burning 6,000 euros worth of gasoline in the process."

Sea, skyscrapers and mountains form concentric circles around the headland that is Monaco. A looming crag, the Tête de Chien, is the backdrop to Monaco-Ville, the medieval quarter built on Le Rocher. The

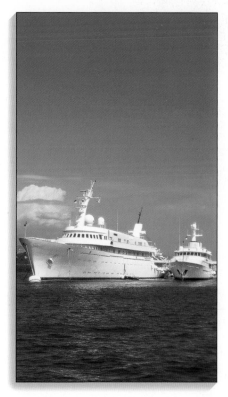

Rock is flanked by two harbours, the artificial Port de Fontvieille to the west and the original Port de Monaco to the east. From here to Monte-Carlo stretches the Condamine quarter, an area in which *belle-époque* villas are fast giving way to high-rise sprawl. Monte-Carlo, a skyscraper-studded hill, has been dubbed "Manhattan-sur-Mer" or "Las Vegas-Plage".

Princely sights

From the Place d'Armes it is a short, steep walk up to the **Palais du Prince** (open Jun–Oct: daily; entrance fee; tel: (00 377) 93 25 18 31), Rainier's official winter residence. The walk, linking the port and the palace, leads through medieval gateways. Until 1863, the gates to the old town were closed at night, much to the annoyance of sociable Monégasques. The final arch, La Rampe Major, opens on to Place du Palais, known as *Placa d'u Palaci* in Mongasque, a Provençal-Genoese dialect. The square is dotted with old cannons, some presented by Louis XIV to the Grimaldi Dynasty.

The salmon-pink palace was pale yellow until it was redesigned by Princess Grace. When a red and white diamond-spangled banner is flying, the Prince is in residence and the Palace is closed to the public. Visitors who arrive at 11.55 will see the changing of the guard, a daily ceremony performed by the Prince's French *carabinieri*. The Constitution forbids the use of Monégasque guards, a precaution designed to prevent a coup d'état. Depending upon the season, the *carabinieri* are dressed in winter blue and red-striped uniforms or in dazzling white.

The State Apartments are sumptuous recreations of palatial 17th- and 18th-century decor. The Cour d'Honneur, an Italianate quadrangle, forms the backdrop for concerts. However, the most appealing room is the Chambre d'York, where the Duke of York, George III's brother, died. He was on his way to visit a mistress in Genoa when he was taken ill off Monaco. Here, reported Horace Walpole, "the poor Duke of York has ended his silly, good-

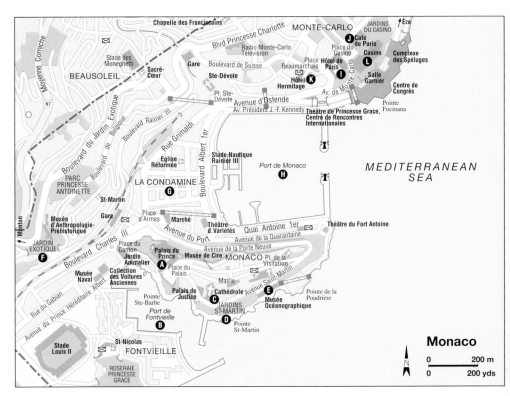

Map on page 246

humoured, troublesome career in a piteous manner." Still, he chose a bedchamber with a frescoed ceiling, Venetian furniture and a gilt-encrusted, canopied bed.

From outside the palace, there are fine views over the **Port de Fontvieille** Ⓑ, a hugely successful development. Built on 30 hectares (74 acres) of reclaimed land, it half-heartedly combines high-rises with Provençal colours. Also down below is the Parc de Fontvieille, the Princess Grace Rose Garden and the Terasses de Fontvieille, a complex of several museums: the **Collection des Voitures Anciennes** (the Prince's vintage cars; open daily; entrance fee; tel: (00 377) 92 05 28 56), a **Musée Naval** (model ships; open daily; entrance fee; tel: (00 377) 92 05 28 48) and a **Musée des Timbres et des Monnaies** (stamps and coins; open daily; entrance fee; tel: (00 377) 93 15 41 50).

In the 1970s, Prince Rainier realised that he had to expand Monaco's economic base so created this quarter as a home to non-pollutant light industry, especially perfumes and electronics. These industries now produce around 30 percent of state revenue while value-added tax provides about 50 percent and, contrary to popular belief, gambling brings in less than 5 percent. As Rainier put it: "Nowadays we probably have as many gardeners as croupiers." In fact, the proliferation of gardeners and gendarmes is proof that Monaco is a civil servants' paradise.

Monaco-Ville

From the Palace, a stroll through the old quarter leads to the cathedral and exotic gardens. This area is a labyrinth of covered passageways, tiny squares, fountains and tangerine-coloured facades. Rue Basse has old porticoed houses with carved lintels and vaulted cellars. But in the height of summer it is hard to appreciate the architecture since the quarter is given over to tawdry tourist trinkets, including Princess Caroline T-shirts and Princess Stephanie's albums. The **Cathédrale** Ⓒ dominates a rocky spur, like the figurehead of a boat.

BELOW: the 253-room Palais du Prince.

The clinical white building was built in 1884 on the site of a medieval church. Designed in neo-Romanesque style with Byzantine flourishes, it is at once majestic and oppressive. The greatest treasures lie in the Chapelle des Princes, the Grimaldi burial chamber. Princess Grace's tomb is nearby, adorned with fresh pink roses. Above is a series of lovely paintings, including the St Nicolas altarpiece by Louis Bréa, the great Niçois artist.

Goldfish and sharks

Just outside the cathedral are the lush **Jardins St-Martin** ⓓ, descending to the sea. Tiers of Aleppo pines and yellow agaves wind around the headland. The gardens are dotted with 18th-century turrets and medieval fortifications. In these manicured and neatly labelled gardens, bossy signs forbid the feeding of goldfish and cats. In fact, the goldfish are fat enough already and the teams of uniformed gardeners are a definite cat-deterrent. Visitors who stop too often are virtually taken in for questioning.

From here the Avenue St-Martin leads to the **Musée Océanographique** ⓔ (open daily; entrance fee; tel: (00 377) 93 15 36 00), founded in 1910 by Prince Albert I. Known as the Navigator Prince, Albert is the best-loved of previous sovereigns. He dedicated his life to the oceans and this "temple of the sea" is his memorial. The undoubted star is the aquarium, a surreal home to weird species: secretive crabs called *dromies* hide in sponges clutched in their back legs; *Bernard l'Hermite* travels with a sea anemone permanently lodged on his back; the noble female octopus waits weeks for her eggs to hatch on her tentacles; as soon as her offspring are born, she dies, exhausted.

One of the most startling sights is not a fish at all but a model of a live coral reef taken from the waters off Djibouti. Children are drawn to the huge tank of cat-sharks and black-tip reef shark, which constantly circle a wrecked boat alive with yellow and blue surgeon fish. Elsewhere a new tank shimmers with the colours of rare

BELOW: the love of money.

Map on page 246

tropical fish. It is a sobering thought that every morning the aquarium occupants devour over 4,000 kg (8,800 lb) of mussels, sardines, seafood cocktail and spinach.

Hanging gardens

From Monaco-Ville a short bus journey or steep walk leads to the equally surreal environment of the **Jardin Exotique ❻** (open daily; entrance fee; tel: (00 377) 93 15 29 80). These tropical gardens are set just below the Moyenne Corniche. A former mayor of Monaco likened them to the Hanging Gardens of Babylon, exotic praise for gardens on the same latitude as Vladivostok. Naturally, it is Monaco's balmy climate that fosters plants normally found in Madagascar or Southern California.

Landscaping the cliffs was a mammoth feat of engineering, taking 20 years to complete. The result is breathtaking: tiered gardens are interlinked by high footbridges and canopies of vegetation; secluded spots are formed by pergolas and arbours; an ornamental pond is enclosed by jungle-like greenery. To weed the gardens specialists have to be suspended in parachute harnesses over the cliff. The stars are the fierce-looking cacti and succulents.

Amongst the 8,000 species of plants are Mexican yuccas, Peruvian monster candles and Moroccan euphorbia that grow up to 15 metres (50 ft) high. Prickly pears, red aloes and downy-eared elephant ears climb up the rocky vaults. The most striking plant is the Mexican echinocactus: it resembles a spiky hedgehog and is better known as "mother-in-law's pillows".

At the foot of the Jardin Exotique is a series of strange caves known as the **Grottes de l'Observatoire**. A precarious descent through the garden is followed by slippery steps leading down to the bottom of the caves. All around are stalagmites and stalactites, ice-blue pools and natural sculptures. The majestic Grande Salle resembles the inside of a cathedral, with Romanesque pillars and baptismal fonts. The galleries are impressive for their silence, broken only by the faint dripping of water.

BELOW: the Hong Kong of the Med.

Builder prince

Between Monaco-Ville and Monte-Carlo is the port-side business area known as **La Condamine** . The railway brought prosperity but lemon groves were supplanted by villas and now skyscrapers. Not for nothing is Rainier known as the Builder Prince. Princess Grace complained that one couldn't sunbathe on the beach after 3pm because of long shadows cast by the skyscrapers. But now no one claims responsibility for the Californian-style patios, hexagonal skyscrapers and a disfigured skyline. The prince's latest building project, completed in 2000, is the seaside Grimaldi Forum, a huge arts and convention centre situated in the northeastern part of Monaco, the Larvotto district.

La Condamine faces the **Port de Monaco** , which is striking enough, particularly if filled with magnificent cruise liners. From the golden years of the 1950s onwards, Aristotle Onassis's boat *Christina* was moored here and often welcomed Princess Grace aboard. The 1960s and '70s saw the jetset take to water, with or without Greek shipping tycoons.

Here, Charles Revlon, the cosmetics tycoon, dreamed up new products on his opulent *Ultima II*. Times have indeed changed: Donald Trump had his boat impounded for failing to settle debts. Current visitors are more likely to be bored Italian industrialists or Brazilian gamblers.

Monte-Carlo

Beyond La Condamine is the district of Monte-Carlo. In the right company, and with the right income, **Monte-Carlo** is still a name to conjure with. However, the only magical area is the Place du Casino and the Square Beaumarchais. As well as the Casino and the Salle Garnier, this golden square boasts the Hôtel de Paris, the Café de Paris and the Hôtel Hermitage, haunts worth visiting for their architecture as well as their atmosphere. Until the building of the Place du Casino, the steep-sided Mont Charles hill was known as a "desert riddled with insalubrious

BELOW: cacti in the Jardin Exotique.

Map
on page
246

caves". In 1886 the new railway brought aristocratic visitors to gamble in a *belle-époque* setting – and the rest is history.

The **Hôtel de Paris** ❶ has a delightful setting, overlooking the lush Casino gardens, the Café de Paris and the sea. Built in 1864, this inspirational hotel set the tone for the rest. It was designed with unbridled extravagance and borrows from an earlier rococo style. Exquisite details include the gracious rotunda with its fan-shaped portico, the curvaceous cupolas and the facades decorated with bare-breasted figureheads. The interior is equally captivating, with caryatids adorning the reception rooms and restaurants.

Alain Ducasse, one of the world's top chefs, presides over the Louis XV restaurant, following in the footsteps of the great Escoffier. The Louis XV is a neo-baroque concoction with cream and gold decor surpassed by a frescoed ceiling. Here, Ducasse pampers the privileged with Italo-Provençal cuisine. Guests include Sophia Loren, Ringo Starr and Roger Moore, all of whom have apartments in Monaco. The Salle Empire restaurant is equally luxurious, decorated with frescoes of bathing nymphs. On its opening night in 1866, the restaurant served caviare and pink champagne, and little has changed since then. Le Grill rooftop restaurant appeals to (slightly) younger jetsetters, including Boris Becker, Björn Borg and various Formula One racing drivers. Still, this motley crew of sportsmen and stars pales in comparison with the procession of grand dukes, royals and statesman who once peopled the hotel. After losing her last 100,000 francs in the Casino, Sarah Bernhardt made a failed suicide bid in her suite here. In more recent times, Onassis retained a suite for his special house guests, including Winston Churchill and his pet parrot. Here, Churchill and Lord Beaverbrook once polished off a bottle of 1815 cognac before breakfast.

In 1943, the Hôtel de Paris was occupied by the Gestapo. In theory, Monaco was neutral but Rainier's grandfather

BELOW: view of Monaco from the corniche road.

Grimaldi Inc.

Thanks to the business acumen of the present ruler, Rainier III, Monaco is now run like a family firm – Grimaldi Inc. The Grimaldi are Europe's oldest reigning family and the last constitutional autocrats. The male line has twice died out but then sovereignty has passed through the female line. Yet the throne is never totally secure.

This old Ligurian family from Genoa were exiled during the medieval political struggle between Guelphs and Ghibellines. The Grimaldi clan found a new power base in Monaco in 1297 and have ruled there ever since. Legend has it that a woman wronged by Rainier I put a curse on the Grimaldi line, denying them lasting happiness.

Until the French Revolution, the princes lived on taxes levied on wine, lemons, tobacco, shipping and playing cards. Menton and Roquebrune formed part of Monaco until 1848 and their loss reduced Monaco's territory by 94 percent. However, the creation of

Monte-Carlo by Charles III delivered Monaco to grand tourism, which flourished until the reign of Louis II, Prince Rainier III's grandfather. Rainier's mother, Princess Charlotte, was the fruit of Louis' liaison with a washerwoman he met in North Africa. Rainier, educated in England and Switzerland, is the first prince to have been born in Monaco and is also the first full-time sovereign. After acceding to the throne in 1949, Rainier set about running Monaco as a business empire, reducing its dependence on gambling.

Rainier's marriage in 1956 to the Hollywood star Grace Kelly brought a new glamour to Monaco, and her tragic death in a car accident in 1982 was a great blow. Grace's legacy lies in the Americanisation of Monaco, from the business ethos to the sophisticated social life, from the street names to the shopping malls. The Gallerie du Sporting is typical Monaco franglais, in keeping with Rainier's mixed marriage. The greatest crisis of his reign was in 1962, when President de Gaulle, trying to stop French citizens settling in Monaco to avoid paying French taxes, sealed off Monaco's borders until Rainier conceded the issue.

In 1997, Monaco celebrated 700 years of independence with great celebrations. However, the fortunes of the principality are far from secure. The 1990s saw a significant drop in tourism and disastrous losses for the casino business. And, as with the rest of the Côte d'Azur, financial scandals began to emerge. In 2000, a French parliamentary commission reported that Monaco's fortune was built on dirty money and that the state-owned casino may be complicit in money-laundering, particularly embarrassing as Rainier is one of the casino's directors.

The rest of the family has not escaped the Grimaldi curse. Princess Stephanie's trail of broken romances (and failed careers) has resulted in three illegitimate children, a scandal involving her bodyguard ex-husband and a Belgian stripper, and a recent liaison with a Swiss elephant-tamer. Princess Caroline, the eldest, lost her second husband to a boating accident in 1990 and now spends most of her time away from Monaco with her new husband, the Prince of Hanover. To cap it all, Rainier's health is in decline, and Prince Albert, his heir apparent, shows no sign of marrying, let alone producing an heir of his own. ❏

LEFT: Rainier III: victim of a woman's curse?

Map
on page
246

supported the Vichy régime. Goering and Himmler used the principality as a place for laundering war spoils. The hotel manager feared for the loss of his finest wines and cognacs so concealed them in a crypt at the bottom of the cellar. The other bottles were drunk but his cache remained intact. It is still the deepest hotel wine cellar in the world and boasts a "champagne alley" with bottles dating back to 1805.

Edwardian grandeur

Situated on the far corner of the square, the **Café de Paris** ❶ was once an equally glamorous location. It was built in 1865 but acquired an art deco interior in the 1920s. The overall effect is seaside Edwardian, with a delicious peaches and cream facade adorned with a fan-shaped portico. Floral mosaics and stained-glass designs lend sophistication to the interior. However, the Café's claim to fame is linked to the womaniser, Edward VII. Legend has it that Escoffier was preparing a special dessert which accidentally caught fire. Edward's

companion was Suzette and the *flambé* was christened *crêpe suzette* in her honour.

Just around the corner on Place Beaumarchais is the **Hôtel Hermitage** ❿, the loveliest of the *belle-époque* hotels. It also lays claim to being the most discreet, not that anywhere with gold-encrusted cupids and rococo guests should be so bold. It has a dramatic setting above the port and opposite the Rock. Built in 1890, the hotel indulges in soft lines and sensual sculptures. With its understated elegance, the glass-domed Jardin d'Hiver is the ideal winter garden. Light is filtered through a stained-glass sunflower, a cool scene complemented by lush ferns and wrought-iron balconies.

The Casino

Terraced gardens and fountains lead down to the green-domed **Casino** ❶ (open daily; pm only; entrance fee; tel: (00 377) 92 16 20 00) and the sea. Amongst the lushness are pineapple-shaped palms, ferns and figs, jacaranda and magnolia. The Casino was

BELOW: the Grimaldis at the baroque Monte-Carlo opera house.

created by Prince Florestan, the founder of Monte-Carlo. The Prince wanted a world stage for Monaco arts and, having lost Monégasque territory to France, also needed to generate new revenue. Inspired by the success of aristocratic tourism in Baden Baden, he realised that good health and gambling were a winning combination.

Early attempts were unsuccessful but the Casino's luck changed when François Blanc, a fraudster, bought the concession. He was helped by the arrival of the railway and by his European gambling monopoly. Business boomed in the *belle époque*.

Occasionally, lucky gamblers would "break the bank". If so, the coffers were ostentatiously refilled since Blanc shrewdly realised, "One winner always attracts a crowd of losers." One lucky loser was a bankrupt Pole who tried to commit suicide. With admirable sense of public relations, the Casino gave him a room in the Hôtel de Paris and presented him with a ticket home. Cunning not charity was the name of the game.

But Lord Salisbury, Queen Victoria's long-serving prime minister, was refused admission to the Casino, having come to the Riviera without his passport. "You see, I'm the man who issues them," was not considered a good enough excuse.

World War I brought the end to grand tourism and Monte-Carlo faced competition from casinos in Cannes, Menton and Nice. In 1951, soon after Prince Rainier came to power, Aristotle Onassis took over the Casino. While Onassis wanted to maintain the Casino as a glamorous preserve, Rainier wanted to open up Monaco to bourgeois tourism. After a showdown in 1962, Rainier wrested control and made the state the principal shareholder.

Gambler's paradise

Today, the Casino retains much of its old glamour and strict rules. A sign forbids ministers of religion or Monégasques to enter the *salles de jeux*. If the Grimaldi attend an opera in the Casino's Salle Garnier, they have to enter through a side door.

BELOW: residents have the highest per capita income in the world.

Map
on page
246

The Casino is decorated in exuberant *belle-époque* style. Daylight filters through stained-glass domes and windows; bronze lamps are held aloft by sculpted nymphs.

To admire the architecture, one should come in the late afternoon but for atmosphere only the late evening will do. In the *salons privés*, serious bets are laid by cigar-smoking gamblers with glazed expressions. Games include roulette, craps, blackjack, baccarat and *chemin de fer*. Spectators eddy from table to table and sound is reduced to low murmurs and sliding chips. No one drinks; gambling is the only addiction.

The entrance staircase boasts a sculpted palm, welcoming one to the Salon des Palmiers and the summery feel of the Casino. Yet the *salons ordinaires* are disappointing. The slot machines seem out of place beside gilded mirrors, chandeliers, cut flowers and Fragonard paintings. In the plush Salon Rose bar, gamblers play on space invaders; on the ceiling, sculpted nudes puff cigars, a reminder that this was once the smoking-room. Just off these public rooms is Le Train Bleu, a chic restaurant modelled on the famous train that brought high society to the Riviera.

High stakes

The *salons privés* are only private insofar as there is a second admission charge. That said, stakes are much higher and non-gamblers are discouraged by the door manager's penetrating gaze. This is no mere doorman but someone with a photographic memory for matching faces to gambling history. The most famous of these "physiognomists" was Monsieur le Broq, who claimed to have memorised over 60,000 faces. The Casino's main "bank" can also be made to vanish down a trap-door in the event of a hold-up.

In the *salons privés* there is a high ratio of croupiers to clients. The croupiers are Las Vegas-trained and form the most powerful lobby in Monaco. When workers went on strike in 1968, the croupiers were

BELOW:
high rollers
at the Casino.

the only ones who picketed in Cadillacs. John Addington Symonds had little good to say of the breed in 1866: "The croupiers are either fat, sensual cormorants or sallow, lean-cheeked vultures, or suspicious foxes."

In the 1970s many of the major players were Arabs. Adnan Khashoggi and Prince Fahd played for $2 milion bets and insisted on playing alone. The Casino encourages the maximum number of players to spread the risk so was not pleased by the Arabs' dramatic winnings. To save its skin, the Casino made a deal: the Arabs could play in private at any time of day or night but had to stay until 6am and stop then, whatever the outcome. The Arabs tired and the Casino won.

Nowadays, the big gamblers tend to be Italian or South American. According to Raoul Bianchieri, the head of SBM: "There are big fortunes in South America, and they are gamesters by temperament." Because of his power in Monaco, Bianchieri is known as "the other prince".

From the Casino, a period lift leads to Le Cabaret, a kitsch restaurant and floor show. Couples are tucked into pink velvet alcoves. The main lighting is provided by bare-breasted Amazons, lamps swathed in gold lamé below the waist. Between courses, artistes perform compulsory card tricks at one's table. After the cabaret, diners are photographed, presented with a plate of chocolates, then expected to dance. For less exhibitionist diners there is Les Privés, a discreet restaurant-bar overlooking the sea.

The **Salle Garnier**, inside the Casino complex, is the prestigious setting for opera, ballet and concerts. It was here that Diaghilev's *Ballets Russes* once performed to great acclaim. Monte-Carlo has a noted orchestra which stages summer concerts in the medieval Fort Antoine.

All the right parties

The Red Cross Gala is the society event of the year, an occasion for the richest society ladies to flaunt their jewels. It is held at the Monte-Carlo Sporting Club, not

LEFT: changing the guard in toy-town. **BELOW:** Princess Caroline.

Map on page 246

a sports club at all. According to Prince Albert, a bobsleigh champion, "to be a good Monégasque, you have to be sporty".

The major event is, of course, the Monaco Grand Prix. This dangerous circuit involves 78 laps around the port, the Hôtel Hermitage and the Place du Casino. The timing is perfect: it takes place immediately after the Cannes Film Festival so there are still plenty of stars around.

Stirling Moss, who won three times, loved the atmosphere. "When I was racing, I'll never forget looking at a beautiful young girl with pale lipstick who was always sitting in front of Oscar's bar. Every time I passed, I blew her a kiss. This sort of thing is only possible in Monaco."

During the Monte-Carlo season, evening is the time for dazzling displays of wealth. Stretch limousines ferry bronzed and bejewelled celebrities between the Hôtel de Paris, the Casino and Jimmy'z, Monte-Carlo's fashionable night spot.

But these are troubled times for the Principality, which celebrated its 700th year in 1997. The Grimaldi family seems beset by tragedy and scandal and there has been a significant drop in tourism *(see page 252)*. Private snapshots of Monaco also reveal the downside. The ultra-discreet set do not stir from their security-conscious apartments, especially since the mysterious death (possibly a murder) of billionaire resident Edmond Safra in his home in 1999. In the Salle Garnier, a world-weary tycoon feigns an interest in the latest cultural offering and wonders why the Grimaldis always select such obscure operas. Next door, in Le Train Bleu, a *grande dame* toys with her caviare, briefly leaving the table to place a losing bet on number 22, her lover's age.

Visitors listen to a Mozart recital in Fort Antoine, the open-air theatre. Monégasque bank clerks and shopkeepers watch their football team play Marseille. A bored croupier polishes his buttons. An Italian tourist wonders how a slice of Parma ham and melon can cost 45 euros. "*Monaco – un rêve, une réalité.*" ❑

BELOW: the glittering Port of Monaco.

Maps:
Area 236
Town 262

MENTON

Still redolent of an earlier era of aristocratic tourism, Menton has a noticeably Italian look and a number of spectacular gardens. Just down the coast are the villas of Cap Martin and the fortified village of Roquebrune

"Nowhere else have I felt such complete happiness," declared Franz Liszt of Menton ❽. Sheltered by mountains, the town basks in an enchanted setting with 300 days of sun a year. In this tropical greenhouse, Mexican and North African vegetation flourishes in a climate at least 2°C warmer than in Nice. *Belle-époque* villas aside, one could easily be in Sicily. But in the 19th century Menton's charm was as a winter sanatorium rather than as a hothouse. Royal visitors such as Queen Victoria and Edward VII helped Menton acquire a reputation as the most aristocratic and anglophile of all the Riviera resorts.

Nowadays the dowager-like image has softened: Menton is cosy rather than genteel, anglophile rather than aristocratic. Certainly, the presence of Italian executives and holiday-makers has revived the town, especially since the joining of Menton with Ventimiglia in 1993, as the European Union's first joint urban community, when frontier posts, municipal and business activities were combined.

Foreign history

Originally Genovese, Menton became part of the Principality of Monaco in 1346 and by and large remained a Grimaldi possession until 1860. However, the Grimaldi astutely placed Menton under the protection of the rising political powers, a form of opportunism still practised by the present Monégasque rulers. In succession, Menton became a Spanish, French and Sardinian protectorate. Given such a cosmopolitan past, it is hardly surprising that Menton can feel so deliciously foreign.

In 1848, Menton rebelled against high Monégasque taxes on oil and fruit. Along with Roquebrune, the town declared itself a republic but this was shortlived and in 1861 Monaco sold both towns to France. This coincided with the beginning of grand tourism and Menton was one of the first health resorts to benefit, thanks to the favourable publicity generated by Dr Bennet. The English doctor promoted Menton's mild climate as perfect for invalids so British and Germans flocked to winter here.

Exploring the town

Set just behind the seafront, the sweetly scented **Jardin Biovès** Ⓐ is a natural introduction to flowery Menton. Facing inland, one's eye is drawn to the gentle gradations of colour and height: lush pink borders and serried ranks of palms and citrus trees that fade to distant mauve hills. The lemon trees are carefully decorated with fairy lights. In the evening glow, the park's cosy prettiness envelops passers-by in a cloying embrace.

PRECEDING PAGES: the old town and beachfront, Menton.
LEFT: a local fisherman.
RIGHT: Catholic imagery.

A voluptuous tone is set by a reclining nude statue and by a fountain dedicated to the "goddess of the golden fruits". Nearby, boughs of sharp Seville oranges and sweet Genoese mandarins intermingle with the Mentonnais lemon, the town's trademark. This oval-shaped lemon, introduced in the 14th century, is noted for its gorgeous scent and unacidic flavour. The Mentonnais boast that it keeps for months longer than its common Portuguese rival.

During the spring *Fête du Citron* the park looks good enough to eat. The fruit, moulded into such shapes as boats and cathedrals, attracts 300,000 visitors every year. When not pressed into promoting the tourist industry, the Menton lemon can be sampled as a refreshing *citron pressé* – at Parisian prices, of course. Menton's sweet aftertaste conceals very sharp marketing.

Overlooking the park is the splendid **Palais de l'Europe**, once the city's grand casino and now home to the helpful tourist office. The present Casino, facing out on to the seafront, is a staid affair, reduced to seaside cabaret, sedate *thés dansants* and low-key gambling. As if in disapproval, St John's Anglican church turns its back on the Casino. The church provides retired British expatriates with spiritual counselling, fêtes and free library books.

On the promenade

In the afternoon, elderly visitors congregate on the **Promenade du Soleil ⓑ** to enjoy the sea views. Along the seafront are vestiges of *belle-époque* villas, epitomised by the charmingly dilapidated Le Pin Doré and similar pastel-coloured hotels. Many of the finest villas have been converted into chic flats or homes for retired French civil servants. Below the Promenade du Soleil sun-seekers stretch out on boulders or on pocket handkerchiefs of sand.

Nearby, genteel dowagers sip afternoon tea in seaside *salons de thé*. Yet in keeping with the changing times, the cafés cater to both ends of the social scale, serving anything from chilled Chablis and bouillabaisse to hot dogs and Coke. In

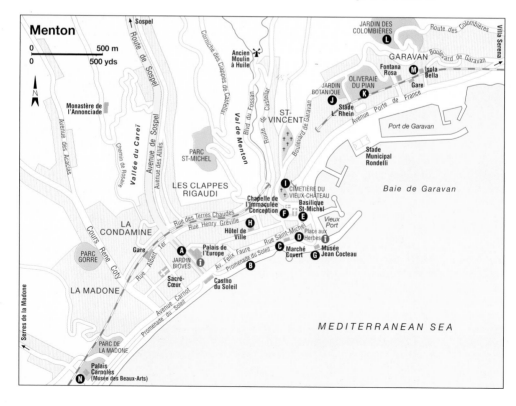

Map on page 262

general, however, Menton's sea views are more memorable than its cuisine.

At the eastern end of the Promenade, the *belle-époque* quarter merges into Vieux Menton, the pedestrianised old town. The **Marché Couvert** ⊙ (open every morning) provides the quirky link between the two quarters. The market, topped by a decorative clocktower, is adorned with comical sculpted faces. The profusion of lemons, figs and artichokes is a match for the market's green, yellow and brown ceramics.

Fish dishes

Rue des Marins, beside the market, is still the centre of Menton's small but thriving fish trade. As the only medieval guild to have survived on the Riviera, it retains a symbolic importance in local eyes. The trade, passed from father to son, is based on small fry such as sardines and anchovies. In spring, anchovies are attracted to Menton's warm water and by May the season is underway. May is also the traditional time for salting and storing. Sardines, still fished

BELOW: the Plage des Sablettes, abutting the old town.

from February to April, are eaten fried with lemon or in a spicy *omelette de poutines*.

Restaurants around the market are a good place to sample the local fish dishes, including *stockfisch*, spiced with garlic and white wine before being flambéed in cognac. A typical accompaniment to fish is *fleurs farcies*, courgette flowers stuffed with cheese, tomatoes and garlic. Aromatic *Côtes-de-Provence Blanc* is a good wine choice.

Beside the Marché Couvert is the Place du Marché, with its flower stalls doing a brisk trade in young lemon trees and cacti. Next door is the **Place aux Herbes** ⊙, a charming arcaded square. Ignore the antique shop, lavender stalls and North African trinket-sellers. Instead, focus on the chestnut trees, fountain and statue, best appreciated from an outdoor café. Place aux Herbes leads to the bustling **Rue St-Michel**, Menton at its most commercial. Avenue Félix Faure and Rue St-Michel provide ample opportunity to stock up on designer luggage, Provençal herbs and lemon-scented soap.

The cathedral quarter

Seen from the old fishing harbour, Vieux Menton is stacked on the hillside, framed by rugged mountains and shimmering reflections. From here, the towers of the cathedral, the **Basilique St-Michel** , and two nearby chapels appear inseparable. From Quai Bonaparte, steep steps lead to a pebble-mosaic courtyard of striking Italianate design. Just above is the pink and ochre cathedral, flanked by two steeples.

The cathedral was begun in 1619 by Honoré II of Monaco, but its facade and atmosphere are essentially baroque. Inside are several heavily restored chapels which were damaged in the 1887 earthquake. Just outside is the Place de l'Église, the setting for Menton's celebrated *Juillet Musicale* and August Festival of Chamber Music. This sunken square has excellent acoustics, framed by the cathedral and chapel yet open to the sea on one side. The unexpected blend of intimacy and sea views has also made it a much sought-after film location.

Next door, the apricot-tinged **Chapelle de l'Immaculée Conception** is a much creamier affair. It was built in 1687 for the Pénitents Blancs, a lay confraternity who sought to return to a simpler faith. The 1887 earthquake damaged the church, but after being restored in 1987 it is now the city's pride and joy. Depending on taste, the baroque interior is either garish or exuberant. It is lit by old coaching lamps but locals gaze up at the *lanteron* to appreciate the natural light. The *pièce de résistance* is the ceiling representing Heaven, a Mediterranean paradise with golden figures and blue skies. In the Hôtel de Ville, Cocteau's pastiche of a Mediterranean marriage shows the same *joie de vivre*.

The cathedral quarter, dating from the 16th century, is the oldest part of town. It is also the poorest, populated by Algerian and Moroccan immigrants as well as Mentonnais craftsmen. Renovation has yet to make an impact on this warren of vaulted brick and cobbled streets. Ramparts from the old fortress have been

BELOW: Cocteau mural in the Salle des Mariages.

Map
on page
262

incorporated into existing buildings. Blind alleys end with tiny stone houses decorated with drying peppers.

Cocteau's local legacy

After running the gauntlet of the lavender sellers on Rue St-Michel, head for the Bastion on the seafront. This fort was built in 1636, when Menton's Spanish rulers feared a French attack. The orange-brick bastion now houses the **Musée Jean Cocteau** Ⓖ (open Wed–Mon; entrance fee; tel: (04) 93 35 49 71), in homage to the painter and poet who once lived locally. Cocteau himself oversaw the restoration of the fort, designing the mosaic flooring and the bright tiling on the four turrets. He donated numerous works to the museum but sadly did not live to see the opening in 1967.

The ground floor, formerly the arms store, contains brilliantly coloured abstractions, powerful self-portraits and *Judith and Holopherne*, Cocteau's first tapestry. Matisse loved it, praising this depiction of seduction, murder and flight as *"la seule vraie tapisserie contemporaine"*. Cocteau dabbled in tapestry, ceramics, photography and sculpture, as well as painting. Throughout the museum are examples of his beautifully crafted jars influenced by Greek, Hellenic and Etruscan designs. The upper floor, once the guards' room, still contains its original vaulted ceiling and brick oven. The highlight is the *Innamorati* collection, a series of love paintings inspired by the lives of Provençal fisher folk. With the sea beating against the bastion walls, the atmospheric setting is reminiscent of the Cap Ferrat tower where Cocteau worked.

Cocteau fans will head inland to the **Hôtel de Ville** Ⓗ to see the **Salle des Mariages** (open Mon–Fri; entrance fee; tel: (04) 92 10 50 00), designed by the artist in the 1950s. Cocteau's touch is evident in the Spanish chairs, the mock panther-skin carpet and the lamps shaped like prickly-pears. As for the murals, Cocteau's inspiration was the Riviera style at the turn of the 20th century, "a mood redolent of art nouveau villas decorated with swirling seaweed, irises and flowing hair".

On the wall above the official's desk, Cocteau depicts the engaged couple trying to read the future in each other's eyes. The mural is full of Provençal symbols, from the sun and swirling sea to the woman's Mentonnais straw hat and her fiancé's fisherman's cap. Cocteau humorously gives the fisherman a fish instead of an eye. The mural on the right features an exotic Saracen wedding, a pretext for a colourful ceremony and extravagant emotions. The bride and groom set off on a white horse amidst rejoicing, sorrow and mystery. Three wise friends bear gifts; a slave girl dances; a jilted girlfriend is comforted by her vengeful brother; a mother-in-law glowers; a gypsy guides the newlyweds towards the future.

Cocteau's aim was to "create a theatrical setting… to offset the officialdom of a civil ceremony". In this he succeeds, bringing wonder and an epic dimension to a dreary register office. Cocteau watched his adopted son get married in this very room. Since then, Menton has become a recherché wedding location, not just a joke to *"épater les bourgeois"*.

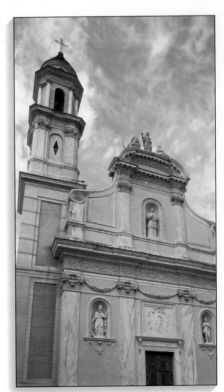

Foreign graves

From Menton it is a pleasant stroll round the bay to **Garavan**, a chic garden sub-urb with the most exotic vegetation in France. At the turn of the 20th century Garavan was in its heyday, a haunt for high society. Glamorous villas with matching landscaped gardens were *de rigueur*. Today, despite encroaching high-rise developments, *belle-époque* villas and art deco follies still survive. Sadly, many luxuriant gardens can only be glimpsed through *chien méchant* signs.

The high inland road to Garavan is more appealing than the seafront route. From the cathedral, climb the winding Rue du Vieux-Château to the **Cimetière du Vieux-Château** ❶ (open daily; free) on the hill. The Italianate cemetery, built over the ancient citadel, spans four terraces, each devoted to a different faith. The tone is set by a smiling marble angel which looks set to soar over the *vieille ville*. The cemetery is noted for its foreign graves, a cosmopolitan cast-list of 19th-century

celebrities who stayed longer than intended. Aubrey Beardsley, the illustrator, is joined by William Webb Ellis, the "inventor" of the game of rugby. Nearby are graves of consumptive English girls who made a vocation of dying poetically. Cats sun them-selves on Prince Youssoupov's tomb, unafraid of Rasputin's murderer.

The **Place du Cimetière**, just outside the cemetery walls, is a popular place for expatriate picnics and gossip. Count on sharing views of the **Vieux Port** and Gar-avan's modern marina. In the distance are signs for "*Frontière*", proof that the wooded headland beyond is, indeed, Italy.

Tropical flora

From the square, the **Boulevard de Gar-avan** leads past terraced gardens and vil-las hugging the coast. Rooftop villas are draped with mimosa, bougainvillaea, lentisks and giant cacti. Number 13, a *belle-époque* mansion built into the old city walls, is surrounded by olive and lemon groves. Next door is an art deco

BELOW: Mentonnais fishermen.

villa with magnificent views of the old port.

Several public paths lead down through lemon groves to the Garavan seafront. One such path, Sentier Villa Noël, leads to the **Jardin Botanique** ❶ (also known as Jardin du Val Rameh; open daily; entrance fee; tel: (04) 93 35 86 72), Menton's most successful park. This lush botanical garden was laid out by Lord Radcliffe, the Governor of Malta, in 1905. The last owner, the retiring Miss Campbell, continued to introduce plants from Asia, Africa and America, making this the most tropical garden in France. It now resembles a cultural melting pot.

Japanese cane bamboos and African succulents compete with Australian eucalyptus and Brazilian bougainvillaea; Arabian date trees and Canary palms dwarf Mexican yucca and Iranian pistachios. The fruit trees smell quite delicious: as well as *citrus amara* and *citrus blanco* lemons, there are also mandarins, bananas, oranges, figs and dates. Even succulents like the deep red aloes look distinctly edible.

Yet the garden does not neglect quieter, more Provençal charms. Sweet-smelling myrtle, rosemary and thyme flourish, as do evergreen lentisks, drooping lilies and a riot of roses. One intimate patch contains an ordinary rockery, except that no rockery is ordinary in Menton. A balmy climate helps, but these plants seem to have been raised on anabolic steroids.

Next door is the **Oliveraie du Pian** ❶, Garavan's public park. It was once part of a Spanish estate but is now a wild olive grove. This variety of olive, *le cailletier*, has been grown here for over 2,000 years and stands out for its stocky trunk and succulent black olives. Some of the gnarled specimens are hundreds of years old. By day, the olive grove is a ball park but on summer nights it is an open-air stage.

Two more gardens

On the far side of the park is Avenue Blasco Ibañez, named after the Spanish novelist who lived in exile here. Shunning the military dictatorship in Spain, Blasco

BELOW:
in the hills
above Menton.

Ibañez settled in the Riviera in 1923. His villa, **Fontana Rosa**, is a piece of self-indulgence, heralded by ceramic portraits of Balzac, Cervantes and Dickens on the gateway. Surrounding the villa is the Spaniard's **Jardin des Romanciers** (open Fri 10am for guided tour; tel: (04) 92 10 33 66), a further tribute to his favourite novelists. The grounds, planted with cypress and Mediterranean shrubs, reflect a pastiche of classical and art-deco styles. A couple of follies take centre stage, adorned by sculpted *putti*, kneeling angels and busts of novelists. Mosaics represent Mediterranean fruit and flowers. It may be kitsch but it's fun. The ceramics have been restored to their former splendour.

A steep walk on Rue Ferdinand Bac leads to the **Jardin des Colombières** ⓛ (group visits only; check at tourist office), arguably the most romantic gardens on the Riviera. The writer and artist Ferdinand Bac longed for an authentic Mediterranean garden, planted with Provençal herbs, box borders and clumps of yews.

The shaded terraces are punctuated by ornamental pools, fountains, classical urns and baroque statues. In fact, the hill-top location and the giant black cypresses closely resemble a French Tuscany.

But if the gardens are Italianate, the exuberant villa defies description. Decorated by Bac in 1926, it borrows freely from Hellenic, Roman and Oriental traditions. A colonnaded atrium contains frescoes of the Ulysses myth while the art deco music room is covered with murals of the nine Muses. In the grounds, a Moorish-style pavilion contains Bac's tomb.

A writer's home

From the gardens, steps cut down to the the Boulevard de Garavan and a turning right leads to **Avenue Katherine Mansfield**, the writer's retreat. The street boasts *belle-époque* villas, from the stuccoed *La Favorite* to *Chrisoleina*, a turreted folly. Before Garavan station, a sign indicates Mansfield's **Isola Bella** ⓜ, a disappointingly small, lemon-coloured villa with a

BELOW: locals shooting the breeze beneath a Cocteau mosaic.

Map
on page
262

disfigured view. Despite suffering from tuberculosis, Katherine wrote some of her best work here, including *The Daughters of the Late Colonel*, an essay on genteel frustation. By contrast, she found Menton liberating, "a heavenly place" with "no division between one's work and one's external existence". Life was centred on "my pale yellow house with its mimosa in a slightly deeper hue". Soon after moving in to the villa, Katherine wrote: "When I die you will find Isola Bella in poker work on my heart."

Mansfield would not have approved of the ugly high-rise sprawl on the Garavan seafront nearby. Nor would she have liked the tacky seafood restaurants lining the quayside. (She admired her maid's knack of turning any dish into an artistic still life, "the fish with its huge, tragic mouth stuffed with parsley".) On Promenade Reine Astrid, just before the Italian border, is **Villa Maria Serena**, whose garden is also worth visiting (open Tue 10am for guided tour; tel: (04) 92 10 33 66).

Palais Carnolès

From Menton, a brisk walk west along the seafront leads to Carnolès. This dull suburb is worth visiting for one sight alone, the **Palais Carnolès** (open Wed–Mon; free; tel: (04) 93 35 49 71). Once a Grimaldi summer home, the villa now houses Menton's **Musée des Beaux-Arts**. The pink and white palace is encircled by parasol pines and 50 different varieties of citrus trees. In 1640, Prince Honoré II built a summer house in the olive groves but Antoine I remodelled it on the Grand Trianon. The well-restored building mostly displays works bequeathed by Wakefield Mori, an eclectic English collector.

The museum's strengths lie in the Italian *Quattrocento* works, 16th-century portraits and modern Riviera landscapes. Amongst the ancient art, the Italian and French madonnas take pride of place. Louis Bréa, often called "Provence's Fra Angelico", is the only home-grown star of the period. The soft and spiritual *Virgin and Child* shows his delicate touch. The rest of the

BELOW: the mildest climate on the Med.

Niçois school cannot compete with the expressive *École de Leonardo* madonna presented here. The ground floor displays a rotating collection of modern art, including Kisling's *Paysage à St-Tropez* and Sutherland's *La Fontaine*, a glowing composition of fountain and leaves.

From Carnolès or Menton, a short drive north leads to the **Monastère de l'Annonciade** (visits arranged at tourist office) and arguably the loveliest views from Menton. By car, take the Avenue de Sospel and turn left into the Route de l'Annonciade. Alternatively, walk along the Chemin du Rosaire, a steep but delightful walk which, until 1936, was the only way of reaching the monastery. The path winds uphill through pine trees and spiky yellow agaves; small shrines represent the stations of the cross.

The path and the monastery were created by Isabelle de Monaco after her miraculous cure from leprosy. Apart from an interruption during the Revolution, a Franciscan community has lived here ever since. Inside the chapel is a bizarre collection of votive offerings, from boats and crutches to a Zeppelin fragment and a strip of parachute from the 1991 Gulf War. The monastery is perched among cypress and olive groves. From its terrace of swaying eucalyptus trees there are coastal views towards Italy, Corsica and Cap Martin.

A fortified village

A few miles west of Carnolès lies **Roquebrune-Cap Martin**, an historic commune sandwiched between Menton and Monaco. In the 1840s, the medieval village of **Roquebrune** ❾ was practically deserted and the wooded headland of Cap Martin was the preserve of sheep and cows. Before the end of the century, however, Cap Martin had been discovered by richer flocks, from Queen Victoria to Empress Eugénie. *Belle-époque* villas sprang up among the olive groves and Cap Martin remains the preserve of the rich today.

From Roquebrune station on the coast it is a short drive or an arduous climb to the

BELOW: the rooftops of Roquebrune.

Maps:
Area 236
Town 262

medieval village. Steep staircases with vertiginous views lead up the reddish-brown cliff. The distinction between castle and village only evolved in the 15th century. Before then, the whole of Roquebrune was a *castellum*, a fortified 10th-century settlement which remains unique in France.

The path finally emerges in Rue de l'Église, beside the parish church, **Ste-Marguerite**. Originally Romanesque, it was heavily restored in the 18th century. The facade is apricot-coloured, like much of Roquebrune, and overlooks a sweet Marian shrine. The welcoming interior is bathed in a soft pink glow.

But the village's vocation is for tourism, not the priesthood. Lavender, honey and carved wood sculptures are Roquebrune's icons, in summer at least. Yet despite being overpriced, overcrowded and over-restored, Roquebrune remains a magical place. The apricot houses, chiselled out of the rock, overhang tiny squares and blind alleys. Narrow passageways burrow through a labyrinth of vaulted archways.

Château de Roquebrune

The geranium-covered walls present a misleadingly decorative picture. This ancient *castellum* was supremely functional. The château battlements commanded views of Mont Agel, Monaco and the coast; there were only two entrances, both heavily guarded. If invaders broke through the defences, they were quickly backed into cul-de-sacs and bombarded with boulders. As the oldest castle in France, Roquebrune was the prototype feudal château for centuries to come.

Roquebrune was built by the Count of Ventimiglia as a means of keeping the Saracens at bay. After a long struggle between the Genoese and the Counts of Provence, Roquebrune became a Grimaldi possession and remained so for five centuries. The grim **château** (open daily; entrance fee; tel: (04) 93 35 07 22), situated on Place Ingram, is largely 13th century, although it was heavily restored in the 20th century by Sir William Ingram. The locals were outraged when the Englishman added a mock

BELOW:
paintings
for sale in
Roquebrune.

medieval *tour anglaise*. The battlements offer magnificent views of the coast.

Rue Grimaldi, the main street, is marred by cute gentrification and craft shops. But the eccentricity and friendliness of the traders sets Roquebrune apart. An artist with an atelier readily discusses local history or produces photos of himself dressed as a Roman centurion. Ever since 1467, when the Virgin saved the town from the plague, 500 Roquebrunois have re-enacted scenes from the Passion every August. A sculptor carves angels and virgins out of olive wood, boasting about his discovery of "*le plus vieil homme de l'Europe*" in a local cave. Roquebrune is, indeed, riddled with prehistoric remains, especially in the famous caves, the Grottes du Vallonet.

Before leaving, stroll down Rue Grimaldi to **Place des Deux Frères**, named after the square's twin crags. In 1890, the square came into being when a huge outcrop was split to create an access road. The result is a success, a release from the slightly claustrophobic feeling of Roquebrune.

Walking to Cap Martin

From the village, it is a pleasant, leisurely downhill stroll to **Cap Martin** ⓾ and the coast. The prettiest route leads along Chemin Souta Riba, a narrow, vaulted path edging round the outside of the village. Views through firs and pines reveal privatised Roman statuary in discreet villas. Soon after Souta Riba joins the Chemin de Menton there is a huge gnarled **olive tree**, reputedly over 1,000 years old. Further on are a couple of chapels, the dilapidated St Roch and the rural de la Pausa, which was built in 1462 as a plague offering. Faded frescoes of olive groves and angels cover the walls.

By the time the path reaches Avenue du Danemark, suburbia is underway. On Avenue Paul Doumer the Roman **Monument de Lumone** is a redeeming feature. These arches and mosaics are all that remain of a Roman settlement on the cape.

Although its olive and lemon groves have receded, Cap Martin is still lusher and less spoilt than Cap Ferrat. However, none of Cap Martin's *belle-époque* villas is open to the public and most bask in smug celebrity. Name-droppers have a field day on Cap Martin. Fragrant Coco Chanel wafted in to entertain German officers during the war. Empress Eugénie liked to play the *grande dame* here but presumably Greta Garbo didn't come for the company. Churchill and Le Corbusier came for the painter's light. Empress Sissy of Austria wintered here after a bad case of *fin-de-siècle* blues. W. B. Yeats came, and died, for reasons of ill-health.

The highlight of the cape is the **Promenade le Corbusier**, a lovely coastal path running west to Monaco and southeast around the cape. The path crosses an olive grove and then hugs the shore. Willows, sea pines and white rocks typify this stretch of coast. The walk towards Monaco passes Le Corbusier's beach house, just before the Pointe de Cabbé (open by appointment only, Tues & Fri; tel: (04) 93 35 62 87). The architect drowned in the sea here in 1965 but had the foresight to design a splendid memorial to himself in Roquebrune cemetery. Cynics label this a supremely Cap Martin gesture. ❏

Map on page 236

LEFT: the view west from Roquebrune. **RIGHT:** religion – the British prefer Anglican protection.

Map
on page
278

THE PERCHED VILLAGES

*For those prepared to leave the coast, a whole new world awaits: high
mountain plateaux, plunging gorges, clear sparkling rivers and, crowning
the most inaccessible peaks, the justly famous "villages perchés"*

A number of the perched villages, such as Ste-Agnès, Gorbio and Peillon, are only a few miles inland, and yet provide a stark and welcome contrast to the urbanised coast. Even villages further into the mountains, such as Utelle, Lantosque or Lucéram, can easily be visited in a day, since the roads are good, if often steep, and rarely busy.

However, it can be particularly pleasant to find a hotel and stay overnight in these beautiful mountains, to fully appreciate the pristine air and star-studded night skies, and to wake up to a deep silence broken only by cow bells. Spring, when the flowers are at their most beautiful, is perhaps the best time to enjoy these unspoilt regions, but during the summer they can provide a cool, refreshing break from the coast.

Above Nice

The perched village of **Falicon** ❶ is close to Nice and well worth a visit. It was the setting for Jules Romains's novel *La Douceur de la Vie,* and was also where Queen Victoria liked to stroll and take her afternoon tea whilst staying in Nice – an event commemorated by a restaurant called Au Thé de la Reine. The old village is very small, filled with covered passages and twisting lanes and is characterised by a series of picturesque little *placettes*, one of which has a rare perpendicular staircase leading to a raised front door. There is a baroque church dating from 1624.

Northeast of Nice and Falicon are two superb examples of *villages perchés*, Peille and Peillon, in the valley of the Paillon river. One has barely escaped the tangle of the Nice's industrial suburbs when these ancient craggy places rise up impossibly elevated above the valley floor.

It is surprising that **Peille** ❷ is not better known. It is a large, almost completely medieval village, with a wonderful variety of features and views. There is parking

either end of the town and two old quarters, both of which date from the 11th century.

Don't miss the Place André Laugier, where there is a pair of 13th-century doors, one Romanesque, one Gothic, and a pair of matched Gothic windows. Behind this is the Place du Mont Agel, surrounded by very old houses, with a Gothic fountain in the centre. The Rue Lascaris leaves the square through the loggia of the ancient palais, and out to a viewing platform. From here, a short path leads to the cemetery and the war memorial. The view extends all the way to Cap d'Antibes.

All the roads leading from Place du Mont Agel are worth exploring: Rue du Moulins has double round-arched windows, probably 15th-century; Rue de la

**PRECEDING
PAGES:**
village women
enjoy a joke.
LEFT: a typical
hill town.
RIGHT: the
Roman Trophée
des Alpes,
in La Turbie.

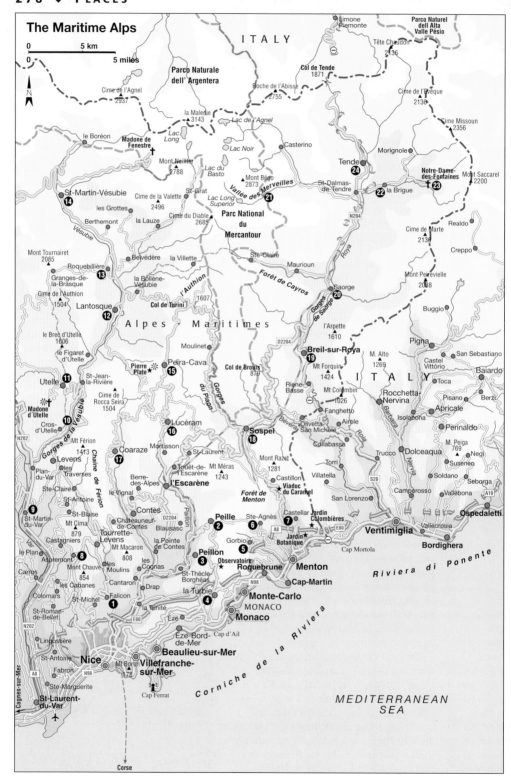

The Maritime Alps

0 —— 5 km

0 —— 5 miles

N

ITALY

Limone Piemonte

Parco Naturel dell Alta Valle Pésio

Parco Naturale dell' Argentera

Col de Tende 1871

Tête Chaudon 2136

Roche de l'Abisse 2755

Cime de l'Évêque 2136

Cime de l'Agnel 2937

la Malédie 3143

Lac de l'Agnel

Cime Missoun 2356

le Boréon

Madone de Fenestre †

Lac Long

Lac Noir

Casterino

Morignole

Tende **24**

Notre-Dame-des-Fontaines † **23**

Mont Saccarel 2200

Mont Neillier 2788

Lac du Basto

Mont Bégo 2873

Vallée des Merveilles

St-Dalmas-de-Tendre

la Brigue **22**

St-Martin-Vésubie **14**

Cime de la Valette 2496

St-Grat

Lac Long Superior

21

Roya

Realdo

les Grottes

Berthemont

la Lauze

Cime du Diable 2685

Parc National du Mercantour

Cime de Marte 2136

Creppo

Vésubie

Mont Tournairet 2085

Belvédère

la Villette

Ste-Claire

Maurioun

Forêt de Cayros

Mont Peirevieille 2088

Roquebillière **13**

la Bollène-Vésubie

Buggio

Granges-de-la-Brasque

Saorge **20**

Pigna

Cime de l'Authion 1504

Alpes   Maritimes

Col de Turini 1607

Gorges de Saorge

San Sebastiano

Lantosque **12**

l'Authion

l'Arpette 1610

Castel Vittório

Baiardo

le Brec d'Utelle 1806

Moulinet

D2204

Breil-sur-Roya **19**

Pisano

Toca

Berzi

le Figaret d'Utelle

Pierre Plate ★

Peïra-Cava **15**

Col de Brouis 875

Mt Forquin 1424

M. Alto 1269

ITALY

Apricale

Perinaldo

Utelle **11**

St-Jean-la-Rivière

Gorges du Planon

Rigne-Basse

Mt Colombin 1026

Rocchetta-Nervina

Isolabona

Barbaira

M. Peiga 769

Negi

Madone d'Utelle ☀†

Cime de Rocca Seira 1504

Bévéra

Olivetta San Michele

Fanghetto

Airole

Roia

Suseneo

Cros-d'Utelle

10

Lucéram **16**

Sospel **18**

Collabassa

Trucco

Dolceacqua

Soldano

Seborga

N202

Mortisson

St-Laurent

Mont Razet 1281

Torri

Nervia

Camporosso

Vallebona

A10

Coaraze **17**

Mt Férion 1413

Mt Méras 1243

Villatella

S20

Castillon

Ospedaletti

Levens

Touët-de-l'Escarène

San Lorenzo

Vallecrosia

Plan-du-Var

les Traverses

Berre-des-Alpes

l'Escarène

Castellar

Jardin Colombières

★

Ventimiglia

Bordighera

Ste-Claire

le Vignal

9

St-Antoine

Contes

D2204

Peille

Ste-Agnès

7

E80

St-Martin-du-Var

St-Blaise

Mt Cima 879

Châteauneuf-de-Contes

Blausasc

2

6

Jardin Botanique

Cap Mortola

Tourrette-Levens

Mt Macaron 808

la Pointe de Contes

Gorbio

5

Riviera di Ponente

Castagniers

8

les Moulins

Peillon

Observatoire ★

Roquebrune

Menton

le Plan

Aspremont

Mont Chauve 854

oles Cognas

3

St-Thècle-Borghéas

Cap-Martin

Carros

les Cabanes

Cantaron

Drap

la Turbie

N98

Monte-Carlo

Colomars

St-Michel

Falicon

1

4

MONACO

St-Roman-de-Bellet

la Trinité

E80

Monaco

N202

Eze

Lingostière

Eze-Bord-de-Mer

Cap d'Ail

St-Antoine

Beaulieu-sur-Mer

Corniche de la Riviera

Fabron

Nice

Mt Boron 178

Villefranche-sur-Mer

Cagnes-sur-Mer

A8

N98

Ste-Marguerite

St-Laurent-du-Var ✈

Cap Ferrat

MEDITERRANEAN SEA

Corse

Map on page 278

Turbie leads down stone steps under an arch to a charming square housing a small **museum** of local history (open summer: Wed, Sat & Sun; pm only).

The finest feature is the large **Église Ste-Marie**, set at the head of the village and created from two adjoining chapels, the oldest being 12th century. Two buttresses span the road, and a slender Romanesque bell tower dominates the village. A picture to the right of the altar shows Peille in the 16th century.

On the side of Montée St-Bernard next to the church are the ruins of a 14th-century castle, part of the original fortifications of the town which were mostly pulled down during the revolution. A very old part of the town lies directly below the castle, across the main road, consisting of very steep stone stairs and covered alleys. The Hôtel de Ville on Rue Centrale is housed in an 18th-century chapel, which has an interesting domed roof.

Dizzy heights

Nearby **Peillon ❸** is regarded as one of the most beautiful of all the perched villages. Approaching from the main road, it seems impossible to believe that 3 km (2 miles) will be enough to reach its dizzy heights among the olives and pines. As the French memorably put it, *"Peillon marque l'extrémité du monde habité."* Its charm is in the entire ensemble, the fantastic position, the winding main "street", which would be better described as a staircase, and the superb views from the top. As you enter the village from the small square shaded by plane trees, there is a fragment of an old archway to the left. There is also a tower of white stone, very clean and well restored.

A number of houses have open top floors in the Renaissance manner. The narrow streets have very steep stone steps through vaulted tunnels and sometimes as many as four front doors leading from someone else's basement. On the edge of the village the **Chapelle des Pénitents Blancs** contains 15th-century frescoes attributed to Jean Canavesio. They can be glimpsed through a grille on the door. Footpaths lead from Peillon across the wonderful wooded mountainside to Peille and La Turbie.

A Roman relic

La Turbie ❹, high above Monte-Carlo, is one of the most magnificent sights of the region. The name La Turbie comes from the Latin *tropaea* (trophy), and it is named after the **Trophée des Alpes** (open Apr–mid-Sept: daily; mid-Sept–Mar: Tues–Sun; entrance fee; tel: (04) 93 41 20 84), a huge Roman monument erected to commemorate the conquest by Augustus of the 45 Alpine tribes who had been attacking Romanised Gaul. Augustus, the first of the Roman emperors, led the campaigns in 15 and 14 BC. The Trophée was built between 13 and 5 BC, probably using the enslaved Alpine tribesmen as labour.

The structure was originally 50 metres (165 ft) high, and even now, 35 metres (115 ft) are still standing after 2,000 years. It consists of a large rectangular base supporting a cylindrical core of 24 huge Doric columns, some of which remain, their load-bearing supports now visible. The columns once supported a masonry tower, surmounted by a stepped cone roof,

RIGHT: a street corner in L'Escarène, north of Peille.

topped with a giant statue of Emperor Augustus as the conquering general.

A nine-line inscription framed by two winged victories exists on the front face, the longest intact Roman inscription to come down to us from antiquity. From the 7th to 10th centuries its upper parts were used as a watchtower against barbarian raids, and parts of its masonry were reused in ramparts to stave off the Saracens.

The trophy crumbles

In the Middle Ages, the Lérins monks destroyed its pagan statues. In the wars between the Guelphs and the Ghibellines, during the 12th and 13th centuries, the villagers took refuge in its passages and stairways. In 1706, it was partially destroyed because of its strategic location and later Louis XIV ordered the destruction of the "castle", not wishing any fortification to fall into the hands of the Dukes of Savoy. The ruins became a quarry and most of the town of La Turbie is built from the very stones which gave it its name. Only one other similar trophy is known, that of Trajan at Adam Klissi in Romania, making this of particular interest.

It is set in a lovely clifftop park, ideal for picnics. There is also a fine museum, displaying the many bits which have been unearthed from the monument, with a large scale model of how it originally looked. From the cliff is a spectacular view over the Mediterranean and to Monte-Carlo below. Yachts and speedboats go about their business and tiny cars crawl along the winding roads, but on the days when Formula One racing cars are in Monte-Carlo for the Grand Prix, the throaty roar is deafening, even 450 metres (1,500 ft) up.

The town itself is small, built in a quarter circle with two surviving town gates, one of which is best seen from the gardens of the Trophée, and many old buildings from the 11th and 13th centuries, particularly lining what used to be the Roman Via Julia. The baroque 18th-century church is built from stones taken from the Trophée and has attractive bands of coloured tiles

BELOW: a hill village in the early 20th century.

1913. COTE D'AZUR - SAINT-JEANNET — Vieille Rue

Map on page 278

on its cupola. The town is utterly charming with a wealth of architectural details embedded in its ochre walls and vaulted arcades, and its narrow cobbled streets dominated by the vast monument.

Up in the mist

Just north of Roquebrune and Menton are a group of hill villages which are just far enough from the bustling coast to have escaped the crowds. It helps that the villages lie at the end of tortuous roads and are literally hidden in mists. Not for nothing are residents of Gorbio and Ste-Agnès known as *les nébuleux*, the mist-dwellers.

Gorbio ❺ sits high on its hill looking out to the Mediterranean, amongst the olives which provided its livelihood until the 19th century, when its inhabitants turned to tourism, catering to the growing-numbers of visitors from Menton. It is famous for its narrow arched streets, and for its snail procession, *la procession aux escargots*, which, disappointingly, is not actually a promenade of snails, but a festival celebrated by the White Penitents when the streets are illuminated by oil flames lit in a multitude of snail shells.

Although close to Menton, **Ste-Agnès** ❻ belongs to medieval Provence, a landscape at once Mediterranean and mountainous. As a quaint *village perché*, Ste-Agnès is the most attractive in the area. Its eagerness to send visitors away with souvenirs rather than memories is the only jarring note.

En route to Ste-Agnès, the familiar olive and lemon groves merge into Provençal *maquis*. As the land climbs to 700 metres (2,300 ft), the olives disappear; sturdy juniper, pine and fir trees jut over the crags. By Ste-Agnès the mists and the temperatures fall, particularly in the early morning. "*Je vais me noyer dans la brume*," ("I'm off to drown myself in the fog,") is almost a cheery greeting in the village.

It is not clear how Ste Agnès acquired her sainthood. One legend has it that she was a Roman empress who sought refuge from a storm in a local grotto and, in thanks, built a chapel on the spot. The

BELOW: medieval walls and doorways in La Turbie.

more colourful version is that Haroun, a Saracen chief, raided the village and selected a Provençale for his harem. The chaste Agnès resisted her kidnapper until he converted to Christianity.

From the 12th century, the village was fought over by the counts of Ventimiglia and Provence. In the 16th century the ancient **château** was dismantled and its stones incorporated into existing houses. The ruins overlook an Italianate cemetery and pine forest. The walk up is especially pungent in spring: woodsmoke wafts through the cherry blossom, herbs and damp pine trees. At the top, if the fog has lifted, there are views towards the Alps, the coast and even Corsica.

A shrine to Ste-Agnès

Just below the château ruins is the village, clustered around the foot of a cliff. Place de la Mairie is lined with medieval buildings, including **Notre-Dame-des-Neiges**, the 17th-century parish church. The honey and herb shops outside are a prelude to the

main assault on Rue Longue. With its neat stone steps and flower-hung archways, well-restored houses and well-trained dogs, Ste-Agnès is almost too perfect. On a summer's day, however, **Rue Longue** mills with enamelists and herbalists, soap-sellers and crystal-engravers, jewellers and dried-flower designers.

Rue Longue leads to **Square Ste-Agnès**, perched on the edge of a ravine. This is where the original chapel was carved into the rock. All that now remains is a small shrine and a cute statue of the saint. The chapel was destroyed during the construction of a wartime fortification system along the border. From 1930, the Italian threat was ever-present so an extension to the Maginot line was created from the coast to the mountains beyond Sospel. Designed as an updated model of a Vauban fortress, **Fort Ste-Agnès** remains an impressive defensive system, only accessible via a narrow drawbridge (open Jul–Sept: daily; Oct–June: Sat & Sun; pm only; entrance fee; tel: (04) 93 35 84 58).

Villagers whimsically attribute their wartime escape to the spirit of Ste Agnès, still lurking in her grotto within the military fort. On 21 January, her saint's day, a dawn concert and carnival are followed by a procession to Notre-Dame-des-Neiges.

Rue des Comtes Leotardi leads out of the village, past covered passageways and medieval ramparts. Along here is the Vieille Auberge, with its promise of *raviolis maison, tarte agnèsoise* and panoramic views. If you're not leaving Ste-Agnès over-fed or laden with pine-scented cologne and Saracen jewels, then consider a walk along mule tracks to Gorbio. The Chemin du Pierre Rochard is named after the wartime parish priest who regularly walked to Menton to bring back rations.

A good place for lunch

Castellar ❼, just east of Ste-Agnès, is perched on a hillside covered with orchards and olives. The village is an acquired taste, historically richer than Ste-Agnès yet somewhat neglected. Entirely lacking in arts and crafts, Castellar is guileless, a traditional hilltop village. To the Niçois, its sole function is to serve

LEFT: a chapel in the trees near Castillon, north of Castellar.

Map
on page
278

Sunday lunch in a rural setting. The rectangular village was laid out with military precision by the Lascaris Seigneurs. It remained in their hands until the Revolution, with peasants continuing to pay such feudal dues as a shoulder of pork for a day's grazing rights. Not until 1792 did Castellar become part of France, an event celebrated by *l'arbre de la liberté* in the **Place de la Mairie**.

From here, the formal grid-pattern is clear: three parallel streets, linked by covered passageways, lead to the church at the end of the village. Two encircling paths trace the outline of the former city walls. **Rue de la République** is lined with sober medieval houses with roughly hewn stone staircases. An old-fashioned bakery produces *fougasse*, biscuits made from almonds and pine kernels.

Equally pleasant aromas waft from La Tour Lascaris, a rustic restaurant housed in the **Palais Lascaris**, the counts' former residence. Although the *salle d'armes* has lost its frescoes, it retains an austere

charm in keeping with the cuisine. Apart from *tourte de courge*, a courgette and aubergine pie, there is *Barba Juan, crêpes* stuffed with mushrooms, cheese and rice. Food is simple and vegetable-based, a reflection of Castellar's peasant roots.

At the end of Rue de la République is **St-Pierre**, a baroque church with an onion-domed bell tower and pinkish facade. From here, Rue Général Sarrail leads back to the Mairie. The first house on the left was a medieval prison but has been converted into a crafts workshop. Opposite is the **Chapelle des Pénitents Blancs**, a restored baroque chapel hemmed in by medieval houses. Further along is the **Chapelle des Pénitents Noirs**, sadly in need of restoration.

Covered passageways on the right lead to **Rue Arson**, the prettiest part of the village, bordering the countryside. A circular medieval tower backs on to the ramparts and, close to the church, is an olive-processing mill and an old wash house. The village is keen to attract visitors but not

BELOW:
a floral retreat.

at the expense of peace and quiet. In short, scruffy Castellar will not succumb to the prettified Ste-Agnès effect.

Into the mountains

Heading north instead of northeast from Nice, the route towards St-Martin-Vésubie takes in more perched villages as well as the spectacular Gorge de la Vésubie. Leave Nice on the N202 and take the D414 to Colomars, where it becomes the ridge road to **Aspremont** ❽, a charming village of concentric picturesque lanes with lots of little winding alleys leading from them. At the foot of the village stands the chapel of St-Claude, built in 1632 to guard the inhabitants against the plague. The church of St-Jacques has an unusual 13th-century Gothic nave, contrasting in style with the other village buildings. Like the rest of the village, the church has been recently restored. A castle once stood at the top of the village, but now only the ramparts remain.

Follow the Rue des Remparts around the top of the village to reach the Place Lean-dre Astraudo, a small square with a fountain; on one side is the highest remaining section of castle wall with corbels and blocked-up windows. There is a stairway to a little children's playground with a superb view of the mountains and a grove of trees marking the position of the castle keep.

Nearby **Castagniers** is a tiny village, largely rebuilt in the 19th century. There is a wonderful view of the Var Valley from the small square in front of the 1817 church.

If you continue up the Var Valley, you will find **St-Martin-du-Var** ❾ just off the main highway. The old village is a small tangle of lanes tucked behind the huge main square. **La Roquette-sur-Var**, high on its hill, was built at a strategic position on the old international frontier with Italy, and at the summit of the village there are the vestiges of a castle. The church of St-Pierre was completed in 1682.

Continuing north on the N202, you come to Plan-du-Var, the last stop for pizza and cold drinks before the **Gorges de la Vésubie** ❿, which lacks any kind of road-

BELOW: La Bollène-Vésubie – the whole village.

Map
on page
278

side refreshment. The gorge is stunning, its steep sides plummeting to the river below, the road winding and tunnelling through the rock. In a car it can be difficult to stop to admire the view; cycling or rambling is a much better way to appreciate it all.

On the Salt Route

At **St-Jean-la-Rivière**, the deep gorge is spanned by a dramatic bridge and the houses are built on top of each other either side of the river. Here, the Vésubie canal, much of which is underground, begins. From here, you can take the steep, winding road to **Utelle** ⓫, one of the villages on the original *route du sel* from the salt flats of Hyères to the Southern Alps, a route which was abandoned in the late-18th century.

Utelle is a very pleasant little town, dependent mainly on olive cultivation. It is built like a star on a rocky outcrop, originally the crossroads of a number of mule paths over the mountains. The hillsides, covered in wild lavender and fragrant herbs, are perfect for walking and picnics.

The 16th-century **Église St-Véran** replaced an earlier one destroyed by the earthquake of 1452. It is a curious mixture of architectural styles, with Romanesque columns and capitals, 18th-century baroque decoration, a Gothic loggia and 16th-century high altar. Don't miss the primitive altarpiece of the Annunciation in the north aisle or the doors with their 12 panels carved with dragons. The village has some intriguing door lintels; near the post office there is one at knee level, carved with esoteric alchemical symbols.

The mountain road continues beyond the village, climbing higher and higher with hair-raising views to the valleys below, until you reach a magnificent wind-blown plateau and the sanctuary of **Madone d'Utelle**. According to legend, it was founded by sailors who were guided to safety during a tempest by a mysterious light on the mountain, and founded the sanctuary in gratitude. The chapel which is usually open, was restored in the mid-1970s, and the building next to it is used as a retreat.

BELOW:
alpine view
from Utelle.

There is a viewing platform with a spectacular 360-degree panorama of mountain peaks and valleys and beyond to the distant sea; on a clear day you can see as far as Cap d'Antibes and even Corsica.

Further up the valley

The main road, the D2565, continues towards Lantosque, climbing all the way. The gorge widens to meadows and pastures; this is an area of pony rides, horses, camping and caravanning.

There can be few things more pleasurable than sitting beneath a parasol at one of the cafés in the lively little square at **Lantosque** , with a distant view of the village of La Bollène-Vésubie clinging to its hilltop further up the valley. Lantosque itself is built on the rocky spine of the hill up which the streets climb in a series of staircases. There is an Italianate influence in the architecture with open loggias on the top floors of many of the older houses.

A little further on is **La Bollène-Vésubie**, a charming town with big, shady

lime trees lining the wider streets. At the top of the village is a pretty baroque church dated 1525. There are no architectural highlights in the village; it is the total ensemble that makes it so delightful.

The D2565 leads on through trout-fishing country to **Roquebillière Vieux**, an equestrian centre. A bridge leads over the river to new **Roquebillière** ⑬, attractively built with uniform red-tiled roofs. High on the mountain, overlooking them both is **Belvédère**, a hill town with a rather good clock and sun-dial on the bell tower and a large barn-like church. The houses are many-storeyed with balconies and top-floor loggias in the mountain tradition. Lavender and jasmine grows everywhere and the views are wonderful.

End of the road

Once beyond Roquebillière, the architecture becomes noticeably alpine, with large overhanging roofs and balconies in the Swiss chalet style. Not for nothing is this area known as the "Suisse Niçoise".

The principal town in this region is **St-Martin-Vésubie** ⑭, a gateway to the Parc National du Mercantour. It is a mountaineering centre and summer retreat, popular with the people of Nice, but even in high season it's a sleepy kind of place. The main shopping and restaurant street is the Rue du Dr-Cagnoli which runs the full length of the town. It has a fast-flowing gutter running down the middle and is lined with Gothic houses with corbels and balconies, the oldest of which are at the bottom, near the church. There is quite a mix of architectural styles, blending Swiss-style chalet roofs and wooden balconies with Italian loggias, Gothic doors and jettied roofs.

At No. 25 is the **Maison Gothique** of the counts of Gubernatis, a national monument. It has a jettied first floor, ornamental frieze and arched ground floor. On one side of the street the buildings lean out over the river and the restaurants have tree-shaded dining terraces in the back. Near the 18th-century **Chapelle des Pénitents Blancs** with its interesting bulb cupola, there is a tiny market place. The baroque church is 17th-century, but possesses a

LEFT: ready for a stroll.

Map on page 278

13th-century virgin which is carried in procession on 2 July to the high mountain sanctuary of Madone de Fenestre, where she remains until the end of September.

From the terrace in front of the church door there is a view looking south to the perched village of Venanson. Behind the east end of the church, to the right, is the Place de la Frairie, a terrace looking out over the Madone de Fenestre river, which has its origins in the Lac de Fenestre in the mountains to the east on the Italian border. The steep river valley can be followed for 13 km (8 miles) along the D94, ending at the Madone de Fenestre chapel.

Back towards the coast

A variety of return routes to the coast are possible. You might go via **Peïra-Cava** ⓯, which was originally a military camp but has developed into a winter sports and holiday resort. The view from the Pierre Plate, which is a ten-minute walk or drive up the small road opposite the Hotel Truchi, is superb. There is parking near the top.

Lucéram ⓰, further south, is situated at the crossroads of ancient paths, in particular the salt route from the coast. Until recently, it depended on mountain farming for survival, mainly olive and lavender cultivation. Today the fortified village, with its tall stacked houses in pastel colours, and its sombre vaulted alleys, depends almost entirely on tourism. It is noted particularly for the church treasures in the 15th-century Église Ste-Marguerite (open Wed–Sun), which include a silver reliquary and retables attributed to Niçois artist Louis Bréa.

Finally, **Coaraze** ⓱ is worth a detour – a restored medieval perched village with concentric lanes, arches, covered passages and public gardens. The church is 17th-century in the *baroque-rustique* style, and there are various modern sundials (one by Jean Cocteau) in the square outside. Visit the cemetery, which uses cement boxes for burials because the rock is so hard that graves are impossible to dig. At the summit of the village is the Place du Château, site of the now demolished castle. ❏

BELOW:
St-Martin-Vésubie, popular in the summer.

Map on page 278

BORDER COUNTRY

In the Bévéra and Roya valleys, not far from the Italian frontier, the terrain is rugged and the alpine scenery spectacular. In the town squares, the architecture, dialect and cuisine betray an Italian ancestry

The **Haut-Pays** resembles Piedmont rather than Provence and, in accent, sounds Italian rather than French. The Italian influence colours the architecture: loggias, arcaded squares and onion-topped bell towers abound. A love of decoration is present in such flourishes as carved lintels, elegant balconies and madonnas in niches. The dreamy Italianate villages strive after colour, with painted facades, *trompe l'oeil* decoration and glinting fish-scale roofs. Sospel and the **Bévéra Valley** mark the transition from the outward-looking Mediterranean world to the inward-looking mountain world. Here olives, lavender and lemons give way to pine, oak, mountain laurel and vivid blue gentians.

The **Haute Roya Valley** begins just northeast of Sospel and from Breil-sur-Roya the mountain atmosphere becomes more pronounced. The rural architecture acquires an alpine sturdiness, with dry stone barns and *cazouns*, the shepherds' primitive shelters.

Sleepy town

The natural gateway to the mountainous hinterland is **Sospel ⑱**, sprawling along the Bévéra Valley. As a great advocate of green tourism, Sospel offers a wide range of walks through classic hill country. Tourism is low key and has not changed the character of this sleepy medieval town.

Sospel was an independent commune by the 11th century and an important trading post on the old Salt Route linking Piedmont with France. Medieval Sospel depended, in turn, on the counts of Ventimiglia, Provence and Savoy but retained a degree of autonomy. This was partly due to the presence of charitable confraternities which played a major role in city life. By the 17th century, Sospel was a noted artistic and intellectual centre but fell into a gradual decline, not reversed by the town's return to France in 1860.

The town did, however, experience brief glory, and much suffering, during World War II. In 1944–45 there were fierce battles in the area and the German forces only withdrew in April 1945. By then, many Resistance workers had been executed and other Sospellois had been deported to Italy. In recognition of Sospel's sacrifices, the town was awarded the *Croix de Guerre*.

The focal point of the town is the **Pont Vieux**, the 11th-century tollgate and bridge spanning the river Bévéra. It is the oldest tollgate in the Alpes-Maritimes and was still in use in the 18th century. Carriages from Nice transported salt, fish, citrus fruits, porcelain and silk towards Piedmont. In the opposite direction came rice, flax, muslin, lace and dry white wine.

PRECEDING PAGES: Place St-Michel, in Sospel.
LEFT: viewing the mountains.
RIGHT: keeping up with the times in Sospel.

Although the bridge was partly blown up in 1944, the stones were fished out of the river and the Pont Vieux was restored in 1953. The left bank of the river, originally outside the city walls, is lined with attractive pastel-coloured buildings.

Beside the old bridge is a small square with an arcaded medieval building and fountain. This faded apricot-coloured building was the **Palais Communal** until 1810, housing both the town council and religious tribunals. Place Garibaldi, the adjoining square, has a series of medieval arcades incorporated into later buildings.

The riverside quarter, stretching from Place Garibaldi to Place Ste-Croix, consists of austere 14th-century houses, once home to Sospel's prosperous merchant class. The houses in Rue de la République contain vast interconnecting wine cellars. In the same street is the Maison de Toia, a sculpted Romanesque *hôtel particulier*.

Medieval Sospel had five confraternities which offered hospitality to pilgrims and made loans to impoverished peasants.

While most Franciscan confraternities were egalitarian, Sospel's were hierarchical: the Pénitents Noirs served the nobility while the Rouges only welcomed local dignitaries; the Blancs were for the bourgeoisie; the Bleus for the young; and the Gris for the poor. The **Chapelle Ste-Croix**, dating from 1518, is still the headquarters of the Pénitents Blancs, who continue to serve charitable purposes.

A beautiful square

From Place Ste-Croix it is a short stroll across the river to the main street, Avenue Jean-Médecin and Place St-Pierre, a market-place overlooking plantain trees. Rue St-Pierre, a medieval street leading to the **cathedral**, is lined with dilapidated houses, including the Romanesque Maison Domérégo. This dingy passage astonishingly opens on to **Place St-Michel**, the most theatrical square in the region. Tucked into a graceful Romanesque clocktower is the cathedral's peaches-and-cream facade: frothy stucco and kitsch gladiatorial figures adorn the exterior.

Opposite the cathedral is the Foyer Rural, also subject to the *trompe l'oeil* effect. This cultural centre used to be the Town Hall until an earthquake shattered the building in 1887. Next door is the Palais Ricci, an arcaded Romanesque mansion which in 1809 welcomed Pope Pius VII on his journey to Tuscany. Curiously, this baroque square echoes Pienza, the Tuscan Renaissance town built by Pius II.

Sospel's cathedral is in its element during a sudden summer thunderstorm. It is also magical in the late evening, when the bells chime and a sliver of moon is visible between the tower and the baroque facade.

The majestic interior is well-preserved and full of light. The highlight is a 15th-century *Madonna* by François Bréa, the renowned Niçois artist. The Virgin, dressed in a gold embroidered dress, stands in front of a Mediterranean coastal scene. Facing Bréa's work is a 15th-century depiction of the Virgin and Christ. The composition features the Pénitents Blancs, who commissioned the work. The painting, awkward and less idealised than Bréa's work, is also more moving.

LEFT: man's best friends.

Map
on page
278

War and resistance

From Place St-Michel, the Montée de Louis Saramito leads up to the ruined castle and abbey. From Sospel, a signposted walk leads all the way through Provençal countryside to Olivetta in Italy. Longer hikes lead south to Castellar, or north to Moulinet and L'Authion, mountainous terrain where the Germans made their last stand at the Battle of Sospel.

War memorials are on every hill but **Fort St-Roch** is the most impressive and now houses a museum dedicated to the local resistance (open Jun–Sept: Tues–Sun; April, May & Oct: Sat & Sun; pm only; entrance fee; tel: (04) 93 04 15 80). Just south of Sospel, St-Roch was built in 1930 against the threat of an Italian invasion. It is virtually an underground village, protected by anti-tank defences where 250 soldiers, with artillery and equipment, could survive for at least three months. Local fears of an invasion were well-founded and although Sospel held out against superior Italian forces, occupation was inevitable, by the Italians in 1940 and the Germans in 1943. By September 1944, the Germans had lost Nice and Menton but hung on to Sospel, despite an Allied advance northwards.

Just 5 km (3 miles) south of Menton, the Allies were told to stay put and wait for the advance across northern Europe. As a result, Sospel suffered even longer in German hands and was exposed to American artillery attacks. In October, the Germans retreated northwards and Hawaiians were the first Allies to enter Sospel. Cries of *"Vive Sospel! Vive la IVème République!"* were shortlived, however, and the battle continued until April 1945.

The Roya Valley

Compared with the Vallée de la Bévéra, the **Roya Valley** is wilder, poorer and more rugged. In the past, routes didn't follow the valley floor because of fears of flooding or landfalls in narrow gorges. Instead, paths were carved along the side of the mountains and through high mountain passes. The Roya's medieval villages,

BELOW: hairpin bends in the Roya Valley.

often perched beside fearsome gorges, were linked only by the old Salt Route.

Until the 19th century, this route was the only way through the region; the Roya Valley did not open up until 1860 when Napoléon III, newly in control of the Comté de Nice, wished to increase trade with Piedmont. The Italian influence, a troubled history, and terrible communications have all helped preserve the Roya in its splendid isolation.

Breil-sur-Roya ⑲ makes an arresting first impression, particularly if reached by rail or via the precarious Col de Brouis. The train from Sospel emerges from a long mountain tunnel and suddenly there is a fish-shaped pattern of pastel houses clinging to a bend in the River Roya. The mountains bank steeply behind the red-tiled houses. A golden angel blows a trumpet from a chapel rooftop.

Breil likes to call itself the "French gateway to the Roya" since until 50 years ago the Italian border ran just north of the village. However, France is only skin deep. *Ciao* is a normal greeting; the *cuisine provençale* tastes of Piedmont; and Italy lies only a few miles east.

Breil was ruled by the counts of Provence, Ventimiglia and Genoa before becoming part of the House of Savoy until 1860. Unlike Sospel, Breil depended almost entirely upon olive growing and farming. The lower slopes are still given over to olives and 500 tonnes are harvested each year. As for farming, the village still operates traditional grazing rights: from October to April more than 2,000 Breil sheep and goats graze on communal land. It was a dispute about this issue that led to an 18th-century revolt against the feudal lords. The event is re-enacted every four years in *Staccada*, complete with mock battles and a show trial.

A church beside the river

A gentle walk along the river leads to Place Brançion in the heart of the medieval village. Open to the river on one side, the square is dominated by an apricot-coloured church, **Sancta Maria in Albis**. This 18th-century baroque facade is echoed by a flamboyant Italianate interior, with a vivid Bréa panel-painting and a fine organ. The church, like many others in the Roya Valley, has a glittering multi-coloured onion dome.

Breil is well-worn hiking country; signed walks lead to medieval watchtowers like La Cruella or to isolated chapels to the west of the village. Longer hikes lead to Sospel or Vesubie.

Although many Breillois are civil servants or coastal commuters, the village is enough of a retirement haven to radiate relaxation. Residents include poets, local historians and the food-writer Mademoiselle Sassi whose book, *Recettes Breilloises*, provides a guide to Breil cuisine.

Breil is, in many ways, untypical of the Roya Valley. The vegetation is lushly Mediterranean and blurs the impact of the brooding mountains. Relative prosperity and an influx of outsiders have diluted its Italian atmosphere. In the Haute Roya, however, the transition to mountainous terrain is complete. The dramatic **Gorges de Saorge**, immediately after Breil,

LEFT: cyclists negotiate a sharp bend.

Map on page 278

announce serious terrain, with high waterfalls, deep forests, wind-blown alpine pastures and mauve-grey canyons.

Roya history

Italian sentiments are not muted in the Haute Roya. From medieval times, the effects of epidemics and wars forced local *seigneurs* to recruit labour from further afield, particularly from Piedmont, Lombardy and Liguria. This Italian influx continued until the 1950s and has left its mark on the language, culture and architecture.

In 1860, unlike the rest of the Comté de Nice, the Upper Roya remained with the House of Savoy, rulers since medieval times. La Brigue, Tende and the other villages in the Upper Roya were in an anomalous position. In the 1860 plebiscite, they voted to rejoin France rather than remain with Piedmont but were refused permission by Cavour, Victor Emmanuel's astute Prime Minister. Cavour's subterfuge was to claim that the region, bordering the game-rich Mercantour, formed part of the King's *terrains de chasse*. The reality had nothing to do with retaining hunting grounds and everything to do with controlling the vital mountain passes.

It was not until a 1947 plebiscite that the Haute Roya was incorporated into France. The head rather than the heart determined this political allegiance: trading links were with the French coast and the French standard of living was far higher. So, while Niçois rightly claim that they were never Italian but merely Piedmontese, the same cannot be said of the distinctly Italian Roya Valley. Since becoming French, there have been no great social changes to this self-sufficient mountain community. The dialects still remain resolutely *Piémontais*, as do the local crafts and traditions.

Shimmering tiles

The most spectacularly sited of all Roya villages is **Saorge 20**. At first sight, it appears suspended between a hazy mountain sky and the lush valley floor. The

BELOW: bridge over the Roya in Breil.

village forms a vast amphitheatre around a sheer cliff. Down below flows the Roya and on the other side of the canyon lie olive groves rising to terraced alpine pastures.

Saorge looks like a traditional *village perché*: it is perched on high for defensive reasons and favours a south-facing slope, both as winter shelter and summer sun-trap. The painted Venetian facades and the bell towers covered in a mosaic of shimmering tiles are also typical of Roya hill-top villages. But the height of the narrow medieval houses, the disparity of street levels and the complexity of the interlinking passages mark Saorge out as a perfect example of a *village empilé*, a "stacked village".

Saorge is set at right angles to the slope so that the equivalent to a 30-storey tower separates the foundations of the lowest house from the roof of the highest one. Each house can be up to ten storeys high, with entrances at five different street levels. The heights are so varied that some streets are merely corridors linking individual apartments rather than houses. This is a medieval version of the complex walkways found in modern shopping malls.

As a fortified village controlling the Col de Tende, Saorge seemed impregnable but was finally captured by the French in 1793. Though it later returned to Piedmont, this former capital of the Roya never regained its prestige. The building of a valley road in the 19th century turned the village into a backwater – only valleys prospered. In 1806, a visiting tax-collector complained of "a road riddled with wolves and bandits, crossed in peril of one's life". The dangers have gone but the isolation remains.

Saorge is a remarkable composition, making it difficult to single out individual attractions. The rough slate roofs, a feature of the Roya Valley, add a severe touch to the 15th-century houses below. The facades are tinted pink, ochre and russet, bathing the village in a warm Ligurian glow at odds with the stark setting. The deepest alleys never see any sunlight.

In the 1960s, at the height of the rural exodus, houses in Saorge sold for 2,000

BELOW: rugged terrain.

Map on page 278

francs; now the average price is 300,000 francs, a sign that many have been snapped up as *résidences secondaires*. The population, a mere 200 in winter, swells to 2,500 in summer. In winter, the shutters are closed and the village only stirs on market day.

Exploring Saorge

At the entrance to the village is a panoramic view of the valley below. On the square itself is a group of peach-coloured buildings, including a chapel and a Mairie crushed against the cliff. From here, Rue Ste-Jeanne d'Arc winds upwards through covered passageways. (The names of streets are usually meaningless in Saorge since most have three names, usually after rival Resistance leaders.)

At the top is **St-Sauveur**, the 15th-century parish church. The forbidding exterior is not misleading; inside is a damp, mauve-tinged interior and a chilly atmosphere not redeemed by a fine Italian organ. Virtually next door is a cheerful café, *Lou Pontin*, a chance to sample *quiques*, a local variant on spinach *fettuccini*.

Cobbled streets lead up to a **Franciscan monastery** set amongst cypresses and olives (open Apr–Oct: Wed–Mon; Nov–Mar: Sat & Sun; pm only; entrance fee; tel: (04) 93 04 55 55). The sunny terrace is a place for contemplation, with telescopic views of Saorge below and of barren mountains beyond. Although the monastery is built around a Romanesque church, it is essentially baroque.

A former mule track leads from the monastery to the **Madone del Poggio**, an isolated Romanesque church topped by an octagonal tower. This graceful sliver of a tower is supported by a honeycomb apse, all that remains of the original abbey. The church and surrounding estate have been in the Davio family for years so the vivid frescoes in the crypt cannot be visited. One consolation is the view of Saorge at sunset. The light shifts across the terraced crescent, colouring the facades sienna and casting deep shadows over the onion-domed towers.

Despite the wonderful scenery, the inhabitants are a disparate, warring group.

The core of the winter community consists of doddering *vieux du pays*, hippies and young professionals. The *vieux* are happy to let run-down shepherds' shacks and outlying farms to the *marginaux*. The hippies lead a pioneer lifestyle, bee-keeping, weaving and tilling the soil. It is subsistence farming – the pastures are known locally as "Siberia" because they receive no sun for four months of the year.

More gorges

Between Saorge and La Brigue the landscape is ravaged by a series of gorges. The building of the Nice-Turin railway brought much-needed work to the Roya villages. Although the line was begun in 1910, work stopped in 1914 and the track was destroyed during World War II. Finally finished in 1972, the result is a spectacular feat of engineering. The 39 viaducts alone make it the most acrobatic line in Europe. The track often does a loop in mountain tunnels so that a train emerges from a tunnel just above its entry point.

RIGHT: Saorge, perfect example of a "stacked village".

Vallée des Merveilles

Cradled in a majestic circle of Alps, the Vallée des Merveilles is aptly named. The valley is a vast open-air museum of prehistory. It is also a Wagnerian landscape of rock-strewn valleys, jagged peaks and eerie lakes. Thanks to the presence of minerals, the lakes are green, turquoise and even black.

Just west of the Lac des Mèsches is the Minière de la Vallaure, an abandoned mine quarried from pre-Roman times to the 1930s. Prospectors came in search of gold and silver but had to settle for copper, zinc, iron and lead. The Romans were beaten to the valley by Bronze Age settlers who carved mysterious symbols on the polished rock, ice-smoothed by glaciation. These carvings were first recorded in the 17th century but investigated only from 1879 by Clarence Bicknell, an English naturalist. He made it his life's work to chart the carvings and died in a valley refuge in 1918.

The rock carvings are similar to ones found in northern Italy, notably those in the Camerino Valley near Bergamo. However, the French carvings are exceptional in that they depict a race of shepherds rather than hunters. The scarcity of wild game in the region forced the Bronze Age tribes to turn to agriculture and cattle-raising. Carvings of yokes, harnesses and tools depict a pastoral civilisation, and these primitive inscriptions may have served as territorial markers for the tribes in the area.

However, the drawings are also open to less earth-bound interpretations. Anthropomorphic figures represent domestic animals and chief tribesmen but also dancers, devils, sorcerers and gods. Such magical totems are in keeping with Mont Bégo's reputation as a sacred spot. Given the bleakness of the terrain, it is hardly surprising that the early shepherds looked heavenwards for help. Now, as then, flocks of cows, sheep and goats graze by the lower lakes. However, the abandoned stone farms and shepherds' bothies attest to the unprofitability of mountain farming.

The Vallée des Merveilles is accessible only by four-wheel drive or on foot, and now, due to vandalism, you can visit the valley only if accompanied by an official guide. Given the mountain conditions, the drawings are only visible between the end of June and October. It is an 8-km (5-mile) drive west from St Dalmas to the Lac des Mèsches. Then follows a 10-km (6-mile) trek through the woods to Lac Long and the rock-carving zone. In the nearby town of Tende, the tourist office can organise a range of trips, and you can also visit the fascinating Musée des Merveilles (see page 303).

The Vallée des Merveilles is part of the Parc National du Mercantour, a vast conservation area worth visiting in its own right. Roughly 90 by 30 km (56 by 19 miles), Mercantour is a wilderness of pine forests, gorges and pastures. There are no permanent residents, just a few hamlets occupied by summer visitors. It is ideal rambling country with an amazing variety of flora and fauna. Wild geraniums, gentian violets and forest fruits are common on the lower slopes, while orchids, edelweiss and rare saxifrage grow higher up.

The park is also a game reserve with ibex, wild boar and mountain goats. The only problem is illegal hunting – the park is often raided to satisfy the local taste for venison. ❏

LEFT: animals inspire many of the rock carvings.

Map on page 278

Just before La Brigue is **St-Dalmas** station, an overbearing piece of Fascist architecture, which served as a communications centre in Mussolini's time. Despite its baroque church and sturdy architecture, St-Dalmas itself is an unremarkable village. It is best-known as a base for excursions into the **Vallée des Merveilles** ㉑ (*see opposite*). This remote valley lies in the heart of a protected zone known as the **Parc National du Mercantour**.

Alpine pastures

La Brigue ㉒ is at once the richest and simplest of Roya villages. Set amidst alpine pastures, La Brigue has always been a remote place, wholly dependent on the wool trade. Until the late 19th century, three-quarters of the population reared the sure-footed breed of sheep known as the Brigasque. After spending the summer in La Brigue, local shepherds took their flocks to winter pastures in Breil, Èze and Menton. The itinerant La Brigue shepherd, dressed in red velvet cap and green corduroy, has entered French folklore as a born storyteller.

The wealth created by the wool trade attracted Jewish merchants, money-lenders and goldsmiths to set up shop in the quarter known as Rû Ghetto. By the 15th century, wool merchants and notables could afford to indulge in artistic patronage. Italian craftsmen were commissioned to build new chapels and to adorn bourgeois homes with engraved lintels. The village was deeply influenced by the Italian Renaissance: the local architecture was enriched by arcaded streets and sculpted columns. Italian frescoes replaced traditional Niçois murals.

As late as the 19th century there was a flourishing crafts tradition in the village. However, La Brigue's return to France in 1947 divided the commune with scant regard for history. The "low" village of La Brigue became French while the "high" village, Briga Alta, remained Italian, along with virtually all the neighbouring hamlets. The population of La Brigue dropped from a peak of 4,000 to a mere 500, making it the same size as it was in the 12th century.

BELOW: Lac du Basto, in the Parc National du Mercantour.

Still, there are compensations for such depopulation. With the exception of one ugly square, there has been little recent development. The remoteness of the location has deterred potential buyers of second homes, as has the impenetrable local dialect and the sense of a closed community. After the War, the villagers may have diversified into cattle-rearing but agriculture is the mainstay. Today's farmers are horse-breeders, cheese-makers and bee-keepers, not to mention amateur fishermen. The river Levense is rich in rainbow trout and the speckled local variety.

The streets of La Brigue

La Brigue, lying along the Levense river, is dwarfed by snow-capped mountains, including the majestic Mont Bégo. The oldest quarter fans out from Rû (Rue) Sec, but the natural introduction to the village is Place St-Martin, an Italianate square. A cluster of trout restaurants border the square and the fast-flowing river. Apart from *truites vivantes* in their tanks, the rustic restaurants offer *gnocchi, lasagne* and *tantifauluza*, a leek tart.

A 17th-century chapel with a leaning *campanile* looms against mauve canyon walls. This is **L'Assuntà,** once the home of the Pénitents Blancs, a chapel which answered to Rome. Decorative Tuscan pillars adorn the facade, creating a purity of line which is not reflected in the interior.

Next door, bordering a more intimate square, is the **Collégiale St-Martin**, the village church. The Romanesque bell tower surmounts a mellow, stone structure. St Martin is said to have preached here before settling in the Loire Valley as bishop of Tours. The interior is the richest in the region, boasting Tuscan decor and striking 16th-century paintings. The ceiling, with its starry blue sky, is reminiscent of Siena Cathedral. Equally Italianate are the frescoes of angels in flight, the vaulted arches and the altar screen.

The works of art, including two attributed to Louis Bréa, are individualistic and memorable. Bréa's *Nativité* portrays a

BELOW: a square in La Brigue.

Map on page 278

luminous Virgin and Child against a dark, craggy background resembling La Brigue. Like Bréa's *Assomption*, also in the church, the painting is a sober yet knowing work. The expressive faces and the delicate handling of drapery are typical of Bréa's artistic gifts.

A baroque venue

In summer, concert-lovers wallow in baroque waves of emotion as the church echoes to the sound of Boccherini and Respighi. The organs in La Brigue have been made by such masters as the Lingiardi brothers. Standard church organs weren't able to play baroque music and opera, still less Piedmontese airs and ballets. However, the church organs in the Roya were all adapted to respond to the 19th-century vogue for *Bel Canto*. On informal occasions the organs play shepherds' folk songs about love and war.

On the far side of the church is another fine Pénitents Blancs chapel, **L'Annonciade**, which contains a collection of religious art. It has a lovely carved baroque facade, also built of the warm local stone. From here, all alleys lead inwards, towards the medieval heart of the village. The cobbled streets are confusingly named in local dialect with Frenchified equivalents, so Rio Secco is also Rû Sec, a reference to the dry river bed that traces the arcaded street.

La Brigue has the greatest variety of decorative slate lintels in the Roya Valley. Made of green and black stone, these lintels are the work of 15th- and 16th-century Italian stonemasons. The lintels usually link a Biblical saying or a wise saw to a pictorial motif, such as a Renaissance dragon, cherubs, shepherds and lambs. Rue Filippi, Rue de la République and Rue Rusca are all good lintel-hunting grounds.

Gods and ghouls

Four kilometres (2 miles) east of La Brigue is **Notre-Dame-des-Fontaines** ㉓ (visits arranged at La Brigue tourist office), arguably the most remarkable chapel in the Riviera hinterland. This simple medieval chapel, overlooking a mountain stream, has been a pilgrimage centre since the 14th century. The chapel is supposedly built

over a Temple to Diana. Legend has it that after a serious drought, the region was saved by a miraculous outpouring of water from this spot. *Jean de Florette* legends aside, the chapel is celebrated for its 15th-century frescoes, painted by Jean Baleison and Jean Canavesio, Ligurian artists.

Baleison's frescoes, decorating the choir, are faded Marian images, painted as refined courtly figures. Jean Canavesio's frescoes, however, are more satisfying compositions, painted around a central figure. What sets his work apart is the drama and intensity of the moral message, designed to provoke pilgrims into repentance. A grotesque *Judas Iscariot* shows the traitor's disembowelment, performed by a demonic monkey. There is a Hieronymous Bosch quality to the most tormented work.

Elsewhere, there are quieter scenes reflecting medieval daily life and landscapes. The *Garden of Gethsemane*, for instance, is full of lush Provençal plants. The artist's palette comes from the region too: the green is crushed slate; the white is

RIGHT: detail of a Canavesio fresco in Notre-Dame-des-Fontaines.

limestone; and the black is burnt oak twigs.

From Notre-Dame-des-Fontaines, walkers can hunt for mushrooms, strawberries and blackcurrants in wooded glades. The enchanting walk back to La Brigue is via a medieval bridge and small orchards. A more strenuous hike leads to **Briga Alta**, the Italian village that once belonged to La Brigue. The villagers still meet during hunting and fishing competitions, a time to celebrate their common heritage: trout, *gnocchi* and *salumeria*, Italian salami.

The head of the valley

Tende ㉔ is as strange as anywhere in the Roya Valley. Despite being a frontier post, it remains a musty, medieval town with its heavy wooden doors closed to the world. But what it lacks in charm, it certainly makes up for in atmosphere.

Tende guards the **Col de Tende**, the old mountain pass connecting Piedmont and Provence. Now bypassed by a road tunnel, the pass was once a fearsome experience. Smollett, crossing it in 1765, was "speechless in front of this celebrated and perilous mountain". Fears of bandits and smugglers aside, the crossing was undoubtedly beset with difficulties: it took six manservants to cut the ice with pickaxes before Smollett could get through.

Approached from La Brigue, Tende is still an impressive sight. The newer part of town hugs the river; behind is stacked the medieval town, rising in tiers to an Italianate cemetery and a stunted tower. The 14th-century tower is all that remains of the feudal château built by the Lascaris dynasty. The town's fortunes are a familiar story of a powerful church and the oppressed, poverty-stricken peasants.

At the start of the 20th century, Tende's farmers and miners were still impoverished: travel was on foot or by mule; bread was a luxury and dried so that it lasted longer. Under Fascism, Tende became a garrison town with over 3,000 Italian soldiers. In 1947 the town, newly French, was deserted by the military, as well as by Italian civil servants and manual workers. The

BELOW: the vast amphitheatre of Saorge *(see page 295).*

Map on page 278

economic decline was only checked in the 1980s, with the opening of a new rail link and ski resorts. The Mercantour park and the Vallée des Merveilles have also helped to attract visitors to the area.

Blackened by time

The *vieille ville* is made of greyish-green schist, a type of slate still quarried nearby. Blackened by time and traffic fumes, these sombre houses set the tone. The overhanging roofs are not decorative, as a glance at the snowy peaks will confirm. Nor is Tende ever hot: "*En été il y a toujours de l'air,*" as the hardy locals say. Only the orange and pink belfries, decorated in Ligurian colours, generate any warmth.

The late Gothic **cathedral**, tucked away down a dark alley, is made of blackened green stone and is badly in need of restoration. The sculpted Renaissance facade is framed by pillars propped on stone lions, an unusual feature in church architecture.

Ancient walnut doors lead to a majestic interior, adorned with a starry Tuscan ceiling and a nave emblazoned with the Lascaris arms, a two-headed eagle. Medieval houses and confraternity chapels are clustered around the cathedral.

The gloomy, claustrophobic atmosphere is intensified by a walk through the *vieille ville*. Thick oak doors are adorned with medieval lintels representing the medieval guilds. **Rue Béatrice Lascaris** climbs through the medieval quarter to the Lascaris tower, ruined ramparts and Italianate cemetery. At the end of covered passageways are blind alleys with views of terraced allotments beside a tinkling mountain stream.

At the northern end of town is a recent addition, the **Musée des Merveilles** (open Wed–Mon; entrance fee; tel: (04) 93 04 32 50). Even if you're not planning a trip to the Vallée des Merveilles (*see page 298*), the museum is worth a visit for the insight it gives into the history and significance of the valley and its bizarre engravings.

Old habits

Out of season *vieille* Tende feels medieval. Locals collect firewood and mule dung in hand-drawn carts; old men strip olive wood; chestnuts are roasted over open fires; dogs tear each other apart in dark corners. The air is rent with sounds of sawing, chopping and howling. Even the smells are unchanged since medieval times: sawdust and woodsmoke, dung and dog's piss, incense and roast chestnuts.

To dispel this oppressive atmosphere one can stroll down to the new town, centred on Place de la République. Here, the aromas vary from *lasagne* and pizza to trout *soufflé* and Piedmontes *polenta*. The stodgy *polenta* dishes are a reminder of Tende's humble origins. Until recently, the poorest people lived on chestnut and cabbage soup or on a pasta made from flour, oil and potatoes. On Sundays, this was supplemented by *une bonne sauce*, generally rabbit.

Game, such as boar and deer, was caught in the woods and sold to wealthier citizens. Nowadays, the local cuisine is on a par with Sospel's but Tende still harbours hunters who stray into the Mercantour, and wild boar are still caught in significant numbers. It is best not to question the provenance of game in local restaurants. ❏

✘ INSIGHT GUIDES
TRAVEL TIPS

CONTENTS

Getting Acquainted

The Côte d'Azur has a particularly varied landscape. In just 2 hours one can travel from the palm-fringed coast to the high peaks of the Alps. In the east, the Parc National du Mercantour covers 686 sq. km (265 sq. miles) of forests, lakes, waterfalls and mountains. While the resorts are fairly built up, the mountains and inland areas are dotted with villages. Along the coast the westernmost stretch is the least developed and further inland lie the region's famous olive groves.

Language: French.

Time Zone: For most of the year, France is one hour ahead of Greenwich Mean Time, so if it is noon in Nice, it is 11am in London, 6am in New York and Toronto and 8pm in Melbourne.

Currency: The euro, divided into 100 cents.

Weights and Measures: The metric system is used in France for all weights and measures.Accurate conversions are given below:
100 grams (gm) = 3.5 ounces
1 kilogram (kg) = 2.2 pounds
10 centimetres (cm) = 4 inches
1 metre (m) = 1.1 yards
1 kilometre (km) = 0.6 miles
1 litre (l) = 1.75 pints

Electricity: Electric current is generally 220/230 volts, but still 110 in a few areas. Current alternates at 50 cycles, not 60 as in the US, so take a transformer for shavers, travel irons, hairdryers etc., which also takes care of the fact that outlet prongs are different.

International Dialling Code: 33 (for France); 377 (for Monaco)

Local Dialling Codes: 04 for the Southeast region.

Climate

An extremely privileged region, both in its natural landscape and its climate, the Côte d'Azur is a popular resort all year round. It enjoys around 2,700 hours of sunshine a year, but the heat is never unbearable because of the sea breezes (nights can be cool). The highest temperatures are in July and August – often over 30°C (86°F). Winter is mild and sunny – frost is a rarity.

There is snow on the mountains, but the heat of the sun means that it is quite possible to ski in a T-shirt. The wettest period is the autumn, but then the area is favoured with short, heavy downpours followed by bright sunshine. Spring, too, can have some wet spells when the sky becomes heavy and overcast. The famous Mistral is the worst aspect of the weather and only really affects the hinterland. This fearsome wind, said to be able to "blow the ears off a donkey", causes considerable damage and can have a depressing effect.

Weather information:
(in English) tel: 08 36 70 12 34. For local forecasts dial 08 36 68 02 followed by the *département* number. Minitel: 3615 METEO. Website: www.meteo.fr

People

CULTURE & CUSTOMS

The history of the region is ancient, with evidence of early human and even Cro-Magnon settlements. Up in the mountains, in the archaeological sites of the Vallée des Merveilles and the Vallon de Fontanelbe, an extraordinary number of stone engravings (over 100,000) bear witness to man's early habitation. The region's later history was inextricably linked with the Greeks, and then the Romans. With the coming of Christianity, Latin became the lingua franca of the area. The Italian influence on architecture, culture and cuisine has been considerable.

Religion plays a great part in the development of any culture and this region is no exception, with much of its religious art dating back to the 15th and 16th centuries.

Recent culture has benefited much from the contribution of artists drawn to the region. Since the arrival of Picasso, Chagall, Matisse *et al*, museums and art galleries have been established and become a magnet for other artists around the world. Indigenous arts and crafts, particularly the pottery and fabrics known as Provençal can be seen all around the region.

Government

For much of its history, the Côte d'Azur, with Nice at its centre, was a disputed area. Its proximity to the Italian border meant that it was mostly controlled by the Italians under the House of Savoy and it did not become French until 1860.

For years the French were ruled by a very centralised form of government, but under the socialists (1981–86) the Paris-appointed *préfets* lost much of their power as the individual *départements* (or counties) gained their own directly elected assemblies for the first time, giving them far more financial and administrative autonomy. Each

Average Daytime Temperatures

January: 12.2°C (54°F)	July: 28.1°C (82.6°F)
February: 11.9°C (53.4°F)	August: 28.4°C (83.1°F)
March: 14.2°C (57.6°F)	September: 25.2°C (77.4°F)
April: 18.5°C (65.3°F)	October: 22.2°C (72°F)
May: 20.8°C (69.4°F)	November: 16.8°C (62.2°F)
June: 26.6°C (79.9°F)	December: 14.1°C (57.4°F)

département still has a *préfet*, but the role is now much more advisory. The *préfecture* is based in the county town of each *département*: Digne in Alpes-de-Haute-Provence, Gap in Hautes-Alpes, Nice in Alpes-Maritimes, and Toulon in Var. These offices handle most matters concerned with the social welfare of their citizens.

Each French *département* has a number which is used as a handy reference for administrative purposes. For example, it forms the first two digits of the postcode in an address and the last two figures on licence plates. The *département* numbers for the Riviera are 06 for Alpes-Maritimes and 83 for Var.

Each *département* is divided into a number of disparately-sized communes whose district councils control a town, village or group of villages under the direction of the local mayor. Communes are now responsible for local planning and environmental matters. Decisions relating to tourism and culture are dealt with at regional level, while the state still controls education, the health service and security.

The Principality of Monaco is generally included as part of the region, but it is largely autonomous. It is still ruled by the Grimaldi family, who acquired it from the Genoese as far back as 1308. In the early 20th century, the then Prince of Monaco signed a treaty with the French to retain its autonomy provided its citizens conformed to French law. This had the perhaps unforeseen effect of attracting tax exiles to the principality (where no income tax was levied).

Economy

The Côte d'Azur is heavily dependent on tourism, but efforts have been made to lessen that reliance. One of the major industries – which is almost an extension of tourism – is the conference trade. The area is probably the most popular in France

for conventions, with the Cannes Film Festival and international music publishing fairs being the best known.

The area also has another glamorous industry: perfumes. Grasse is the perfume capital of the world.

There is hardly any heavy industry in the region. However, the Var valley is continuing to attract electronics and related businesses. To the west, the business park of Sophia-Antipolis is a magnet for high-tech industries and is often spoken of as France's Silicon Valley.

There is also an emphasis on scientific research, with centres set up for the study of astronomy, oceanography and health care. An off-shoot of the interest in health can be seen in the growth of treatment centres for thalasso-therapy (sea-water cures) and balneotherapy (bathing cures).

Planning the Trip

Entry Regulations

To visit France, you need a valid passport. All visitors require a visa except for citizens of EU countries.

Citizens of the USA, Canada, Australia or New Zealand do not need a visa for stays of up to three months. If you are unsure, check before you travel with the French consulate in your country.

Visitors who stay in France for more than 90 days should apply for a *carte de séjour*.

Customs

You are permitted to take any quantity of goods into France from another EU country as long as they are for personal use and tax has been paid on them in the country of origin. Customs can still question visitors.

Quantities accepted as being for personal use are:
● up to 3,200 cigarettes, 400 small cigars, 200 cigars or 3kg loose tobacco
● 10 litres of spirits (over 22 per cent alcohol), 90 litres of wine (under 22 per cent alcohol) or 110 litres of beer
From outside the EU you can bring in:
● 200 cigarettes, 100 small cigars, 50 cigars or 250g loose tobacco
● 1 litre of spirits (over 22 per cent alcohol) and 2 litres of wine and beer (under 22 per cent alcohol)
● 50g perfume
Visitors can also carry up to €10,000 in currency

Animal Quarantine

Animal quarantine laws have been revised and it is now possible for your pets to re-enter Britain without quarantine. Conditions are stringent, however, with tough health requirements and restricted points of entry.

For further information you are advised to contact the Ministry of Agriculture, or the French consulate if you are abroad.

Once in Europe, travelling between countries other than Britain and the continent requires only a valid vaccination certificate.

Health Care

The **International Association for Medical Assistance to Travellers** (IAMAT) is a non-profit-making organisation which anyone can join free of charge (a donation is requested). Benefits include a membership card (entitling the bearer to services at fixed IAMAT rates by participating physicians) and a traveller clinical record (a passport-sized record completed by the member's own doctor prior to travel). A directory of English speaking IAMAT doctors on call 24-hours a day is published for members.

EU nationals staying in France are entitled to use the French Social Security system, which refunds up to 70 per cent of medical expenses (but sometimes less, e.g. for dental treatment).

To get a refund, British nationals should obtain form **E111** before leaving the UK (or E112 for those already in treatment). This form is open-ended; you don't need a new one every time you travel. Even so, the refund can take time and involve a certain amount of red tape to obtain, so you can be out of pocket for a long time before you get the money. Travel insurance can be a better option.

If you undergo treatment while in France the doctor will give you a prescription and a *feuille de soins* (statement of treatment). The medication will carry vignettes (little

stickers), which you must stick onto your *feuille de soins*. Send this, the prescription, and form E111 to the local Caisse Primaire d'Assurance Maladie (in the phone book under *Sécurité Sociale*). Refunds can sometimes take over a month to come through.

Nationals of non-EU countries should take out travel and medical insurance before leaving home. Consultations and prescriptions have to be paid for in full, and are reimbursed, in part, on receipt of a completed fiche.

To contact the **International Association for Medical Assistance to Travellers (IAMAT):**

US: 417 Center Street, Lewiston, NY 14092, tel: (716) 754 4883.
Canada: 1287 St Claire Ave, W. Toronto, M6E 1B9, tel: (416) 652 0137 or 40 Regal Road, Guelph, Ontario, N1K 1B5, tel: (519) 836 0102

Pharmacies

Pharmacies in France are good, but expensive, and many toiletries will be cheaper in the supermarket. The staff are well qualified however, and able to advise on many minor ailments – they may be able to help with minor wounds and other basic medical services. All pharmacies can be identified by a neon green cross, Most open from 9am or 10am to 7pm or 8pm.

If the pharmacy is closed there will be a sign indicating the nearest *pharmacie de garde*, which will also offer a night time service. If you can't find a pharmacy, consult the Gendarmerie.

Money

The unit of currency in the France (and in most other countries of the European Union) is the **euro** (abbreviated €). There are 100 **cents** in a euro. Banknotes come in the following denominations: €5, €10, €20, €50, €100, €200 and €500. Coins in circulation are: 1 cent, 2 cents, 5 cents, 10 cents, 20 cents, €1 and €2.

Banks displaying the *Change* sign will change foreign currency

and, in general, at the best rates (you will need to produce your passport in any transaction). If possible avoid hotels or other independent bureaux which may charge a high commission.

You will find most major international **credit cards** accepted, though American Express is sometimes refused due to high charges to the retailer.

Cards issued by French banks have a security microchip (*puce*) in each card. The card is slotted into a card reader, and you key in a PIN number to authorise the transaction. There are sometimes problems when you present cards issued by UK or US banks with magnetic strips, and your card might be rejected. Explain the problem and suggest that they telephone for confirmation that the card is valid.

The French Tourist Office recommends the following explanation: "*Les cartes internationales ne sont pas des cartes à puce, mais a bande magnetique. Ma carte est valable et je vous serais reconnaisant d'en demander la confirmation auprès de votre banque ou de votre centre de traitement.*"

You can withdraw euros from bank and post office automatic cash machines using various foreign cards and your PIN number. The machine will indicate which cards it accepts, and very often also have user instructions in English. Check with your bank before leaving home that your card will work in this way.

Eurocheques are no longer accepted.

What to Bring

You should be able to buy anything you need in France. There will be plenty of things you will want to buy so leave space in your suitcase or pack another fold-up bag.

Pharmacies offer a wide range of drugs, medical supplies and toiletries, along with expert advice, but you should bring any prescription drugs you need. Spare glasses or contact lenses are a good idea.

Sunscreen and anti-mosquito products are advisable in summer. If you bring electrical equipment you will need adaptors.

Clothing will depend on your destination and when you travel; you will only need to dress up for big city restaurants or casinos. Summer wear is very casual, not to say minimal, although be prepared to dress up for dinner after a day on the beach. Dress appropriately for visiting churches; a scarf or shirt is always useful as a cover-up.

Most sports equipment can be hired but you should bring personal equipment such as walking boots with you.

In big cities you will find English language newspapers and magazines, and English bookshops, but elsewhere you will need your own reading matter. Ensure you have up-to-date local guides, phrase books and maps, though the latter are increasingly available in supermarkets. Electronic translators can be really useful. Don't forget essentials like passport, driving licence, insurance documentation, special passes and credit card emergency numbers.

Maps

In France maps can be bought most cheaply in hypermarkets or service stations. Tourist offices usually provide free maps.

The **Institute Géographique National** (IGN) is the French equivalent of the British Ordnance Survey, and their maps are excellent. Those covering the Riviera are listed below:

Red Series (1:250,000, 1 cm to 2.5 km) sheet 115 covers the region at a good scale for touring.

Green Series (1:100,000 (1 cm to 1 km) are more detailed, corresponding roughly to individual *départements* – sheet nos. 67 and 68 cover most of the region, for the far north, sheets 60 and 61 are necessary.

Also available is the IGN tourist map *Alpes Maritimes* and highly detailed 1:50,000 and 1:25,000 scales, which are ideal for walkers.

For planning your route IGN 901 covers the whole of France at a scale of 1 cm to 10 km and is regularly updated.

Good mountain maps for walkers and winter sports are produced by Didier Richard, mostly at a scale of 1:50,000, but a few at the more detailed 1:25,000 scale.

Stockists in London include: **Stanfords International Map Centre**, 12–14 Long Acre, Covent Garden WC2, tel: 020 7730 1354 **The Travel Bookshop**, 13 Blenheim Crescent, London W11 2EE, tel: 020 7229 5260

IGN Maps are also available from their agent in the UK: **World Leisure Marketing**, 11 Newmarket Court, Derby, DE24 8NW, tel: 0800 838080. www.map-guides.com.

Getting There

BY AIR

There are an increasing number of low-cost flights to the Riviera. **Go** (0802 838 383; www.go-fly.com) now flies to Nice from Stansted and Bristol. Low-cost flights to Nice are also operated by **Easyjet** (UK 0870 6000 000; Nice 04 93 21 48 33; www.easyjet.com) from Luton and Liverpool.

Air France (UK 0845 0845 111; US 1-800 237 2747; France 08 02 80 28 02; www.airfrance.com) operate flights from Paris to Nice. There are no direct Air France flights to the South from the UK.

British Airways (UK 0345 222111; US 1-800 247 9297; France 08 02 80 29 02; www. britishairways.com) flies to Nice from Heathrow and Manchester. **British Midland** (UK 0870 6070 555; France 08 00 05 01 42; www.britishmidland.com) fly direct to Nice from Heathrow and East Midlands, and via either of these two airports from Aberdeen, Belfast, Edinburgh, Glasgow, Leeds, Manchester and Teesside.

From the US, most flights involve a Paris connection. **Delta** (US 1-800 241 4141; France 08 00 35 40 80; www.delta.air.com) have a daily

Public Holidays

A list of major public holidays is given below. It is common practice, if a public holiday falls on a Thursday or Tuesday for French business to *faire le pont* (bridge the gap) and have the Friday or Monday as a holiday, too. Details of closures should be posted outside banks etc. a few days before the event but it is easy to be caught out, especially on Assumption day in August, which is not a holiday in the UK.

New Year's Day: 1 January
Easter Monday: (but not Good Friday)
Labour Day: Monday closest to 1 May
Ascension Day
8 May: (to commemorate the end of World War I)
Whit Monday: (Pentecost)
Bastille Day: 14 July
Assumption Day: 15 August
All Saints' Day – Toussaint: 1 November
Armistice Day: 11 November
National holiday in Monaco: 19 November
Christmas Day: 25 December

flight from New York to Nice, and another to Lyon, 200 km (120 miles) north of Avignon.

From Paris, **Air Inter** (France 08 02 80 28 02) runs hourly *navettes* (shuttle flights) from Orly to Marseille and Nice.

TAT (France 08 03 80 58 05) flies from Paris to Toulon-Hyères.

Air Liberté (France 08 03 09 09 09) flies from Paris Orly to Nice.

AOM French Airlines (France 08 03 00 12 34) have flights from Paris Orly to Nice, Marseille, and Toulon-Hyères.

Note: the 20-minute taxi ride from Nice airport is not value for money – so take the bus instead.

Helicopter transfer services operate from Nice to Cannes and Monaco (transfers can be included in ticket prices).

BY SEA

Deciding which ferry to take depends on your starting point in the UK and how much driving you want to do in France. Since the opening of the Channel Tunnel, ferry services have become increasingly competitive. It's worth shopping around for discounts and special offers.

The following companies operate across the English Channel to various ports. All carry cars as well as foot passengers.

Brittany Ferries offer sailings from Portsmouth to Caen, and Poole to Cherbourg (summer only), and St Malo: The Brittany Centre, Wharf Road, Portsmouth PO2 8RU; tel: 0870 536 0360; www.brittany-ferries.com.

P&O sail from Portsmouth to Cherbourg, St Malo and Le Havre, and also operate the short sea route from Dover to Calais: Channel House, Channel View Road, Dover CT17 9TJ; tel: 0870 242 4999; www.poef.com.

Hoverspeed Fast Ferries operates a Superseacat service from Newhaven to Dieppe, crossing in 2 hours: International Hoverport, Dover CT17 9TG; tel: 08705 240 241; www.hoverspeed.co.uk.

BY TRAIN

From the UK, Eurostar trains run to Lille and Paris Gare du Nord. Services for the South depart from the Gare de Lyon The TGV high-speed track has now reached Marseille, reducing the journey time to about 3 hours. From Paris Gare de Lyon, 10–12 trains a day depart for Marseille. Nine TGVs per day depart for Nice (journey time now approximately 5 hours). All these stations connect with the local train network.

Sleepers

A comfortable way to get to the south is by overnight sleeper. The cheapest alternative is the couchette, which has six beds per carriage with an ad hoc mix of men,

women and children. The *voiture-lit* is more private, with a carriage for up to three people. You can travel first- or second-class, and reservations must be made well in advance.

Tickets

In the UK, tickets for journeys in France can be booked from any British Rail station or travel centre or the **International Rail Centre** at Victoria Station (020 7834 2345). Otherwise visit the **Rail Europe Travel Shop** (179 Piccadilly, 0870 584 8848) or book on line at www.raileurope.co.uk. For journeys on the TGV you always have to book in advance.

Remember that before you get on the train you have to date-stamp your ticket in the orange *composteur* machine at the station. It will say *compostez votre billet*. SNCF central reservations and information is on 08 36 35 35 35, open 7am–10pm daily. Phone or Minitel reservations (3615 SNCF) have to be collected and paid for within 48 hours.

Discounts and Passes

A variety of passes and discounts are available within France *(see page 317)*. A Eurodomino pass allows unlimited travel on France's rail network for 3–8 days duration within one month, but this must be bought before travelling to France. Discounted rates are available to children aged 4–11, or young people aged 12–25.

US visitors can also find a good choice of discounts and passes, including Eurailpass, Flexipass and Saver Pass. These can be bought in the US before you travel. Call (212) 308 3103 for information, and 1-800 223 636 for reservations.

Bicycles

Within the region there are designated trains which will carry bicycles, but for long-distance journeys they must be carried separately, and will need to be registered and insured. This may take a while, but you can arrange

for your bicycle to be delivered to your final destination. To take bikes on the Eurostar you will have to check them in 24 hours in advance of travel or, alternatively, be prepared to wait 24 hours at your destination.

BY BUS

The cheapest way to get to the Riviera is by bus, though you need to be prepared for a long journey. Eurolines (UK 01582 404511, France 08 36 69 52 52) has regular services from London to Avignon, Marseille and Nice.

For local bus information see page 317.

BY CAR

Many drivers are daunted by the thought of a long drive (1,200 km/745 miles from London and over 900 km/560 miles from Paris), before even starting their holiday. Indeed, in high season the roads can become very crowded. For those in a hurry, the autoroute from Paris to Nice (A6, A7, A8) takes about eight hours, but toll fees can add up dramatically along the way. For travellers driving from the port of Calais, it is now possible to travel all the way to the Riviera by motorway.

However, if speed is not of the essence and you intend to make the drive part of your holiday, follow the green holiday route signs to your destination – these form part of a national network of *bison futé* routes to avoid traffic congestion at peak periods. You will discover parts of France you never knew existed and are more likely to arrive relaxed. The first weekend in August and the public holiday on the 15th are usually the worst times to travel, so avoid them if you can.

All autoroutes have *péage* toll-booths, where payment can be made by cash or credit card. For information on French motorways see www.autoroutes.fr.

Channel Tunnel

Le Shuttle carries cars and their passengers from Folkestone to Calais on a simple drive-on-drive-off system (journey time 35 minutes). Payment is made at toll booths (which accept cash, cheques or credit cards). Prepaid tickets and booked spaces are available, but no booking is necessary as you can just turn up and take the next available service.

Le Shuttle runs 24 hours a day, all year round, with a service at least once an hour through the night. Information and bookings from Le Shuttle Customer Services Centre, PO Box 300, Folkestone, Kent CT19 4QW; tel: 0990 353 535. In France, tel: 08 01 63 03 04.

Business Travellers

Contacts are vital for anyone trying to do business in the region, and it helps a great deal if you are willing to meet people personally.

Chambres de Commerce et d'Industrie can provide local information and a calendar of trade fairs is available from the Chambre de Commerce et d'Industrie de Paris, 27 Av de Friedland; tel: 01 42 89 70 00; fax: 01 42 89 78 68. Most major banks can refer you to lawyers, accountants and tax consultants, and some also provide specific expatriate services.

On the Côte d'Azur in particular, business tourism is of vital importance to the region's economy, and has been developed alongside its regular tourist industry. Nice, Cannes and Monte-Carlo all attract visitors to the trade fairs and other events that take place annually. The larger hotels depend on the conference trade for a major part of their business. The international airport at Nice, with direct flights to much of Europe and the US means that it is an ideal venue for top-flight companies who can afford to indulge their higher paid executives.

Cannes, Nice and Monte-Carlo all have huge, modern convention centres in very attractive locations. The **Palais des Festivals** in Cannes is at the west end of La Croisette and plays host to the annual Film

Travelling with Children

The Riviera is more the kind of place that attracts adults to its glamorous beaches and nightlife than a family resort, and young families would be well advised to stay away from the crowds (and high prices) of the high season. The coastal resorts to the west are more easily approached by car and therefore more attractive to families. To get anywhere near the beaches of Nice or Cannes in August could be a nightmare with young children in tow (remembering the difficulties of parking). However, the private beaches of the Riviera *do* cater well for children, and have beach clubs providing various amusements (for a fee). Some of the public beaches have the same kind of facilities (expect to pay for the morning/afternoon session).

In France generally, children are treated as people, not just nuisances. It is pleasant to be able to take them into restaurants (even in the evening) without heads turning in horror. French children, being accustomed to eating out from an early age, are on the whole well behaved in restaurants so it helps if one's own offspring understand that they can't run wild.

Many restaurants offer a children's menu; otherwise, they will often split a *prix-fixe* menu between two children. If travelling with very young children, you may find it practical to order nothing specific but request an extra plate and give them morsels from your own dish. It is a good introduction to foreign food without too much waste. French meals are generous enough (*nouvelle cuisine* excepted) to allow you to do this without going hungry yourself, and you are unlikely to encounter hostility from *le patron* (or *la patronne*). Another option is to order a simple, inexpensive dish from the *à la carte* menu, such as an omelette.

Most hotels have family rooms, so children do not have to be separated from parents, and a cot (*lit bébé*) will often be provided for a small supplement. It is a good idea to check availability if booking in advance. Some of the hotels offer a baby listening or child-minding service.

Listed below are some fun places to take the kids:

Jardin D'Oiseaux Tropicaux
Route de Valcros, La Londe
tel: 04 94 35 02 15.
A unique collection of exotic birds and rare plants in landscaped woodland. Open daily.

Le Village des Tortues
Gonfaron
tel: 04 94 78 26 41
"Tortoise Village" is a refuge and study centre where children and adults can observe different kinds of tortoises. Open Mar–Nov: daily

Aquatica
Route 98, Fréjus
tel: 04 94 51 82 51
A huge waterpark with varied attractions. Open Jun–Sept: daily (weather permitting).

Parc Zoologique de Fréjus
Le Capitou, Fréjus
tel: 04 94 40 70 65.
An eco-friendly zoo. Open daily.

Base Nature
Fréjus
tel: 04 94 17 05 60.
Large seafront park with beaches, a nature reserve, and varied sport and leisure activities. Open daily.

Marineland
4 km (2 miles) north of Antibes
tel: 04 93 33 49 49.
Marine park/entertainment complex with waterslides. Open daily.

Museum of Oceanography
Ave St-Martin, Monaco
tel: 00 377 93 15 36 00.
A fascinating aquarium with impressive displays of whale skeletons and stuffed marine fauna. Open daily.

Festival. In Nice, the **Acropolis** is set in splendid gardens studded with statues by famous artists, while Monte-Carlo's **Grimaldi Forum** puts on both conferences and major cultural events. Most larger hotels also have conference facilities.

BUSINESS INFORMATION

BFM on 96.4 FM is a business radio station. Les Echos gives stock quotes on the website www.lesechos.com. Minitel service 3615 CD has real-time stock quotes. Business directories Kompass France and Kompass Régional also give company details and detailed French market profiles on 3617 KOMPASS. *The French Company Handbook*, which lists all companies in the 120 Index of the Paris Bourse, is available from the *International Herald Tribune* (France tel: 01 41 43 93 00) or from Paul Baker Publishing, 37 Lambton Rd, London SW20 0LW; tel: 020 8946 0590 (price £50).

Travellers with Disabilities

TRAVEL

Le Shuttle (UK tel: 0990 353 353) – the Channel tunnel car-on-a-train service – allows disabled passengers to stay in their vehicle. Eurostar trains (UK special requests, tel: 020 7928 0660) give wheelchair passengers first-class travel for second-class fares.

Most ferry companies offer facilities if contacted beforehand. Vehicles fitted to accommodate disabled people pay reduced tolls on autoroutes.

Autoroute Guide

An autoroute guide for disabled travellers (*Guides des Autoroutes à l'usage des Personnes à Mobilité Réduite*) is available free from Ministère des Transports, Direction des Routes, Service du Contrôle des Autoroutes, La Défense, 92055 Cedex, Paris; tel: 01 40 81 21 22.

Useful Websites

Transport
www.sncf.fr
www.britrail.co.uk
www.eurostar.co.uk
www.raileurope.com

Accommodation:
www.chatotel.com (chateaux & independent hotels)
www.fuaj.org (youth hostels)
www.relaischateaux.fr
www.campingfrance.com
www.gites-de-france.fr

Restaurants
www.bottin-gourmand.com
www.calvacom.fr/savoy

Weather
www.meteo.fr

Regional
provence.web.fr
Listing of villages, hotels,

Taxis
If you are disabled, a French taxi driver cannot refuse to take you. Moreover, he or she must help you into the vehicle and is obliged to transport a guide dog for a blind passenger.

HOLIDAYS AND ACCOMMODATION

Gîtes Accessible á Tous lists *gîte* accommodation equipped for the disabled. It is available from: Maison de Gîtes de France, 59 Rue St-Lazare, 75009 Paris; tel: 01 49 70 75 85; fax: 01 42 81 28 53.

The French Federation of Camping and Caravanning (Fédération de Camping-Caravanning) guide indicates which camp sites have facilities for disabled campers. It is obtainable from Deneway Guides, Chesil Lodge, West Bexington, Dorchester DT2 9DG; tel: 01308 897 809, price £8.95.

The Michelin Green Guide – Camping/Caravanning France lists sites with facilities for the disabled.

restaurants with links to all main towns and cities.
www.visitprovence.com
Tourist website in both French and English of French government tourist information on sights, tours, specialist walks, hotels and restaurants and a variety of practical information.
www.provence-beyond.com
English language website with information on lesser known places, and also offering personally tailored tours for a fee.
www.riviera-reporter.com
Local English language magazine site with archive of articles on a variety of practical and political subjects and links to other relevant government/advice sites.
www.crt-riviera.fr
French government tourist site with information on sights, accommodation and travel.

The Association des Paralysés publishes *Où Ferons Nous Étapes?* which lists accommodation suitable for disabled travellers. The Association is at 22 Rue du Père Guérain, Paris 75013; tel: 01 44 16 83 83.

ACCESS

It is not particularly easy for disabled visitors to travel on the Riviera and access can be a problem. Even if museums, monuments, hotels, restaurants and other places claim in their advertising to have access for disabled people, it's always wise to check beforehand exactly what they mean. They may be able to accommodate wheelchair users but not have accessible toilets, for example. Small villages with steep streets and inaccessible cliff-top castles can be a nightmare to negotiate with a wheelchair. Bigger cities are sometimes better equipped with facilities, but don't bank on it. Basically, try to check out your route as much as possible in advance.

Disabled parking is usually available and indicated with a blue wheelchair sign. The international orange disabled parking disc scheme is also recognised in France (don't forget to bring the disc with you).

To hire a wheelchair or other equipment enquire at a local pharmacy.

Students & Young People

Student & youth discounts

Students will be able to find a good range of discounts; to qualify for reduced entry prices to museums, cinemas and theatres you need an International Student Identity Card from CROUS (see below) or from travel agents specialising in student travel. ISIC cards are only valid in France if you are under 26. Under 26s can also get up to 50 per cent discounts on certain trains with the Carte 12/25 (see page 318), or buy the Carte Jeune (€20 from FNAC) which gives discounts on museums, cinema, theatre, travel, sports clubs, restaurants, insurance and some shops.

Studying in France

Foreign students in France can get information on courses, grants and accommodation from the **Centre Regional des Oeuvres Universitaires et Scolaires (CROUS)**, 69 Quai d'Orsay, 75007 Paris; tel: 01 44 18 53 00; or from local cultural exchange and language courses.

The **Socrates-Erasmus Programme** is a scheme that enables EU students with a reasonable level of French to spend a year of their degree following appropriate courses in the French university system. The UK office publishes a brochure and helps with general enquiries. Contact details: In Britain: UK Socrates-Erasmus Council, RND Building, The University, Canterbury, Kent CT2 7PD. 0122 7762712 In France: Agence Erasmus, 10 pl de la Bourse, 33081 Bordeaux Cedex 05 56 79 44 02 mj.bio.ndini@socrates-fr.org.

Other useful organisations include:
Central Bureau for Educational Visits and Exchanges
Seymour Mews House, Seymour Mews, London W1H 9PE
tel: 020 7486 5101.
Centre des Échanges Internationaux
1 rue Jolzen, Paris 75006
tel: 01 40 51 11 71
Sporting and cultural holidays and educational tours for 15–30-year-olds. Non-profit making.
Alliance Français
101 boulevard Raspail, Paris
tel: 01 45 44 38 28
Non-profit, highly regarded French language school, with beginners' and specialist courses.
Souffle
BP 133, 83957 La Garde Cedex
tel: 04 94 21 20 92
fax: 04 94 21 22 17
An umbrella organisation for courses in French.

Local Language Courses
International School of Nice
15 ave Claude Debussy,
06200 Nice
tel: 04 93 21 04 00
Actilangue
2 rue Alexis Mossa, 06000 Nice.
tel: 04 93 96 33 84
fax: 04 93 44 37 16.
French courses.
Azurlingua
25 boulevard Raimbaldi,
06000 Nice
tel: 04 93 62 01 11
fax: 04 93 62 22 56
www.azurlingua.com
Language holidays.
Centre International d'Antibes
38 bd d'Aguillon, Antibes
tel: 04 92 90 71 70
fax: 04 92 90 71 71
www.cia-France.com
French tuition.
Institut d'Enseignement de la Langue Française sur la Côte d'Azur (ELFCA)
66 avenue de Toulon,
83400 Hyères
tel: 04 94 65 03 31
fax 04.94 65 81 22
www.elfca.com
French tuition.

Tourist Offices Abroad

UK
French Government Tourist Office,
178 Piccadilly, London W1V 0AL
tel: 0891 244 123
fax: 020 7493 6594
email: piccadilly@mdlf.demon.co.uk
www.franceguide.com
A French travel centre with information, books and guides.
USA
444 Madison Ave, NY NY 10022
tel: 410 286 8310
fax: 212 838 7855
www.franceguide.com
Canada
1981 Ave McGill Collège,
Suite 490, Montreal, Quebec
tel: 514 288 4264
fax: 514 845 4868
Australia
Level 22, 25 Bligh St, Sydney,
NSW 2000
tel: 02 9231 5244
Ireland
10 Suffolk St, Dublin
tel: 1 679 0813
fax: 1 679 0814

Practical Tips

Office workers normally start early – 8.30am is not uncommon, but often stay at their desks until 6pm or later. This is partly to make up for the long lunch hours (from noon or 12.30 for two hours) which are still traditional in banks, shops and other public offices. On the Riviera, while the smaller traders still keep to these hours – many closing until 3pm at lunchtime, the larger department stores now tend to stay open. Many companies, too, are beginning to change to shorter lunchbreaks as employees appreciate the advantages of getting home earlier to their families in the evenings.

Banks on the Riviera are normally open 8.30am–noon and 1.30–5pm, Monday–Friday. However, some bureaux de change are open on Sunday.

Tipping

You do not usually need to add service to a restaurant bill in France. A charge of 10 per cent is added automatically as part of the bill. (To be sure, check that it says "*Service compris*" on the menu, or ask ("*Est-ce que le service est compris?*") Taxis also include service, but won't mind a bit extra.

Media

Newspapers

Regional **newspapers**, such as *Nice-Matin*, with national and international as well as local news, have a far higher standing here than in the UK and are often read in preference to national dailies such as *Le Monde*, *Libération* and *Le Figaro*. British and American dailies, notably *The Times* and the *International Herald Tribune*, are widely available, as are local English-language publications aimed at the tourist and expatriate community.

Look out for the *Riviera Reporter* which gives an irreverent, insider's view of the region. (www. riviera-reporter.com)

Radio

France Inter is the main national radio station (FM 87.8 MHz). It broadcasts English-language news twice a day in summer (generally 9am and 4pm). An all-English station is Monte-Carlo's Riviera Radio (106.3 and 106.5 MHz), which has 24 hours of world news, regional broadcasts and small ads.

Television

France has six terrestial TV channels. **TF1**, the largest, has been privatised since 1987, and features movies, game shows, dubbed soaps, audience debates and the main news at 8pm.

France 2 is a state-owned station featuring a mix of game shows, documentaries and cultural chat shows.

F3R is more heavyweight than the first two channels and shows local news, sports, excellent wildlife documentaries and a late-night Sunday Cinema, *Minuit*, with classic films in the original language (VO for *version originale*). It also has a news and documentary programme, *Continentales*, which is broadcast five days a week with news broadcasts from around Europe in the original language with French subtitles.

Canal+ offers a roster of satellite and cable subscription channels with recent movies (sometimes original language), exclusive sport and late-night porn.

Arte is an excellent Franco-German hybrid, specialising in intelligent arts coverage and films in the original language. From 5.45am–7pm, Arte's wavelength is shared with the educational channel, **La Cinquième**.

M6 is a daytime channel with a base of music videos supplemented by magazine programmes such as *Culture Pub*.

Any suitably connected television can supplement these channels with a range of internationally broadcast satellite stations.

Postal Services

Post Offices (PTTs) open Mon–Fri 9am–noon and 2–6pm, Sat 9am–noon. In large towns they may not close for lunch, but in small villages, they may only be open for a short time in the morning. Before you start queuing check that you are at the right counter; in larger post offices, each counter has specific services. If you only want **stamps**, look for the sign, "*Timbres*". Standard-weight letters within France and most of the EU require a €0.46 stamp.

You can also buy stamps at tobacconists *(bureaux de tabac)* and some shops selling postcards. Large post offices and *maisons de la presse* (newsagents) also offer **fax** and **photocopying** services; many supermarkets also have coin-operated photocopiers. **Minitel** *(see page 316)* is gradually being replaced by the Internet and is now not always available in post offices.

POSTE RESTANTE

Mail can be kept *poste restante* at a post office, addressed to Poste Restante, Poste Centrale (for the main post office), then the town postcode and name. A small fee will be charged and you will need to show your passport to collect your mail.

URGENT MAIL

Urgent post can be sent *par exprès*. The Chronopost system is also fast but expensive. However, packages weighing up to 25g are guaranteed delivery within 24 hours.

Telephones

French telephone numbers are all 10 figures, always written – and spoken – in sets of two, e.g. 01 23 45 67 89. Regional telephone numbers are prefixed as follows: Paris, Ile de France region 01; Northwest 02; Northeast 03; Southeast and Corsica 04, and Southwest 05. When dialling from outside the country omit the zero. If you want numbers to be given singly rather than in pairs, ask for them "*chiffre par chiffre*".

Note that the international phone code for Monaco is 00 377. When phoning a Monégasque number from inside the principality, you must dial the code. If you're phoning from France, dial 00 377 then the number. To phone abroad – including France – from Monaco, use the international prefix 00 then the country code (33 for France).

The international access codes for US phonecards are as follows:

AT&T: 0800 99 00 11.
MCI: 0800 99 00 19.
Sprint: 0800 99 00 87.

Phone Directories

Phone directories (*annuaires*) are found in all post offices and in most cafés. The *Pages Blanche* (White Pages) lists names of people and businesses alphabetically. The *Pages Jaunes* (Yellow Pages) lists businesses and services by category. Both are also now available on the Internet at:
www.pagesjaunes.fr
www.pagesblanches.fr

PUBLIC PHONES

You should be able to find functioning telephone boxes (*cabines publiques*) in every sizeable village. Coin-operated phones take most coins but card phones are now more usual. Buy a phone card (*une télécarte*) from post offices, stationers, railway stations, some cafés and bureaux de tabacs, if you think you will need to use a public callbox.

Some cafés, restaurants and shops have metered phones but these may cost more. If you need to make a phone call in a small village with no public phone, look out for a blue *téléphone publique* plaque on a house. The proprietor is officially appointed to allow you to use the phone and charge the normal amount for the call.

MAKING A PHONE CALL

Lift the receiver, insert card or coin, then dial the number. When you replace the receiver, any unused coins will be returned to you. If you wish to make a follow-on call and have coin credit left, do not replace the receiver but press the *Appel Suivant* button and then dial the new number.

The cheapest times to telephone are weekdays 7pm to 8am and at weekends.

International Calls

To make an international call dial 00 followed by the country's international call number. This can be found in the front of the

Embassies and Consulates

You can find a full list of embassies and consulates in the *Pages Jaunes* under *Ambassades et Consulats*. For general enquiries or problems with passports or visas, you should try the local consulate first. They will be able to advise you whether you need to consult the Embassy in Paris, or a local honorary consul. It is also advisable to phone first, in case you need to make an appointment. Otherwise, the answerphone should give an emergency contact number.

Embassies and Consulates in Paris
Australian Embassy, 4 Rue Jean-Rey, 15th, tel: 01 40 59 33 00. Open 9am–6pm Mon–Fri; Visas 9.15am–12.15pm Mon–Fri.
British Embassy, 35 Rue du Fbg-St-Honoré, 8th, tel: 01 44 51 31

00. Open 9.30am–1pm, 2.30–6pm Mon–Fri. *Consulate*, 16 Rue d'Anjou, 8th, tel: 01 44 51 33 01/ 01 44 51 33 03. Open 2.30–5.30pm Mon–Fri.
Canadian Embassy, 35 Ave Montaigne, 8th, tel: 01 44 43 29 00. Open 9am–noon, 2–5pm Mon–Fri. *Visas*, 37 Ave Montaigne, tel: 01 44 43 29 16. Open 8.30–11am Mon–Fri.
Irish Embassy, 12 Ave Foch, 16th. *Consulate*, 4 Rue Rude, 16th, tel: 01 44 17 67 00. Open for visits 9.30am–noon Mon–Fri; by phone 9.30am–1pm, 2.30–5.30pm Mon–Fri.
New Zealand Embassy, 7 Rue Léonard de Vinci, 16th, tel: 01 45 00 24 11. Open for visas 9am–1pm Mon–Fri.
South African Embassy, 59 Quai d'Orsay, 7th, tel: 01 53 59 23 23. Open 8.30am–5.15pm Mon–Fri, by

appointment. *Consulate*, 9am–noon.
US Embassy, 2 Ave Gabriel, 8th, tel: 01 43 12 22 22. Open 9am–6pm Mon–Fri, by appointment. *Consulate/Visas*, 2 Rue St-Florentin, 1st, tel: 01 43 12 22 22. Open 8.45–11am Mon–Fri. *Passport service*, 9am–3pm.

Consulates in the South
British: 24 Ave Prado, 13006, Marseille, tel: 04 91 15 72 10, fax: 04 01 37 47 06.
US: 12 Blvd Paul Peytral, 13286, Marseille, tel: 04 91 54 92 00, *and* 31 Rue du Maréchal Joffre, 06000, Nice, tel: 04 93 88 89 55.
Canadian: 10 Rue Lamartine, 06000, Nice, tel: 04 93 92 93 22.
Irish: 152 Blvd J.F. Kennedy, 06160, Cap d'Antibes, tel: 04 93 61 50 63, fax: 04 93 67 96 08.

Pages Jaunes (Yellow Pages) section of the phone directory or on the information panel in a telephone box.

Reverse Charge Calls

You cannot make a reverse charges call (call collect) within France but you can to countries which will accept such calls. To do so, go through the operator and ask to make a PCV (*pay-say-vay*) call. Telephone calls can only be received at call boxes displaying the blue bell sign.

Free Calls

Numéros verts are free numbers, usually beginning with 08. To dial one from a public telephone you still need to insert a card or money first. The coins used will be returned immediately after the call. The card will not be debited for the amount.

Minitel

Minitel is the precursor of the Internet in France, a computer-based videotext information terminal connected to the telephone, and can be found in most homes, cafés and hotels.

Post offices have the Minitel as a telephone directory (on 3611) and information resource. However, it is now being superseded by the Internet. To use the Minitel for information key in 3611, wait for the beep and press *Connexion*. Type in the name and address that you want, and press *Envoi*.

Mobile Phones

If you are using a British-based mobile in France dial as if you are a local subscriber. To call from one British phone to another use the international code even if you are both in France.

Tourist Information

The *Maison* or *Bureau de Tourisme* is sometimes still called the *Syndicat d'Initiatif* in small villages. Where there is no tourist office the *mairie* (town hall) can provide local information on places to stay,

sights to see, local festivals, etc. Tourist offices can provide a wide variety of information and will often book hotels and supply local maps free of charge.

Regional Tourist Offices

Comité Regional du Tourisme de Provence-Alpes-Côte d'Azur, Les Docks, Atrium 10.5, BP 46214, 10, Place de la Joliette, 13567 Marseille Cedex 2, tel: (04) 91 56 47 00, fax: (04) 91 56 47 01.
Comité Regional du Tourisme Riviera Cote d'Azur, 55 Promenade des Anglais, BP 602, 06011 Nice, tel: (04) 93 37 78 78, fax: (04) 93 86 01 06, www.crt-riviera.fr
Office de tourisme et des congres de la Principauté de Monaco, 2a Boulevard des Moulins, 9800 Monaco, tel: 00 377 92 16 61 16, fax: 00 377 92 16 60 00, www.monaco-congres.com

Security and Crime

Sensible precautions regarding personal possessions are all that should be necessary. Be aware of pickpockets in cities, and be careful on trains, especially when travelling at night – make sure doors are securely locked.

Drivers should follow the rules of the road and always drive sensibly. Heavy on-the-spot fines are given for traffic offences such as speeding, and drivers can be stopped and breathalysed during spot checks. Police are fairly visible on the main roads of France during the summer months.

Lost Property

To report a crime or loss of belongings, visit the local *gendarmerie* or *commisariat de police*. Telephone numbers are given at the front of local directories, or in an emergency, dial 17. If you lose a passport, report first to the police, then to the nearest consulate. If you have the misfortune to be detained by the police for any reason, ask to telephone the nearest consulate for a member of staff to come to your assistance.

Emergencies

Ambulance – dial 15
Police – dial 17
Fire (Sapeurs-Pompiers) – dial 18
In the case of a serious accident or medical emergency, phone either the Police, the Sapeurs-Pompiers or for an ambulance, or alternatively call the Service d'Aide Médicale d'Urgence (SAMU) which exists in most large towns and cities. Though primarily a fire brigade, the Sapeurs-Pompiers are trained paramedics, and both they and the police have medical back-up and work in close contact with SAMU.

In case of credit card loss or theft, call the following 24-hour services, which have English-speaking staff:
American Express 01 47 77 72 00
Diners Club 01 49 06 17 17
MasterCard 01 45 67 84 84
Visa 08 36 69 08 80.

Gay Riviera

Local gay organisations and social centres are advertised in the local press. General information is available from Radio FG (98.2 MHz) and national magazines *Têtu* and *Lesbia*. If you need help or more information, try the Paris-based Centre Gai et Lesbien, tel: 01 43 57 21 47. Gay and lesbian bars and clubs include the following:

Cannes

Zanzibar, 85 Rue Félix-Faure. One of France's oldest gay bars

Nice

Le Baby Doll, 227 Blvd de la Madeleine. Lesbian club.
Blue Boy Enterprise, 9 Rue Spinetta. Nice's best gay club, everyone welcome, floorshows.
Cherry's Café, 36 Rue des Ponchettes, crowded gay bar overlooking the Prom.

St-Tropez

Le Pigeonnier, 13 Rue de la Ponche. Popular gay club.

Getting Around

Domestic Travel

Public transport on the Côte d'Azur is fairly efficient and avoids the problem of finding a parking space. It is really only sensible to take a car if you are touring. Roads to and around the main resorts get completely choked up during July and August and you can spend as much time getting to the beach as you spend on it. Parking in the main resorts is costly. In most towns parking meters have now generally been replaced by *horodateurs*, pay-and-display machines, which either take coins or cards (100F or 200F, available from tabacs).

Car hire is expensive, but bikes are readily available. Most railway stations hire them out and they do not necessarily have to be returned to the same station.

Bikes are carried free of charge on buses and some trains (*Autotrains*); on other, faster services you will have to pay (check before you travel – some services have high charges for carrying cycles).

Travelling by a combination of bike and bus or train can be an excellent way of touring and viewing the region.

BY BUS

Details of routes and timetables are generally available free of charge. The main source of information for bus travel is available from Agence Sunbus, 10 Avenue Félix Faure, Nice, and also from local tourist offices. There are good services from the airport to all the major resorts, but inland services can be infrequent. When boarding a bus tickets should be punched in the machine next to the driver; passes should be shown to the driver.

BY TRAIN

Reservations and Information
The Metrazur rail network links all the coastal towns. Further services run inland. Two scenic mountain lines depart from Nice: the Roya valley line via Sospel, and the privately operated Train des Pignes which runs up the Var Valley to Digne-les-Bains.
SNCF national reservations and information: tel: 08 36 35 35 35; www.sncf.fr; open 7am–10pm daily.
Rail information in English: tel: 08 36 35 35 39.

Fares and Deals
Fares vary according to whether you travel on a peak "white" day or a cheaper, less-busy "blue" day.

Excursions

Boat trips are the most obvious excursions that come to mind on the Côte d'Azur and many companies offer trips for a just a few hours or a whole day. However, you may prefer to take a trip on a steam train, in a four-wheel drive or in the air. Some possibilities are listed below:

Train
The "Train des Pignes" run by Chemins de Fer de Provence line goes from Nice to Digne and a trip on it is a grand way to take in some of the sights. It climbs as high as 900 metres (2,950 ft) at Saint-André les Alpes. All-inclusive day trips, 150 km (95 miles) each way (Tuesday–Thursday) include a meal, wine and coffee and a guided village tour.

On most Sundays from mid-May to mid-October, a steam train runs from Puget-Theniers to Annot and back. Information from Chemins de Fer de Provence, 33 Avenue Malaussena, 06000 Nice, tel: (04) 93 88 34 72.

It is also worth taking a trip along the SNCF Nice-Cuneo line which passes through some splendidly wild landscapes and also offers sights of spectacular engineering in the form of bridges and viaducts. For further information, contact SNCF, tel: 08 36 35 35 35.

Sea
Take a trip to Monaco, the Îles de Lérins (where the "Man in the Iron Mask" was confined in the fortress on Ste-Marguerite Island), the Hyères Islands, or even a day trip to Corsica. Or go out in the evening to watch fireworks from the sea.

From Le Lavandou: Compagnie des Transports Maritimes, 15 Quai Gabriel Péri, 83980 Le Lavandou, tel: (04) 94 71 01 02.

From Ste-Maxime/St-Tropez: Transports Maritime, Plan-de-la-Tour, 83120 Ste-Maxime, tel: (04) 94 96 51 00.

Bateau Bleu, tel: (04) 94 95 17 46. Departures from St-Raphaël and St-Tropez,

Calanques de la Corniche d'Or (Estérel), tel: (04) 94 95 17 46. Departures from St-Raphaël.

SNCM Ferryterranée, Quai du Commerce, 06005 Nice Cedex, tel: (04) 93 13 66 66. Day trips to Corsica with two hours ashore (ports vary).

Photo Safari: Trips from June–October (according to the movements of the whales) from Antibes or Beaulieu-sur-Mer, lasting 10–12 hours. The cost includes boat hire and a two-man crew (maximum 8 passengers). Contact: Guigo Marine, Port Vauban, Avenue du 11 Novembre, 06600 Antibes, tel: (04) 93 34 70 70.

Stations have leaflets showing the calendar of blue and white days. You can save on TGV fares by purchasing special discount cards. The *Carte 12/25* gives 12 to 25-year-olds a 50 per cent reduction. Pensioners benefit from similar terms with a *Carte Vermeil*. A *Carte Enfant* entitles a child under 12 and up to three accompanying adults to travel at a 50 per cent reduction, or 25 per cent on white days. Couples are entitled to a *Découverte a deux*, 25 per cent reduction for return journeys on "blue" days. There are also advance purchase discounts available.

All tickets purchased at French stations have to be put through the orange machines at the stations to validate them before boarding the train. These are marked *"compostez votre billet"*.

BY CAR

British, US, Canadian and Australian licences are all valid in France and you should always carry your car's registration document and insurance (third party is the absolute minimum, but it is advisable to ask your insurance company to provide you with added cover).

Additional insurance cover, which can include a get-you-home service, is offered by a number of organisations, including the British and American Automobile Associations and Europ-Assistance, Sussex House, Perrymount Road, Haywards Heath RH16 1DN, tel: (01444) 442211; in the US, Europ-Assistance Worldwide Services Inc., 1133 15th Street,

Suite 400, Washington DC 20005, tel: (202) 347 7113.

For co-ordination with automobile clubs from other countries, mainly assistance with breakdown, contact:

FFAC (Federation Français des Automobiles Club et des Usagers de la Route)
8 pl. de la Concorde
75008 Paris
tel: 01 53 30 89 30
fax: 01 53 30 89 29.

Car Hire

Hiring a car is an expensive business in France, partly because of the high VAT (TVA) rate of 33 per cent on luxury items. Some fly-drive deals work out reasonably well if you're only going for a short visit – Air France, for instance, offers a fly-

Rules of the Road

The use of seat belts (front and rear if fitted) and crash helmets for motorcyclists is compulsory. Children under 10 are not permitted to ride in the front seat unless the car has no rear seat.

Priorité à la droite: An important rule to remember is that priority on French roads is always given to vehicles approaching from the right, except where otherwise indicated. In practice, on main roads the major road will normally have priority, with traffic being halted on minor approach roads with one of the following signs:
● STOP
● *Cédez le passage* – give way
Vous n'avez pas la priorité – you do not have right of way
● *Passage protégé* – no right of way

Particular care should be taken in towns, where you may wrongly assume you are on the major road, and in rural areas where there may not be any road markings (watch out for farm vehicles).

The French recently changed the rules concerning roundabouts – in theory, drivers already on the roundabout now have priority over those entering it, but beware.

Some drivers still insist that priority belongs to the drivers entering a roundabout.

Speed limits: Speed limits are as follows: 130 kph (80 mph) on toll motorways; 110 kph (68 mph) on dual carriageways; 90 kph (56 mph) on other roads except in towns where the limit is 50 kph (30 mph). There is now a minimum speed limit of 80 kph (50 mph) on the outside lane of motorways during daylight with good visibility and on level ground. Speed limits are reduced in wet weather as follows: toll motorways: 110 kph, dual carriageways: 100 kph, other roads: 80kph.

On-the-spot fines can be levied for speeding. On toll roads, the time is printed on the ticket you take at your entry point; your average speed can thus be calculated and a fine imposed on exit. Nearly all motorways (*autoroutes*) are toll roads, so you will need to have some cash with you (especially small change) if you intend to use them, although toll booths will now accept payment by Visa and there is always a manned booth.

Autoroutes are designated "A" roads and national highways "N"

roads. "D" roads are usually well maintained, while "C" or local roads, may not always be so.

Accidents and Emergencies: You must carry a red triangle to place 50 metres (160 ft) behind the car in case of a breakdown or accident. In an accident or emergency, call the police (dial 17) or use the free emergency telephones (every 2 km/1 mile) on motorways. It is useful to carry a European Accident Statement Form (obtainable from your insurance company) which will simplify matters in the case of an accident.

Unleaded petrol (*essence sans plomb*) is now widely available in France. Leaded petrol is no longer available, and has been replaced by a substitute unleaded petrol for leaded fuel vehicles. If in doubt, a map showing the location of filling stations is available from main tourist offices.

For information about current road conditions, contact: Autoroute, tel: 93 49 33 33; CRIR, tel: 91 78 78 78. In the Alps you may need snow chains, which can be bought cheaply at hypermarkets or hired from garages.

drive service to Nice, with daily departures. French Railways offer a good deal on combined train/car rental bookings. Weekly rates are often better than daily hire and it can be cheaper to arrange before leaving for France. Major car-hire companies are listed below:

Ada Central reservations
01 55 46 19 99
www.net-on-line.net/ada
Avis 01 55 38 68 60
www.avis.com
Budget 08 00 10 00 01
www.budget.com
Europcar 08 03 35 23 52
www.europcar.com
Hertz 01 39 38 38 38
www.hertz.com
Rent-a-Car 08 36 69 46 95
www.rentacar.fr

BY TAXI

There are 29 taxi ranks in Nice, but you can also hail them in the street. They cost around €1.50 per kilometre. Note that the taxi fare from Nice airport to the centre is a rip-off. It's better to take the bus.

Nice Centrale de Taxi
tel: (04) 93 13 78 78

COACH TRIPS

Day or half-day trips with commentary take in many of the sights along the coast and inland, and are less expensive than going by sea or air.

Details of the many coach operators are available from local tourist offices or bus/coach stations.

OVERLAND

Access to many of the sites of the Vallée des Merveilles is now forbidden unless a guide is conducting a tour. One way of getting around is by four-wheel drive, although it can be costly – upwards of €150 a day. The Association des Taxis

Routes

Following a tourist circuit, or route is a sure way of getting to see the major sights of a region. Local tourist offices will help with suggestions. Some of the major routes are given below:

Route des Hauts Lieux de Provence: this covers an extensive area, in the west of the region, from Toulon to Fréjus and as far north as Draguignan. It takes in, among other sites, the Cité Episcopale de Fréjus and the Roman Arenas, the Château de Grimaud, the Château d'Entrecasteaux and the Palais des Comtes de Provence à Brignoles.

Accompagnateurs des Merveilles will take you up to the Vallée des Merveilles (from late June to late October) for a day trip, including a guided tour of the archaeological site. For guides, contact the Bureau des Guides du Val des Merveilles, Tende, tel: (04) 93 04 77 73.

HITCH-HIKING

Hitch-hiking is best organised through an agency, such as: **Allô-Stop**, 8 rue Rochambeau, Paris, tel: 01 53 20 42 42; open 9am–6.30pm Mon-Fri; 9am–1pm, 2–6pm Sat; credit cards: MasterCard and Visa.

The agency fee is €5–12, depending on distance; and then around 4 cents per km paid direct to the driver. Contact the agency well in advance to arrange a convenient lift. Avignon, Marseille and Nice are all popular destinations.

WALKING

The hinterland behind the coast, the national parks of Mercantour and Luberon and of course, the mountains offer superb opportunities for walkers. There are also a number of coastal paths, for example the Sentier du Littoral which follows the coast south from La Favière (Var), and can easily be

Côtes de Provence Wine Route: much of this route takes in the same area as the Route des Hauts Lieux de Provence. For details of vineyards open to the public and offering tastings and direct wine purchase, contact the Syndicat des Vins Côtes de Provence, 83460 Les Arcs-sur-Argens, tel: (04) 94 73 31 01.

Circuit sans frontière de Nice à Turin: as its name suggests, this road leads all the way from Nice to Turin, and its aim is to cover, in particular, all the major religious sites en route.

achieved in a day's walk. All the main footpaths in France form part of the national network of long-distance footpaths (Sentiers de Grandes Randonnées or GR). The major footpaths in the region are the GR5 which goes from Nice all the way up to Amsterdam; the GR51, from Theoule to Castellar, overlooking the coast; the GR52 from Menton to the Vallée des Merveilles and the GR4 to the Gorges du Verdon.

It should be noted that both the Parc National du Mercantour and the Vallée des Merveilles enforce a code of country behaviour and it is forbidden to enter many of the sites in the latter without a guide.

The French Ramblers' Association, Fédération Française de la Randonnée Pédestre (FFRP) in Paris publishes Topoguides (guide books incorporating IGN 1:50,000 scale maps) to all France's footpaths, in French. However, there is a series of guide books in English published by Robertson-McCarta called *Footpaths of Europe*, which are based on the French topoguides with IGN maps and include information about accommodation along the way. Titles appropriate to the region are: *Walking the GR5: Larche to Nice*, and peripherally, *Walking the GR5: Modane to Larche* and *Walks in Provence*. All these titles are available by mail order from Compass Books.

IGN Blue series maps at a scale of 1:25,000 are ideal for walkers, and they also publish maps of the national parks. Didier-Richard are specialist publishers of walking maps, at a scale of 1:50,000. Useful sheets are *No. 1 Alpes de Provence*, *No. 9 Mercantour*, *No. 19 Haute-Provence* and *No. 26 Au Pays d'Azur*.

French topoguides are available from all recommended bookshops in the region.

The **Comité Regional pour la Randonnée Pédestre** organises a variety of activities throughout the year: guided walks taking a day, a weekend or more; as well as themed walks, flora or wildlife for example.

Various walking holidays with accommodation either in hotels or under canvas are available. Some are organised through package operators in the UK, others are bookable through the French organisations such as Clés de France, the agency for the French National Parks.

For more information on walking see page 336.

IN THE AIR

Tourist flights in helicopters are offered by:
Héli-Air St-Tropez, tel: 04 94 97 15 12.
Héli-Air Monaco, tel: 00 377 92 05 00 50.

Where to Stay

Accommodation

Accommodation on the French Riviera includes grand city hotels or seafront palaces, country villas or gîtes, campsites and a range of small town hotels, country auberges and chambres d'hôtes. During the summer it is advisable to book, especially in the coastal regions, but outside the peak holiday period (between mid-July and mid-August, when the French head south en masse) you should find accommodation easily. Some hotels in remoter areas may close between November and February, and most camp sites will be closed during the winter months.

Hotels

All hotels in France conform to national standards and carry star-ratings, set down by the Ministry of Tourism, according to their degree of comfort and amenities. Prices (which are charged per room, rather than per person) range from as little as €35 for a double room in an unclassified hotel (i.e. its standards are not sufficient to warrant a single star, but it is likely to be clean, cheap and cheerful), to around €100 for the cheapest double room in a 4-star luxury hotel.

Hotels are required to display their menus outside, and details of room prices should be visible either outside or in reception, as well as on the back of bedroom doors. It is possible for a hotel to have a 1-star rating, with a 2-star restaurant.

When booking a room you should normally be shown it before agreeing to take it; don't hesitate to ask. Supplements may be charged

for an additional bed or a cot (*lit bébé*). You may be asked when booking if you wish to dine, particularly if the hotel is busy – and you should confirm that the hotel's restaurant is open (many are closed out of season on Sunday or Monday evenings).

Lists of hotels can be obtained from the French Government Tourist office in your country or from regional or local tourist offices in France.

If you just want an overnight stop to break a journey, you may find clean, modern, basic chains like Formule 1 handy.

Hotel Guides

Various guides can be obtained from the French Tourist Office (in person or by sending £1 in stamps towards P & P). These include *Châteaux & Hotels de France* (hotels and B&Bs in private chateaux) and *Relais du Silence* (hotels in chateaux or grand houses, in peaceful settings.) www.silencehotel.com

Logis de France is France's biggest hotel group, with over 5,000 private hotels in small towns and the French countryside. Most of these hotels are one- or two-star and they vary greatly in facilities, atmosphere and levels of service. Contact the Fédération Nationale des Logis et Auberges de France, 83 Ave d'Italie, 75013 Paris; tel: 01 45 84 70 00, or the French Government Tourist office for a *Logis de France* handbook. (Free of charge to personal callers.)

Bon Weekend en Villes is an excellent value tourist office promotion has been going since 1991, offering two nights (either Fri–Sat or Sat–Sun) for the price of one. The offer is usually valid between November and March, and year round in some towns. You need to book at least 8 days in advance. Contact the French Government Tourist Office for further information.

Bed & Breakfast

Bed and breakfast (*chambre d'hôte*) accommodation is fairly widely available in private houses, often on working farms, whose owners are members of the Fédération Nationale des Gîtes Ruraux de France. Bookings can be made for an overnight stop or a longer stay. Breakfast is included in the price and evening meals – usually made with local produce and extremely good value – are often available.

Welcome Guides Bed and Breakfast in France lists B&Bs, including chateaux. UK booking service, tel: 01491 578803, fax: 01491 410806. www.bedbreak.com

If you do not wish to book anything in advance, just look out for signs along the road (usually in the country) offering *chambres d'hôtes*. You will be taking pot luck, but you will be fairly safe for a bed off-season and may be delighted by the good value of the simple farm food and accommodation on offer.

Gîtes

Rural *gîtes* are a good way to appreciate a holiday in the South, though most will be found in rural areas away from the coast. Accommodation can range from simple farms to grand chateaux. All have been set up with the help of government grants, aimed at restoring rural properties, and are regularly inspected by the *Relais Départemental* (the county office of the national federation) and given an "*épi*" (ear of corn) classification. Prices average €250–350 per week in August for a 2–4 person *gîte*.

Gîtes are self-catering, and you should check exactly what you need to supply. Sometimes they may be quite remote and you will need your own transport. *Gîte* owners will be able to advise about shopping, local sights and activities, bicycle hire, and so on.

Brittany Ferries are UK agents for Gîtes de France; bookings can be made through The Brittany Centre, Wharf Rd, Portsmouth PO2

8RU; tel: 0870 5360 360. The list of *gîtes* in the Brittany Ferries brochure is only a selection of those available.

In France, contact the **Maison de Gîtes de France**, 59 Rue St Lazare, 75009 Paris; tel: 01 49 70 75 85; fax: 01 42 81 28 53. The Gîtes de France brochure, *Gîtes Accessible á Tous*, lists *gîte* accommodation with disabled access and services. You can also investigate *gîtes* on the web at www.gites-de-france.com.

Various UK-based tour operators also offer a range of self-catering accommodation as part of a package holiday. Try the following:
Something Special, 01279 630 401
French Life, 0870 444 8877
French Expression, 020 7431 1312
Individual Travellers, 08700 771771
Direct Travel, 020 8641 6060.

Youth Hostels

To stay in most hostels (*auberges de jeunesse*) you need to be a member of the International Youth Hostels Association, or join the Federation Unie des Auberges de Jeunesse. Contact the following for more information:
Fédération Unie des Auberges de Jeunesse (FUAJ), 27 rue Pajol, 75018 Paris, tel: 01 44 89 87 27, fax: 01 44 89 87 10. The federation is affiliated to the International Youth Hostel Federation.
American Youth Hostelling International, PO Box 37613, Dept USA, Washington DC 20013/7613, tel: 0202 783 6161.
Youth Hostels Association, Trevelyan House, 8 St Stephens Hill, St Albans, Herts, AL1 2DY, tel:

01727 855215. To book youth hostels abroad, tel: 01629 581418, fax: 01629 581062.

Camping

French camp sites (*les campings*), often run by local councils, can be remarkably comfortable and well appointed. Prices range from €8 to around €20 per night for a family of four, with car, caravan or tent. Coastal camp sites can get crowded in high season. Camping rough (*camping sauvage*) is generally not permitted though it may be worth asking the landowner. Fire is an ever present risk in the region.

Camp sites are graded from one-star (minimal comfort, water points, showers and sinks) to four-star luxury sites, which allow more space for each pitch and offer above-average facilities. The majority of sites are two-star. *Aire naturelle de camping* and *Camping à la Ferme*, tend to be cheaper with very minimal services.

The *Guide Officiel* of the French Federation of Camping and Caravanning (FFCC), available from French Government Tourist Offices, lists 11,600 sites nationwide, and indicates those that have facilities for disabled campers. *The Michelin Green Guide – Camping/ Caravanning France* is very informative and also lists sites with facilities for the disabled.

Reservation Services
Canvas Holidays (UK), tel: 01383 644000, fax: 01203 422010
Select Site Reservations (UK), tel: 01873 859 876, fax: 01873 859 544.

The Gîte d'Etape

Gîtes d'étape offer very basic accommodation for walkers or cyclists, often in remote mountain areas; expect communal accommodation, bunk beds, shared bathrooms, etc. You will need to make reservations, especially in busy periods. *Gîtes de neige*, *gîtes de pêche* and *gîtes équestre* offer similar facilities.

Mountain refuges (*réfuges*) offer similar accommodation and may also provide drinks and meals. They range from large and solid stone houses to very basic huts. Many are open only June–Sep; they should be booked in advance. Prices vary between €8 and €15 per person. Lists of refuges are available from local tourist offices.

Avis Car Away (camping cars; France), tel: 01 47 49 80 40, fax: 01 47 49 80 50, www.aviscaraway.com

Hotels by Region

This hotel list names the region's most famous hotels and also suggests others that have a certain interest or distinctive charm. It is by no means exhaustive. It should be noted that prices on the Côte d'Azur tend to be higher than in other regions of France, but it is still possible to find reasonably priced accommodation. Opening and closing dates and room prices may vary.

Note: hotels are listed in accordance with the order of the *Places* chapters.

HYÈRES AND THE MASSIF DES MAURES

Aiguebelle
(just outside Le Lavandou)
Les Roches
1 Ave des Trois Dauphins, 83980 Le Lavandou
Tel: (04) 94 71 05 07
Fax: (04) 94 71 08 40
Set on the cliffs with fabulous sea-views, a luxurious modern hotel tastefully decorated and furnished. Private beach, fresh-water swimming-pool. Closed: mid November–mid December and early January–early March. Credit cards: AmEx, Diners Club, MasterCard, Visa. €€€
Beau Soleil
Aiguebelle
Tel: (04) 94 05 84 55
Fax: (04) 94 05 70 89
Reasonably priced hotel where the rooms have balconies and you can dine under the plane trees. €€

Hyères
Hotel du Soleil
2 Rue des Remparts
Tel: (04) 94 65 16 26
Fax: (04) 94 35 46 00
soleil@hotel-du-soleil.fr
A friendly and peaceful hotel close to the Parc St-Bernard. €€

Porquerolles
Mas du Langoustier
Tel: (04) 94 58 30 09
Fax: (04) 94 58 36 02
langoustier@compuserve.com
Luxurious establishment in an old Provençal *mas* on the Ile de Porquerolles, surrounded by exotic gardens, with a fabulous restaurant. Closed Nov–Apr. Credit cards: AmEx, Diners Club, MasterCard, Visa. Rooms: full-board only. €€€

Port Cros
Le Manoir
Tel: (04) 94 05 90 52
Fax: (04) 94 05 90 89
A tropical atmosphere with large garden and colonial-style family house. Comfortable rooms, some with balcony. Closed: early October–early May. Credit cards: MasterCard, Visa. €€€

Price Categories

The prices of the hotels are indicated as follows:
€ = Budget: under €60
€€ = Moderate: €60–120
€€€ = Expensive: €120–250
€€€€ = Luxury: over €250
All prices given are for the hotel's standard double room, per night. Breakfast is not normally included.

ST-TROPEZ AND ITS PENINSULA

La Croix-Valmer
Souleias
Plage de Gigaro
Tel: (04) 94 55 10 55
Fax: (04) 94 54 36 23
Modern hotel in extensive grounds overlooking the unspoilt beach of Gigaro. Spacious rooms, swimming-pool, tennis courts, private yacht. Closed: Nov–mid-March. Credit cards: Eurocard, Diners Club, Visa. €€

Grimaud
La Boulangerie
Route de Collobrières
Tel: (04) 94 43 23 16
Fax: (04) 94 43 38 27
Simple and comfortable, a small

friendly hotel quietly situated in the Maures hills. Swimming-pool and tennis courts. Closed: mid October–early April. Credit cards: Visa. €€
Hostellerie du Coteau Fleuri
Place des Penitents
Tel: (04) 94 43 20 17
coteaufleuri@wanadoo.fr
Closed 10 Nov–15 Dec, and from 5–20 Jan. An old hostelry on the side of a hill with a rustic dining room and little terrace. Credit cards: AmEx, Diners Club, CB. €€

Plan-de-la-Tour
(10km/6 miles from Ste-Maxime)
Mas des Brugassières
1.5 km (1 mile) south of the village
Tel: (04) 94 55 50 55
Fax: (04) 94 54 50 51
Away from the coast in the Maures hills. A small hotel with rooms on to either the terrace around the swimming-pool or a private terrace. Tennis courts. Open: all year round. Credit cards: AmEx, Diners Club, Visa. €€

Ramatuelle
Le Baou
Av Gustav Etienne. Ramatuelle
Tel: (04) 94 79 20 48
Fax: (04) 94 79 28 36
hostellerie.lebaou@wanadoo.fr
Large modern rooms with balconies and lovely views. €€€
La Ferme d'Augustin
Plage de Tahiti
Tel: (04) 94 55 97 00
Fax: (04) 94 97 40 30
An old farm with a Mediterranean garden. Rustic atmosphere and furniture. All rooms with sea-view. Closed: mid October–mid March. Credit cards: Visa. €€

St-Tropez
Bastide de St-Tropez
Route des Carles
Tel: (04) 94 55 82 55
Fax: (04) 94 97 21 71
bst@wanadoo.fr
The height of luxury in the heart of the vineyards. Some of the rooms and suites with private garden and jacuzzi. Open: all year round. Credit cards: AmEx, Diners Club, MasterCard, Visa. €€€

Hôtel Byblos
Avenue Paul Signac
Tel: (04) 94 56 68 00
Fax: (04) 94 56 68 01
saint-tropez@byblos.com
107 rooms. Legendary glamorous
hotel still popular with the Johnny
Hallyday set. €€€€

Lou Cagnard
18 Avenue P. Roussel
Tel: (04) 94 97 04 24
Fax: (04) 94 97 09 44
Very reasonably priced hotel near
the port and with a pretty courtyard.
No credit cards. €€

La Ponche
3 Rue des Remparts
Tel: (04) 94 97 02 53
Fax: (04) 94 97 78 61
Once a favourite of Picasso's, this
hotel was originally a row of little
fishermen's cottages in the old
town. Excellent restaurant. €€€

Résidence de la Pinède
Plage de la Bouillabaisse
Tel: (04) 94 55 91 00
Fax: (04) 94 97 73 64
Residence.pinede@wanadoo.fr
On the famous Bouillabaisse
beach, under the pine trees. The
hotel has been refurbished to
provide comfortable rooms and
suites. A member of the Relais et
Châteaux group. Closed: 25
October–20 March. Credit cards:
AmEx, Diners Club, MasterCard,
Visa. €€€€

Le Yaca
1 Boulevard d'Aumale
Tel: (04) 94 55 81 00
Fax: (04) 94 97 58 50
e.mail: hotel-le-yaca@wanadoo.fr
An attractive old Provençal residence
in town, tastefully refurbished.
Accommodation built around a
swimming-pool and gardens. Closed:
15 Oct–20 Dec and 10 Jan–10 April.
Credit cards: AmEx, Diners Club,
MasterCard, Visa. €€€

ST-RAPHAËL, FRÉJUS AND THE ARGENS VALLEY

Les Arcs
Le Logis du Guetteur
Place Château
Tel: (04) 94 99 51 10
Fax: (04) 94 99 51 29

This pretty hotel occupies the site
of a 13th-century château with
beautiful views of the rooftops and
vineyards below. Closed February.
€€

Fréjus
Aréna
145 Blvd Général de Gaulle,
Tel: (04) 94 17 09 40
Fax: (04) 94 52 01 52
Situated in the old town with a
swimming-pool, a garden and an
excellent restaurant serving
regional specialities. €€

Sable et Soleil
158 Rue Paul Aréne
Tel: (04) 94 51 08 70
Fax: (04) 94 33 49 12
guyduale@free.fr
A 1950s building under the
pines with a pergola. Plain but
adequate rooms at a reasonable
price. No restaurant. Closed mid-
Nov–mid-Dec. Credit cards:
Eurocard, Visa. €

St-Raphaël
Bleu Marine
Port Santa-Lucia.
Tel: (04) 94 95 31 31
Fax: (04) 94 82 21 46
Recently restored with swimming-
pool and view of the port. Some
of the rooms have balconies and
there is a good restaurant. All
credit cards. €€

Golf de Valescure
Ave des Golfs
Tel: (04) 94 52 85 00
Fax: (04) 94 82 41 88.
New traditional-style *mas*
surrounded by pine trees, rooms
with terraces and an elegant club
house. All credit cards.
€€

CANNES

Carlton Intercontinental
58 Blvd de la Croisette
Tel: (04) 93 06 40 06
Fax: (04) 93 06 40 25
cannes@interconti.com
Cannes' world-famous waterfront
luxury hotel. The rooms and lobby
have recently been completely
renovated and are now more

splendid than ever. Health centre
and casino on the top floor. Open:
all year round. Credit cards: AmEx,
Diners Club, MasterCard, Visa.
€€€€

Martinez
73 Blvd de la Croisette
Tel: (04) 92 98 77 00
Fax: (04) 93 38 97 90
martinez@concorde-hotels.com
Given a trendy new look in 2002,
this Art Deco palace is where the
stars love to stay during the
festival. It has three restaurants,
most notably the Palme d'Or.
Closed mid Nov–last week in Dec.
Credit cards: AmEx, Diners Club,
Eurocard, Visa. €€€€

Splendid
4 Rue Felix Faure
Tel: (04) 97 06 22 22
Fax: (04) 93 99 55 02
hotel.splendid@wanadoo.fr
19th-century mansion with a homely
atmosphere but no restaurant.
Credit cards: AmEx, Diners Club,
Eurocard, Visa. €€

ANTIBES AND THE PLATEAU DE VALBONNE

Antibes
Relais du Postillon
8 Rue Championnet
Tel: (04) 93 34 20 77
Fax: (04) 93 34 61 24
postillon@atsat.com
It is hard to find a bargain in high
season on the Côte d'Azur, but
Postillon in the old town of
Antibes is pretty close to one. The
15-room hotel is pleasant enough –
but not beside the sea. Good
restaurant. €

Biot
Hotel des Arcades
Place des Arcades
Tel: (04) 93 65 01 04
Fax: (04) 93 65 01 05
A 15th-century mansion offering
accommodation that combines
antique furniture with modern
convenience. The restaurant is
also an art gallery, and meals and
rooms are reasonably priced.
Closed mid-November–mid-
December. €€

Cap d'Antibes
Hotel du Cap-Eden Roc
Boulevard Kennedy
Tel: (04) 93 61 39 01
Fax: (04) 93 67 76 04
edenroc-hotel@wanadoo.fr
Beautifully set on the water's edge in extensive wooded grounds. Recently refurbished, very comfortable rooms. Heated swimming-pool, tennis courts. Closed: Nov–Mar. Credit cards: AmEx, Diners Club, Mastercard, Visa. €€€€

Juan-les-Pins
Belles Rives
Boulevard Edouard-Baudoin
Tel: (04) 93 61 02 79
Fax: (04) 93 67 43 51
info@bellesrives.com
Close enough to town to enjoy the atmosphere, but far enough from the noise and crowds. This 1930s villa has retained all the charm of its era, when it was the home of Zelda and F. Scott Fitzgerald. Closed Nov–mid March. All credit cards. €€€
Garden Beach Hotel
15–17 Boulevard Baudoin
Tel: (04) 92 93 57 57
Fax: (04) 92 93 57 56
contct@lemeridien-juanlespins.com
On the site of the former casino, in the centre of town and with a nice terrace overlooking the bay. Open: all year round. Credit cards: AmEx, Diners Club, MasterCard, Visa. €€€
Juan Beach
5 Rue de l'Oratoire
Tel: (04) 93 61 02 89
Fax: (04) 93 61 16 63
juan.beach@atsat.com
Reasonable rates in this old family house with simple rooms and summer dining in a flowery garden. Closed Dec–Mar. Credit cards: Eurocard, Visa. €€

Mougins
Le Moulin de Mougins
Notre Dame de Vie
Tel: (04) 93 75 78 24
Fax: (04) 93 90 18 55
mougins@relaischateau.fr
An old mill restored by celebrated chef Roger Vergé with three rooms and a couple of apartments overlooking the garden. €€€

Les Muscadins
18 Boulevard Courteline
Tel: 93 90 00 43
Fax: (04) 92 92 88 23
muscadins@alcyonis.fr
On the edge of the village, an attractive hotel with a good view of the Bay of Cannes. Only 8 bedrooms, each different, all nicely furnished and decorated. Closed: 1 February–1 April and 1–15 December. Credit cards: AmEx, Diners Club, MasterCard, Visa. €€€

GRASSE AND THE LOUP VALLEY

Grasse
La Bastide St-Antoine
48 Ave Henri Durant
Tel: (04) 93 70 94 94
Fax: (04) 93 70 94 95
info@jacques-chibois.com
Better known for its restaurant owned by the acclaimed M. Chibois this beautiful 18th-century *bastide* has 11 rooms. Credit cards: AmEx, Diners Club, Eurocard, Visa. €€€

CAGNES, VENCE AND THE VAR VALLEY

Cagnes-sur-Mer
Le Cagnard
Rue du Pontis-Long
Tel: (04) 93 20 73 21
Fax: (04) 93 22 06 39
res@lele-cagnard.com
Situated in the little winding back-streets not far from the Château Grimaldi, a charming hotel with a rustic atmosphere. Wooden beams, low ceilings and attractive old furniture. Member of the Relais et Châteaux group. Open: all year round. Credit cards: AmEx, Diners Club, MasterCard, Visa. €€€

Roquefort Les Pins
Auberge du Colombier
Tel: (04) 92 60 33 00
Fax: (04) 93 77 07 30
info@auberge-du-colombier.com
A small friendly hotel set away from the coast in a beautiful well-established garden commanding a fine view down to the Mediterranean.

Swimming-pool and tennis courts. Closed: 10 January–10 February. Credit cards: AmEx, Diners Club, MasterCard, Visa. €€

St-Paul-de-Vence
La Colombe d'Or
Place du Général de Gaulle
Tel: (04) 93 32 80 02
Fax: (04) 93 32 77 78
A lovely old building on the edge of the village, once frequented by artists such as Picasso, Matisse, Miró and Léger, whose works still adorn the walls. Private courtyard and swimming-pool. Closed mid-Nov–mid-Dec. Credit cards: AmEx, Diners Club, MasterCard, Visa. €€€
Mas d'Artigny
Route de la Colle
Tel: (04) 93 32 84 54
Fax: (04) 93 32 95 36
email: contact@mas-artigny.com
Beautifully situated in the woods between St-Paul and la Colle with a splendid 360° view of the sea and the mountains. Open: all year round. Credit cards: AmEx, Visa. €€

Vence
Château du Domaine St-Martin
Route de Coursegoules
Tel: (04) 93 58 02 02
Fax: (04) 93 24 08 91
st-martin@webstore.fr
True luxury set on the hills above Vence, with a magnificent view of the coast. Extensive grounds, swimming-pool. A member of the Relais et Châteaux group. Closed: 20 November–10 March. Credit cards: AmEx, Diners Club, MasterCard, Visa. €€€
Villa Roseraie
Avenue Henri Giraud
Tel: (04) 93 58 02 20
Fax: (04) 93 58 99 31
Small friendly hotel in a 1930s villa. Pretty garden and pool. No restaurant. Closed: January. Credit cards: AmEx, Visa. €€

NICE

Hotel Beau Rivage
24 Rue Saint Francois-de-Paule
Tel: (04) 92 47 82 82

Fax: (04) 92 47 82 83
nicebeaurivage@new-hotel.com
118 rooms. 1930s hotel with a
private beach. Matisse had an
apartment here and Nietzsche and
Tchekhov are counted among other
famous visitors of the past.
Thoroughly modernised since then,
the hotel is comfortable and ideally
situated in the old town. €€€

Grimaldi
15 Rue Grimaldi
Tel: (04) 93 16 00 24
Fax: (04) 93 87 00 24
zesse@le-grimaldi.com
Charming little B&B, with all rooms
beautifully furnished in different
fabrics. Credit cards: AmEx, Diners
Club, Eurocard, Visa. €€

Hotel Négresco
37 Promenade des Anglais
Tel: (04) 93 16 64 00
Fax: (04) 93 88 35 68
direction@hotel-negresco.com
The last vestige of Nice's era of
splendour at the end of the 19th
century with its famous dome
dominating the the Baie des Anges.
Period furniture from the 16th and
18th century, and priceless paintings
and tapestries. Open: all year
round. Credit cards: AmEx, Diners
Club, MasterCard, Visa. €€€€

La Pérouse
11 Quai Rauba-Capéu
Tel: (04) 93 62 34 63
Fax: (04) 93 62 59 41
lp@hroy.com
At the east end of the Promenade
des Anglais, conveniently situated
between the old town and the port.
The rooms have splendid views of
the Baie des Anges. Swimming-
pool. Open: all year round. Credit
cards: AmEx, Diners Club,
MasterCard, Visa. €€€

Hotel Windsor
11 Rue Dalpozzo
Tel: (04) 93 88 59 35
Fax: (04) 93 88 94 57.
windsor@webstore.fr
57 rooms. An exotic garden
surrounds the swimming pool and
there is an aviary with tropical
birds. The rooms are comfortable
and some are individually decorated
by contemporary artists. A
Moroccan-style hammam adds
to the originality. €€

CAP FERRAT AND THE GOLDEN TRIANGLE

Beaulieu-Sur-Mer
La Réserve de Beaulieu
5 Boulevard Leclerc
Tel: (04) 93 01 00 01
Fax: (04) 93 01 28 99
reserve@wanadoo.fr
A luxurious late 19th-century villa,
beautifully situated on the coast
with private beach and harbour.
Swimming-pool in the garden.
Closed: mid November–mid
December. Credit cards: AmEx,
Diners Club, MasterCard, Visa. €€€

Price Categories

The prices of the hotels are
indicated as follows:
€ = Budget: under €60
€€ = Moderate: €60–120
€€€ = Expensive: €120–250
€€€€ = Luxury: over €250
All prices given are for the
hotel's standard double room,
per night. Breakfast is not
normally included.

Èze
Château Eza
Tel: (04) 93 41 12 24
Fax: (04) 93 41 16 64
chateza@webstore.fr
Accessible only on foot (your
baggage is carried up by donkey),
this 400-year-old castle is perched
on top of the cliff and overlooks
260 km (160 miles) of coast.
Beautifully decorated rooms with
antique furniture, oriental rugs,
some with fireplace. Closed:
November–March. Credit cards:
AmEx, Diners Club, MasterCard,
Visa. €€€€

St-Jean-Cap-Ferrat
Brise Marine
58 Avenue Jean Mermoz
Tel: (04) 93 76 04 36
Fax: (04) 93 76 11 49
info@hotel-brisemarine.com
A small hotel in an attractive
terraced garden. Some of the
rooms overlook the sea. Closed:
end October–1 February. Credit
cards: Visa. €€

La Voile d'Or
Yachting Harbour
Tel: (04) 93 01 13 13
Fax: (04) 93 76 11 17
reservation@lavoildor.fr
An Italian villa in a garden
overlooking the yachting harbour.
Rooms of all sizes, attractively
decorated. Two pools. Closed: 31
October–1 March. Credit cards:
Visa. €€€

MONACO

Abela Hotel
23 Avenue des Papalins,
Fontvieille, Monte-Carlo
Tel: (00 377) 92 05 90 00
Fax: (00 377) 92 05 91 67
A little way out of the centre,
a comfortable modern hotel
overlooking the new harbour. Open:
all year round. Credit cards: AmEx,
Diners Club, MasterCard, Visa. €€

Hôtel Hermitage
Square Beaumarchais
Tel: (00 377) 92 16 40 00
Fax: (00 377) 92 16 38 52
Beautiful Edwardian architecture,
spacious comfortable rooms.
Swimming-pool and fitness centre.
Open: all year round. Credit cards:
AmEx, Diners Club, MasterCard,
Visa. €€€€

Hôtel de Paris
Place du Casino
Tel: (00 377) 92 16 30 00
Fax: (00 377) 92 16 38 49
hp@sbm.mc
The most prestigious of Monaco's
luxury hotels. Indoor swimming-pool
and fabulous restaurant. Open: all
year round. Credit cards: AmEx,
Diners Club, MasterCard, Visa.
€€€€

MENTON AND ROQUEBRUNE

Menton
Chambord
6, Avenue Boyer
Tel: (04) 93 35 94 19
Fax: (04) 93 41 30 55
hotel-chambord@wanadoo.fr
Three-star hotel just off the
Promenade du Soleil. Closed mid-

Dec–mid-Jan. No restaurant. Credit cards: AmEx, Diners Club, MasterCard, Visa. €€

Hotel de Londres
15 Avenue Carnot
Tel: 93 35 74 62
Small central hotel, popular during the lemon festival. Open: 23 December–31 October. Credit cards: AmEx, Diners Club, MasterCard, Visa. €€

Roquebrune

Vista Palace Hotel
Grande Corniche
Tel: (04) 92 10 40 00
Fax: (04) 93 35 18 94
info@vistapalace.com
A modern luxury hotel high above Monaco with wonderful views. Spacious rooms, pool and fitness centre. Closed during February. Credit cards: AmEx, Diners Club, MasterCard, Visa. €€€

Westminster
14, Avenue Laurent
Tel: (04) 92 41 41 40
Fax: (04) 93 28 88 50
Closed: Feb–Nov. Close to the railway with terraced gardens. Most rooms have a garden view. No restaurant. Credit cards: Visa. €€

THE PERCHED VILLAGES

Peillon

Auberge de la Madone
Tel: (04) 93 79 91 17
Fax: (04) 93 79 99 36
c.millo@club-internet.fr
A simple country hotel, whose rooms offer splendid views of the hill-top village and valley. Closed

20 October–20 November and from 7–31 January, and on Wednesdays. Credit cards: CB. €€

Annexe Lou Pourtail
A less expensive but charming alternative owned by the proprietors of the Auberge de la Madone. No restaurant. €

Utelle

Bellevue
Utelle 06450 Lantosque
Tel/fax: (04) 93 03 17 19
Quiet, family hotel open in July and August, with stunning views and swimming-pool. Credit cards: CB. €

BORDER COUNTRY

Sospel

Hotel des Etrangers
9 Boulevard de Verdun
Tel: (04) 93 04 00 09
Fax: (04) 93 04 12 31
sospel@ifrance.com
Swimming-pool on site, English spoken and proprietor is expert on local history. Closed Nov–March. Credit cards: AmEx, Diners Club, MasterCard, Visa. €€

Tende

Le Prieuré
St-Dalmas-de-Tende
Tel: (04) 93 04 75 70
Fax: (04) 93 04 71 58
contact@leprieure.org
Three-star hotel with good restaurant in lovely valley. Organises summer trips to Vallée des Merveilles. Credit cards: AmEx, Diners Club, MasterCard, Visa. €

Where to Eat

Eating Out

One of the great pleasures of visiting the Riviera is its glorious food, and wherever you go you will find a wide variety of different establishments from simple fish restaurants to the great classics. But beware: along the coast restaurants may be over-priced and disappointing. Never forget the option of creating your own meal from a visit to the market and a *charcuterie*. A crisp baguette, ham, local cheese, tomatoes, and fresh grapes or peaches can make a better beach picnic than the expensive offerings of the seaside concessions.

Many hotels will have their own restaurants, or restaurants will also have rooms to rent. This selection includes good regional restaurants with typical local dishes as well as some of the great stars of French cuisine.

Inland it is always worth seeking out typical local restaurants and sampling the specialities of the region. Increasingly, the regional produce is itself the focus of the great chefs who compete in their stylish treatment of peasant food and traditional dishes. (*See pages 109–113*).

Smoking

Although some restaurants are divided into *fumeurs* and *non fumeurs* (smoking and non-smoking), smoking is still widely accepted in France and you may need to specify if you prefer a non-smoking section.

Reading the Label

The best wines produced within the region are from the Côtes de Provence *appellation*, especially the rosés of the Massif des Maures. To the west of the Riviera, the lower Rhône valley produces some even better wines, in particular the famous Châteauneuf-du-Pape.

Like elsewhere in France, the wines are graded according to their quality and this must be shown on the label. The grades are as follows:

● Vin de table: usually inexpensive everyday table wine. The quality can vary.

● Vin de pays: local wine.

● VDQS (*vin délimité de qualité supérieure*): wine from a specific area; better than *vin de table*.

● AOC (*appellation d'origine controlée*): Good quality wine from a specific area or château where strict controls are imposed on the amount of wine produced each year.

● *Mis en bouteille au château*: bottled at the vineyard. Also indicated by the words, *récoltant* or *producteur* around the cap.

● *Négociant*: a wine that has been bought by a dealer and usually bottled away from the estate. However, this is not necessarily to the detriment of the wine; there are many excellent *négociants*.

Cafés

Although there has sadly been a significant decline in the number of French cafés in recent years, they remain an institution, good for morning coffee, reading the paper, drinks or snack meals. In smaller towns and villages they are very much the centre of local life. Note that if you drink at the bar it is usually cheaper than sitting at a table.

Restaurant Listings

As with the hotels, the purpose of this list is to mention some of the region's most famous restaurants, and to recommend others that are particularly attractive or interesting. The restaurants are grouped in accordance with the layout of the book, and then in alphabetical order. Credit cards accepted in the restaurants are listed at the end of each entry.

HYÈRES AND THE MASSIF DES MAURES

Aiguebelle
Les Roches
1 Ave des Trois Dauphins
Tel: (04) 94 71 05 07

Beautiful beach setting and good food inspired by the flavours of Provence. Credit cards: Visa, AmEx. €€€

La Garde-Freinet
La Faucado
Route Nationale, 83310
La Garde-Freinet
Tel: (04) 94 43 60 41
Traditional Provençal décor and traditional Provençal cuisine served on a beautiful open-air terrace. All credit cards. €€

Hyères
Potiniere
27 Ave de la Mediterannée
Tel: (04) 94 00 51 60
Excellent value tasty seafood cuisine served at the hotel's restaurant overlooking the port. All credit cards. €

Porquerolles
Restaurant l'Olivier
Le Mas du Langoustier
Ile de Porquerolles
Tel: (04) 94 58 30 09
Expensive, exclusive island dining, but worth the trip for lunch even if you don't stay at the hotel. Try the fish soup, the sea bass stuffed with olives and tomatoes and the exquisite desserts. Credit cards: AmEx, DC, MC, V. €€€

ST-TROPEZ AND ITS PENINSULA

Gassin
Villa de Belieu
Tel: (04) 94 56 40 56
A beautiful setting in a wine *domaine*. Four excellent menus. Credit cards: AmEx, Visa, MasterCard, Diners Club. €€

Grimaud
Café de France
Place Neuve
Tel: (04) 94 43 20 05
Simple Provençal food, served on a shady terrace set back from the village square. Credit cards: Visa. €

St-Tropez
La Bouillabaisse
Quartier la Bouillabaisse
Tel: (04) 94 97 54 00
In an old fisherman's cottage serving excellent fresh fish from the terrace right by the beach. Credit cards: Visa, AmEx. €€

La Cascade
5, Rue de l'Eglise
Tel: (04) 94 54 83 46
Lively Caribbean atmosphere and Caribbean specialities. Credit cards: Visa. €€

Le Café
Place des Lices
Tel: (04) 94 97 44 69
Traditional bistro with hearty fare on the site of the Café des Arts, the original hangout of the Places des Lices *boules* players. Credit cards: AmEx, MC, Visa. €

Leï Mouscardins
Tour du Portalet
Tel: (04) 94 97 29 00
Superb quayside dining with a

Price Categories

The prices of the restaurants are indicated as follows:
€ = Budget: under €25
€€ = Moderate: €25–50
€€€ = Expensive: over €50
These are average menu prices per person, not including wine or coffee. Note that menu prices at lunchtime are often half the price of the evening menu.

seasonal menu of original fish and
vegetable dishes. Thought by many
to be St-Tropez's best restaurant.
Credit cards AmEx, Diners Club,
MasterCard, Visa. €€€

L'Olivier
Route des Carles
Tel: (04) 94 97 58 16
A country-house restaurant with
garden, serving elegant cuisine
based on the flavours of Provence.
All credit cards accepted. €€

Le Relais des Caves du Roy
Hotel Byblos,
Avenue Foch
Tel: (04) 94 56 68 20
Superb Provençal dishes make this
one of St-Tropez's finest. All credit
cards accepted. €€€

ST-RAPHAËL, FRÉJUS AND THE ARGENS VALLEY

Les Adrets-de-l'Estérel
Auberge des Adrets
Route Nationale 7, towards
Mandelieu
Tel: (04) 94 82 11 82
Good food in a pleasant setting.
Closed: Mon. Credit cards: Visa. €€

Les Arcs
Le Logis du Guetteur
Place Château
Tel: (04) 94 99 51 10
Sophisticated menu in a beautiful
setting above the village. Tables on
the terrace offer great views of the
rooftops and surrounding vineyards.
All credit cards accepted. €€

Auribeau-sur-Siagne
Auberge de la Vignette Haute
Tel: (04) 93 42 20 01
Rustic setting and romantic
atmosphere. The dining room is lit
by 400 oil lamps. Credit cards:
Visa, AmEx, Diners Club. €€€

Lorgues
Chez Bruno
Route de Vidauban
Tel: (04) 94 85 93 93
Expect rich menus based around
truffles and foie gras at this
beautifully situated, extremely
popular restaurant. All credit cards
accepted. €€€

St-Raphaël
Pastorel
54, Rue de la Liberté
Tel: (04) 94 95 02 36
Good traditional food with a
Provençal touch. Credit cards: Visa,
AmEx, Diners Club. €€

CANNES

La Côte
Carlton Intercontinental Hotel
58 Boulevard de la Croisette
Tel: (04) 93 06 40 23
Elegant dining-room, excellent
cuisine. Credit cards: Visa, AmEx,
Diners Club. €€€

Neat
11 Square Merimée
Tel: (04) 93 99 29 19
The only English chef, so far, to
earn a Michelin star in France,
Richard Neat serves modern
French cuisine at his highly rated
restaurant not far from the Palais
des Festivals. Credit cards: AmEx,
Diners Club, MasterCard, Visa.
€€–€€€

La Palme d'Or
Hôtel Martinez
73, Boulevard de la Croisette
Tel: (04) 92 98 74 14
Imaginative gastronomic cuisine
with a taste of the Mediterranean.
One of Cannes' top restaurants,
with a view of the Bay and the
Lérins Islands. Credit cards:
Visa, AmEx, Diners Club. €€€

La Pizza
3, Quai St-Pierre
Tel: (04) 93 39 22 56
The best-known pizza place in the
region – plenty of atmosphere. €

Le Royal Gray
Hôtel Gray d'Albion
38 Rue des Serbes
Tel: (04) 92 99 79 60
Master chef Jacques Chibois has
been voted chef of the year many
times. Widely recognised as the
best restaurant in Cannes. Credit
cards: Visa, AmEx, Diners. €€

Villa de Lys
Hôtel Majestic
14 Blvd de la Croisette
Tel: (04) 92 98 77 00.
Chef Bruno Oger is one of the
region's rising-star chefs and serves
good traditional fare along with
oriental inspired offerings in this
hotel restaurant. Credit cards: AmEx,
Diners Club, MasterCard, Visa. €€

ANTIBES AND THE PLATEAU DE VALBONNE

Antibes
Auberge Provençale
Place Nationale
Tel: (04) 93 34 13 24
Attractive dining-room and beautiful
courtyard in summer. Credit cards:
Visa, AmEx, Diners Club, €

Bacon
668 Boulevard de Bacon
Tel: (04) 93 61 50 02
Celebrated restaurant famous for
its fish dishes and in particular its
superlative bouillabaisse. Credit
cards: Visa, AmEx, Diners Club. €€

La Bonne Auberge
Route Nationale 7
Tel: (04) 93 33 36 65
One of the best restaurants in the
area. Credit cards: Visa, AmEx. €€€

Casa Pablo
1 Rue de la Touraque
Tel: (04) 93 34 21 54
An unpretentious, pretty restaurant
near the ramparts. Credit cards:
Visa, AmEx, Diners Club. €

Don Juan
17 Rue Thuret
Tel: (04) 93 34 58 63.
Excellent service and good pizzas
and Provençal dishes. €

Biot
Les Arcades
16 Place des Arcades
Tel: (04) 93 65 01 04

Classical Provençal cuisine in the dining room of a 15th-century house, which doubles as an art gallery. All credit cards. €€

Auberge du Jarrier
30, Passage de la Bourgade
Tel: (04) 93 65 11 68
Comfortable old auberge serving elegant French cuisine with a Mediterranean flavour. All credit cards accepted. €€

Les Terraillers
11 Route du Chemin Neuf
Tel: (04) 93 65 01 59
An elegant restaurant just outside the village in a beautiful vaulted cellar. Attractive terrace in summer. Closed: November and Wednesdays. Credit cards: Visa, AmEx, Diners Club. €€

Golfe-Juan
Le Bistrot du Port
53 Boulevard des Frères Roustan
Tel: (04) 93 63 70 64
Mainly fish dishes. Attractive terrace on the old port. Closed: Sunday evenings and Monday. Credit cards: Visa. €€

Juan-les-Pins
Belles Rives
Boulevard Baudointel
Tel: (04) 93 61 02 79.
Elegant hotel and restaurant set right on the water's edge, once the residence of F. Scott Fitzgerald. Credit cards: Visa, AmEx. €€

La Terrasse
La Pinède
Avenue Gallice
Tel: (04) 93 61 20 37
Recognised as one of the region's best restaurants, with a palm-shaded terrace. All credit cards accepted. €€€

Mougins
L'Amandier
Place du Commandant Lamy
Tel: (04) 93 90 00 91
This is Roger Vergé's second restaurant *(see below)*, in the old village. Credit cards: Visa, AmEx, Diners Club. €€€

Le Bistrot de Mougins
Place du Village
Tel: (04) 93 75 78 34
Set in a beautiful vaulted stone

Dining Habits

It is essential to be aware of dining hours in the region. Most people stop for *le midi*, and often lunch will start as early as midday. By one o'clock it is almost too late, and they may not serve at all beyond 2pm. Evening meals are usually at 8pm and in smaller or country places you may not get dinner after 9pm.

At the height of the season, or if you have a particular place in mind, reservations are recommended. Restaurants often have outdoor tables for fine weather, even in towns and cities, where you may find yourself sitting on the pavement or in an inner courtyard.

The French usually eat salad after the main course and sometimes with the cheese. Cheese comes before dessert. You will almost always be given bread with your meal. Water will be supplied if asked for, and should be safe to drink.

You will find wine lists often reflect the region, so all the wine regions will have predominantly local wines on the list. The restaurateur will usually be delighted to advise you. All restaurants will offer a *vin de pays* by the carafe *(pichet)* or demi-carafe and this is almost always good value for money and perfectly drinkable.

cellar, excellent Provençal cuisine. All credit cards. €€

La Ferme de Mougins
10 Avenue Saint Basile
tel: (04) 93 90 03 74
A Provençal residence built of stone, set in an idyllic garden. Credit cards: Visa, Eurocard, Diners Club, AmEx. €€

Le Moulin de Mougins
424 Chemin du Moulin
Tel: (04) 93 75 78 24
The most famous restaurant in this village full of famous restaurants. Roger Vergé's *"cuisine du soleil"* is known worldwide Credit cards: Visa, AmEx, Diners Club. €€€

Valbonne
L'Auberge Fleurie
1016 Route de Cannes
Tel: (04) 93 12 02 80
Excellent value regional cuisine with particularly good desserts. €

GRASSE AND THE LOUP VALLEY

Le Bar-sur-Loup
La Jarrerie
Route de Grasse
Tel: (04) 93 42 92 92
Offers a traditional and elegant atmosphere and good cuisine, plus an atmospheric setting in a former

monastery. Closed: January, Monday evenings and Tuesdays. Credit cards: Visa. €€

Cabris
Auberge du Petit Prince
15 Rue Frédéric Mistral
Tel: (04) 93 60 63 14
A country inn serving good food and offering an attractive terrace. Closed: mid November–mid December, Thursday evenings and Fridays. Credit cards: Visa, AmEx, Diners Club. €

Coursegoules
L'Escaou
Tel: (04) 93 59 11 28
Restaurant in this mountain village, serving rustic Provençal cuisine with superb views from its terrace. Credit cards: Visa. €

Grasse
La Bastide St-Antoine
48 Ave Henri Dunant
Grasse
Tel: (04) 93 70 94 94
Hard to find but worth the search, this new restaurant set in an old olive grove outside Grasse is currently fashionable for its wonderful, value-for money gourmet menu, specialising in truffles and mushrooms. Credit cards: AmEx, Diners Club, MasterCard, Visa. €€

Tourrettes-sur-Loup
Chez Grand'Mère
Place Mirabeau
Tel: (04) 93 59 33 34
Very popular for North African
specialities and meats grilled on
the open fire. Reservations
recommended. €
Le Petit Manoir
21 Grand'Rue
Tel: 93 24 19 19.
Elegant restaurant serving fine
cuisine. Credit cards: Visa,
Eurocard. €€

CAGNES, VENCE AND THE VAR VALLEY

Cagnes-sur-Mer
Le Cagnard
Rue du Pontis Long
Haut-de-Cagnes
Tel: (04) 93 20 73 21
The cuisine is elegant and beautifully
presented. Charming dining-room in
what was once the 14th-century
castle's guardroom. Credit cards:
AmEx, Diners Club, Visa. €€€
Entre Cour et Jardin
102 Montée de la Bourgade
Tel: (04) 93 20 72 27
Friendly restaurant in a little village
street with art exhibitions in the
courtyard twice a year. Credit cards:
Visa. €€
La Table d'Yves
85 Montée de la Bourgade
Haute-de-Cagnes
Tel: (04) 93 20 33 33
Hearty Provençal dishes, some of
the best fish soup in the region,
delicious pasta and excellent
lamb, all served in a charming
village setting. All credit cards
accepted. €€

La Gaude
La Seguinière
Tel: (04) 93 24 42 92
An attractive villa with plenty of
atmosphere. Jazz on Saturday
evenings. Garden in summer. All
credit cards accepted. €€

St-Paul-de-Vence
La Colombe d'Or
1 Place du Général de Gaulle
Tel: (04) 93 32 80 02

The dining-room is hung with the
works of Matisse, Picasso, Léger,
Delaunay and others, while the
terrace must be the most beautiful
in the region. Good, traditional
cuisine. Credit cards: AmEx, Diners
Club, Visa. €€€

Vence
Restaurant Jacques Maximin
689 Chemin de la Gaude
Tel: (04) 93 58 90 75
Exotic garden setting for this
legendary French chef to produce
his classic and unusual dishes,
drawing on the best produce of the
surrounding region. Credit cards:
AmEx, Diners Club, MasterCard,
Visa. €€€

Price Categories

The prices of the restaurants are
indicated as follows:
€ = Budget: under €25
€€ = Moderate: €25–50
€€€ = Expensive: over €50
These are average menu prices
per person, not including wine or
coffee. Note that menu prices at
lunchtime are often half the price
of the evening menu.

NICE

Auberge de Bellet
St-Roman de Bellet
Tel: (04) 93 37 92 51
In Nice's most famous vineyard of
the same name. Vintage wines and
delicacies such as lobster, pigeon,
and garlic stew. All credit cards. €€
Le Chantecler
Hôtel Negresco
37 Promenade des Anglais
Tel: (04) 93 16 64 00
Nice's finest restaurant offers
elegant cuisine with a
Mediterranean touch. It is run
by Alain Lorca, typical of a new
generation of Provençal chefs
who bring an original light twist
to the region's delicacies. Credit
cards: AmEx, Diners Club,
Eurocard, Visa. €€€
Le Comptoir
20 Rue Saint-Francois-de-Paule
Tel: (04) 93 92 08 80

A 1930s-style bar and restaurant,
excellent for late-night dining.
Credit cards: AmEx, Diners Club,
Visa. €
Nissa-Socca
5, Rue Ste-Réparate
Tel: (04) 93 80 18 35
Arrive early or be prepared to wait.
Popular and unpretentious, serving
Niçois specialities: fresh pasta,
vegetable fritters. Excellent value.
Closed: Sundays and Monday
lunchtimes. Note: credit cards
not accepted. €
Le Safari
1 Cours Saleya
Tel: (04) 93 80 18 44
Big café with outside tables in
flower market street. Try the *bagna
cauda*, a hot anchovy dip with raw
vegetables. Credit cards: Visa,
AmEx. €

CAP FERRAT AND THE GOLDEN TRIANGLE

Beaulieu-sur-Mer
Le Metropole
15 Boulevard Leclerc
Tel: (04) 93 01 00 08
Fish specialities in a discreetly
luxurious setting. Closed:
November–20 December. Credit
cards: Visa, MasterCard. €€€
La Réserve
5 Boulevard Leclerc
Tel: (04) 93 01 00 01
Excellent cuisine in an elegant
Renaissance-inspired setting.
Emphasis on fish dishes. Credit
cards: AmEx, Diners Club, Eurocard,
MasterCard, Visa. €€€

Èze
Château de la Chèvre d'Or
Rue du Barri
Tel: (04) 92 10 66 66
Light, classical cuisine in a
medieval château with superb sea
views. Closed: December, January,
February and Wednesdays. Credit
cards: Visa, AmEx, Diners Club.
€€€
Chateau Eza
Tel: (04) 93 41 12 24
Former residence of the Prince of
Sweden, suspended high above the
sea. Closed: late October–early

April. Credit cards: AmEx, Diners Club, Eurocard, Visa. €€€

St-Jean-Cap-Ferrat
Le Provençal
2 Avenue Denis Semeria
Tel: (04) 93 76 03 97
Imaginative, gastronomic cuisine with a Mediterranean flavour.
Closed: Sundays. Credit cards: AmEx, Visa. €€
La Voile d'Or
Yacht Harbour
Tel: (04) 93 01 13 13
High prices justified by the idyllic setting overlooking the pretty harbour and the exquisite cuisine.
Closed: November–March. Credit cards: AmEx, Visa. €€€

MONACO

Bar et Beouf
Ave Princess Grace, Monte-Carlo
Tel: (00 377) 92 16 60 60
An Alain Ducasse establishment where his protégé, Didier Elena, offers exquisite cuisine in a stylish Philippe Starck interior. All credit cards. €€€
Le Café de Paris
Place du Casino
Tel: (00 377) 92 16 20 20
Recently completely renovated in fine 1920s style, this brasserie deserves a visit as one of the sights of Monte-Carlo. The crêpe suzette was invented here. Credit cards: Visa, AmEx, Diners Club. €€
Louis XV
Hotel de Paris.
Place Monte-Carlo.
Tel: (00 377) 92 16 38 40
The most celebrated Alain Ducasse establishment, this glittering restaurant in the Hôtel de Paris serves sophisticated updates of sturdy Mediterranean peasant cuisine – at a price. The terrace overlooks the Casino. All credit cards accepted. €€€
Polpetta
2 Rue Paradis
Tel: (00 377) 93 50 67 84
Offering hearty Italian food, which is perhaps the best value for money in Monaco. Credit cards: Visa. €

MENTON AND ROQUEBRUNE

Menton
Le Lion D'Or
7 Rue des Marins.
Tel: (04) 93 35 74 67
Good value local favourite serving fresh fish straight from the sea.
Credit cards: MasterCard, Visa. €€

Roquebrune
Au Grand Inquisiteur
Rue du Château
Tel: (04) 93 35 05 37
Restaurant in a medieval setting in the old village. Credit cards: Visa. €
Le Vistaero
Grande Corniche
Tel: (04) 92 10 40 20
Fabulous view over Monaco and the coast towards Nice, along with excellent food. Credit cards: AmEx, Diners Club, Visa. €€€

THE PERCHED VILLAGES

Peillon
Auberge de la Madone
Tel: 93 79 91 17
A true Provençal inn offering authentic regional cuisine and lovely mountain views. Note: credit cards not accepted. €€

BORDER COUNTRY

Breil-sur-Roya
Castel du Roy
Route de Tende
Tel: (04) 93 04 43 66
Charming riverside restaurant with tranquil, tree-shaded terrace serving specialities of the region.
Credit cards: Visa. €

La Brigue
Le Mirval
Rue St-Vincent Ferrier
Tel: (04) 93 04 63 71
The most charming restaurant in La Brigue, situated outside the village, beside the river. Local specialities include trout, spinach ravioli and game. Open April–November only.
Credit cards: AmEx, Diners Club, MasterCard, Visa. €

Culture

The Riviera has a wealth of cultural events, especially in the summer months, when there are festivals of music, theatre and dance. Cannes is known for its film festival, and Nice and Juan-les-Pins for jazz, but more and more smaller towns and villages also stage their own celebrations.

Traditional festivals also abound, celebrating everything from flowers to lemons. The Riviera also has a magnificent legacy of art and there are a number of important art museums – in Nice, St Paul de Vence, St Tropez and Antibes. There are also many smaller museums and galleries offering a huge variety of art and crafts. In larger towns like Nice, Cannes and Monte-Carlo you will find opera, theatre and cinema venues.

For information on exhibitions and concerts, contact local tourist offices. The useful booklet *Terre de Festivals* (available from tourist offices) covers summer arts festivals in the region; it can also be found online at www.festival.cr-paca.fr. Tickets for festivals can often be bought directly at tourist offices or at branches of Fnac (www.fnac.fr) and Virgin, or via France Billet, tel: (04) 42 31 31 31).

Diary of Events

January
Cannes: MIDEM (International Disc and Music Publishing Festival)
Menton: Theatre season
Monaco: Monte-Carlo Rally; International Circus Festival
Nice: Festival of Birds

February
Isola 2000: Snow Carnival
Menton: International Lemon Festival
Nice: Carnival and Battle of Flowers

March

Antibes: Café Theatre Festival
Grasse: Carnival
Monte-Carlo: MANCAS – contemporary and film music festival; Spring Arts Festival (continues until end of April)

April

Cannes: MIP-TV (International TV festival)
Monte-Carlo: Biennial of Sculpture (odd numbered years, until end of September); Monte-Carlo Tennis Open
Roquebrune-Cap-Martin: Costumed procession of lanterns to the castle on Good Friday

May

Cannes: Film Festival
Fréjus: Fleuriades – flower festival
Grasse: Expo Roses – international rose show
Monaco: Formula One Grand Prix
Nice: May Festival and International Youth Folk Festival; Art Jonction International
St-Tropez: The Bravades festival is in honour of the Roman soldier Torpes from whom St-Tropez takes its name

June

Antibes: International Young Soloist Festival
Cannes: International Cabaret-Theatre Festival
Fréjus: Arênes de l'Automobile: exhibition of collector's cars
Monte-Carlo: Fires of Saint Jean folk festival
Nice: Sacred Music Festival
Roquebrune-Cap-Martin: Theatre Festival
Whole region: Fête de la Musique (21 June)

July

Antibes: International Jazz Festival. Musiques au Coeur opera festival
Fréjus: Forum des Arts et de la Musique – concerts, classical dance, theatre
Golf-Juan: Jean Marais Festival (theatre and music)
Grasse: International Festival of Military Music
Juan-les-Pins: Jazz à Juan

Monte-Carlo: Season of concerts in the Palais du Prince courtyard; Fireworks Festival and Monaco carnival
Nice: International Folk Festival; Grande Parade du Jazz – Nice's famous Jazz Festival
Sospel and nearby towns: Les Baroquiales – music and opera in alpine churches
Vallauris: Biennale de Céramique Contemporaine – ceramics on display every two years
Vence: Classical concerts in the cathedral and open air
Villefranche-sur-Mer: Venetian Festival
Whole region: Bastille Day (14 July, all France) – fireworks and celebrations

August

Antibes: International Fireworks Festival
Fréjus: Fête du Raisin – wine-tasting and feasting
Grasse: Festival of Jasmine
Menton: International Chamber Music Festival
Monte-Carlo: Feast of Saint Roman folk festival
Roquebrune-Cap-Martin: Costumed procession to the castle
Vallauris: Pottery Festival

September

St-Tropez: Grape-picking festival
Whole region: Journées du Patrimoine – historic monuments and official buildings open free to the public

October

Monte-Carlo: Season of Symphony Concerts

November

Cannes: Festival International de la Danse
Monte-Carlo: National holiday (19 November) – parades, ceremonies and spectacles (fireworks the previous evening)

December

Fréjus: Foire aux Santons – Provençal craftsmen exhibit *santons* (small clay figures of saints used for religious purposes).

Nightlife

Apart from Paris, the Côte d'Azur has the most exciting nightlife in France. The casino at Monte-Carlo was the first in the country to open in 1865 (at a time when they were not permitted in the rest of France). It saved the principality from bankruptcy and the rich and famous came flocking to try their luck. What started as a Victorian novelty has now been tinged by a touch of Las Vegas and it has been joined by plenty of other casinos along the coast, some of them incorporating nightclubs or cabarets.

Bars and Nightclubs

If gambling is not your style, you can enjoy your evenings at a nightclub or bar, or by soaking up the atmosphere at a pavement café. Bigger towns like Nice or Monte-Carlo also offer opera, theatre and cinema.

Local tourist offices will keep you up to date with what is going on, as will the local English-language and French papers. Following is a list of discothèques, nightclubs, and cafés/restaurants where you can be entertained as you dine. Many of the luxury hotels also have piano bars. You will need a healthy bank account for most of them.

Antibes

La Siesta, Pont de la Brague, tel: (04) 93 33 31 31. Restaurant, bar, casino and nightclub. Shows June–September.

Cannes

Jimmy's. Palais des Festivals, tel: (04) 92 98 78 00. Fashionable disco.
Les Coulisses, 29 rue de Commandant André, tel: (04) 92 99

17 17. Fashionable nightclub, especially popular during film festival.

Le Queens, 48 bd de la République, tel: (04) 93 90 25 58. Big, funky club popular with locals and festival goers alike.

Zanzibar, 85 Rue Félix-Faure, tel: (04) 93 39 30 75. Long-established gay bar and club.

Juan-les-Pins

Le J's, av Georges Gallice, Juan-les-Pins, tel: (04) 93 67 22 74. nightclub.

Whisky à Gogo, La Pinède, tel: (04) 93 61 26 40.

Monte-Carlo

La Rascasse, Quai Antoine, tel: (00 377) 93 25 56 90. All-night pub, with outdoor terrace with jazz and rock and a restaurant.

Le Sporting Club, av Princess Grace, tel: (00 377) 92 16 22 77. Fashionable Eurotrash rendezvous.

Jimmy'z, place du Casino, tel: (04) 93 50 80 80. Smart, expensive discothèque.

Nice

Le Bar des Oiseaux, 5 rue Saint-Vincent, tel: (04) 93 80 27 33. Live bands and live birds.

Blue Boy Enterprise, 9 rue Spinetta, tel: (04) 93 44 68 24. An all-night gay club with drag shows.

Dizzy Club, 26 quai Lunel, tel: (04) 93 26 54 79. Piano-bar and dancing.

Ste-Maxime

Café de France, pl Victor Hugo, tel: (04) 94 96 18 16. Classic bar with people-watching terrace.

St-Tropez

Bar du Port, 7 Quai Suffren, tel: (04) 94 97 00 54 Minimal, retro-style bar.

Café de Paris, 15 Quai Suffren, tel: (04) 94 97 00 56. Old bar, redesigned by Philippe Starck to attract a trendy crowd.

Les Caves du Roy, Hôtel Byblos, tel: (04) 94 97 16 02. Legendary club in Hotel Byblos, still a favourite of Johnny Hallyday.

L'Esquinade, 2 Rue du Four, tel: (04) 94 97 87 45. Famous, Bardot-era nightclub. One of the originals.

Le Papagayo, Résidence du Port, tel: (04) 94 97 07 56. This has long been the place to spot famous faces.

Le Pigeonnier, 13 Rue de la Ponche, tel: (04) 94 97 84 26. Popular gay club.

Le VIP Room, residences du Nouveau Port, tel: (04) 94 97 14 70. St-Tropez's latest, most fashionable nightclub.

Theatres and Cinemas

Monte-Carlo

Théâtre du Fort Saint-Antoine, av de la Quarantaine, tel: (00 377) 9325 6612. Theatre-in-the-round for summer night concerts.

Le Cabaret du Casino, pl du Casino, tel: (00 377) 92 16 36 36. Classic French cabaret.

Nice

Opéra de Nice, 4 rue St-François-de-Paule, tel: (04) 92 17 40 40. Classic venue for symphony, ballet and opera.

Théâtre de Nice, promenade des Art, tel: (04) 93 13 90 90. French and foreign classics and contemporary work.

Théâtre de la Photographie et de L'Image, 27 bd de Dubouchage, tel: (04) 92 04 99 70. A restored "belle epoque" theatre with photography shows and coffee bar.

Cinématheque de Nice, 3 Esplanade Kennedy, tel: (04) 92 04 06 66. Recent films in their original version with sub-titles.

Casinos

Note that entrance to most casinos is around €12–20 (although some are free) and restricted to those aged over 21 years of age. Many require you to show your passport.

The main gaming venues are as follows:

Antibes

La Siesta, Route de Bord de Mer, tel: (04) 93 33 31 31. Open: June–September. Huge nightclub and casino.

Cannes

Carlton Casino Club, Carlton Intercontinental, 58 la Croisette, tel: (04) 92 99 51 00. Open: every day 4pm–4am. Also has restaurants, piano bar and disco.

Casino Croisette, Palais des Festivals, tel: (04) 92 98 78 00.

Monte-Carlo

Casino de Monte-Carlo, Place du Casino, tel: (00 377) 92 16 23 00. The original and still the most famous where formal dress is required. Open: all year: main salon from noon, private rooms from 3pm. The casino also has a separate cabaret venue and several restaurants.

Nice

Casino Ruhl de Nice, 1 Promenade des Anglais, tel: (04) 93 87 95 87. Open: daily 5pm–5am (4pm–4am in winter). Also offers a restaurant, disco and cabaret.

Shopping

Shopping Areas

Over the years most major towns in France have made the sensible decision to keep the town centre for small boutiques and individual shops. Many of these areas are pedestrianised and so rather attractive (although beware – some cars ignore the *voie piétonnée* signs). The large supermarkets, hypermarkets, furniture stores and DIY outlets are grouped on the outskirts of the town, mostly designated as a *Centre Commercial*. This laudable intent is, however, somewhat marred by the horrendous design of some of these centres – groups of garish functional buildings which make the town's outskirts very unattractive. In the case of Nice, for example, there are vast hypermarkets, out by the airport to the west of the town.

These *Centres Commercials* are fine for bulk shopping, for self-catering or for finding a selection of wine to take home at reasonable prices, but otherwise the town centres are far more interesting. It is here that you will find the individual souvenirs that give a taste of the region, alongside the beautifully dressed windows of delicatessens and pâtisseries.

Nice itself has glamorous shopping districts to attract its wealthy tourists. The **Masséna quarter** is a pedestrianised area of chic boutiques, where you will also find the main department stores, Galeries Lafayettes and La Riviera. In **Cannes**, head for the city centre, particularly Rue d'Antibes with its confectioners and luxury boutiques. The **Cannes English Bookshop** (on rue Bivouac Napoleon) is a well-stocked emporium and worth a visit.

Markets

The heart of every French town is its market, and the markets of the Côte d'Azur and Provence are possibly the most colourful and lively of any in the whole of France. In many towns the market is held every day (except Monday); they mostly start early in the morning and close at midday. The French themselves usually visit early to get the best of the produce.

Some of the best general daily markets are in **Nice** (Cours Saleya), **Antibes** (Cours Masséna, covered market), **Cannes** (Marché Forville, also the flower market, Jardin des Allées – not Saturday), **Grasse** (Place aux Aires), **Menton** (Esplanade du Carei, and covered market), **Toulon** (Cours Lafayette), **Monte-Carlo** (Place d'Armes), **St-Maxime** (covered market, Rue Fenand Bessy, open all day in summer). Other markets which are well worth a visit, but not held daily are as follows (mornings): **St-Tropez** (Tuesday and Saturday), **Fréjus** (Wednesday and Saturday, Place des Poivriers, also **Fréjus Plage**, Place de la République, Tuesday and Friday, June–September), **Hyères** (Tuesday, Place de la République, Saturday, Avenue Gambetta), **Le Lavandou** (Thursday), **Draguignan** (Wednesday and Saturday), **Ste-Maxime** (Old Town, Thursday; Marché du Capet, Avenue Georges Pompidou, Monday).

Another attraction are the specialist markets. All the above have flower stalls, but Nice, where the flower market is open all day, and **Cannes** are especially colourful. Antique and second-hand (*brocante*) markets are also very popular; those listed below are held regularly and are open all day unless otherwise indicated.

Antibes: Place Audiberti, Thursday; also Cours Masséna for bric-à-brac and crafts, Tuesday and Friday afternoons.
Cagnes: Place du Château, Sunday.
Cannes: Allées de la Liberté, Saturday.
Menton: Place aux Herbes, Friday.
Nice: Rues A. Gauthier/C.

Ségurane/E. Philibert, also the flea market, Place Guynemer, both daily except Sunday; philatelist's market, Square Durandy, Rue Pastorelli, Sunday morning.
Ste-Maxime-sur-Mer: Marché des Artisans (craft market), Thursday.
La Seyne-sur-Mer: Les Sablettes, Saturday, plus a flea market, Place B. Frachon, alternate Sundays except in July.
Vence: L'Ara, Wednesday.
Villefranche-sur-Mer: Place A. Pollonais, Sunday.
There are also antique and craft fairs and *marchés exceptionnels*, held at various points throughout the year, such as harvest times. Check with the local tourist office for details.

Buying Wine Direct

You may be tempted by all the signs you see along the road for *dégustations* – tastings. Many wine producers and farmers will invite you to try their wines and other produce with the aim of making a sale. This is a good way to try before you buy and can sometimes include a visit to a wine cellar. Also, the wine should be cheaper here than in the supermarket, and it can be more reliable to buy something you have tried and know you like. To taste and buy a range of different wines at one establishment, try the following:

Maison des Vins, Route Nationale 7, Les Arcs-sur-Argens, tel: 04 94 99 50 20.
Les Maîtres Vignerons de St-Tropez, La Foux junction, 4 km (2 miles) west of St-Tropez, tel: 04 94 56 32 04.

Shopping Tips

Food shops, especially bakers, tend to open early; boutiques and department stores open from 9am, but sometimes not until 10am. In town centres, just about everything closes from noon until 3pm apart from the department stores which usually stay open. Most shops close in the evening at 7pm. Out of town, the hypermarkets are usually open all day until 8 or even 9pm. Most shops are closed Monday mornings and large stores generally all day. If you want to buy a picnic lunch, remember to buy everything you need before midday. Good delicatessens (*charcuterie*) have a selection of delicious ready-prepared dishes, which make picnicking a delight.

Tax Refunds (Detaxe)

A refund (average 13 per cent) on value added tax (TVA) can be claimed by non-EU visitors if they spend over €180 in any one shop. The shop will supply a *detaxe* form and you will need to have it stamped by customs when you leave the country. You send a stamped copy back to the shop, which will refund the tax, either by bank transfer or by crediting your credit card. *Detaxe* does not cover food, drink, antiques or works of art.

Complaints

If you have a complaint about any purchase, return it in the first place to the shop as soon as possible. In the case of any serious dispute, contact the Direction Départementale de la Concurrence et de la Consommation et de la Répression des Fraudes.

Sport

Participant Sports

The Riviera offers a huge range of sports and activities to choose from. Apart from lying on the beach, of course, you can indulge in surfing, windsurfing and waterskiing.

Antibes and Cannes are major watersports centres, and the Iles de Lérins and Iles de Hyères offer some of the best diving in the Med. For detailed listings pick up the *Watersports Côte d'Azur* brochure from main tourist offices or go to www.france-nautisme.com.

The sea is usually warm enough for swimming from June to September, and almost every town will have a municipal pool, though it may only be open in school holidays. Even small villages often have a tennis court, though you may have to become a temporary member to use it – enquire at the local tourist office or *mairie* (town hall) which will also provide details of all other local sporting activities.

The mountains and river valleys offer walking, riding, cycling and climbing, river rafting and canoeing, and skiing in the winter months.

General information on sports and activities can be obtained from local tourist offices. Many UK tour operators offer holidays tailored to specific activities.

WATER SPORTS

It is not necessary to be a millionaire and member of the most fashionable yacht club to enjoy the pleasures of the sea. Of course, if you wish to hire a luxury yacht for a week's cruise, being a millionaire might help. You also need money to enjoy some of the beaches. Only 70

per cent are open to the public, the rest (nearly 150 beaches) are privately owned (usually by hotels) and an entrance fee is charged. Most of the private beaches have a good range of equipment for hire: windsurfers, dinghies, catamarans, water skiing, parascending etc.

To hire a boat, or a yacht, for a day or longer, all you need really do is stroll around the pleasure ports of the resorts and ask. Another source of information is the local *syndicat d'initiative* or tourist office. For scheduled cruises, *see* page 317.

Sailing & Windsurfing
Comité Regional de Voile Côte d'Azur, Espace Antibes, 2208 Route de Grasse, 06600 Antibes, tel: (04) 93 74 77 05

Scuba Diving
Fédération Française d'Etudes et de Sports Sous-Marins, 24 Quai Rive-Neuve, 13007 Marseille, tel: (04) 91 33 99 31, fax: (04) 91 54 77 43

Canoeing & Kayaking
Fédération Française de Canoe-Kayak et des Sports Associés en Eau-Vive, 87 Quai de la Marne, 94340 Joinville-le-Pont, tel: (01) 45 11 08 50, fax: (01) 48 86 13 25
Ligue Régionale Alpes-Provence, 14 Ave Vincent Auriol, 30200 Bagnols-sur-Ceze, tel: (04) 66 89 47 71

Fishing
Here you have a choice of sea or fresh-water fishing. The season opens around the second Saturday in March. For freshwater fishing you will need to be affiliated to an association. For general information and addresses of local fishing associations, contact:
Conseil Superieur de la Pêche, 134 Avenue de Malakoff, 75016 Paris, tel: (01) 45 01 20 20.

CLIMBING

Beyond the coast there are many opportunities for climbers. You can find guides for day outings or clubs that will organise beginners' courses.

For further information contact:
Club Alpin Français, 14 Ave Mirabeau, Nice, tel: 04 93 53 37 95.

CYCLING

Cycling is a wonderful way to enjoy the region (see page 310 for advice on transporting your own bike). If you don't have you own bike, you can rent cycles locally from bike shops or youth hostels. You might also consider a package cycling holiday, with accommodation booked in advance and your luggage transported for you. The IGN 906 Cycling France map (see page 309) gives details of routes, cycling clubs and places to stay.

More details are available from: **The Touring Department Cyclists Touring Club**, Cotterell House, 69 Meadrow, Godalming, Surrey GU7 3HS, tel: 01483 417 217. Their service to members includes competitive cycle and travel insurance, free detailed touring itineraries and general information sheets about France, while their tours brochure lists trips to the region. The club's French counterpart, **Fédération Française de Cyclotourisme** is at 8 rue Jean-Marie-Jégo, 75013 Paris, tel: 01 44 16 88 88.

GOLF

The Riviera has many excellent golf courses and the weather means golf can be played all year round. Most of the clubs provide lessons with resident experts.
Fédération Française de Golfe, 68 rue Anatole France, Le Vallois, Perret, tel: 01 41 49 77 00, fax: 01 41 49 77 01
Golf de la Grand Bastide, Chateauneuf de Grasse. tel: 04.93 77 70 08, 18 holes, open all year.
Golf Opio-Valbonne, Opio. tel: 04 93 12 00 08, 18 holes, open all year.
Golf de Valescure, Avenue Paul l'Hermite, 83700 Saint-Raphaél, tel: 04 94 82 40 46, fax: 04 94 82 41 42, 18 holes, open all year.

SKIING

The Maritime Alps are popular for skiing and there are several large resorts, such as Auron, Valberg and Isola 2000. They are only a few hours from the coast and, at certain times of the year, you could conceivably combine beach and skiing in one day.
Fédération Française de Ski, 50 Avenue des Marquisats 74000 Annecy. tel: 04 50 51 40 34, www.ffs.fr
Auron: Office du Tourisme, tel: 04 93 23 02 66.
Isola 2000: Office du Tourisme, tel: 04 93 23 15 15.

WALKING

Walking holidays are an increasingly popular way to enjoy the less trammelled parts of the Riviera, especially inland in the mountains. Ensure you are suitably equipped with water, warm clothing and good boots. There is an excellent network of signposted footpaths, (sentiers de grand randonée; long-distance footpaths) but ensure you have a good map. (For information on maps see page 309) Local tourist offices or ramblers' organisations may organise guided walks of local sights, plants or wildlife. For local information, contact the relevant tourist office, or the following: **Fédération Française de Randonnée Pedestre**, 14 Rue Riquet, 75009 Paris. tel: 01 44 89 93 90, fax: 01 40 35 85 48.
Comité Departemental de la Randonnée Pédestre, 4 Ave de Verdun, Cagnes-sur-Mer, tel and fax: 04 93 20 74 73

Spectator Sports

Probably the most famous event in the whole region is the prestigious **Monte-Carlo Car Rally**, held in January. First staged in 1911, this road trial continues to attract the top names in the sport. Another lesser-known rally is held in November at St-Tropez; the 20-km

(12-mile) **Rolls-Royce Rally**. The other big motoring event is the **Monte-Carlo Grand Prix** in May, one of the most decisive contests in the competition for the world motor racing championship.

April is the time for the International Tennis championships in Monte-Carlo, the **Monte-Carlo Open**, which is complemented by another "open", this time the **Golf Tournament** which takes place in early July. Another golfing event is the **Professional Golf Open** at Mougins (Cannes) which is held every April.

The major horse-racing venue is the **Côte d'Azur Hippodrome** at Cagnes-sur-Mer where meetings are held during the day from December to May and in the evenings in July and August. One of its major events takes place in February. There is also an **international show-jumping competition** in Cannes during May. Hyères is popular for racing, and meetings are held at the **Hippodrome** there during the spring and autumn. Fréjus hosts a **horse show** in June.

There are all kinds of sailing and other water-sport events, with most of the major competitions taking place at Mandelieu-la-Napoule, just west of Cannes, including the **Grand Prix de la Corniche d'Or** (April), "**Les Vieilles Ecoutes**" (July), the **International Rowing Regatta** (August) and the **Grand Prix de la Ville** (October). Other events are the **International Marathon** in the Baie des Anges, Nice in April, the **Transgolfe Windsurf Regatta** in St-Tropez in July and the **Royal Regattas** in September in Cannes to coincide with the **International Pleasure Boat Festival**; there is also a **Boat Show** at Beaulieu-sur-Mer in May.

Language

French is the native language of more than 90 million people and the acquired language of 180 million. It is a Romance language descended from the Vulgar Latin spoken by the Roman conquerors of Gaul. It still carries the reputation of being the most cultured language in the world and, for what it's worth, the most beautiful. People often tell stories about the impatience of the French towards foreigners not blessed with fluency in their language. In general, however, if you attempt to communicate with them in French, they will be helpful.

Since much of the English vocabulary is related to French, thanks to the Norman Conquest of 1066, travellers will often recognise many helpful cognates: words such as *hôtel*, *café* and *bagages* hardly need to be translated. You should be aware, however, of some misleading "false friends" (*see page 339*).

Words & Phrases

How much is it? *C'est combien?*
What is your name? *Comment vous appelez-vous?*
My name is... *Je m'appelle...*
Do you speak English? *Parlez-vous anglais?*
I am English/American *Je suis anglais/américain*
I don't understand *Je ne comprends pas*
Please speak more slowly *Parlez plus lentement, s'il vous plaît*
Can you help me? *Pouvez-vous m'aider?*
I'm looking for... *Je cherche*
Where is...? *Où est...?*
I'm sorry *Excusez-moi/Pardon*
I don't know *Je ne sais pas*

The Alphabet

Learning the pronunciation of the French alphabet is a good idea. In particular, learn how to spell out your name.
a=ah, **b**=bay, **c**=say, **d**=day **e**=er, **f**=ef, **g**=zhay, **h**=ash. **i**=ee, **j**=zhee, **k**=ka, **l**=el, **m**=em, **n** =en, **o**=oh, **p**=pay, **q**=kew, **r**=ehr, **s**=ess, **t**=tay, **u**=ew, **v**=vay, **w**=dooblah vay, **x**-=eex, **y** ee grek, **z**=zed

No problem *Pas de problème*
Have a good day! *Bonne journée!*
That's it *C'est ça*
Here it is *Voici*
There it is *Voilà*
Let's go *On y va. Allons-y*
See you tomorrow *A demain*
See you soon *A bientôt*
Show me the word in the book *Montrez-moi le mot dans le livre*
yes *oui*
no *non*
please *s'il vous plaît*
thank you *merci*
(very much) *(beaucoup)*
you're welcome *de rien*
excuse me *excusez-moi*
hello *bonjour*
OK *d'accord*
goodbye *au revoir*
good evening *bonsoir*
here *ici*

there *là*
today *aujourd'hui*
yesterday *hier*
tomorrow *demain*
now *maintenant*
later *plus tard*
this morning *ce matin*
this afternoon *cet après-midi*
this evening *ce soir*

On Arrival

I want to get off at...
Je voudrais descendre à...
Is there a bus to the Louvre?
Est-ce qu'il ya un bus pour le Louvre?
What street is this? *A quelle rue sommes-nous?*
Which line do I take for...? *Quelle ligne dois-je prendre pour...?*
How far is...?
A quelle distance se trouve...?
Validate your ticket
Compostez votre billet
airport *l'aéroport*
train station *la gare*
bus station *la gare routière*
Métro stop *la station de Métro*
bus *l'autobus, le car*
bus stop *l'arrêt*
platform *le quai*
ticket *le billet*
return ticket *aller-retour*
hitchhiking *l'autostop*
toilets *les toilettes*
This is the hotel address
C'est l'adresse de l'hôtel

Basic Rules

Even if you speak no French at all, it is worth trying to master a few simple phrases. The fact that you have made an effort is likely to get you a better response. More and more French people like practising their English on visitors, especially waiters in the cafés and restaurants and the younger generation. Pronunciation is the key; they really will not understand if you get it very wrong. Remember to **emphasise each syllable**, but not to pronounce the last consonant of a word as a rule (this includes the plural "s") and always to drop your "h"s. Whether to use **"vous"** or **"tu"** is a vexed question; increasingly the familiar form of "tu" is used by many people. However it is better to be too formal, and use "vous" if in doubt. It is very important to be polite; always address people as **Madame** or **Monsieur**, and address them by their surnames until you are confident first names are acceptable. When entering a shop always say, "Bonjour Monsieur/ Madame," and "Merci, au revoir," when leaving.

Time

At what time? *A quelle heure?*
When? *Quand?*
What time is it? *Quelle heure est-il?*
● Note that the French generally use the 24-hour clock.

I'd like a (single/double) room... *Je voudrais une chambre (pour une/deux personnes) ...*
....with shower *avec douche*
....with a bath *avec salle de bain*
Does that include breakfast? *Le prix comprend-il le petit déjeuner?*
May I see the room? *Je peux voir la chambre?*
washbasin *le lavabo*
bed *le lit*
key *la cléf*
elevator *l'ascenseur*
air conditioned *climatisé*

On the Road

Where is the spare wheel? *Où est la roue de secours?*
Where is the nearest garage? *Où est le garage le plus proche?*
Our car has broken down *Notre voiture est en panne*
I want to have my car repaired *Je veux faire réparer ma voiture*
It's not your right of way *Vous n'avez pas la priorité*
I think I must have put diesel in the car by mistake *Je crois que j'ai mis du gasoil dans la voiture par erreur*
the road to... *la route pour...*
left *gauche*
right *droite*
straight on *tout droit*
far *loin*
near *près d'ici*
opposite *en face*
beside *à côté de*
car park *parking*
over there *là-bas*
at the end *au bout*
on foot *à pied*
by car *en voiture*
town map *le plan*
road map *la carte*
street *la rue*
square *la place*
give way *céder le passage*

dead end *impasse*
no parking *stationnement interdit*
motorway *l'autoroute*
toll *le péage*
speed limit *la limitation de vitesse*
petrol *l'essence*
unleaded *sans plomb*
diesel *le gasoil*
water/oil *l'eau/l'huile*
puncture *un pneu de crevé*
bulb *l'ampoule*
wipers *les essuies-glace*

Shopping

Where is the nearest bank (post office)? *Où est la banque/Poste/ PTT la plus proche?*
I'd like to buy *Je voudrais acheter*
How much is it? *C'est combien?*
Do you take credit cards? *Est-ce que vous acceptez les cartes de crédit?*
I'm just looking *Je regarde seulement*
Have you got...? *Avez-vous...?*
I'll take it *Je le prends*
I'll take this one/that one *Je prends celui-ci/celui-là*
What size is it? *C'est de quelle taille?*
Anything else? *Avec ça?*
size (clothes) *la taille*
size (shoes) *la pointure*
cheap *bon marché*
expensive *cher*
enough *assez*
too much *trop*

Emergencies

Help! *Au secours!*
Stop! *Arrêtez!*
Call a doctor *Appelez un médecin*
Call an ambulance *Appelez une ambulance*
Call the police *Appelez la police*
Call the fire brigade *Appelez les pompiers*
Where is the nearest telephone? *Où est le téléphone le plus proche?*
Where is the nearest hospital? *Où est l'hôpital le plus proche?*
I am sick *Je suis malade*
I have lost my passport/purse *J'ai perdu mon passeport/porte-monnaie*

a piece *un morceau de*
each *la pièce (eg ananas, €2 la pièce)*
bill *la note*
chemist *la pharmacie*
bakery *la boulangerie*
bookshop *la librairie*
library *la bibliothèque*
department store *le grand magasin*
delicatessen *la charcuterie/le traiteur*
fishmonger's *la poissonerie*
grocery *l'alimentation/l'épicerie*
tobacconist *tabac (can also sell stamps and newspapers)*
markets *le marché*
supermarket *le supermarché*
junk shop *la brocante*

Sightseeing

town *la ville*
old town *la vieille ville*
abbey *l'abbaye*
cathedral *la cathédrale*
church *l'église*
keep *le donjon*
mansion *l'hôtel*
hospital *l'hôpital*
town hall *l'hôtel de ville/ la mairie*
nave *la nef*
stained glass *le vitrail*
staircase *l'escalier*
tower *la tour (La Tour Eiffel)*
walk *le tour*
country house/castle *le château*
Gothic *gothique*
Roman *romain*
Romanesque *roman*
museum *la musée*
art gallery *la galerie*
exhibition *l'exposition*
tourist information office *l'office de tourisme/le syndicat d'initiative*
free *gratuit*
open *ouvert*
closed *fermé*
every day *tous les jours*
all year *toute l'année*
all day *toute la journée*
swimming pool *la piscine*
to book *réserver*

Dining Out

Table d'hôte (the "host's table") is one set menu served at a fixed price.

Table Talk

I am a vegetarian *Je suis végétarien*
I am on a diet *Je suis au régime*
What do you recommend? *Que'est-ce que vous recommandez?*
Do you have local specialities? *Avez-vous des spécialités locales?*
I'd like to order *Je voudrais commander*
That is not what I ordered *Ce n'est pas ce que j'ai commandé*
Is service included? *Est-ce que le service est compris?*
May I have more wine? *Encore du vin, s'il vous plaît?*
Enjoy your meal *Bon appétit!*

Prix fixé is a fixed price menu.
A la carte means dishes from the menu are charged separately.
breakfast *le petit déjeuner*
lunch *le déjeuner*
dinner *le dîner*
meal *le repas*
first course *l'entrée/les hors d'oeuvre*
main course *le plat principal*
drink included *boisson compris*
wine list *la carte des vins*
the bill *l'addition*
fork *la fourchette*
knife *le couteau*
spoon *la cuillère*
plate *l'assiette*
glass *le verre*
ashtray *le cendrier*

Breakfast and Snacks

baguette **long thin loaf**
pain **bread**
petits pains **rolls**
beurre **butter**
poivre **pepper**
sucre **sugar**
confiture **jam**
oeufs **eggs**
...à la coque **boiled eggs**
...au bacon **bacon and eggs**
...au jambon **ham and eggs**
...sur le plat **fried eggs**
...brouillés **scrambled eggs**
tartine **bread with butter**
crêpe **pancake**

croque-monsieur **ham and cheese toasted sandwich**
croque-madame **...with a fried egg on top**
galette **type of pancake**
pan bagna **bread roll stuffed with salad Niçoise**
quiche **tart of eggs and cream with various fillings**
quiche lorraine **quiche with bacon**

First course

An *amuse-bouche*, *amuse-gueule* or appetizer is something to "amuse the mouth", served before the first course
anchoiade **sauce of olive oil, anchovies and garlic, served with raw vegetables**
assiette anglaise **cold meats**
potage **soup**
rillettes **rich fatty paste of shredded duck, rabbit or pork**
tapenade **spread of olives and anchovies**
pissaladière **Provençal pizza with onions, olives and anchovies**

La Viande – Meat

bleu **rare**
à point **medium**
bien cuit **well done**
grillé **grilled**
agneau **lamb**

False Friends

False friends are words that look like English words but mean something different.
le car motorcoach, also railway carriage
le conducteur bus driver
la monnaie change (coins)
l'argent money/silver
ça marche can sometimes mean walk, but is usually used to mean working (the TV, the car etc.) or going well
actuel "present time" (*la situation actuelle* the present situation)
rester to stay
location hiring/renting
personne person or nobody, according to context
le médecin doctor

Slang

métro, boulot, dodo nine-to-five syndrome
McDo McDonald's
branché trendy (literally "connected")
C'est du cinéma It's very unlikely
une copine/un copain friend/chum
un ami friend but *mon ami*, boyfriend; also *mon copain*
un truc thing, "whatsit"
pas mal, not bad, good-looking
fantastic! fantastic! terrible!

andouille/andouillette **tripe sausage**
bifteck **steak**
boudin **sausage**
boudin noir **black pudding**
boudin blanc **white pudding (chicken or veal)**
blanquette **stew of veal, lamb or chicken with a creamy egg sauce**
boeuf à la mode **beef in red wine with carrots, mushroom and onions**
à la bordelaise **beef with red wine and shallots**
à la Bourguignonne **cooked in red wine, onions and mushrooms**
brochette **kebab**
caille **quail**
canard **duck**
carbonnade **casserole of beef, beer and onions**
carré d'agneau cassoulet **rack of lamb stew of beans, sausages, pork and duck, from southwest France**
cervelle **brains (food)**
chateaubriand choucroute **thick steak Alsace dish of sauerkraut, bacon and sausages**
confit **duck or goose preserved in its own fat**
contre-filet **cut of sirloin steak**
coq au vin **chicken in red wine**
côte d'agneau **lamb chop**
daube **beef stew with red wine, onions and tomatoes**
dinde **turkey**
entrecôte **beef rib steak**
escargot **snail**
faisan **pheasant**
farci **stuffed**
faux-filet **sirloin**
feuilleté **puff pastry**
foie **liver**

foie de veau **calf's liver**
foie gras **goose or duck liver**
pâté
gardiane **rich beef stew with olives
and garlic, from the Camargue**
cuisses de grenouille **frog's legs**
grillade **grilled meat**
hachis **minced meat**
jambon **ham**
lapin **rabbit**
lardon **small pieces of bacon,
often added to salads**
magret de canard **breast of duck**
médaillon **round meat**
moelle **beef bone marrow**
mouton navarin **stew of lamb with
onions, carrots and turnips**
oie **goose**
perdrix **partridge**
petit-gris **small snail**
pieds de cochon **pig's trotters**
pintade **guinea fowl**
Pipérade **Basque dish of eggs,
ham, peppers, onion**
porc **pork**
pot-au-feu **casserole of beef and
vegetables**
poulet **chicken**
poussin **young chicken**
rognons **kidneys**
rôti **roast**
sanglier **wild boar**
saucisse **fresh sausage**
saucisson **salami**
veau **veal**

Poissons – Fish

Armoricaine **made with white wine,
tomatoes, butter and cognac**
anchois **anchovies**
anguille **eel**
bar (or loup) **sea bass**
barbue **brill**
belon **Brittany oyster**
bigorneau **sea snail**

Bercy **sauce of fish stock, butter,
white wine and shallots**
bouillabaisse **fish soup, served
with grated cheese, garlic
croutons and** rouille, **a spicy sauce**
brandade **salt cod purée**
cabillaud **cod**
calmars **squid**
colin **hake**
coquillage **shellfish**
coquilles Saint-Jacques **scallops**
crevette **shrimp**
daurade **sea bream**
flétan **halibut**
fruits de mer **seafood**
hareng **herring**
homard **lobster**
huître **oyster**
langoustine **large prawn**
limande **lemon sole**
lotte **monkfish**
morue **salt cod**
moule **mussel**
moules marinières **mussels in
white wine and onions**
raie **skate**
saumon **salmon**
thon **tuna**
truite **trout**

Légumes – Vegetables

ail **garlic**
artichaut **artichoke**
asperge **asparagus**
aubergine **eggplant**
avocat **avocado**
bolets **boletus mushrooms**
céleri **grated celery**
rémoulade **with mayonnaise**
champignon **mushroom**
cèpes **boletus mushroom**
chanterelle **wild mushroom**
cornichon **gherkin**
courgette **zucchini**
chips **potato crisps**

How do I make an outside call?
Comment est-ce que je peux
téléphoner à l'exterieur?
**I want to make an international
(local) call** Je voudrais une
communication pour l'étranger
(une communication locale)
What is the dialling code? Quel
est l'indicatif?
**I'd like an alarm call for 8
tomorrow morning.** Je voudrais
être réveillé à huit heures
demain martin
Who's calling? C'est qui à
l'appareil?
Hold on, please Ne quittez pas
s'il vous plaît
The line is busy La ligne est
occupée
**I must have dialled the wrong
number** J'ai dû faire un faux
numéro

chou **cabbage**
chou-fleur **cauliflower**
concombre **cucumber**
cru **raw**
crudités **raw vegetables**
épinard **spinach**
frites **chips, French fries**
gratin dauphinois **sliced potatoes
baked with cream**
haricot **dried bean**
haricots verts **green beans**
lentilles **lentils**
maïs **corn**
mange-tout **snow pea**
mesclun **mixed leaf salad**
noix **nut, walnut**
noisette **hazelnut**
oignon **onion**
panais **parsnip**
persil **parsley**
pignon **pine nut**
poireau **leek**
pois **pea**
poivron **bell pepper**
pomme de terre **potato**
radis **radis**
roquette **arugula, rocket**
ratatouille **Provençal vegetable
stew of aubergines, courgettes,
tomatoes, peppers and olive oil**
riz **rice**
salade Niçoise **egg, tuna, olives,
onions and tomato salad**

Numbers

0	zéro	10	dix	20	vingt
1	un, une	11	onze	21	vingt-et-un
2	deux	12	douze	30	trente
3	trois	13	treize	40	quarante
4	quatre	14	quatorze	50	cinquante
5	cinq	15	quinze	60	soixante
6	six	16	seize	70	soixante-dix
7	sept	17	dix-sept	80	quatre-vingts
8	huit	18	dix-huit	90	quatre-
9	neuf	19	dix-neuf		

vingt-dix
100 cent
1000 mille
1,000,000 un
million
● Number 1 is
often written
like an upside
down V. Number
7 is crossed.

salade verte **green salad**
truffe **truffle**

Fruits – Fruit
ananas **pineapple**
cavaillon **fragrant sweet melon from Cavaillon in Provence**
cerise **cherry**
citron **lemon**
citron vert **lime**
figue **fig**
fraise **strawberry**
framboise **raspberry**
groseille **redcurrant**
mangue **mango**
mirabelle **yellow plum**
pamplemousse **grapefruit**
pêche **peach**
poire **pear**
pomme **apple**
raisin **grape**
prune **plum**
pruneau **prune**

Sauces – Sauces
aioli **garlic mayonnaise**
béarnaise **sauce of egg, butter, wine and herbs**
forestière **with mushrooms and bacon**
hollandaise **egg, butter and lemon sauce**
lyonnaise **with onions**
meunière **fried fish with butter, lemon and parsley sauce**
meurette **red wine sauce**
Mornay **sauce of cream, egg and cheese**
Parmentier **served with potatoes**
paysan **rustic style, ingredients depend on the region**
pistou **Provençal sauce of basil, garlic and olive oil; vegetable soup with the sauce.**
provençale **sauce of tomatoes, garlic and olive oil.**
papillotte **cooked in paper**

Dessert – Puddings
Belle Hélène **fruit with ice cream and chocolate sauce**

Non, Non, Garçon

Garçon is the word for waiter but is never used directly. Say *Monsieur* or *Madame* to attract his or her attention.

clafoutis **baked pudding of batter and cherries**
coulis **purée of fruit or vegetables**
gâteau **cake**
île flottante **whisked egg whites in custard sauce**
crème anglaise **custard**
pêche melba **peaches with ice cream and raspberry sauce**
tarte tatin **upside down tart of caramelised apples**
crème caramel **caramelised egg custard**
crème Chantilly **whipped cream**
fromage **cheese**
chèvre **goat's cheese**

In the Café

If you sit at the bar (*le zinc*), drinks will be cheaper than at a table. Settle the bill when you leave; the waiter may leave a slip of paper on the table to keep track of the bill. The French enjoy bittersweet aperitifs, often diluted with ice and fizzy water.

drinks *les boissons*
coffee *café*
...with milk or cream *au lait or crème*
...decaffeinated *déca/décaféiné*
...black/espresso *express/noir*
...American filtered coffee *filtre*
tea *thé*
...herb infusion *tisane*
...camomile *verveine*
hot chocolate *chocolat chaud*
milk *lait*
mineral water *eau minérale*
fizzy *gazeux*
non-fizzy *non-gazeux*
fizzy lemonade *limonade*
fresh lemon juice served with sugar *citron pressé*
fresh squeezed orange juice *orange pressé*
full (eg full cream milk) *entier*
fresh or cold *frais, fraîche*
beer *bière*
...bottled *en bouteille*
...on tap *à la pression*
pre-dinner drink *apéritif*
white wine with cassis, blackcurrant liqueur *kir*
***kir* with champagne** *kir royale*
with ice *avec des glaçons*
neat *sec*

red *rouge*
white *blanc*
rose *rosé*
dry *brut*
sweet *doux*
sparkling wine *crémant*
house wine *vin de maison*
local wine *vin de pays*
Where is this wine from? *De quelle région vient ce vin?*
pitcher *carafe/pichet*
...of water/wine *d'eau/de vin*
half litre *demi-carafe*
quarter litre *quart*
mixed *panaché*
after dinner drink *digestif*
brandy from Armagnac region of France *Armagnac*
Normandy apple brandy *calvados*
cheers! *santé!*
hangover *gueule de bois*

Days and Months

Days of the week, seasons and months are not capitalised in French.

● **Days of the week**
   Monday *lundi*
   Tuesday *mardi*
   Wednesday *mercredi*
   Thursday *jeudi*
   Friday *vendredi*
   Saturday *samedi*
   Sunday *dimanche*
● **Seasons**
   spring *le printemps*
   summer *l'été*
   autumn *l'automne*
   winter *l'hiver*
● **Months**
   January *janvier*
   February *février*
   March *mars*
   April *avril*
   May *mai*
   June *juin*
   July *juillet*
   August *août*
   September *septembre*
   October *octobre*
   November *novembre*
   December *décembre*
● **Saying the date**
   20th October 2002, *le vingt octobre, deux mille deux*

Further Reading

History and Culture

France in the New Century, by John Ardagh. London: Penguin, 2000. Up-to-date tome on modern France.
Inventing the French Riviera, by Mary Blume. Thames and Hudson. Excellent account of emigré Riviera.
The Identity of France, by Fernand Braudel. Fontana Press. Unputdownable analysis, weaving major events with everyday life, by one of France's best historians
A Traveller's History of France, by Robert Cole. London: The Windrush Press. Background reading.
On the Brink: the Trouble with France, by Jonathan Fenby. Little Brown, 1998. Witty account of French politics and life today.
When the Riviera was Ours, by Patrick Howarth. Century Hutchinson. The development of the Riviera as a tourist resort.
Travels in the South of France, by Stendhal. John Calder. Record of a journey made by the author in 1838.
The French, by Theodore Zeldin. How the French live today.

Fiction

The Rock Pool, by Cyril Connolly. Oxford University Press.
Tender is the Night, by F. Scott Fitzgerald. Penguin.
Collected Short Stories, by Katherine Mansfield. Penguin.
Bonjour Tristesse, by Françoise Sagan. Penguin.
Perfume, by Patrick Süskind. 1985. Well-written best-seller set in the perfumed world of Grasse.

Food and Art

A Table in Provence, by Leslie Forbes. Webb & Bower. Recipes.
A Life of Picasso. Vols I and II, by John Richardson. Cape, 1996.
A History in Art, by Bradley Smith. New York: Doubleday, 1984. The

history of France seen through the eyes of artists.
The Unknown Matisse, by Hilary Spurling. Knopf, 1998.
The Food Lover's Guide to France, by Patricia Wells. London: Methuen. Regional dishes, best restaurants, shops and markets from food critic at the *International Herald Tribune*.

Other Insight Guides

The following **Insight Guides** highlight other French destinations: *France, Paris, Normandy, Brittany, Loire Valley, Burgundy, Provence, Southwest France* and *Alsace*.

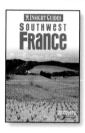

Insight Pocket Guides are designed for the short-stay visitor and contain full-size fold-out maps. Titles in this series include *French Riviera, Paris, Brittany, Corsica, Loire Valley, Côte D'Azur, Provence* and *Alsace*.

Insight Compact Guides are handy mini-encyclopedias packed with facts, photographs and maps; titles include *French Riviera, Paris, Normandy, Brittany, Burgundy* and *Provence*.

Insight Fleximaps combine clear, detailed cartography with essential travel information. The laminated finish makes the maps durable, waterproof and easy to fold. Titles include: *French Riviera, Provence, Corsica* and *Paris*.

Feedback

We do our best to ensure the information in our books is as accurate and up-to-date as possible. The books are updated on a regular basis, using local contacts, who painstakingly add, amend and correct as required. However, some mistakes and omissions are inevitable and we are ultimately reliant on our readers to put us in the picture.

We would welcome your feedback on any details related to your experiences using the book "on the road". Maybe we recommended a hotel that you liked (or another that you didn't), as well as interesting new attractions, or facts and figures you have found out about the country itself. The more details you can give us (particularly with regard to addresses, e-mails and telephone numbers), the better.

We will acknowledge all contributions, and we'll offer an Insight Guide to the best letters received.

Please write to us at:
Insight Guides
PO Box 7910
London SE1 1WE
United Kingdom
Or send e-mail to:
insight@apaguide.demon.co.uk

ART & PHOTO CREDITS

Index

Numbers in italics refer to photographs

A
B
C
D
E
F
G
H
I
J
a
b
c
d
e
f
g
h
i
j
k
l